EMPIRE OF THE BLACK SEA

EMPIRE OF THE BLACK SEA

The Rise and Fall of the Mithridatic World

Duane W. Roller

OXFORD
UNIVERSITY PRESS

OXFORD
UNIVERSITY PRESS

Oxford University Press is a department of the University of Oxford. It furthers
the University's objective of excellence in research, scholarship, and education
by publishing worldwide. Oxford is a registered trade mark of Oxford University
Press in the UK and certain other countries.

Published in the United States of America by Oxford University Press
198 Madison Avenue, New York, NY 10016, United States of America.

Library of Congress Cataloging-in-Publication Data
Names: Roller, Duane W., author.
Title: Empire of the Black Sea : the rise and fall
of the Mithridatic world / Duane W. Roller.
Description: New York : Oxford University Press, 2020. |
Includes bibliographical references and index.
Identifiers: LCCN 2019033327 (print) | LCCN 2019033328 (ebook) |
ISBN 9780190887841 (hardback) | ISBN 9780197673171 (paperback) |
ISBN 9780190887865 (epub) | ISBN 9780190887858 | ISBN 9780197500552
Subjects: LCSH: Mithridates VI Eupator, King of Pontus, approximately 132 B.C.–63 B.C. |
Pontus—Kings and rulers. | Pontus—History. | Black Sea Region—History. |
Rome—History—Mithridatic Wars, 88-63 B.C.
Classification: LCC DS156.P8 R65 2020 (print) | LCC DS156.P8 (ebook) |
DDC 939/.33—dc23
LC record available at https://lccn.loc.gov/2019033327
LC ebook record available at https://lccn.loc.gov/2019033328

1 3 5 7 9 8 6 4 2

Paperback printed by Marquis, Canada

CONTENTS

PART II
MITHRIDATES VI THE GREAT

ILLUSTRATIONS

MAPS

FIGURES

PREFACE

Over a period of more than two centuries, the Pontic dynasty of northern Asia Minor evolved from modest beginnings into one of the most powerful states in the Greco-Roman world. Its founder, Mithridates I, was a refugee from the unforgiving and violent politics of the years after the death of Alexander the Great in 323 BC. The dynasty culminated in its last and most famous king, Mithridates VI the Great, who died in 63 BC. Pontos was originally the north central portion of what is today modern Turkey, but at its peak the kingdom controlled central Asia Minor and most of the coastal Black Sea, with trade and commercial connections into Armenia, toward the Iranian plateau, the Caucasus, and the barbarian hinterland north of the sea. Eventually Pontos was rivaled only by Ptolemaic Egypt and the lengthening reach of the Roman Republic.

Much of the modern interest in the ancient Pontic kingdom has centered on the career of Mithridates the Great, but he was merely the last representative of a dynasty that began in the early third century BC as the world that had been left in disarray by the death of Alexander the Great settled into a number of hereditary and contentious monarchies. Pontic power was slow to develop, but by the end of the third century BC Pontos had become one of the major regional states of the Hellenistic world. With the arrival of the Romans in Asia Minor, early in the following century, local politics became tangled with the effects of Roman policy, and the history of the last century of the Pontic dynasty is one of ever more complex relations with that power. After the accession of Mithridates VI around 120 BC, the dynasty both reached its peak and began its decline, eventually yielding to the inexorable power of Rome, as was to happen to the other surviving kingdoms founded after Alexander's death.

This study is the first thorough analysis in English of the dynasty as a whole, with detailed attention given to its origins and entire history. The author has positioned himself for this endeavor by his extensive earlier writings on the eastern dynasties of the Hellenistic and Roman world, especially an analysis of the Pontic kingdom as reconstituted by Marcus Antonius (Mark Antony) in 37 BC, and the career of the most famous descendant of the Mithridatids, Queen Dynamis of Bosporos, the granddaughter of Mithridates VI.[1] The present work extends from the world of the successors of Alexander the Great to the Roman era and draws heavily on the concept of the allied king or queen, monarchs on the fringes of the Roman world who entered into a symbiotic relationship with that power, for better or worse, most famously Cleopatra VII and Herod the Great.

There are certain difficulties inherent in writing a study of the Pontic dynasty. As in all historiography, sources can be deficient or lacking, and the emphasis placed in ancient literature on certain events or personalities may reflect more the survival of the sources than their perceived contemporary importance. Moreover, after the arrival of the Romans the extant writings begin to reflect the victor's point of view, a well-known problem in late Hellenistic history and most pernicious in the case of Cleopatra VII. And, as always, women, regardless of their importance, tend to be faint or virtually nonexistent in the narrative.

As before, the author wrote the book in his study in Santa Fe, having conducted research in the Harvard College Library and the library of the University of California at Berkeley, as well as utilizing the excellent interlibrary loan services of the Ohio State University. He would particularly like to thank the Emeritus Academy of the Ohio State University for grant support. Among the many who assisted in the completion of this work, he would like especially to thank Stanley Burstein, David Braund, Emma Dodd of Numismatic Ars Classica, Amelia Dowler of the British Museum, Patric-Alexander Kreuz, Kenneth Lapatin, Lee Patterson, Letitia K. Roller, Lisbet Thoresen, Stefan Vranka and many others at Oxford University Press, Claudia Wagner, and Wendy Watkins and the Ohio State University Center for Epigraphical and Paleographical Studies.

Map 1 Localities mentioned in the text

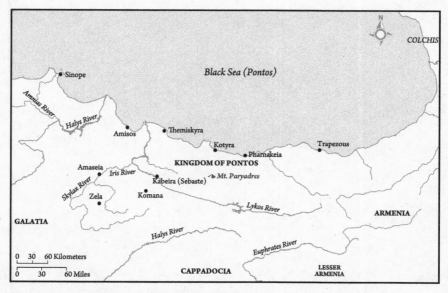

Map 2 Pontos during the period of the Mithridatic dynasty

GENEALOGICAL CHART

This chart is greatly simplified, designed to show the line of descent from Mithridates I the Founder to the royal children of Mithridates VI the Great. Ruling personalities in Pontos and Bosporos are shown in capitals. For a more complete stemma, see Richard D. Sullivan, *Near Eastern Royalty and Rome* (Toronto 1990), stemma 2 (as well as the other stemmata in that volume), and *BNP Chronologies*, 110–11.

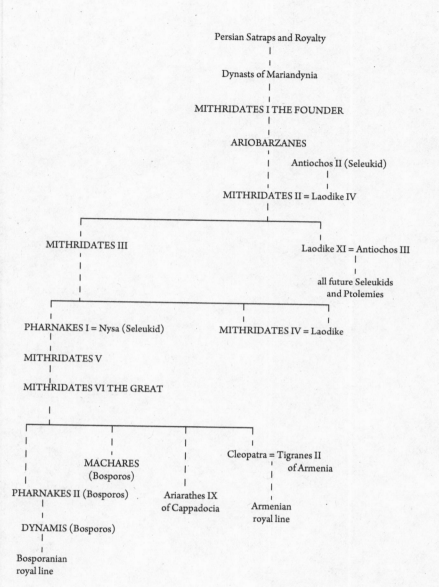

Persian Satraps and Royalty
|
Dynasts of Mariandynia
|
MITHRIDATES I THE FOUNDER
|
ARIOBARZANES
| Antiochos II (Seleukid)
| |
MITHRIDATES II = Laodike IV
|

MITHRIDATES III   Laodike XI = Antiochos III
| |
| all future Seleukids
| and Ptolemies

PHARNAKES I = Nysa (Seleukid)   MITHRIDATES IV = Laodike
|
MITHRIDATES V
|
MITHRIDATES VI THE GREAT
|

| MACHARES   Cleopatra = Tigranes II
| (Bosporos)   of Armenia
| |
PHARNAKES II (Bosporos)   Ariarathes IX |
| of Cappadocia   Armenian
DYNAMIS (Bosporos)   royal line
|
Bosporanian
royal line

Introduction

In early 63 BC, Mithridates the Great, king of Pontos, who ruled a territory that included most of the Black Sea coast, was in residence at his palace at Pantikapaion, just north of the sea. For thirty years he had been fighting the Romans for dominance in Asia Minor and beyond, and although he had won numerous victories, the overall trajectory was one of steady defeat for the king as Roman power spread to the east. He had been forced to abandon his traditional capital of Sinope, on the south shore of the sea, and retreat to the farthest corner of his kingdom at Pantikapaion, one of the most remote cities of the Greco-Roman world, where winters were unimaginably cold and the barbarian threat was ever present. Many of his allies and much of his family had abandoned him. Although he planned an invasion of Italy by going up the Danube and south through the Alps, imitating his famous predecessor Hannibal, he devoted most of his time to botany and pharmacology, in the long-standing tradition of scholarly royalty. But eventually he realized that he had no other options, and thus asked a bodyguard to kill him. Thus ended the career of one of the most remarkable leaders of classical antiquity, the man whom his younger contemporary Cicero called "the greatest king since Alexander [the Great]."[1]

Mithridates—the sixth king of Pontos to bear that name—is the best known and last ruler of a dynasty that extended back to the early third century BC and his ancestor Mithridates I the Founder. Mithridates I was a product of the world after the death of Alexander in 323 BC. Alexander had left no plans for the organization of his vast empire, and thus there were forty years of political maneuvering, often violent, as the territories that he had left coalesced into three major kingdoms and several minor ones, which extended from the Greek peninsula to India. One of these was Pontos.

Part I of this study examines the Pontic kingdom from its origins in the generation after Alexander to the death of Mithridates V around 120 BC.

Mithridates I the Founder—probably descended from the Persian aristocracy—emerged as a follower of Alexander's successor King Antigonos I Monopthalmos ("the One-Eyed") but eventually became a threat and had to flee for his own survival into the rugged mountains of northern Asia Minor. He declared himself king at some time early in the third century BC and began to rule a sprawling unorganized territory that eventually became the kingdom of Pontos, establishing his capital at his new city of Amaseia on the Iris River. In time he acquired the port of Amastris on the Black Sea, which provided the emergent kingdom with an outlet to the rest of the world and resulted in significant economic benefits. The Founder survived until 266 BC, when he was succeeded by his son Ariobarzanes.

Ariobarzanes, who ruled for a decade, is little known. His son Mithridates II was the first to establish the international profile of the Pontic state. He participated in a collective effort to give aid to the island of Rhodes after an earthquake in the early 220s BC, and, more importantly, married the Seleukid princess Laodike IV. The Seleukids were one of the major empires that had been established after the death of Alexander, and the largest territorially—extending at their peak from the Aegean to India—and their acceptance of a dynastic marriage with the king of Pontos is proof of the latter's legitimacy as an important ruling power. One of the couple's daughters, Laodike XI, married back into the Seleukid family, becoming the wife of King Antiochos III in 222 BC, and therefore all successive Seleukids were descended from Pontic royalty. When their daughter Cleopatra I married Ptolemy V of Egypt, the Pontic line also became the ancestors of the remainder of that dynasty. Thus much of the subsequent royalty of the Hellenistic world—into the Roman period—was descended from Mithridates II and Laodike IV, including its most famous representative, Cleopatra VII.

Mithridates II devoted his last years to expanding the kingdom, especially to the south and west, and along the Black Sea coast, dying sometime after 220 BC. His grandson Pharnakes I was one of the powerful kings of the dynasty. He came to the throne early in the second century BC and profited from significant changes in the political dynamics of Asia Minor, including the expulsion of his relatives the Seleukids from all of the territory except the southeast, and the arrival of the Romans, who were in pursuit of their nemesis Hannibal.

Pharnakes adopted a more aggressive policy than his predecessors, attempting to spread Pontic control in all directions. He seized the Greek city of Sinope, on the Black Sea, and made it his new capital. His reign was largely one of warfare with his neighbors, with varying success, until the Romans curbed his expansionism. Efforts were more successful beyond areas of Roman interest, to the north and east, and he established diplomatic relations with cities on the west coast of the Black Sea. He also seems to have been the first Pontic monarch to reach out to the traditional Greek world, especially Athens, where he may have commissioned the building of the Middle Stoa in the Agora. He fostered Greek art in his kingdom. Yet in retrospect his ambitions exceeded his ability, and his wars caused financial problems.

Pharnakes died in the early 150s BC and was followed by his brother Mithridates IV, who established good relations with the Romans and the Greek island of Delos, where he and his sister-wife Laodike were commemorated. He died by 149 BC, to be succeeded by his nephew Mithridates V, who sent aid to the Romans in their last war with Carthage. During his reign the kingdom of Pergamon was willed to the Romans, causing major changes to the politics of western Asia Minor, with the Romans gaining territory there for the first time. Pontos was now the largest and wealthiest regional state, and its policy, at first, was to support Rome. But the Pontic kingdom was thrown into chaos around 120 BC when Mithridates was assassinated by his inner circle, to be succeeded by his adolescent son Mithridates VI.

Part 2 of this study is centered on the career of Mithridates VI the Great, who reigned from around 120 BC to 63 BC. His career is well documented, and inevitably any study of the Mithridatic dynasty emphasizes his era. He was the only Pontic king who had a significant afterlife and who entered popular culture. After contentious early years, when his claim to the throne was far from secure due to the issues surrounding the death of his father, he embarked on an ambitious program of expansionism, beginning with encircling the Black Sea. He brought the cities on its north coast—the region called the Bosporos—under his control. He also acquired the western part of Armenia, known as Lesser Armenia. By the end of the second century BC he controlled not only the traditional land of Pontos but the regions all around the Black Sea to its east and north into Bosporos and beyond.

Needless to say, such activities soon caught the attention of the Romans. Much of the territory he acquired was beyond their area of concern, but they could not have looked with disinterest at such an aggressive monarch, whose kingdom was not far from their eastern provinces. Moreover, there were persistent rumors that he would next move into the lower Danube and even go as far as the Adriatic, something quite relevant to the Romans. Yet internal chaos at Rome as well as their own wars—in Africa and Gaul, and with their Italian allies—prevented any early Roman response, something that encouraged the king. But when he moved directly west of Pontos to the borders of Roman territory, it was another matter.

An alliance with the king of Greater Armenia, Tigranes II (who married Mithridates's daughter, probably in the 90s BC), increased Mithridates's influence, and the two kings created a major power base: Tigranes's possessions extended toward the Iranian plateau and into Syria. Thus Pontos and Rome began to slip toward open warfare. Yet the king continued to cultivate the Greek states, and a monument to him was erected on the island of Delos in 102/1 BC.

By 89 BC Rome was ready to respond to Mithridates's expansionism, and after futile negotiations, war broke out in that year. The reasons were complex, and in part rose from the increasing dysfunctionality in Rome during the early first century BC. The war quickly turned into an outright attempt to expel the Romans from Asia Minor and perhaps even the Greek peninsula; most notoriously, the king ordered the killing of thousands of Romans and Italians in the Roman cities of Asia, as a response to the predatory ways of the tax collectors and businessmen. He also established a Pontic puppet government in Athens, but in time that famous Greek city was sacked by the Roman proconsul Lucius Cornelius Sulla, who carried the war to Asia and forced the king to accept highly unfavorable peace terms in 85 BC.

Mithridates spent the next decade rearming and reestablishing his position. A desultory series of campaigns and diplomatic activities between 83 and 81 BC was identified by ancient sources as the Second Mithridatic War, but it offered few benefits to either side. The king continued to mobilize, and his invasion of Bithynia—a territory to the west of Pontos that had just been acquired by Rome—precipitated the third and final war in 73 BC. It was more lengthy and complex than the previous ones, and after initial successes the king's fortunes began to fail, as the two proconsuls sent against him, Lucius Licinius Lucullus (73–66 BC) and Gnaeus Pompeius (Pompey the Great, 66–63 BC) steadily forced him into a defensive position. By late 66 BC the king was in full retreat, abandoning Pontos and making an epic journey around the east side of the Black Sea to take up residence in Pantikapaion, where he was eventually killed at his own request. Traditional Pontos was provincialized and the Bosporanian territories placed under the rule of his son, Pharnakes II, who was closely supervised by the Romans.

NAMES, PLACES, AND PEOPLE

The modern handling of proper names from antiquity (whether personal or toponymic) is a difficult problem. In the complex multilingual world of Greece and Rome, names could vary depending on what language they were presented in. People would even use different versions of their own names when speaking or writing different languages. Moreover, ancient names passed through the latinization of medieval times, so that the forms often used today may bear little resemblance to anything familiar to the original users or residents. There is no easy way of dealing with these issues, and the orthography used in this book, insofar as possible, attempts to balance historical accuracy with modern familiarity.

Three names used frequently herein deserve special note. "Mithridates" is a Persian theophoric name ("Given by Mithra," the ancient south Asian divinity who was prominent in Persia), documented as early as the sixth century BC[2] and exceedingly common in the Persian and eastern Greek worlds thereafter. The original spelling was "Mithradata" or "Mithradates," but "Mithridates" is more common in Greek and Latin, although the earlier form also survived, especially in inscriptions.[3]

Pontos is a district of north-central Asia Minor, which became the core of what modern sources regularly call "the kingdom of Pontos," but this is essentially a late construct, probably from no earlier than the Roman period.[4] Territorial boundaries were fluid in antiquity, and kingship could be more a declaration of status rather than an assertion of ruling a specific region. Yet, for convenience, the term "kingdom of Pontos," or just "Pontos," is used herein to describe the regions ruled, or claimed, by the Pontic kings from Mithridates I through VI.

Finally, one of the more ambiguous terms from antiquity is the toponym "Asia." It could mean the entire continent or merely the peninsula that is modern Turkey and generally called "Asia Minor" today. In addition the toponym was applied to the new Roman province created on the Aegean coast in the late second century BC. The term "Asia Minor" is useful today but anachronistic to the period under discussion.[5] Greek and Roman sources tend to describe Asia Minor in term of ethnicities—Cappadocians, Cilicians, and the like—rather than by any collective term. In this volume, "Asia Minor" is used for the entire region and "Asia" for the Roman province, except in a few cases where the continent is meant.

SOURCES

As with much of Hellenistic history, the ancient sources for the Mithridatic dynasty and its era are scattered. Any specialized study of the kingdom, if such ever existed, has been lost. The standard historians of the period, such as Polybios, Diodoros, Livy, Appian, and Dio, as well as Memnon and Justin, provide most of the extant literary information. Their value and detail vary: Polybios's account does not go far beyond the middle of the second century BC, and Livy's history is highly fragmentary for the period in question. Almost all of Appian's *Mithridateios* is about Mithridates VI the Great. A history of Herakleia Pontika by its citizen Memnon, existing today only in a Byzantine summary, is useful, as are other fragmentary and limited sources cited in the notes. As always, inscriptions and coins provide some of the best evidence, especially for the years before the accession of Mithridates VI. Documentation of his reign is far more thorough, with a variety of Greek and Latin sources that are listed in chapter 6.

The only previous survey of the entire Pontic dynasty is Eduard Meyer's *Geschichte des Königreichs Pontos* (Leipzig 1879), which, although seminal in its importance, is long out of date. It was Meyer who popularized the anachronistic term "kingdom of Pontos" for the territory ruled by the Mithridatic kings. Other more recent sources focus heavily on Mithridates VI and are discussed at the beginning of chapter 6. Some of these have brief summaries of the earlier years of the dynasty, such as Théodore Reinach's *Mithridate Eupator, Roi de Pont* (Paris 1890) or Brian C. McGing's *The Foreign Policy of Mithridates VI Eupator, King of Pontus* (Leiden 1986), but the emphasis is always on the last generation of the kingdom. Also valuable for the period after Roman involvement in Asia Minor are David Magie's *Roman Rule in Asia Minor* (Princeton 1950) and A. N. Sherwin-White's *Roman Foreign Policy in the East, 168 B.C. to A.D. 1* (Norman 1983). Other material is cited in the notes and bibliography. Although by necessity the present work includes a thorough study of Mithridates VI, it is also an attempt to survey the entire dynasty from the time of Mithridates I the Founder to its end as rulers of a Hellenistic state.

PONTOS TO 120 BC

Chapter 1

Pontos

THE FIRST EXPLORATION OF THE PONTIC REGION

What is commonly called the kingdom of Pontos flourished for hundreds of years in the territory south of the Black Sea, with most of its kings named Mithridates. By the Roman period, queens were also independent rulers of the territory. Pontos was the northern part of the long peninsula that today is modern Turkey, but which was generally called "Asia" in antiquity (with a localized sense and different from the identical term for the entire continent). The name "Pontos" was transferred from the Greek name for the Black Sea and was an ancient Greek word for "sea." This was a poetic term, used many times by Homer in the *Iliad* and the *Odyssey*, first appearing when Achilles, having lost his friend Briseis, looks despondently over the dark *pontos*.[1]

In early times Greek seafarers discovered the narrow straits of the Hellespont and Bosporos, at the northeast corner of the Aegean, an event perhaps reflected in the quest of Jason and the Argonauts for the Golden Fleece. The straits led to another sea that was only tenuously connected to the Mediterranean. This (the modern Black Sea) came to be called the "Pontos," rather than by any indigenous name. Since *pontos* is connected to words meaning "pathway" (Latin *pons*, or "bridge" is related)—seas were pathways to other lands—applying this term to a newly discovered sea reached by a pathway from the Aegean was particularly appropriate.[2]

Exploration of the Pontos meant awareness of its coasts, especially those on the southern side. The Argonauts, said to have been active in the generation before the Trojan War, would have sailed along this coast in their journey to

Colchis, a far-off locale consistently placed at the southeastern corner of the sea. Although in later times coastal cities remembered the passage of the Argonauts, intensive Greek knowledge of the region did not come until after 700 BC, when cities such as Miletos in Ionia sent out expeditions and established trading outposts along the Black Sea coast, which in time grew into independent cities.[3]

Later—exactly when is not known—the term "Pontos" came to be applied to the territories just to the south of the sea, the rugged coastal strip of northern Asia Minor and its mountainous hinterland. This is a reversal of the normal way in which seas were named, which usually reflected the ethnym of the inhabitants on their shores.[4] The name Pontos for the territory south of the sea was firmly in place by the late fifth century BC, because in 400 BC the Greek adventurer Xenophon, during his famous retreat from Mesopotamia across the mountains of eastern Asia Minor to the Black Sea and the Greek world, was perfectly familiar with the term as applied to a territory.[5] Why this rare transference from sea to land occurred is not understood, but it was presumably a shortening of a phrase such as "the lands on the coast of the Pontos."

Despite Xenophon's awareness of the toponym, the region of Pontos was still little known to Greeks in 400 BC, except for the coastal cities: Xenophon's ignorance of the landscape and its inhabitants, and his ill-advised crossing of the mountains in winter, demonstrates this. He encountered numerous groups of hostile mountain peoples, who were nominally subjects of the Persian empire. Yet any Persian presence was minimal, despite organization of the region into the nineteenth satrapy of the empire. The locals were occasionally used as mercenaries, especially during the Persian invasions of Greece in the early fifth century BC,[6] but it is clear that Persian administration of the region was slight, and effective Persian control did not extend north of the watershed between the Mediterranean and the Black Sea.[7] The coastal Greek cities remained enclaves of hellenism generally free of the Persians: Xenophon's relief in reaching the Greek world at Trapezous is apparent.[8] As the Persian empire began to deteriorate—something already underway in Xenophon's time—the region of Pontos, with its Greek cities, hardy mountaineers, and a limited Persian presence, was ripe for revolt and the establishment of a new order that blended hellenism and Persian culture and brought both to the indigenous population. Even as Xenophon passed through Pontos, events were occurring to its west that within a century would establish the long-lived Mithridatic dynasty.

THE LANDSCAPE

Political boundaries were often fluid in antiquity, depending on ethnic movements, territorial claims not always implemented, and relations with adjoining states. Nevertheless, during the flourishing years of the kingdom of Pontos—from the early third century BC into the Roman period (not considering the great but temporary expansionism of Mithridates VI in the late second century and early first centuries BC)—its kings and queens ruled a district covering at most about 450 miles of the southern Black Sea coast, from a point between Herakleia Pontika and Amastris in the west into the less organized region of Colchis in the east, at the southeastern corner of the sea. Colchis itself was often under Pontic control; in the early first century AD the queen of Pontos, Pythodoris, also took the title "queen of the Colchians."[9]

Pontos is defined by a narrow coastal plain and precipitous mountains in the interior whose summits become higher from west to east. In the west is the ridge of Mount Olgassys (modern Ilgaz Dağları), beginning in the region of Paphlagonia and extending for about eighty miles into Pontos. It lies roughly parallel to the coast and sixty to seventy-five miles from it, rising to 8,488 feet. East of this range the summits are lower for nearly two hundred miles in an area of deep river valleys that forms the heartland of interior Pontos. Farther east rises the other great mountain of Pontos, Paryadres (largely modern Canik Dağları and Dogu Karadeniz Dağları), again parallel to the coast and only forty miles from it, extending for about seventy miles and rising to over ten thousand feet. In fact, the Paryadres are not so much a range as the beginning of the high plateau of eastern Asia Minor and Armenia, culminating in Mount Ararat of biblical fame.

Despite their ruggedness, these mountains are cut by a number of large rivers. The most famous is the Halys (modern Kızılırmak), which flows in a great arc from a source south of the Paryadres, passing through Cappadocia and then heading north in western Pontos, reaching the Black Sea after a course of 840 miles (the longest river completely in Asia Minor). It was notable in Greek history from early times, remembered as the boundary between the Aegean and Mesopotamian worlds as well as for the engineering feats of Thales of Miletos. By Pontic times its importance as a political boundary had diminished, but it was still a significant geographical one.[10]

More important in Pontic history was a network of shorter rivers in the central part of the territory. The major stream is the Iris (modern Yeşilırmak), whose source is south of the Paryadres. It flows west-northwest and then enters a series of canyons, passing first the great temple city of Komana and then the Pontic metropolis of Amaseia, eventually reaching the Black Sea after 260 miles, just thirty-five miles southeast of the mouth of the Halys. The Iris has two important tributaries. The Lykos (modern Kelkit Çay) flows north of and parallel to the upper Iris, past the site of Kabeira, which, as Sebasteia, became the capital of Pontos in the Augustan period. The other tributary is the Skylax (modern Çekeretırmak), which comes from the southwest and joins the Iris just above Amaseia. These rivers are never far from one another, surrounded by rugged mountains and generally flowing through deep gorges that create fertile basins that were the economic and cultural heartland of inland Pontos. The Halys—whose source is only a few miles from the upper Lykos—curves around this region to the south, to some extent defining Pontos, although at its southernmost point it is well into Cappadocia, which often had close political connections with Pontos. The upper Lykos is only about thirty miles from the upper Euphrates, across the watershed of Asia Minor, and this divide was itself the southern boundary of the eastern portions of Pontos.

THE EARLIEST SETTLEMENTS ON THE COAST

Hittites and Assyrians may have been the first non-indigenous people to reach the Black Sea coast, coming overland from the south. Greek settlement began in the eighth century BC, but the story of Jason and the Argonauts, who passed along the coast in their quest for the Golden Fleece, hints at earlier Greek interest in the region from the Aegean world, allegedly in the generation before the Trojan War.

The oldest cities in Pontos were on the coast and generally of Greek origin. Sinope (modern Sinop, fig. 1.1) was probably the first, founded by the Ionian city of Miletos.[11] Its fine location (the best on the western part of the southern Black Sea coast) gave it early prominence. The city controlled an extensive trading network, since it was located at the end of an ancient route from the Mediterranean (five days away) and Mesopotamia.[12] There was access to the resources of the interior as well as contact with the territories to the north, directly across the Black Sea, known as the Kimmerian Bosporos (not the more familiar Bosporos between the Black Sea and the Aegean, but the modern Crimea and Sea of Azov

Figure 1.1 Sinope, location of ancient town. Shutterstock 111781768.

region). In fact, one could cross from Sinope, situated at the northernmost part of Asia Minor, to the Kimmerian Bosporos without losing sight of land. Sinope also established its own settlements toward the east, in the direction of Colchis. The wealth and hospitality of the city were famous: Xenophon was well received by the locals in 400 BC and given large amounts of barley and wine, and in the Roman period the geographer Strabo called it "the most notable city" of the region, famous for its magnificent public buildings.[13]

Although Sinope was an independent state in the early years of its existence, in time the city and its wealth came to be coveted by the major powers and, later, by the dynasts of the Hellenistic world. After the Persians spread west in the sixth century BC, Sinope was technically part of their empire (or at least adjacent to it), and in the fourth century BC the names of Persian officials began to appear on its coinage: around 364–362 BC the city was controlled by the satrap of Cappadocia, a certain Datames, and a generation later Ariarathes.[14] Datames, like his contemporary Mausolos of Halikarnassos, was one of the players in the collapse of Persian power in the western part of the empire. Originally a member of the palace guard of King Artaxerxes II, he began to take an independent posture in central Asia Minor. Yet his ambitions soon raised suspicions at court, and he was assassinated in 362 BC by a certain Mithridates, one of the ancestors of the later Pontic royal line.[15] Unlike Mausolos, Datames was ultimately unsuccessful in creating his own state, yet he briefly brought Sinope (and probably other coastal cities) under his control, whether authorized to do so by the Persian government or not. His successor Ariarathes also claimed Sinope, perhaps with more legitimacy insofar as the Persians were concerned. He was satrap of Cappadocia at the time of Alexander the Great and until he was defeated by Eumenes of Kardia, one of Alexander's companions and successors, in 322/1 BC.[16] But his control of Sinope had in some way come to an end; by 333 BC the city was again issuing coins in its own name.[17] Nevertheless, the fortunes of Sinope, which indirectly involved the originators of the future Pontic royal line, demonstrate the political realities of the fourth century BC, events that allowed the kingdom of Pontos to emerge at the end of that century. The wealth and location of Sinope continued to make it a goal for ambitious dynasts, especially as Pontos developed as a recognizable state, and in 183 BC King Pharnakes I suddenly and successfully attacked the city and incorporated it into the Pontic empire, making it the new capital.[18]

About eighty miles along the coast to the southeast was another important Greek city, Amisos (modern Samsun), whose early history is obscure but which was perhaps founded in the early sixth century BC by Miletos. It too was located at a point where trade from the interior reached the Black Sea, the outlet for a rich hinterland especially productive of fruit and nuts. It is uncertain when Pontos assimilated Amisos, but in the middle of the third century BC King Mithridates II had a presence in the city.[19]

How much farther east the kingdom extended in its early days is uncertain: King Pharnakes I founded Pharnakeia (modern Giresun) about one hundred miles east of Amisos, perhaps shortly after annexing Sinope. In all probability this was a demonstration of presumed Pontic power in this direction. Seventy miles farther to the east was Trapezous (modern Trabzon), another early Greek foundation and an outpost of Sinope. It may have come under Pontic control at the same time as its mother city, but this is not certain, and Trapezous remained more connected to Armenia than Pontos until the late first century BC.[20] Beyond Trapezous was Colchis, certainly under Pontic control by the early first century BC, when Strabo's great-uncle Moaphernes was royal governor and a local dynasty, perhaps related to the Pontic one, had been deposed.[21]

At the west end of Pontos was its final coastal city, Amastris, which had an unusual history. It was founded shortly after 300 BC by Amastris, the niece of Dareios III of Persia. She had been married to Dionysios, the tyrant of nearby Herakleia Pontika. Probably because she was no longer welcome in that city after the death of her husband and with her children ruling, she established Amastris, about sixty miles to the northeast, a rare example at this early date of a woman founding a city. She ruled there as queen until she was killed by her sons around 284 BC. Such instability at Amastris may have led King Ariobarzanes of Pontos to seize it a few years later, evidently with the connivance of Amastris's successor, a certain Eumenes, who turned toward Pontos to resist annexation by Herakleia.[22] Ariobarzanes's acquisition of the city is the first documented example of Pontic expansionism on the coast.

THE INTERIOR

Despite the greater antiquity of the coastal cities, the kingdom of Pontos actually had its origins in the interior. Inland, the earliest location associated with the Pontic kingdom is Kimiata, perhaps on a southern spur of Mount Olgassys near modern Ilgaz. Epigraphical information suggests that the site may have been farther west and actually named Kimista, at modern Asar Kale, where extensive Hellenistic remains have been found.[23] Kimista lies about sixty miles west of Kimiata, on the right (here south) bank of the Billaios River, and just within the traditional territory of Paphlagonia. The site—whether Kimiata or Kimista— was the refuge of a certain Mithridates, who was probably a descendant of the assassin of Datames the satrap of Cappadocia. Mithridates fled to the region in 302 BC for the reasons noted in Chapter 2.

If Mithridates ended up in Kimista (rather than Kimiata), it would require an emendation of the relevant passage in Strabo's *Geography*, not something to be done lightly, since Strabo was quite well informed about both the region and the history of the Mithridatic dynasty. Regardless, either site would have suited Mithridates's needs, although Kimiata would have been more defensible, since it was an ancient fortress, perhaps of Hittite origin, probably with no townsite.[24]

Whether it was in the region of the Kimiatene or Kimistene that Mithridates (who came to be known as Ktistes, "the Founder") established himself in 302 BC, preparatory to claiming the rule of Pontos, either site demonstrates that the future king retreated into the remote mountainous region of north-central Asia Minor, caught in the complex web of intrigues that marked the generation after the death of Alexander the Great. He created for himself a stronghold in Paphlagonia near the western border of Pontos. Mithridates, who may have

Figure 1.2 Amaseia. Shutterstock 1087007765.

previously been based in Mysia, to the southwest, perhaps saw the opportuni-
ties of creating a kingdom from the large unorganized territory to his east. Both
Kimiata and Kimista are little known and seem to have played no further role in
Pontic history.

The most important town in interior Pontos was Amaseia (modern Amasya;
fig. 1.2). Because it was the hometown of Strabo, who was born there in the late
60s BC and may also have lived in the region in the early first century AD, there
is more information about this city than any other in Pontos.[25] It was not an
ancient foundation, but had been established by Mithridates I probably shortly
after he seized Kimiata, which lies slightly over one hundred miles to the west.
He made it the capital of Pontos, a role that continued until the acquisition of
Sinope in 183 BC, and Amaseia remained an important city thereafter and into
late antiquity.

Strabo described its situation in the valley of the Iris River, whose gorge is
over three thousand feet deep. It was both a city and a fortress. The modern visi-
tor to the site cannot fail to be impressed by its situation, and most of the features noted by Strabo are still visible, especially the fortifications and also the
tombs and cenotaphs of the kings of Pontos, including that of Mithridates I (fig.
1.3).[26] Strabo also mentioned the royal palace, bridges across the river, and a

Figure 1.3 Amaseia, royal tombs. Shutterstock 1143719102.

sophisticated hydraulic system. The survival of the palace means that it probably remained a royal city even after the official capital was moved to Sinope.

THE RELIGIOUS STATES

Amaseia was the only major city in interior Pontos before the time of Mithridates VI; most of the region consisted of villages, royal preserves, and temple states. These states were a peculiar feature of the Pontic landscape, religious entities that consisted of shrines to a particular divinity, and which also possessed the surrounding hinterland. They could be extensive territorially and functioned as independent political units.[27] Many of those in Asia Minor were Hittite in origin, and the concept may have come from Mesopotamia. They were wealthy and prosperous, often controlled by hereditary dynasties. Their rulers had royal privileges, such as the father and son named Archelaos at Komana, or Aba at Olbe in western Cilicia, who succeeded her husband and ruled as priestess-queen in the 30s BC as an allied monarch of both the Romans and Ptolemies.[28] These states and their rulers were an important element in the political fabric of Asia Minor from the Bronze Age into Roman times.

Kabeira (modern Niksar), about sixty miles east of Amaseia, was a royal estate from at least the time of Mithridates VI. Its importance was because of its proximity to an ancient shrine of Men—the local moon god—which lay just to the northeast at Ameria (near modern Ardıçlı). The god was instrumental in the legal authority of the Pontic kings, who swore their oaths in his name. Since the sanctuary was officially dedicated to Men of Pharnakes, it was established by someone of that name (probably well before the Pontic king Pharnakes I), a name known in Persian royalty at least from the sixth century BC. By Roman times, when Amaseia and Sinope had been annexed, Kabeira had become the most important urban center in interior Pontos and was designated the new capital of the territory. Queen Pythodoris had named it Sebasteia by the early first century AD, and it may have been here that Strabo spent his last years and completed his *Geography*. The visible remains are medieval, but they include Roman elements.[29]

None of the temple states was more famous than Komana, at modern Kılıçlı on the right bank of the Iris, about fifty miles upstream from Amaseia and twenty-five miles southwest over the divide from Kabeira. It was an outpost of Komana in Cappadocia, which was of Hittite origin. Both were dedicated to the war goddess Ma and were almost identical in their rites. The cult became part of the Pontic religious establishment early in the history of the kingdom, and its priests, who wore a royal diadem, were second only to the king. There was a biannual festival called the Procession of the Goddess, perhaps occurring at the solstices or equinoxes. As with many religious festivals, it became a great gathering event with people coming from throughout Asia Minor and beyond. It was especially known for its Armenian market. The environment of Komana was luxurious—its rich vineyards were particularly of note—and there was an extensive resident population, including many temple prostitutes.[30]

Although the cult existed throughout the period of the Mithridatic dynasty, a list of the priest-kings is only available from the time of Mithridates VI into the Augustan period. They were politically active: the first known, Dorylaos, an ancestor of Strabo, was also an important member of the royal court and was involved in the military activities of the era.[31] A later priest-king, Archelaos, married Berenike IV of Egypt (the sister of Cleopatra VII) and served briefly as co-ruler of Egypt.[32] His son, also named Archelaos, succeeded to the office of priest-king and was the father of the fourth Archelaos, the scholarly king of Cappadocia in the Augustan period.[33] At that time the shrine and its cult had declined in importance, and the few later priest-kings recorded were essentially political appointees of little merit. The site has been identified, but there are virtually no remains of the great shrine that once housed six thousand temple slaves.[34]

There was another shrine at Zela, about thirty miles west of Komana. It was dedicated to the Persian deities Anaitis, Omanos, and Anadates, whose festival was still celebrated in the Augustan period. Since the cult was Persian, it dated from at least that era, but it was locally believed to have actually had Assyrian origins. It does not seem to have had the independent political profile of Komana and was subject to the Pontic kings as an outpost of Persian cult. Yet like Komana it had temple slaves flourishing in an abundant environment. It also had a closer relationship to the population as a whole, because the Pontic people made their oaths on the most important matters at the site. It has been located near modern Zile, but the visible remains are Byzantine and later.[35]

Thus in a piecemeal fashion extending over two centuries, the kingdom of Pontos spread from its origins around Kimiata into the Iris River system around Amaseia and Komana and to the coast. The boundaries were never stable, and it underwent almost constant expansion from the establishment of Amaseia around 300 BC to the great ambitions of Mithridates VI, who sought to rule all Asia Minor and the Black Sea coast, if not more. Pontos came into existence as an independent state in the era of the collapse of the Persian empire, and, unlike the rest of Asia Minor, the region was hardly coveted and not even visited by Alexander the Great. It was only when Pontic aspirations—or, specifically, those of Mithridates VI—collided with Rome that the kingdom ceased to acquire territory.

DEMOGRAPHY

As was the case with much of Asia Minor, the population of Pontos was mixed between the various ethnic elements that had long inhabited the region. The ability of the shrine at Zela to continue flourishing into the Roman period is evidence of the importance of a Persian survival. The Persians had nominally been in control of the region for over two hundred years, and the Mithridatic dynasty was evidently descended from its ruling aristocracy. It is probable that ordinary

Persians had come to Pontos for trade and mercantile reasons, and their descendants still survived in the Augustan period.

The Greek cities on the coast provided a Hellenic element, and Greeks penetrated into the interior for commerce. Greek personal names existed at the village level, documented by numerous funerary inscriptions. There were Greek-language schools, and these gave the population an awareness of Greek literature and mythology. Generally there is no evidence for these schools previous to the Roman imperial period, yet one suspects that use of the Greek language began much earlier, perhaps no later than the second century BC.[36] Northern Asia Minor was rich in Greek mythology, even if some of this was imposed by infiltration of traditions from the coastal Greek states into the interior. Nevertheless, the myths were a subject of fascination to everyone: villagers would put Homeric verses on their tombstones. The Argonauts had passed through the region, and a generation later the Trojan War was fought to the west of Pontos, with Trojan allies coming from Paphlagonia and perhaps farther east, well into the area of Pontos. King Priam of Troy had in his youth battled the Amazons on the Sangarios River just west of Pontos.[37] Although Homeric knowledge of northern Asia Minor remains disputed, there seem to have been Pontic traditions about local involvement in the Trojan War.[38]

The Amazons were another feature of the Greek mythological tradition closely associated with Pontos. Like most mythical peoples, they tended to be just beyond the limits of civilization, and at the time of the death of Mithridates VI they were in the Caucasus,[39] but they were originally in or around Pontos. Themiskyra, said to be their homeland, was on the large estuary of the Iris River in the heart of coastal Pontos; whether any Amazons remained in Pontos in historical times is not known.

The Amazons were connected with Alexander the Great, who had a relationship with their queen Thalestria; thus traditions about him are on the border of myth and history.[40] Alexander never entered Pontos—the closest he came was Ankyra, just beyond it to the west, in the summer of 333 BC—but he was inevitably a powerful force in the hellenized image of the Pontic world, especially to Mithridates VI, who sought to stress connections with his famous predecessor at every opportunity and was said to have had tokens of him at the time of his own death.[41]

Thus over the years the ruling aristocracy as well as the general population of Pontos became more hellenized (especially after the capital was moved to Greek Sinope), with Greek becoming the official language by at least the second century BC.[42] As with the allied kings and queens of the Roman era, the kings of Pontos could be different things to different people, stressing their Persian origins yet creating a Hellenistic monarchy at the royal court that sought contacts with the Greek and eventually the Roman world. And the Greek and Persian people of Pontos would have their own relationships with the ruling elite.

In addition, there were other ethnic forces in Pontos. Vestiges of earlier peoples survived, although their visibility remains speculative. Enigmatic references to Syrians in northern Asia Minor (from as early as the fifth century BC) may refer to an Assyrian presence, and in Hellenistic times it was believed that the Assyrians had reached the Black Sea, perhaps following the ancient trade route across Asia Minor to Sinope.[43] The Hittites had been active in at least the southern part of the future Pontic kingdom. If there were Pontic peoples who claimed descent from either of these groups, they may have been connected to the great sanctuaries, whose origins were certainly ancient, but such memories easily become mythical. The shrine of Anaitis at Zela, although said to have been established by the Persians, was additionally associated with the semi-mythical Assyrian queen Semiramis.[44]

The final ethnic component of Pontos was the indigenous mountain population. Strabo recorded some of those subject to Queen Pythodoris in the early first century AD, such as the Tibarenians and Chaldaians, inland from Trapezous. They had been around for some time: in the late sixth century BC the Tibarenians, at least, had paid tribute to the Persians and were civilized enough to participate in the invasion of Greece half a century later.[45] These and other ethnic groups who were still recognizable in Hellenistic and Roman times were generally in the more rugged eastern areas of Pontos, toward Armenia and Colchis. Yet by the Augustan period the kings and queens of Pontos claimed to rule them.[46] Whether this was reality or a politically correct fiction is by no means certain, since monarchs always insisted that they exercised more control over fringe populations than they actually did. But it is clear that the inhabitants of the Pontic realm became less civilized and less hellenized farther to the east, and at Trapezous the non-Greek element was strong enough that as late as the second century AD public inscriptions were visible that contained incorrect Greek.[47] Nevertheless, this ethnic diversity was typical of the Hellenistic world, and Pontos was no different from many other contemporary political entities in its ability to bring these diverse elements together in order to create a cohesive state.

THE PONTIC ECONOMY

Pontos was primarily agricultural. There is an extensive amount of evidence on the economy from the account of Strabo, which, is somewhat eulogistic and is essentially limited to the period of Augustus and Tiberius, but the data can often be extrapolated back into earlier times. Strabo emphasized the fertility of the plains and river valleys; particularly notable were the plains of Themiskyra and Phanaroia. The town of Themiskyra (modern Terme) was on the coast about twenty-five miles southeast of Amisos and was probably a Milesian foundation. Although modest, it was the seaport for the largest coastal plain in Pontos, which extends for about fifty miles along the shore and twenty-five inland, remembered as where Herakles had encountered the Amazons. The plain was luxuriant in grasses, with all kinds of cattle and horses, and produced a variety of cereal grains. Its interior, next to the mountains, yielded fruit and nuts. It was well watered, since the lower Iris and other streams crossed it. As such, it was a microcosm of the agrarian abundance of the most fertile parts of Pontos.[48]

Somewhat different was the inland plain of Phanaroia, which spread along the Lykos River from Kabeira about thirty miles to its junction with the Iris. Never more than five miles wide, it was said to be the most productive part of Pontos and was notable for its olives, vines, and other crops. The commodities produced in the two plains were probably the core of the Pontic economy, with cereals and vines also important around Sinope as early as the fifth century BC.[49]

Other products were also significant. Timber for shipbuilding, always a necessity in the Greco-Roman world, was available in the coastal regions west of Sinope, as well as wood for furniture (maple and a variety called *orokaryon*, not otherwise documented but probably similar to walnut).[50] The fertility of Pontos also meant that it was abundant in wild animals, which could be caught for local food, but the land was rare in any kind of sheep, and thus wool—or at least types soft enough to be useful—was only produced in the Gadilonitis region between the mouth of the Halys and Amisos.[51] But one lake, Stiphane (modern Ladık Gölü, today only an intermittent vestige of its predecessor), lying twenty miles northeast of Amaseia, was noted for its fish, although no other details were provided.[52] There was also a vigorous tuna (*pelamydes* in Greek) industry all along the south coast of the Black Sea. The tuna migrated from the Maiotis (the modern Sea of Azov, on the north side of the sea) and traveled along the east and south coasts, and eventually into the Aegean. Thus the Pontic fishermen had an early chance to harvest it, although the fish did not reach maturity until they passed Sinope. Towns farther east also caught them when they were not yet full grown. By the second century BC, Pontic salted fish was a major export product, but according to Cato the Elder, the price—three hundred drachmas a jar—was exorbitant.[53]

There were other resources beyond agriculture, timber, and fishing. Mining was important, especially the realgar works near Pimolisa, on the Halys River (at modern Osmancık). Realgar (arsenic sulfide) was an orange mineral, primarily used for coloring. The mines were state-owned in the early imperial period and probably had been a royal monopoly previously. The miners were slaves and worked under terrible and often deadly conditions.[54] Silver had been mined in early times in the mountains of eastern Pontos: it was believed that the Homeric reference to the "birthplace of silver" referred to this region. This had been an important mining district since prehistoric times; early Greek settlement may have been connected with a search for metals, something implicit in the story of the Golden Fleece.[55] By Roman times precious metals were no longer found, although there were still local iron mines.[56]

Sinope profited because of the ancient trade route from the interior. This was so important that a type of red ochre from Cappadocia was called "Sinopean" because it was shipped from there to the rest of the Greco-Roman world, a fine example of identifying an item not from its point of origin but from the most familiar place on the trade route. The ochre was mercury sulfide, also known as minium, cinnabar, or miltos, used as a red dye for painting and also medicinally.[57]

Amomum (or amomon, *Amomum sublatum*) was an important export from Pontos, although it is not certain whether it was produced in the region or imported from elsewhere (perhaps India, arriving in Pontos from the Caspian region and Colchis). It is an aromatic and a type of cardamom, used medically (primarily to reduce inflammation) and as a constituent of perfumes.[58]

Sinopean ochre, and perhaps amomum and even iron, demonstrates how Pontos could profit from being an intermediary on the trade routes from the east and south to the Greco-Roman world. The cities on the coast had long maintained relations with the Greek heartland, and as the Pontic kingdom expanded and became more stable, it also reached out to the Aegean through trade and political connections. King Pharnakes I and his queen, the Seleukid princess Nysa, were honored by Athens in the early second century BC, probably before the annexation of Sinope.[59] A few years later, in the 170s BC, a Pontic grain and oil merchant—his name and hometown are not preserved on the inscription mentioning him—was also recognized by the Athenians, presumably an indication that trade between Pontos and Athens was well established.[60] These records show that Pharnakes I and Nysa, along with their subjects, were actively involved in spreading the Pontic presence through the Greek world, using both their prestige and the benefits of Pontic commodities.

The land of Pontos included extensive royal and temple holdings: it seems unlikely that all the seventy-five fortresses built by Mithridates VI were totally for defense but were instead probably royal estates or even regional granaries.[61] The great temple sanctuaries were notable for their prosperity, through both agriculture and the income received from those visiting the shrines. They were also involved in the slave trade. The coastal cities would have owned land in their hinterland that contributed to their wealth; although established as free Greek cities, in time they became integral parts of the kingdom. And presumably, as everywhere, there were farms and villages that functioned outside of the state economy.

Thus by the time that the kingdom of Pontos began to be organized, in the early third century BC, the territory was already a diverse region with Hittite, Assyrian, Persian, and Greek elements, as well as various indigenous populations. It had a developing economy, based on agricultural and mineral resources. Nevertheless, except for the Greek cities, it was as yet largely outside of the mainstream of the developing Hellenistic world, and thus ripe for the establishment of a new kingdom, a feature of the fluid politics of the era.

Chapter 2

The Founder

ANCESTRY

The state of Pontos was created in the early third century BC by Mithridates I, known in antiquity as "the Founder," who established himself at the fortress of Kimiata (or Kimista) and used it as a base to create his kingdom.[1] He was descended from several generations of Persian satraps and dynasts, but the evidence for the origin of his family is full of contradictions. An ancestry from the highest levels of the Persian aristocracy was promulgated in later days, although the veracity of this is far from certain. Assertion of a famous ancestry was common among the Hellenistic dynasts, and one can perhaps be dismissive of many of these claims, yet the sources are consistent that Mithridates I was a descendant of either Dareios I of Persia or one of his six co-conspirators who helped put him on the throne in 522 BC.[2] Alexander the Great was also mentioned among his ancestors, which is highly improbable. But the strongest argument against descent from Dareios or his circle is that several sources do not give the name of the famous ancestor; in fact, Polybios, the earliest extant author to record the claim, merely wrote that the Mithridatic line came from "one of the seven Persians," a suspicious vagueness.

Yet despite the unanimity of the ancient sources, such an ancestry has generally been rejected since at least the nineteenth century. To be sure, one has every reason to do so, given the proclivity of people of power to create heroic genealogies for themselves, but there is nothing unreasonable in assuming that the Mithridatic kings were related to the Persian aristocracy, and it should not be seen merely as an attempt to find favor with the Persian element of the kingdom.[3] In fact, one could argue that especially in the later years of the dynasty, a Greek or Macedonian ancestry would have been more politically viable.

On balance, then, descent from one of the seven Persians seems probable, but the exact line cannot be proven. Another possibility is Dareios's son Gobryas, who commanded the Mariandynians in the war against Greece, which suggests that he had connections with northwestern Asia Minor.[4] Mariandynia was the mountainous district south of Herakleia Pontika, not far from the western boundary of the future Pontic kingdom. By the end of the fourth century BC, a certain Mithridates seems to have been the dynast of Mariandynia, assuming that this is the toponym reflected in the incomprehensible (and otherwise unknown) name "Arrhine" or "Marine" in the extant text of Diodoros. This Mithridates, who died in 302 BC, was preceded by Ariobarzanes (later to be another Pontic royal name), who had died in 336 BC, and was followed by another Mithridates, someone who greatly expanded his territory and in all likelihood was the Founder.[5]

These conclusions have a degree of speculation about them and are based on determining the proper interpretation of the mysterious Arrhine/Marine. The relationships between the three known Mariandynian dynasts (Ariobarzanes-Mithridates-Mithridates) are not clear. It is unlikely that power passed from father to son, and the two dynasts named Mithridates were probably uncle and nephew. Yet Diodoros outlined a dynasty that was typical of the local rulers who came to power in the last years of the Persian empire. After Alexander the Great passed through Asia Minor in the 330s BC, the local satraps and dynasts tended to change their allegiance from the Persians to Alexander, and then to his successors, whose territories were always fluid. The earlier Mithridates, in power 336–302 BC, became caught in the rivalries of the era: he first supported Antigonos I Monopthalmos, satrap of Phrygia and nominal ruler of Asia Minor, but when Mithridates's attentions drifted toward Cassander, another of Alexander's successors, who had assumed the title of king of Macedonia in 305 BC, he was killed at the obscure town of Kios, on the Aegean, and the second Mithridates, probably his nephew, inherited his possessions.[6] The younger dynast may have already fled to Kimiata in Paphlagonia, a necessary act of self-preservation.

Another possible ancestor was Artabazos, perhaps the person of that name who was a commander in Xerxes's invasion of Greece and satrap of Daskylion. This too would give the Mithridatids a connection with northwest Asia Minor, where Daskylion is located.[7]

THE PROBLEM OF KIOS

The introduction of Kios into the narrative of the formative years of the Mithridatic dynasty raises another problem of interpretation. The text of Diodoros describing the death of the elder Mithridates is ambiguous:

> At about this time [302 BC], Mithridates, who was subject to Antigonos but seemed to be turning his support to those around Cassander, was killed around Kios in Mysia, having ruled it and Arrhine [or Marine] for thirty-five years.[8]

The problem is the antecedent of "it." Since the late nineteenth century this has been universally accepted as referring to Kios, thus leading to the assumption that this was the seat of the ancestors of the Founder.[9] Kios (modern Gemlik) lies at the head of a bay of the same name on the southern side of the Propontis, the sea between the Hellespont and the Thracian Bosporos. It was a Milesian foundation that remained relatively obscure. After its participation in the Ionian revolt against Persia of 499 BC, it was little involved in the events of Greek history. There is no evidence of a Persian presence in the city: it paid tribute to Athens in the fifth century BC and was organized according to Greek civic institutions. The city was destroyed by Philip V of Macedonia in 202 BC and refounded by Prousias of Bithynia, who then named it after himself.[10] Its location, facing west in extreme northwestern Asia Minor, seems odd for the seat of a dynasty that was able to assert itself in Pontos, hundreds of miles to the east. Moreover, Strabo, in his discussion of the town, made no mention of it being the ancestral seat of the Mithridatic family, whose history was of great interest to the geographer; in fact, he had just mentioned Mithridates I the Founder and his acquisition of Kimiata.[11] There is no doubt that the Founder's assumed uncle, the elder Mithridates, was killed at Kios in 302 BC, but the suggestion that this obscure town was the seat of a dynasty that had ruled there for nearly a century seems improbable.

It is better to see the matter of Kios as a diversion and conclude that the antecedent of Diodoros's "it" is Mysia, a construction—admittedly ambiguous—that he used elsewhere with more clarity.[12] Despite almost universal acceptance of the idea that the Mithridatic dynasty originated at Kios, there is, oddly, no further significant association of Mithridates I or his descendants with this place—strange if it were the ancestral seat—and any relevance of Kios to the dynasty beyond the death of the elder Mithridates is simply not viable. Kios (by now called Prousias) was taken by Mithridates VI when he conquered Bithynia in 73 BC, but this seems merely a routine event, not reacquisition of the historic home of the dynasty.[13] The ancestral region of the Mithridatic family was clearly Mysia, and almost certainly included Mariandynia, two territories not far from one another that would be well positioned for the Founder's retreat into the interior, either after his relative's death at Kios or more probably even earlier, when the unforgiving politics of the last quarter of the fourth century BC became a threat to his survival.

THE SUCCESSORS

It is well known that when Alexander the Great died at Babylon on 13 June 323 BC, he left no coherent plans for succession. The eastern Mediterranean entered into a forty-year period of complex diplomacy and frequent warfare, with the rise and fall of dynasts and potential dynasts. Years of uncertainty ensued before the new Hellenistic world settled into the three great kingdoms of the Ptolemies in Egypt; the Seleukids in Syria, the Levant, and southern Asia Minor; and the Macedonians in the Greek peninsula. These were accompanied by numerous free cities, federal associations, and lesser dynasties such as that which emerged in Pontos.[14] Much of what happened during this era is not immediately relevant to the origins of the Pontic kingdom, but several personalities stand out among the successors of Alexander whose actions were an essential part of the creation of the Mithridatic world, and who were all known to Mithridates I.

Antigonos I Monophthalmos (ca. 382–301 BC) was a companion of Alexander and took part in the eastern expedition as far as Phrygia, where he was appointed satrap of that region.[15] He managed Alexander's affairs in central Asia Minor and after the king's death adopted a policy of consolidating his power in both northern Asia Minor and the Greek peninsula. His son Demetrios Poliorketes ("Besieger of Cities," 336–283 BC), who was raised in Phrygia and as a young man became a friend of Mithridates I, served as his father's commander in Greece.[16] Father and son were the first of Alexander's successors to declare themselves kings, probably in 306 BC, thus creating the formal structure of the new Hellenistic state, although at first the title was more an honorific than that of a ruler of a specific territory and was awarded because of military victories.[17]

Another important successor of Alexander involved in the genesis of the Pontic kingdom was Cassander (ca. 354–297 BC), who was not part of the eastern expedition but generally remained in Macedonia. After Alexander's death he and Antigonos formed an alliance, but in the inevitable ways of the Hellenistic world, this did not last long, and within a decade the two were at odds, largely over territorial issues in the Greek peninsula. Cassander declared himself king (of Macedonia) shortly after Antigonos and Demetrios took the title, and this may have aggravated the rivalry.[18] Caught in the midst of it was the ancestor of Mithridates I, who had been a supporter of Antigonos but was killed at Kios—perhaps on his way to Macedonia—as he was transferring his loyalty to Cassander.

Seleukos I (ca. 358–281 BC), another companion of Alexander and a member of the eastern expedition, became satrap of Mesopotamia and in time extended his control to the Mediterranean, founding the Seleukid empire. He repeatedly attempted to obtain much of central and northern Asia Minor, and thus would become involved in the formative years of the Pontic kingdom.[19] His successors and those of Mithridates I would regularly intermarry, and in time the Seleukid kings and queens would also be descendants of the Founder.

And finally, there was Lysimachos (ca. 355–281 BC), of Thessalian origin, who participated in the eastern expedition and was given control of Thrace after Alexander's death. By 313 BC he was extending his power into northwestern Asia Minor, and he also declared himself king around 306 BC.[20]

The history of the early Hellenistic period defies any simple narrative, with the constant shifting alliances and territories and innumerable battles. Yet Antigonos, Demetrios, Cassander, Seleukos, and Lysimachos were to play a particularly significant role in events connected with the career of the Founder and the establishment of the Pontic kingdom.

THE EARLY CAREER OF THE FOUNDER

Mithridates I would be known to ancient historians even if he had never become king; he was a minor player in the circle around Antigonos and his son Demetrios in the last quarter of the fourth century BC.[21] His exact lifespan is difficult to determine because the data are contradictory, but some reasonable suggestions may be made. According to Diodoros, after the death of his homonymous uncle he ruled Cappadocia and Paphlagonia for thirty-six years.[22] The statement was placed by Diodoros under events of 302 BC, and thus would assume a death date of 266 BC. To be sure, Pontos was not mentioned, but Cappadocia and Paphlagonia make some sense: Cappadocia can be a general term for anywhere in central Asia Minor, including Pontos,[23] and Paphlagonia was the location of Mithridates's original retreat, Kimiata. Diodoros was probably vague about details, including the exact territorial limits, and it is unlikely that Mithridates exercised any official power from as early as 302 BC, but this is probably not a major issue.

According to Hieronymos of Kardia, Mithridates died at age eighty-four.[24] Hieronymos moved in the same circles as Mithridates—he too was attached to Antigonos I and Demetrios—and wrote a history extending from the death of Alexander to around the middle of the third century BC. One would expect him to have been well informed about the world that he functioned in, and he probably knew Mithridates. His information would suggest that Mithridates was born about 350 BC, perfectly reasonable for the known elements of his career. But Plutarch in his biography of Demetrios emphasized that Mithridates and Demetrios were essentially the same age and were youthful companions. The birth date of Demetrios is well attested as around 336 BC, since sources are consistent in making him twenty-two years of age when he was in Syria during the winter of 314/313 BC.[25] It is clear that two people born about fourteen years apart could hardly be described as of the same age or "youthful companions."

Presumably one piece of the data is wrong. Either Mithridates was born over a decade later, or he did not die in 266 BC at age eighty-four. Other elements of the tradition seem solid: the story that Mithridates and Demetrios were friends in their youth is well documented, and there would be little reason for it to be a fabrication, whereas the age at death could easily be an error. Without proof, it seems better to assume that Mithridates was born in the 330s BC, the same decade as Demetrios. This removes another difficulty in the chronology of his career, since if he were born in 350 BC, most of his activities as king of Pontos would have been in old age, and thus he would have been closer to the generation of Alexander the Great, which seems improbable. The later birthdate would mean he reached maturity after 310 BC, which fits with other elements of his career.

Young Mithridates attracted attention from the dynasts of the era because of his character: he was notable for his bravery and had been raised from childhood as a soldier.[26] Where he grew up is not known; his father, who is obscure today, was probably Ariobarzanes, the brother of the elder Mithridates, dynast of Mysia and Mariandynia, although the evidence for the family and upbringing of Mithridates I remains confused, and there are many contradictions. But it is clear that as soon as he reached adulthood, he attached himself to the retinue of Eumenes of Kardia, satrap of Paphlagonia and parts of Cappadocia, which may suggest that Mithridates was raised in his territory. Eumenes—probably a relative of his compatriot Hieronymos, the historian—had been Alexander's secretary and was part of the eastern expedition. In the years after Alexander's death he sought to preserve his position as satrap, resulting in a series of conflicts with Antigonos I. Eventually, in early 315 BC, at Gabiene on the Iranian plateau, Eumenes was captured and killed.[27] Fighting on his side was Mithridates, who had already proven himself through his ability. His activities during the battle are not known, but afterward he was somehow able to avoid the fate of his patron and join the side of the victor, Antigonos.

Before long Mithridates and Antigonos's son Demetrios became close friends.[28] Plutarch's account calls Mithridates a *hetairos*, or companion, of Demetrios, which can have legal force within the Macedonian aristocracy but not necessarily in this case, since the two were about the same age. Presumably as a new member of Antigonos's entourage Mithridates would naturally gravitate to his coeval son. No details are provided about the relationship or how long it lasted. But eventually Antigonos became suspicious of Mithridates; what happened is not known, but given the constantly shifting loyalties of the era, Mithridates had in some way become a threat. His relative the elder Mithridates would fatally change his allegiance from Antigonos to Cassander in 302 BC, but this was probably later; yet some years earlier Antigonos may have had similar concerns about another member of the family. Antigonos and Cassander were often at odds during these years, and the former had a reputation for ruthlessness. Eumenes and the elder Mithridates would be only two of many supposed rivals that he eliminated.

As recounted by the sources, Antigonos dreamed that he was walking across a large and beautiful field and sowing it with gold dust, but Mithridates reaped the harvest and took it away to the region of the coastal Black Sea.[29] To be sure, this is a standard after-the-fact dream prophecy of future greatness, a formula using an agricultural metaphor that goes back at least to the dream that Astyages of Media had about Cyrus of Persia.[30] Even if one is dismissive of Antigonos's dream, Mithridates did something that caused the ever-suspicious satrap to believe that he was no longer reliable, and thus he resolved to kill him. He told his son Demetrios about his plans but swore him to silence.

But Demetrios would not allow his friend to have such a fate. The two went for a walk alone on the seashore, and Demetrios used his spear to write "Flee, Mithridates" in the sand, thereby keeping the vow of silence given to his father. Mithridates understood and immediately left the court of Antigonos at night with a handful of companions. He took refuge in a stronghold somewhere in Cappadocia, here used in the generic sense of central Asia Minor. However much the dream may be questioned—as well as the message scratched in the sand, which has the characteristics of the prophecy that comes true despite attempts to avoid it happening—for some reason Mithridates terminated his association with Antigonos and departed. What is lacking in the extant accounts is either a location or date for the event. The only certainty is that it happened sometime between the battle of Gabiene (winter 315/314 BC) and the death of Antigonos (301 BC). Conventionally, Mithridates's flight has been associated with the death of his ancestor at Kios in 302 BC, but this is unlikely. By that time both the younger Mithridates and Demetrios would have been in their thirties, hardly the youthful companions implied in the tale. Moreover, the event had to have taken place when Demetrios and Antigonos were together at a coastal location. Demetrios (who, along with his father, declared himself king in 306 BC) is pictured as being young and still under his father's control, very much his subordinate. By 314 BC he had been posted to Syria by his father, and thereafter they generally operated separately.[31] Thus the walk on the beach was in all probability within a year or two after the battle of Gabiene: long enough for the two young men to become friends but before Demetrios left for Syria. A probable location is the Phoenician city of Tyre, which Antigonos and Demetrios besieged in 314 BC.[32]

By the end of 314 BC, then, Mithridates was on his own, having left the court of Antigonos and his friend Demetrios, and had retreated somewhere into the interior of Asia Minor, or perhaps even to his uncle's residence in Mysia. Eventually he ended up at Kimiata or Kimista in Paphlagonia, but this may not have been for some time, perhaps not even until after the death of both his uncle and Antigonos in 302 and 301 BC, respectively.[33] Even though Mithridates had distinguished himself on the battlefield and had won the favor (for a while) of one of the most powerful early Hellenistic dynasts, his total obscurity for many years need not cause concern; such invisibility is part of the sporadic nature of the records of Hellenistic history, and Mithridates, although a talented young man, had no significant support or power base. To go into hiding, even for an extended period of time, would have been the best means of surviving the turbulent politics of the era. But eventually he gained a following—many came to him, wherever he was—and this became the basis of the kingdom of Pontos.[34]

KING MITHRIDATES I

According to Diodoros, Mithridates I was king of Cappadocia and Paphlagonia for thirty-six years; the statement was placed in the context of the death of his uncle and other events of 302 BC.[35] Although the comments are unlikely to be accurate in detail—it is improbable that Mithridates had any formalized sense of a territory to rule at that early date—they probably reflect a feeling that 302 BC was an important year in his personal history. The death of his uncle meant that he inherited some territory: his father Ariobarzanes was obscure and may already have been dead, and there are no other known heirs. Moreover, in 302 BC the political organization of northwestern Asia Minor underwent certain changes that may have favored the rise of Mithridates I.

It was at about that time that Lysimachos established himself in the region. As satrap of Thrace he had long shown interest in expanding his power across the northern Aegean into Asia Minor. An opportunity presented itself with the death of Dionysios, the ruler of Herakleia Pontika, around 306 BC. His widow, Amastris, inherited control of the city, but her rule was never secure—there was opposition within her family to a woman of power—and before long she married Lysimachos. This not only strengthened her position but gave him access to an important seaport on the Black Sea.[36] In 302 BC Lysimachos was involved in campaigns against Antigonos in interior Asia Minor, but by later in the year he had been forced back north and entered winter quarters in the Plain of Salon, a fertile cheese- and cattle-producing district (the modern Bolu region of Turkey). The plain is about forty miles south of Herakleia and within the ancient territory of Mariandynia, the region held by the elder Mithridates, who was killed at Kios at about the same time. Lysimachos may have gone into Mariandynia to prevent Antigonos from claiming the territory. In the spring of 301 BC Lysimachos, having recently declared himself king, moved south, and in a decisive battle at Ipsos in Phrygia, Antigonos was caught between him and Seleukos I—with Cassander providing troops—and was killed. This not only established Lysimachos as master of much of Asia Minor but effectively created the Seleukid empire.[37]

Where Mithridates the Founder was during these months is not documented, but it is hard to imagine that he was not somehow involved in these momentous events that took place in and around his territory. When Lysimachos spent the winter in the Plain of Salon, he was not only in the traditional territory of Mithridates's uncle but only one hundred miles from Kimiata on a well-traveled route, where Mithridates may already have established himself. It seems probable that Mithridates—already having serious complaints against Antigonos—offered his support to Lysimachos at this time, and perhaps even accompanied him to Ipsos. After the battle, Lysimachos, now the unquestioned ruler of northern Asia Minor, embarked on a major reorganization of the region. One of his actions, which had far-reaching consequences, was to designate a retainer, Philetairos of Tios, as the commander of the fortress of Pergamon in Mysia, entrusting him with a treasury of nine thousand talents.[38] Pergamon was still unimportant at this date, but in time Philetairos, with extensive funds available, declared himself independent and established the local dynasty, which was to rule much of western Asia Minor for 150 years and contribute brilliantly to the art and culture of the Hellenistic world.

How Mithridates fit into Lysimachos's plans is not known. Like Philetairos, he was as yet of little importance, but Lysimachos would have realized that he was useful, especially as a buffer to Seleukid claims to the region, and thus he may have confirmed Mithridates's possession of portions of Mariandynia, Mysia, and the Paphlagonian regions around Kimiata, thus establishing the initial territorial basis of the future Pontic kingdom. Mithridates was not yet strong enough to declare himself a king, which would probably offend his new patron (in all likelihood he merely took the title of satrap), or to consider organizing his new possessions into a coherent state, but the blessing of Lysimachos gave him credibility, and thus he could consider 302 BC, the year of the death of his uncle, as the moment that his rule began.

Over the next two decades support for Mithridates I increased, especially as Lysimachos's interests turned more toward Bithynia, to the west of Pontos. Yet given the vagueness of territorial limits and topographical terminology, it is not possible to determine exactly what Mithridates ruled. It was said that he gained control of Cappadocia and lands along the Black Sea because the Macedonians—presumably Lysimachos—were engaged elsewhere. The suggestion that Mithridates held Cappadocia is an exaggeration—it was a vast, sprawling area in central Asia Minor that had its own rulers—but he probably encroached onto its northern regions, around the Halys River.[39] To some extent the information in the sources about the limits of his territories is tainted by the ambitions of his descendant Mithridates VI the Great two centuries later, who often justified his own territorial claims by asserting that the districts in question had always been under Pontic control.[40]

At some time in the thirty-six years after 302 BC, Mithridates declared himself king, following the pattern of the era. The major dynasts—Lysimachos, Seleukos I, Ptolemy I, and Demetrios Poliorketes—had done so in the last decade of the fourth century BC; by the following century, lesser dynasts also assumed the kingship. The first may have been Zipoites of Bithynia, in 297 BC or slightly earlier.[41] Mithridates may have become king in 281 BC, since the Byzantine chronographer Georgios Synkellos reported that the Mithridatic dynasty had existed for 218 years at the time of the death of Mithridates VI in 63 BC.[42] Yet Synkellos's data (or that preserved in the manuscripts) are suspect, since he also recorded that there were ten kings of Pontos through Mithridates VI, but by all other accounts there were only eight.[43] Thus Mithridates's assumption of kingship was possibly as early as 297 BC. This is when the Pontic era began, and it is also contemporary with the kingship of his neighbor Zipoites.[44] But 281 BC was the year of the death of both Lysimachos and Seleukos I, the last of the major successors who had known Alexander, and that year saw a major reorganization of the fortunes of northern Asia Minor.

The Macedonians were said to have objected to the change of Pontos from satrapy to kingdom but could not prevent it. This suggests that Mithridates may have taken advantage of the instability after the death of Lysimachos, when there were seven kings or claimants to the Macedonian throne in four years, until Antigonos II Gonatas, a son of Demetrios Poliorketes, took control in 277 BC and established the Antigonid dynasty that would last for the century remaining to the Macedonian kingdom. Mithridates may well have seen his chance during these years to move from satrap to king.

During his reign he founded the city of Amaseia, which remained the capital of the new kingdom until his descendant Pharnakes I moved it to Sinope in 183 BC. No date for the establishment of Amaseia can be determined, but it was during the Founder's reign, since he was buried there.[45] Amaseia lies a hundred miles east of the original stronghold of Kimiata, at the other end of Mount Olgassys and farther away from any districts claimed by the Macedonians, Bithynians, or

Seleukids. It is securely in the deep valley of the Iris, but with access to the rich plains of Phanaroia and Themiskyra as well as the Black Sea coast.

Yet the new kingdom was still in its formative stage; it is significant that there seem to be no coins from the reign of Mithridates I.[46] Pontic coinage probably did not begin until the time of his grandson, Mithridates II, who came to the throne around 255 BC. Nevertheless, in declaring himself king and building a new capital, Mithridates I not only inserted himself into the dynastic ideology of the era but well deserved the epithet of the Founder.

SOLIDIFYING THE KINGDOM

Mithridates would have had two priorities regarding his new kingdom: to protect his south and west from Macedonian and Seleukid ambitions, and to secure a foothold on the Black Sea. Although Amisos and Sinope were the nearest seaports, both were stable Greek cities that offered little opportunity for assimilation by Pontos. But farther west along the coast at Amastris the situation was more uncertain. When Queen Amastris, who had ruled the city that she founded for about fifteen years, was killed in 284 BC, her husband, Lysimachos, gave the city to a certain Eumenes, probably the brother of Philetairos of Pergamon.[47] Before long Lysimachos was dead, and Eumenes ruled Amastris without any obligations. Ariobarzanes, the son and future successor of Mithridates (who enters the historical record at this point), opened negotiations with Eumenes, who promptly and unexpectedly handed the city over to the Pontic kingdom, despite military threats and even an offer of payment from its mother city of Herakleia Pontika. Eumenes may have been acting on behalf of Pergamene interests, believing that they were better served by restraining the power of Herakleia.[48] The result was the most important territorial acquisition by Mithridates I beyond the original core of Pontos, since it gave the kingdom a port on the Black Sea and a bulwark against the expansionism of Herakleia.

With the death of Lysimachos at Seleukid hands in early 281 BC, Seleukos I sought to extend his power into northern Asia Minor by threatening Herakleia. He had already made an alliance with Pergamon. Ambassadors sent by Herakleia to Seleukos were not received, and the government of the city reached out to its neighbors, including Mithridates (as well as Byzantion and Chalkedon, on the Bosporos).[49] Nothing is known about the response, if any. Probably at the same time Seleukos sent his commander Diodoros into Cappadocia, with the result that Diodoros was killed and his army lost.[50] "Cappadocia" often includes "Pontos," and it may be that the Seleukid strategy was to neutralize Mithridates, who was beginning to demonstrate his regional power. If so, this obviously failed, and Mithridates's elimination of a Seleukid army may have been one of the factors that led him to declare himself king: the original kings, Antigonos Monopthalmos and Demetrios Polioketes, had taken the title when they defeated a Ptolemaic army.

Yet Seleukos's campaign against northern Asia Minor (and indeed Macedonia itself) was stillborn when he was assassinated later in 281 BC by a member of his staff, Ptolemy Keraunos (a son of Ptolemy I of Egypt), who had his own desire for Macedonia and indeed was declared its king.[51] The collapse of Seleukid ambitions in northwestern Asia Minor meant that Mithridates would have a freer hand to tend to the security and expansion of his kingdom.

The relationships that Mithridates had with Herakleia Pontika and Amastris are difficult to untangle and seem to change without viable explanations. Part of this is the deficiency of source material and the fact that the king, as a minor dynast, only entered the historical record when his activities impacted on the major powers. In addition, his paramount interest was the safety of his kingdom (which included any necessary territorial acquisitions), but this meant that he had to follow a narrow path and be sensitive to the ever-changing alliances and power bases of the era. Acquisition of Amastris was, to some extent, serendipitous; the relationship with Herakleia was somewhat more complex. As the most powerful city on the western coast of the southern Black Sea, it had to be both favored and contained.

An unexpected change in the dynamics of northern Asia Minor occurred in 278 BC, when several groups of migrating Celts entered the region.[52] These bands had been on the move for well over a century, coming from their homeland in modern France; one of them had attacked Rome in the early fourth century BC. In time others crossed the Hellespont, and although they were probably more peaceful and organized than Greek and Roman sources imply, they were seen as a danger, in fact an existential threat to the Hellenistic world and to civilization in general. Resistance to and defeat of them became part of the received view of the history of the third century BC, best visible today in the surviving art of the Pergamene kingdom. Greek sources called them the Galatians, from the same root as Latin "Galli" (English "Gauls"). In time various accommodations were achieved, and they settled in the lightly populated region of central

Asia Minor that came to be called Galatia, gradually becoming hellenized. They became notable as mercenaries, serving in most battles in the region well into the Roman period.[53]

Regardless of the actual nature of the Galatians, before long it was realized that they could be useful in the never-ending dynastic wars of the era. Mithridates understood their utility, according to the obscure historian Apollonios, who wrote a history of Karia (probably his home region) at an uncertain date.[54] His account is confused, but it recorded that Mithridates and his son Ariobarzanes allied with the Galatians and engaged the Ptolemies, defeating them and driving them into the sea. There is no date for the event, but it must have occurred during the last decade of the king's life. The context is probably the Ptolemaic operations in Karia during the reign of Ptolemy II (who came to the throne in 281 BC).[55] As a result of the campaign the Galatians allegedly founded several cities, most notably Ankyra (modern Ankara). The city had been visited by Alexander and thus already existed, but Arrian's account of his campaign (written in the second century AD) is anachronistic—the term "Galatia" is used—and the city may have been renamed by the Galatians (the name, unusual for an inland location, was said to refer to the anchors taken as spoils in the campaign against the Ptolemies).[56] Another Galatian foundation that may have helped Mithridates was Tauia (later Tavium, near modern Büyük Nefes), about eighty miles east of Ankyra and just south of the Pontic kingdom, an old Hittite center.[57] Ankyra—whenever the name was applied—and Tauia were thus towns controlled by an ally and therefore a theoretical barrier against perceived Seleukid and Ptolemaic incursions from this direction.

One element of the last years of the Founder was the appearance of his son and successor Ariobarzanes, named after his grandfather and born, in all probability, around 300 BC. No one else is known from Mithridates's immediate family, and the failure of the sources to mention any wives demonstrates that he did not have enough status to connect with one of the major dynastic families of the era, unlike his grandson Mithridates II, who married a Seleukid princess. Ariobarzanes is the only recorded child of Mithridates I, and while his father was still alive he obtained the city of Amastris for the kingdom and took part in the expedition against the Ptolemies. Apollonios's phrasing, that "Mithridates and Ariobarzanes" led the campaign, suggests that by the 270s BC the son had been raised to a level of co-rule with his father.

The Founder died in 266 BC. He was buried in the first of the royal tombs in Amaseia, high above the Iris River (fig. 1.3); visitors to the site today can still see the facade and enter the chamber. He had been in power thirty-six years, although it was only in the last fifteen—after the almost simultaneous deaths of Lysimachos and Seleukos I—that the Pontic kingdom began to coalesce and he could call himself king. He had moved his royal seat from the isolated fortress of Kimiata—probably not suitable for a townsite—to the new capital of Amaseia, and had established a foothold on the coast at Amastris. He solidified his southern border by establishing relations with the newly arrived Galatians. He ruled during what was arguably some of the most unstable years of the Hellenistic era, yet he skillfully balanced his own needs against those of the great powers, playing a role in terminating any Ptolemaic, Seleukid, and Macedonian aspirations in north-central Asia Minor. He was also indirectly involved in the demise of Seleukos I, although before long the Pontic kings would realize that the Seleukids were probably their best allies, as later marriage alliances demonstrate. By the time of his death and the transfer of power to Ariobarzanes, Pontos had emerged as one of the new powers in Asia Minor.

Chapter 3

The Kingdom Becomes
an Independent State

ARIOBARZANES

The reign of the son of Mithridates I, Ariobarzanes, is not well documented. He had been assisting his father for a number of years, involved in the matter of the Galatians and in acquiring the city of Amastris for the kingdom. He came to the throne in 266 BC, at perhaps thirty-five years of age, and was the only ruling member of the family to hold the name Ariobarzanes (Ariyabardana), which is known from at least the fifth century BC, when an earlier Ariobarzanes—perhaps the great-grandfather of the king—was an important player in events of northwest Asia Minor for a number of years, eventually receiving Athenian citizenship.[1]

King Ariobarzanes ruled Pontos for slightly over a decade. The only documented event of his reign was a deteriorating situation with the Galatians.[2] Details are not preserved, but after Ariobarzanes's death the Galatians invaded the kingdom. Nothing else is known about his reign; like the case of his father, his family relationships remain invisible except for the identity of his son Mithridates II. Even his death date cannot be determined precisely: it was during the reign of the Seleukid king Antiochos II (261–246 BC), perhaps after 250 BC.

MITHRIDATES II

When Mithridates II came to the throne in (probably) the early 240s BC, he was believed to be weak, perhaps because of his youth, and the Galatians, once the allies of the kingdom, attacked.[3] Evidently, the results of the invasion were serious enough that there was famine, and Mithridates appealed for help to Herakleia Pontika, which sent grain to the city of Amisos, from which it was transported to the interior. Implicit in this is that any past differences between Pontos and Herakleia had been settled, and that by this time Pontos controlled Amisos. This city, situated at the western end of the fertile Plain of Themiskyra and just fifteen miles from the mouth of the Iris River, was well placed as a seaport for shipment of commodities into Pontos proper, and acquisition of it probably occurred during the reign of Ariobarzanes or even earlier, but details are lacking.

Herakleia already had its own issues with the Galatians—there had been a previous attack—which may have encouraged the city to seek as a new ally its opponent of a generation previously. This earlier encounter took place just after the death of Nikomedes I of Bithynia (sometime between 255 and 253 BC), and presumably the Galatian attack on Pontos was a few years later. The help that Herakleia sent to Pontos resulted in a second threat by the Galatians against the city, which sent an embassy to them led by the historian Nymphis.[4] His diplomatic skills were probably less effective than his payment of five thousand gold pieces to the Galatian army and an additional two hundred each to the officers, and the Galatians withdrew and seem to have had no further interest in either Herakleia or the territory of Mithridates.

During the reign of Mithridates II the kingdom reached legitimacy as an international power, albeit a minor one. His marriage arrangements, which are discussed later, are proof of this, as well as the king's response to an earthquake that struck the island of Rhodes in 227 or 226 BC. The event can be dated with some precision because of the list of contemporary kings in Polybios's account.[5] The earthquake was devastating (although it was noted that it provided a fine opportunity for urban renewal), and its major casualty was the famous Colossus, which was over a hundred feet high but had stood for only half a century.

Many of the rulers of the Mediterranean world promptly gave aid to the Rhodians. Polybios listed ten kings and one queen who made contributions. As expected, the major kings (Ptolemy III, Seleukos II, and Antigonos III) donated lavish amounts, but the account mentions kings from as far away as Sicily (Hieron II and Gelon), as well as Queen Chryseis of Macedonia (the wife of Antigonos and mother of Philip V). Except for the Sicilian kings, who are listed separately, the monarchs are presented in order of importance, beginning with Ptolemy and the other major kings, and continuing down to regional dynasts, some of whom are otherwise unknown. Sixth on the list is Mithridates II; the amount that he gave is not specified, although Polybios noted that it was similar to that provided by his more powerful colleagues. The account of the donations of the eleven monarchs is the first extant report of such a collaborative effort by the Hellenistic rulers, coming slightly over a century after the death of Alexander the Great, at a time when the Hellenistic world, although never free of dynastic rivalries and warfare, had reached an era when cooperation was seen to have its own virtue.

Moreover, it marks the entry of the Mithridatic kingdom into global politics. To be sure, Mithridates II had already been engaged in marriage alliances, but these were pointed in one direction, toward the Seleukids. Now, however, in the early 220s BC, he was able to stand alongside his royal colleagues and take part in an effort that affected the entire Mediterranean world from Sicily to the Levant and Egypt, unlike the foreign policy of his predecessors, which had been limited to the defense of the kingdom or accommodation with the Seleukids alone.

Yet Mithridates did not rank high among the kings of the East: below Prousias I of Bithynia, who reigned just to the west of Pontos, and above a certain Lysanias, who ruled some principality in Asia Minor (perhaps in Karia) that cannot be identified today. Yet the Rhodian donations demonstrate the position of the Mithridatic kingdom in the world of the late third century BC.

MARRIAGE ALLIANCES

Mithridates's standing among contemporary kings was not only due to his participation in the relief of Rhodes but also because of his astute marriage connections. The women of the Mithridatic dynasty before his time remain anonymous, suggesting that the royal wives were not of significant dynastic importance. But Mithridates II, seeking to increase his legitimacy among the great powers of the era, reached out to the Seleukids for a marriage partner. At the time of his accession, the extent of the Seleukid kingdom far exceeded that of any of the other major states, from the Aegean to India and south into the Levant, with repeated attempts to gain a foothold in the Black Sea coastal regions.[6] The kingdom was at its territorial peak—although soon inexorable contraction would set in—and obviously desired some of Mithridates's possessions. The king probably realized the futility of any military opposition, but connections through marriage might be a way of establishing a peaceful relationship with the larger and more powerful kingdom.

Thus Mithridates II sought marriage with a Seleukid princess. The evidence is scant but credible, yet so vague that not even her name is known with certainty. It was probably Laodike (IV), as that was the name of her mother (Laodike I) and two of her daughters (Laodike X and XI).[7] Like so many Hellenistic royal names, it had heroic antecedents: the original Laodike was a Trojan princess, a daughter of King Priam,[8] and a later Laodike (XIV) was the matriarch of the Seleukid dynasty, the wife of a certain Antiochos (an officer of Philip II of Macedonia) and the mother of Seleukos I, the companion of Alexander the Great and the first Seleukid king.[9] It is thus no wonder that the name should become frustratingly common in the early Hellenistic period, and at least six holders of it are known from the royalty of the mid-third century BC, with more later, to the everlasting confusion of both ancient and modern commentators.

The marriage between Mithridates II and Laodike IV is solely documented in the *Chronicle* of Eusebios, to be sure a late source—from the early fourth century AD—but the report is unlikely to have been made up.[10] The sparse account merely states that one of the daughters (unnamed) of the Seleukid monarchs Antiochos II and Laodike I married Mithridates II. No date is provided, but the suggestion is that it was before the death of her father in 246 BC. Since Mithridates II had not been long on the throne, and Laodike IV had grown children by the 220s BC, this suggests a date of around 250 BC for the marriage, but dates between 250 and 240 BC have all been suggested. This connection between the two dynasties was a momentous event in the self-image of the Pontic kingdom, and may mark the beginning of a Pontic chronological era, although the evidence is far from certain.[11] A century later Pontos seems to have been using the Seleukid era, but this need not be a contradiction.[12]

By 246 BC Seleukos II, Laodike IV's brother, was on the Seleukid throne, ruling until 226 BC. Before his accession the Seleukids may have seen the marriage as a way of controlling northern Asia Minor to their advantage in the turbulent final years of Antiochos II. In a way, the Seleukids were protecting their north and west as they entered a period of increasing contention with the Ptolemies to their south.[13] Only a few months after the start of his reign, Seleukos II began a war against Ptolemy III of Egypt (the so-called Third Syrian War of 246–241 BC); preparations were surely underway before Antiochos II died and perhaps even at the time of the marriage. Moreover, Seleukos had to face internal contention with his brother, Antiochos Hierax ("the Hawk"), a rivalry exploited by their mother, Laodike I, who was now the Seleukid dowager queen. Further evidence that Seleukos was seeking to stabilize (or at least have fewer worries about) his northern frontier is that he allegedly gave Greater Phrygia to Mithridates as a dowry, although this should perhaps be treated cautiously since the assertion was made over a century later by Mithridates VI to support his claim to the territory.[14]

Mithridates II and Laodike IV had at least two children, both named Laodike (X and XI). Whether the little-known Mithridates III was also her child is not certain, and Laodike IV drops from the historical record after the birth of her children. Her homonymous daughters are difficult to distinguish. One, perhaps the younger (Laodike X), was given to her uncle Antiochos Hierax in some sort of hostage situation that is not fully understood.[15] Later she married Achaios, a cousin of the Seleukid ruling line, who claimed the title of king in 221 BC. He established himself at Sardis and was killed there in 213 BC by Antiochos III, the successor of Seleukos II. Laodike X seems to have survived her husband's death and gained a following at Sardis, but disappears from the historical record at that point. Whether she was the Laodike who was the mother of the Greco-Baktrian king Eukratides I, who came to the throne around 170 BC and whose coinage provides his mother's name, remains speculative.[16]

Her older sister, Laodike XI, was also of importance. In 222 BC she married Antiochos III, who came to the Seleukid throne in that year. The wedding took place at Seleukeia on the Euphrates, situated at an important crossing of the river in Commagene. It was a magnificent spectacle, and afterward the royal couple went to Antioch on the Orontes, the Seleukid capital, where Laodike was given the title of queen. This was the first time that one of the major Hellenistic kings took a spouse from one of the lesser (and non-Macedonian) dynasties, definite proof of the emergence of Pontos as an important state.[17]

By 204 BC Laodike XI had received the title of "sister-queen"—although she and Antiochos III were actually first cousins—perhaps an attempt to imitate the sibling marriage of the Ptolemaic dynasty.[18] In that year King Antiochos III wrote to Anaximbrotos, his satrap of Karia, stating that he was increasing the honors given to Laodike and establishing a cult of her, with chief priestesses who themselves were of royal origin.[19] The letter made it clear that Laodike was still alive at that time. Another inscription, from the Elamite town of Susa, although heavily restored, suggests that the cult also existed there in 177/176 BC, but that the queen was dead by then. Yet during her reign she acted independently, or as an equal partner with her spouse: around 204 BC the city of Teos (one of the twelve Ionian cities, north of Ephesos) granted her and her husband divine honors for services rendered, especially in relieving the city from Pergamene control. On the inscription recording the event, Laodike's goodwill toward the city is particularly noted, and a statue of her, as well as one of her husband, was set up in the local agora.[20] She was also honored through the construction of a springhouse in her name. Her independent profile was reinforced a few years later (probably in 197 BC) when she told the city of Iasos (in Karia) that they were to receive on her behalf a ten-year endowment of grain; in response the citizenry established a cult of her and the king.[21] This was an early example of philanthropy by a Hellenistic royal woman, something that in time would become a common trait, culminating in the activities of the aristocratic women of the Roman imperial period.

Laodike had eight, or perhaps nine, children, and it is through these numerous offspring that her legacy among the eastern dynastic network was assured. Two of her sons became Seleukid kings, Seleukos IV (ruled 189 or 187–175 BC) and Antiochos IV (ruled 175–164 BC), and between them they were the ancestors of all the subsequent Seleukid kings to the last, Philip II, who was forced out by the Romans in 65 BC. Her daughters made significant dynastic marriages. One was engaged to Demetrios I, king of Baktria. This took place around 200 BC when Demetrios made a visit to the Seleukid court before he was king.[22] He came to the throne shortly thereafter and allegedly embarked on an expedition to India, although the information is confused and unclear.[23] Because his wife—Laodike XI's daughter—is not named or ever heard from again, she may have died shortly after the marriage.

Another daughter, Antiochis, married Ariarathes IV of Cappadocia, perhaps also around 200 BC. Antiochis and Ariarathes were seemingly unable to have children, and she convinced her husband to accept two of her own children—Ariarathes and Holophernes—as his own. The father of these children is not known, and Ariarathes IV was allegedly unaware that they were not his. The younger Ariarathes was sent to Rome to be educated in 172 BC, an early instance of what would become a common practice for the children of Hellenistic royalty, and Holophernes was banished to Ionia.[24] By that time Antiochis and Ariarathes IV actually had had children (a son and two daughters). The son, originally named Mithridates, became King Ariarathes V of Cappadocia around 163 BC.[25] Clearly there are unexplained issues regarding the children of Antiochis. Nevertheless, the story provides an interesting insight into the dynastic maneuvering of the era, and of Hellenistic royalty generally, and also the indisputable fact that only the mother can know the parentage of children. The descendants of Antiochis, who was the granddaughter of Mithridates II of Pontos, ruled Cappadocia until the dynasty ended in 96 BC; Antiochis herself was killed at Antioch at the time of the death of her brother Antiochos IV in 164 BC, for unknown reasons.

Laodike XI and Antiochos III had another daughter, Laodike (V), whose career is unclear because of the many homonymous women of the era. She probably married in sequence her brothers Antiochos IV and Seleukos IV and also became high priestess of the cult of her mother, and perhaps was the mother of Antiochos V, who ruled briefly in the 160s BC. She may also have been the first Seleukid queen to be depicted on coinage.[26]

Yet the daughter of Antiochos III and Laodike XI whose impact was to be most prominent among future generations was the one who also brought the most famous Hellenistic dynastic name into the history of the eastern Mediterranean. Why her parents chose to name her Cleopatra is not known; it does not seem to have been used among royalty since the death of the sister of Alexander the Great a century previously.[27] The name also had some mythological authority, most notably as the wife of Meleagros in the Kalydonian Boar Hunt tale, but there was little indication that it would become so famous.

Cleopatra became an important player in the political ambitions of her parents. In 204 BC, the Egyptian king, Ptolemy IV, died mysteriously, and his successor, Ptolemy V, was a child. This resulted in a period of instability in Egypt, quickly exploited by the Seleukids.[28] Warfare between the Ptolemies and Seleukids was imminent, due to territorial disputes in the Levant and interior Syria. But then Antiochos III announced that he and Ptolemy V had concluded a marriage alliance—how much Ptolemy knew about this is uncertain, but he was convinced to agree—and in the winter of 194/193 BC sixteen-year-old Ptolemy married ten-year-old Cleopatra, who became Cleopatra I of Egypt.[29] The ceremony took place at Raphia on the Egyptian-Levantine border. Although neither survived long, all the remaining Ptolemaic rulers to the end of the dynasty in 30 BC were descended from the royal couple, whose children were Ptolemy VI, Ptolemy VIII, and Cleopatra II. Thus the granddaughter of Mithridates II of Pontos became the great-great-grandmother of her most famous namesake, Cleopatra VII, the last Ptolemaic ruler of Egypt and the companion of the triumvir Marcus Antonius.

These dynastic interactions are complex and often baffling to modern readers, and were equally so in antiquity. The Hellenistic penchant toward homonymity has long been a source of confusion. But the sheer number of prominent royal personalities who were descended from Mithridates II of Pontos shows not only the connectivity between the eastern dynasties but also the emergent importance of Pontos in the royal network of the era. Mithridates II did not know that his descendants would include, in addition to future rulers of Pontos to the end of the dynasty, Seleukid, Ptolemaic, Cappadocian, Armenian, Parthian, and Mauretanian royalty, with connections to Baktria and the Roman aristocracy.

THE LAST YEARS OF MITHRIDATES II

The marriage alliances are certainly the most important feature of the reign of Mithridates II, as they positioned him and his kingdom within the mainstream of the politics of the second half of the third century BC. With a Seleukid princess for his wife and, later, his daughter as Seleukid queen, he was inevitably drawn into the internal problems of the Seleukid state, which reverberated throughout Asia Minor. In particular there was the civil war between Seleukos II and Antiochos Hierax, brothers of Mithridates's wife, which began around 246 BC and continued for nearly a decade.

The sequence of events during these years is far from certain, but when war broke out between the brothers, Mithridates at first sided with Hierax.[30] Before open hostilities began, Seleukos had given his brother command of the Seleukid territories in Asia Minor, in part to counteract growing Pergamene strength and ambitions. Moreover, Seleukos and Ptolemy III were moving toward war over territorial issues in the Levant, and placating Hierax may have been to assure his support in this matter.

But Hierax quickly established a strong power base in Asia Minor, largely independent from the central Seleukid government; he did so by making alliances with the Galatians and Mithridates II. Hierax was still an adolescent—one report is that he was only fourteen—and it was at this time he gained his surname, "the Hawk," because of his adolescent aggressiveness, which made him seem like a bird of prey. His sister Laodike IV was probably not yet married to Mithridates; in fact, at some time during these years she was actually in the entourage of Hierax.[31]

Hierax eventually saw his chance and declared war on his brother, with the aid of Mithridates II and the Galatians. This seems to have occurred only after Seleukos II and Ptolemy III came to terms, which seems strategically unwise, and Seleukos promptly invaded the territories of Hierax's coalition. Around 240 BC, near Ankyra, a battle was fought in which Seleukos was defeated. He was suspected to have been killed, and allegedly Hierax was devastated at the report and elated when it turned out to be false.[32] This may be a paradigm for the regret felt by siblings whose inability to get along with one another leads to disaster, and there is no evidence of any long-term reconciliation. In fact, after the battle near Ankyra, Hierax's fortunes began a steady decline. Mithridates was no longer mentioned as an ally (neither were the Galatians), and although Hierax survived for over a decade more, he became an adventurer, wandering as far as Mesopotamia and Europe, and suffering a series of defeats until, fleeing Pergamene retribution, he died in Thrace around 226 BC.[33] But during his last years Mithridates II was no longer a part of his world, and it may be that after Seleukos's recovery from the battle near Ankyra Mithridates received some of the territory Hierax had claimed, and perhaps his sister in marriage, in an attempt to repair the damage done to northwest Asia Minor by her brother.

Given Mithridates's new legitimacy as king of an important state, due to his marriage alliances as well as his participation in the collaborative project to restore Rhodes, it was only natural that he should seek ways to expand his kingdom. If the report of his descendant Mithridates VI is to be believed, he received portions of Phrygia after the Ankyra battle, as part of the dowry for his wedding with Laodike IV.[34] But the Greek cities on the coast were still an issue. The kingdom had acquired Amisos at some uncertain date before the accession of Mithridates II, and the next region for assimilation was Sinope, which lies between Amisos and Herakleia, seventy-five miles along the coast from the former. In 220 BC Mithridates prepared to attack the city; whether he actually did so is ambiguous in Polybios's account.[35] The Sinopeans built elaborate defenses around the city and its port, not knowing whether the king would come by land or sea, perhaps an indication that it was believed he had substantial forces available. They also appealed to Rhodes for assistance, which sent a vast amount of support in terms of men, supplies, and funds, as well as a thousand jars of wine. Unfortunately, exactly what happened is not known, for Polybios, as was his custom, broke off his account in order to move to another contemporary topic, and the remainder of the story is not extant in the preserved portions of his history.[36]

At this time the Rhodians, despite the effects of the earthquake of a few years previously, were the preeminent maritime power of the eastern Mediterranean and, as can be seen, had interests as far as the Black Sea. In fact, a few years earlier, they had gone to war against Byzantion because that city was restricting trade from the sea to the Mediterranean world through what were considered exorbitant customs duties.[37] Mithridates, despite his previous assistance to the Rhodians in their time of need, may have realized that any engagement that would bring them against him would be unwise. Either his attack on Sinope never happened, or he was unsuccessful in taking the city. It was only forty years later that King Pharnakes I, his grandson, acquired Sinope for the kingdom.

Whatever happened between Mithridates II and Sinope, it is the last event associated with his kingship, and presumably he died shortly thereafter, having been on the throne about thirty years. He had come to power as a king thought to be so weak that the Galatians saw his accession as an opportunity for invasion; when he died, his kingdom was an international power and his daughter was the Seleukid queen. During those years Pontos evolved from a minor kingdom with ambitions limited to northern Asia Minor to an emergent major power with complex dynastic interests. The marriage alliances, in particular, gave Pontos new status. Another demonstration of the importance of the kingdom is its first coinage, although the date of its inauguration is far from certain, and it has been attributed to as early as Mithridates I or as late as Mithridates III.[38] The earliest coins seem to be gold staters with the head of Athena on the obverse and a Nike on the reverse, and with the Greek legend "of king Mithridates" (demonstrating that Greek was the official language of the kingdom). They are direct imitations of coins of Alexander the Great; even though the Pontic dynasty was not born out of his successors, and the Mithridatic kings were not related to those associated with Alexander, it is a clear statement that the self-image of Pontos was that it deserved to be placed within that world. These coins seem to fit into the ideology of the era of Mithridates II, when Pontos sought to prove its credentials as a respected member of the Greek world. Foregoing any connection with the environment of the defunct Persian empire (and thus the ancestors of the dynasty), Mithridates II instead located himself in the new culture of the legacy of Alexander, a solid means of creating legitimacy and a view forward rather than backward. This was an attitude that would be sustained to the end of the dynasty and his most famous descendant, Mithridates VI the Great. Moreover, a gold issue was an astute move, since gold coinage was the mark of a dominant state. It is probably the earliest gold coinage in Hellenistic northern Asia Minor, solid proof of the kingdom's view of itself in the third century BC.

Chapter 4

The Arrival of the Romans

MITHRIDATES III

The planned attack by Mithridates II on Sinope around 220 BC is the latest event associated with his reign. Thirty years later a new king, Pharnakes I, was on the Pontic throne and was part of a grand coalition fighting against Eumenes II of Pergamon, a conflict that took place in the early 180s BC.[1] Whatever had happened in the previous thirty years, the activities of the rulers of Pontos were not significant enough to warrant the attention of the major extant sources. An account may have appeared Polybios's *Histories*, which become fragmentary after 216 BC (the end of Book 5); Diodoros's *Bibliotheke*, another potential source, is also deficient for the period in question. Thus the Pontic kingdom during these years remains invisible to the modern reader.

Since both Mithridates II and Pharnakes I are well documented, the lack of any information about either during this interval means it can be assumed that the former died shortly after 220 BC and the latter came to the throne not long before 190 BC. This presumes an intervening king, and it is possible to conclude that he was Mithridates III, not mentioned in the extant literature and only cited on an inscription from Delos as the father of Mithridates IV. He was probably but not certainly the son of Mithridates II and Laodike IV. According to Plutarch, in his account of the escape of Mithridates I from the entourage of Antigonos I Monophthalmos, there were eight kings in the Pontic line, until the Romans brought the dynasty to an end. Appian confirmed this, and also added that six of the kings were named Mithridates. Since two kings with other names are known (Ariobarzanes and Pharnakes I), there is a missing Mithridates, who can only be placed between Mithridates II and Pharnakes I, since after Pharnakes there is no gap in the king list. The last ruler of the

50

Hellenistic Pontic kingdom was Mithridates the Great, who died in 63 BC and must be Mithridates VI.[2]

Thus Mithridates III ruled most if not all of the period between 220 and 190 BC.[3] Yet essentially nothing is known about his reign, or the Pontic kingdom, during those thirty years, until Pharnakes I was on the throne by 190 BC. In fact, extrapolating back from the early years of Pharnakes, there is no evidence of any significant achievement, changes, or issues in foreign policy during the previous reign.

Mithridates III is also documented by his tomb, located at Amaseia between those of his father and son, Mithridates II and Pharnakes I,[4] and his presumed coinage, a series of silver issues with a royal portrait on the obverse, facing right, showing a prominent nose, thick lips, a close-cropped beard, and a wrinkled brow.[5] The quality of the portrait is high, demonstrating that the king had access to Greek die cutters who created a realistic and individualized portrait, in the fashion of Hellenistic representations of foreign royalty. On the reverse is the Greek legend "of King Mithridates" and a seated Zeus, remindful of the statue of the god at Olympia. There is also a star and crescent symbol, which appears here for the first time on Pontic coinage, and which would remain through the issues of Mithridates VI (fig. 4.1). This is some kind of dynastic device, not fully explained. The coins attributed to Mithridates III are not certainly identified with that king, but the portrait strongly resembles that on the coinage of his son Pharnakes I, a younger version of the same physiognomy.[6]

(a) (b)

Figure 4.1 Coin of Mithridates VI with star and crescent: obverse and reverse. American Numismatic Society 1967.152.390. Courtesy American Numismatic Society.

THE HELLENISTIC WORLD, 220–190 BC

The period from 220 to 190 BC was one of profound change in Hellenistic Asia Minor, most notably due to the arrival of the Romans and their involvement in the affairs of the region. Mithridates III was not the only new king who came to the throne around 220 BC. His brother-in-law Antiochos III became Seleukid king in 222 BC, and in the same year Philip V came to power in Macedonia and in the following one Ptolemy IV in Egypt. Meanwhile, Attalos I of Pergamon, the grandnephew of Philetairos, who had been on the throne for twenty years, was contending with the Seleukids for dominance of Asia Minor. In the Levant, there was repeated and sporadic warfare between the Seleukids and the Ptolemies, with the former generally gaining a more dominant position.[7]

But it was in the traditional Greek world that the future was being decided. Piracy in the Adriatic had brought the Romans to Illyria in 229 BC, but an adventurer, Demetrios of Pharos (modern Hvar in Croatia), resisted the Romans and supported the pirates. The Romans, occupied with the Gauls in the Celtic territories north of Italy, tended at first to ignore Demetrios's activities, but eventually, in 219 BC, a consular army was sent against him. Demetrios promptly sought refuge with Philip V of Macedonia. Two years later the first official contact was made between Rome and Macedonia when an embassy was sent to Philip requesting the extradition of Demetrios. Yet the Romans were in no position to enforce the demand, since the previous autumn Hannibal had crossed the Alps and invaded Italy. Philip, on the other hand, saw this as an opportunity to remove the Romans from the eastern Adriatic—dangerously close to his own interests—and began to attack Roman outposts in what has come to be called the First Macedonian War. An attempt by Ptolemy IV to negotiate a truce was the first Roman contact with the Ptolemaic kingdom.

By 215 BC Philip V had made an alliance with Carthage, and then with Prousias I of Bithynia, thus extending his reach to all three continents. This caused Attalos I of Pergamon to ally with the Romans, which brought Roman interests into Asia Minor. Although the Romans remained largely occupied with Hannibal, the Aegean world was polarizing into a Roman coalition (including Pergamon and a number of southern Greek states, especially Athens and Sparta) and a Macedonian one (including Bithynia and much of Central Greece).

When the Second Punic War came to an end in 201 BC, Rome turned its attention to the east, with the Second Macedonian War beginning the following year. A Roman embassy was sent to Athens, which ordered Philip to cease war on the Greek states and to compensate Attalos (who was present) for injuries received. This was the first time that the Romans gave orders to a Hellenistic power, and compliance was expected. The Roman ambassadors continued east and opened negotiations with Antiochos III and Ptolemy V in an attempt to end the Fifth Syrian War. This was the first official meeting between Rome and the Seleukids.

Needless to say, Philip ignored the Roman ultimatum, and the Second Macedonian War lasted until 197 BC, when he was defeated at Kynoskephalai in Thessaly. The terms of the settlement included the surprising statement that not only were the Greek cities in Europe to be free and independent but those in Asia Minor as well. Philip had claimed some territory in western Asia Minor, and this was the Romans' primary concern, but the decree was a stronger rebuke to the active territorial interests of Antiochos III. To be sure, he protested, and in the following year the Romans ordered him to release any cities in Asia that he controlled and not to invade Europe. In return, in the winter of 194/193 BC, Antiochos attempted to establish an official agreement of friendship and alliance with the Romans; this was at the same time that he strengthened his relations with Ptolemy V by marrying his daughter Cleopatra I—the grand-daughter of Mithridates II—to him. Yet the Romans refused any adjustment of the previous order.

In the autumn of 192 BC, Antiochos attacked Demetrias, the Macedonian royal city in Thessaly, thus invading Europe, and Rome declared war. Within a year—after a loss at Thermopylai—he returned to Asia. The Romans followed, and they defeated Antiochos again in early 189 BC at Magnesia By Sipylos. At the Seleukid royal residence of Apameia, in Phrygia, a treaty was concluded in which Antiochos agreed to withdraw from essentially all of Asia Minor and to pay an immense indemnity, which greatly assisted the Roman economy.[8] The treaty, preserved in detail by the ancient sources, sets out in precise specifics the disposition of western and southern Asia Minor, as far north as Phrygia and Mysia. In addition to eliminating Seleukid control in all but extreme southeastern Asia Minor, it greatly increased the power and extent of Pergamon: King Eumenes II, who had succeeded his father Attalos I in 197 BC, received not only an indemnity from Antiochos but additions to his territory, including footholds in Europe. Rome was now able to dictate the future of the kingdoms, dynasties, and cities in Asia Minor.

Of particular interest was the presence in Antiochos's entourage of the famous Carthaginian leader, Hannibal. After his defeat by the Romans in the Second Punic War and further difficulties at Carthage, he had fled to the Seleukids in 195 BC, becoming one of Antiochos's major advisors, although with a low opinion of his strategic abilities. Needless to say, Hannibal's primary goal was vengeance against the Romans, who considered him a destabilizing influence in Asia Minor.[9] Thus one of the many conditions of the treaty of Apameia was that Antiochos give up Hannibal, but he slipped away to Crete. He was next reported at the Armenian court of King Artaxias I, although this seems rather far afield from his other travels and is dubious. Then he came to Bithynia, as an advisor—militarily and architecturally—to Prousias I, continuing his agitation against the Romans. He took up residence on an estate—poignantly named Libyssa in memory of his homeland—writing anti-Roman pamphlets until his suicide in 183 BC.[10] Despite his desultory last years, the mutual obsessions between him and the Romans were an important element in Asia Minor in the 180s BC and affected the policies of the regional dynasts, including those of Pontos.

Nevertheless, the long extant list of participants in the various campaigns of the generation after 220 BC makes no mention of Pontos or its kings, although some territory may have been lost to Pergamon as part of the treaty of Apameia in 189 BC. This is probably why Pharnakes I would send ambassadors to Rome a few years later regarding an issue with Pergamon.[11]

THE ACCESSION OF PHARNAKES I

The exact dates of the reign of Pharnakes I are not known (fig. 4.2).[12] As noted, he probably came to the throne around the time of the Apameia treaty, succeeding his father, the ephemeral Mithridates III. His successor, Mithridates IV, became king between 160 and 155 BC, and the last dated event of Pharnakes's reign was when he and his wife Nysa received honors from Athens during the archonship of Tychandros in 160/159 BC.[13] Within five years Mithridates IV was on the throne, who was not the son but the brother of Pharnakes. After his reign the succession returned to the direct line with Pharnakes's son Mithridates V.[14] There was also a second Pharnakes, the great-grandson of the first, who in the 40s BC briefly attempted to reconstitute the Pontic kingdom after the death of his father, Mithridates VI. The name Pharnakes marks an unexplained break

Figure 4.2 Coin of Pharnakes I: obverse and reverse. British Museum 1872,0709.131. Photograph © The Trustees of the British Museum.

from the onomastics of the Pontic dynasty and may suggest that Pharnakes was not the firstborn son of Mithridates III. It was a historic Persian name (Farnaka), most notably held by the uncle of Dareios I, who was administrator of the palace at Persepolis between 505 and 497 BC.[15]

In the Apameia arrangement, the Romans and Eumenes II of Pergamon profited the most. In addition to acquiring a substantial indemnity, Eumenes's territory was greatly enlarged, receiving the Thracian Chersonesos (the long narrow peninsula on the northern side of the Hellespont); its major city, Lysimacheia (founded by Lysimachos in 309 BC); and much of Phrygia, part of Mysia, and various cities as far south as Ephesos and inland to Tralleis and Sardis. If Pontos also possessed any part of Phrygia at that time—as Mithridates VI was to claim a century later—the kingdom had cause for concern at the growing power of Pergamon, now situated on its margins.[16]

Yet other than the Seleukids—who were to play no future role in the destiny of Asia Minor beyond its extreme southeastern portions—the real losers in the Apameia treaty were the Bithynians. Bithynia had emerged as an independent state in the second half of the fifth century BC and, not without effort, generally managed to retain its independence against the Persians, Alexander the Great, and the successor dynasties. Its historic territory was extreme northwestern Asia Minor, extending inland from the coasts of the Propontis and Bosporos. Zipoites, who came to power in 328 BC, may have been the first minor dynast to declare himself king, in 297 BC. In 230 BC, a vigorous monarch, Prousias I, began his rule. After half a century on the throne, he was followed by his son Prousias

II, who reigned from 182 to 149 BC. In 74 BC the great-grandson of the latter, Nikomedes IV, willed the kingdom to Rome.

Because of territorial proximity, the interests of Bithynia and Pontos could often be intertwined, and after the Apameia treaty both states realized the dangers of Pergamene expansionism. Due to the treaty, Bithynia had lost its claim to Mysia (the historic hinterland of Pergamon), which Prousias I had acquired during a period of Pergamene weakness in the late 190s BC. It is unlikely that Prousias had seized the city of Pergamon itself, but he probably held the lands to its northeast, adjoining the traditional Bithynian homeland. Thus Prousias had every reason to find fault with the treaty of Apameia, and the arrival of Hannibal at his court would make the Romans especially interested in his kingdom. Soon Prousias enlisted Pharnakes I of Pontos to his cause.

The early years of Pharnakes were marked by his involvement as a Bithynian ally in the war against Pergamon, his sudden acquisition of the coastal city of Sinope, and the first contacts with Rome. Pontos had not been directly affected by the Apameia treaty, and this may have encouraged Pharnakes to adopt a more aggressive posture than his predecessors, becoming involved in the overall destiny of Asia Minor rather than limiting himself to the territorial concerns of his own region.

Pergamon had benefitted the most from the treaty, and thus it was perhaps natural that the other states in the region would feel a need to contain this expanded power. Bithynia had suffered the most, and the appearance of Hannibal may have been the catalyst for assembling a coalition in the early 180s BC against Eumenes II of Pergamon. Prousias and Hannibal were of a similar age (around sixty) and seem to have had an instant rapport; the king came to rely on the Carthaginian for both strategic and tactical advice.[17]

Prousias and Hannibal perhaps made a visit to Pharnakes in Pontos to enlist his support.[18] The other members of the coalition were the Galatian tetrarch Ortiagon, a man noted for his culture and bravery, who had unfulfilled visions of uniting all the Galatians, and Philip V of Macedonia.[19] Ortiagon is not heard from again and may have been killed in the war; Philip probably only provided logistical support.[20]

The war did not go well for the coalition. Although Hannibal, in his last campaign, managed some striking tactical maneuvers—especially when he threw jars full of snakes onto the Pergamene ships—the Pergamene forces defeated the coalition in a land battle at Mount Lypedron, an unknown location in Bithynia. This may be the victory celebrated by the Telmessians (presumably the inhabitants of the Karian town of Telmessos, which was a Pergamene possession at the time) in December 184 BC. The effusive inscription, from a location far away from the presumed area of conflict, suggests that it may be a commemoration of the end of the war.[21]

For a war that lasted nearly five years, it is astonishingly poorly documented. Despite this, it is clear that the coalition forces lost, although not easily. Eumenes's greatest fear was Philip V of Macedonia, who probably had greater resources than the other participants. Near the end of the war, perhaps in late 184 BC, Eumenes sent his brother Athenaios to Rome to complain about Philip's involvement.[22] Philip was also destabilizing Thrace, close to territories that Eumenes had acquired under the Apameia treaty. In addition, Philip and Pharnakes sent envoys to Rome, the first official contact between the kingdom of Pontos and the Romans. Sparta and Rhodes also sent representatives, and Livy pointed out that never before had there been so many people from Asia Minor in Rome. The Romans took all this seriously and sent out a commission to investigate.[23]

The Rhodians had come to Rome not because of the Pergamene-Bithynian war but because of another matter entirely, the sudden seizure by Pharnakes of the city of Sinope, where they had interests. Sinope had become an enclave in the midst of the expanding coastal territories of Pontos, especially after the kingdom acquired Amisos. It lay at the end of an ancient trade route from Mesopotamia and was the closest city in Asia Minor to the rich territories on the north shore of the Black Sea. It would be a major asset to Pontos, which would thus effectively control all the central part of the southern coast of the sea and also possess an excellent staging point for the north shore. Mithridates II had attempted to take the city around 220 BC; now, forty years later, his grandson took advantage of the distractions due to the Pergamene-Bithynian war and successfully obtained it. It may be that Pharnakes withdrew from the wartime coalition in order to pursue a policy more relevant to the future of his kingdom, believing that those who might object were otherwise occupied. Presumably the capture of Sinope, which required a long siege, was, at the latest, during 183 BC.[24]

There is no extant report on the seizure itself, only the rather horrified reaction to it. Rhodes, whose connections with the region went back half a century—ever since Mithridates II had threatened Sinope—called the action a "crime" (*atychia*), or, in Livy's Latin, a "calamity" (*clades*). The following year the Roman commissioners reported that Pharnakes was greedy and arrogant. Even Strabo, who would normally take the Pontic side of things, since his ancestors were involved in the Pontic royal government, wrote that the city had been "enslaved." Clearly Pharnakes, however reasonable his actions seemed in terms of Pontic domestic policy, offended all sides.[25]

Pharnakes's acquisitions were not limited to the city of Sinope itself. Sinope possessed a string of settlements to the east, most notably Kotyros (modern Ordu), about 150 miles away, beyond the Pontic town of Amisos, and Kerasous (near modern Giresun), thirty miles farther east. Even more to the east was the most important city on this part of the coast, Trapezous (modern Trabzon), the limit of Sinopean control, at the borders of Armenia. The evidence is uncertain, but it is probable that Pharnakes also took possession of these towns, either peacefully or otherwise, when he acquired Sinope, with the possible exception of Trapezous, which may only have come under Pontic control at the time of Mithridates VI.[26]

As part of this expansion of Pontic territory, Pharnakes became the first of its kings to found a city and name it after himself. The new settlement of Pharnakeia (at modern Giresun) was populated—as was common with Hellenistic foundations—from towns in the region, especially Kotyros and Kerasous (which Pharnakeia was near). The town seems never to have become particularly important, probably because it was situated between the ancient centers of Amisos and Trapezous.[27]

Regardless of the distaste toward the seizure of Sinope expressed by the Rhodians and Romans, and perhaps others, the city became the major port of the expanding Pontic kingdom. Pharnakes was probably the first to develop a Pontic navy, which would have been based at Sinope.[28] In annexing this ancient trade center and seaport, Pontos for the first time moved away from being a state oriented solely in northern Asia Minor and began to look north, across the Black Sea toward the little-known lands on its north shore and beyond. Moreover, Pharnakes now controlled approximately four hundred miles of the southern Black Sea coast. Sinope became the new Pontic capital and the seat of its royalty, who thereafter were born and buried there.[29]

THE WAR BETWEEN PERGAMON AND PONTOS

Exactly why Pharnakes sent a delegation to Rome is far from clear, since the sources only refer vaguely to the existence of matters in dispute, without any specifics. It is possible that the king wanted to be involved in any settlement of the war between Pergamon and Bithynia, and may also have felt a need to justify his seizure of Sinope. In addition, the war may have impacted on Pontic claims to parts of Phrygia and Galatia. The various embassies arrived in Rome, probably late in 183 BC, and the Senate agreed to send commissioners to Asia Minor—led by a certain Marcus (who cannot be otherwise identified)—to investigate the matter of Sinope and the dispute between Pharnakes and Eumenes.[30]

It is difficult to structure events in an exact chronological sequence, and there are gaps in the narrative, but it seems that while Marcus's commission was gathering evidence, Pharnakes, having finished with Sinope, moved against Galatia, Paphlagonia, and Cappadocia, presumably the portions that Pergamon held but which he considered to belong to Pontos. When Marcus returned to Rome, his report, which was not favorable toward Pharnakes, may have led to an attempt at a truce.[31]

But Pharnakes persisted in his military activities, despite a Roman order to stand down, and sent his general Leokritos to Galatia in winter—perhaps early 180 BC—with a force of reportedly ten thousand. Leokritos is the first person known in Pontic history who was not a member of the royal family. His name shows that Pharnakes had Greek commanders in his army, and he may have been a descendant of the Leokritos who had died at Athens in 287 BC in a revolt against Demetrios Poliorketes.[32] Greek commanders would become a standard element of the Pontic military to the end of the dynasty.

In Galatia, Leokritos was able to gain the support of two local chieftains, Kassignatos and Gaizatorix, but only briefly. When the Pergamene army showed up a few months later, under the command of Eumenes and his brother Attalos (the future king Attalos II), the chieftains sought Pergamene protection, which was refused, although Kassignatos may have eventually ended up as a Pergamene cavalry commander.[33] In Paphlagonia, Pharnakes seized the treasury of another chieftain, Morzios of Gangra, who was probably the most powerful regional leader.[34]

The Pergamene army quickly moved against the invasion of Galatia, but by the time they arrived, Leokritos had withdrawn, so the army advanced on Pontos proper. En route they joined with Ariarathes IV of Cappadocia at Parnassos, just northeast of Lake Tatta. He had his own complaint against Pharnakes, who had also seized his treasury. Shortly thereafter the combined forces heard that another Roman commission had arrived demanding a truce: the commissioners sought out Pharnakes, who showed no interest in their proposal. Nevertheless the Romans insisted that the king send a delegation to Pergamon to meet Eumenes.

This was probably Eumenes's suggestion, because he felt that a meeting between the two kings and the Romans would demonstrate Pharnakes's unreliability and arrogance. Yet the conference broke up with no solution, and the war continued.

It was now probably the spring of 180 BC, and the war became more aggressive. Leokritos appeared at Teion (or Tios), on the Black Sea between Herakleia and Amastris. This was traditionally an outpost of Herakleia but had been given to Pergamon in the Apameia treaty, perhaps in part because it was the home of Philetairos, the founder of the Pergamene dynasty.[35] But given Pontos's consistent expansionism along the coast, it was a natural locality for Pontos to acquire, and Leokritos attacked the city. Under a truce, a mercenary force was to be given safe conduct away from the city, but Leokritos, under orders from Pharnakes, killed them all as they were leaving, an action that further lowered the international reputation of the king. Nevertheless, possession of Teion moved the effective Pontic territory farther west along the coast to a point almost halfway between Amastris and Herakleia. Meanwhile, Eumenes had blockaded the Hellespont, thus eliminating movement in and out of the Black Sea.[36] The goal was to block seaborne supplies to Pontos, perhaps aggravated by fear of a Pontic fleet in the Aegean, but the action did not meet with the approval of the Rhodians, who had interests in the Black Sea, and Eumenes soon withdrew.

At this point the Seleukid king, Seleukos IV, attempted to enter the war on Pharnakes's side.[37] He was Pharnakes's cousin and had come to the throne just after the time of the Apameia treaty that had severely constrained his father. An offer of five hundred talents from Pharnakes may have eased his decision. He evidently moved his army some distance north but soon remembered that crossing the Tauros mountains would be a direct violation of the treaty. He had been visited shortly before by Titus Quinctius Flamininus, who had been involved in Roman affairs in Greece and Asia Minor for many years (he had defeated Philip V at Kynoskephalai in 197 BC) and who may have told Seleukos that it was unwise to break the treaty.[38] Unfortunately Diodoros's account, the major extant source, breaks off and does not provide the full details of why Seleukos started and then withdrew, but he never came to his cousin's aid.

With the failure of Seleukos to help, Pharnakes was in an untenable position. Presumably the combined Pergamene and Cappadocian armies were within his territory. Joining them was the new king of Bithynia, Prousias II, who had succeeded his father Prousias I probably in 182 BC and turned against the historic allies of Bithynia in order to support Pergamon. His reign, which lasted until

149 BC, was marked by discontent; he was weak, uneducated, and ignorant, and eventually was killed in a palace revolt led by his son Nikomedes II.[39]

Thus Pharnakes was forced—presumably by the Romans—to sign a peace treaty, probably in the autumn of 180 BC (or perhaps the following spring). The text was preserved verbatim by Polybios.[40] The disputing parties were Eumenes, Prousias, and Ariarathes on one side and Pharnakes and a certain Mithridates on the other. This Mithridates had not been mentioned previously by Polybios and cannot easily be identified. He may be the "satrap of [Lesser] Armenia" named later in the same passage, or a ruler of Sophene. Both were adjoining territories to the southeast of Pontos, and the satrap may have been a relative of Pharnakes and might reasonably be expected to have been allied with him.[41] In the treaty, the king was enjoined not to invade Galatia and to withdraw from Paphlagonia and Cappadocia, to make restitution to the inhabitants of those regions, and to return those whom he had deported to their homes. The treasuries of Morzios and Ariarathes were also to be restored. He was to evacuate Teion (which was given to Bithynia) and pay an indemnity of nine hundred talents. The treaty records some additional insights into the nature of the war and Pharnakes's ambitions, such as his invasion of Paphlagonia and the alliance with Mithridates of Lesser Armenia or Sophene (which show attempts to expand Pontic control east and west of what was previously claimed), as well as the massive deportations that the war involved. Pharnakes had gained nothing and had become responsible for a large financial burden, which was still affecting the kingdom nearly twenty years later.[42]

There is much more of interest in the text of the treaty. Three regional dynasts are listed in addition to the participating major kings: Artaxias I of Greater Armenia; a certain Akousilochos, who is otherwise unknown but whose territory was probably east of Pontos; and Gatalos the Sarmatian, who was north of the Black Sea and whose involvement suggests Pontic aspirations in that direction. Also mentioned are four cities: Herakleia, Mesembria, Chersonesos, and Kyzikos. Herakleia, of course, had been involved in the affairs of northwest Asia Minor for some time and had long had a contentious relationship with the Pontic kingdom. Mesembria (modern Nesebur in Bulgaria) had been founded on the west coast of the Black Sea in the late sixth century BC, and its inclusion in the treaty is the first hint of worries regarding possible Pontic expansion toward that area. Chersonesos was on the north shore of the sea, in modern Crimea, and was another example of Pontic interests toward the north. Kyzikos, a Milesian settlement on the Propontis, had historic relations with the Pergamene dynasty.[43]

The text of the treaty noted that all the cities were independent, although it cannot be determined whether they, or the three dynasts mentioned, were actually involved in the war. It is more probable that the war had caused widespread awareness of Pontic ambitions among the states and cities around the Black Sea, and those that were the most prominent would wish to be certain that their interests were upheld.

It had been less than a decade since the Apameia treaty had seemingly brought peace to Asia Minor, yet its arrangements were in danger of being disrupted: even the Seleukids were attempting to assert their traditional interests in the region. All four of the cities might have seen a danger in Pontic aggression, especially since Teion and Sinope had already succumbed to it. Herakleia was only forty miles farther along the coast from Teion; Chersonesos was one of its settlements. Kyzikos and Mesembria could have been persuaded by Herakleia that Pontos was a threat.[44] The Sarmatians had associations with Chersonesos.[45] The connectivity between the places mentioned in the treaty shows the extensive concern about Pontic intentions—almost around the entire circuit of the Black Sea—a harbinger of the actual Pontic territorial acquisitions over the next century: Pharnakes would conclude an agreement with Chersonesos in 155 BC.[46]

It is probable that all the signatories to the treaty other than Mithridates of Lesser Armenia or Sophene were opposed to Pharnakes and his ambitions. Moreover, the Romans were almost certainly involved and probably dictated some if not all of the terms, since they may have been particularly worried at the threat of a Seleukid move back into northern or western Asia Minor. Thus the reach of Roman interests also essentially encircled the Black Sea. To them, Pharnakes was a destabilizing influence, and their entry into the political dynamics of Pontos would hardly have caused them to look favorably on its king. This first impression on both sides was remembered when the Romans repeatedly went to war against Pharnakes's grandson, Mithridates VI, who cited the treatment of his grandfather as one of the reasons for war.[47]

PONTOS AFTER THE PERGAMENE WAR

Thus Pharnakes's ambitions were curtailed by means of the treaty of late 180 BC. Although he was to remain on the throne for another twenty years, or more, several of his adversaries and allies had passed from the scene. Prousias I of Bithynia died in 182 BC after ruling for half a century. His friend and ally Hannibal, facing Roman demands for his extradition and under house arrest at Libyssa, had drunk poison in 183 BC, thus, as he said, relieving the Roman people from their lengthy worries.[48] The Romans had pursued him for nearly twenty years after the end of the Second Punic War, and their obsession with him had been one of the reasons that they had become involved in Asia Minor. Yet the death of Hannibal only came after the Romans were too deeply implanted to change direction.

In Macedonia, Philip V was to die at Amphipolis a few months after the treaty restraining Pharnakes was signed and was succeeded by his son Perseus, who unsuccessfully attempted to restore Macedonian power but lost his kingdom in the process.[49] He was deposed by the Romans in 168 BC, and the independent kingdom of Macedonia came to an end.

Despite the emphasis of Pharnakes's expansionism toward the west and south, the treaty reveals that he was moving in all directions, not only toward Cappadocia, Galatia, Bithynia, and Pergamon but north into the Chersonesos across the Black Sea and east into Armenia. He also attempted to connect with the Seleukids to the southeast, but the Romans told Seleukos IV not to become involved.

Armenia was another matter. The treaty is the first evidence for Pontic interests in that direction. Armenia is located in the high uplands just to the east of Asia Minor proper, extending north into the southern Caucasus, between the southeastern Black Sea and the Caspian Sea. It reaches its highest point at Mount Ararat (16,854 feet); the sources of the Tigris and Euphrates also lie in the territory near one another. Although Armenia was known to the Mesopotamian and Levantine world from earliest times—both the source of the Euphrates and Mount Ararat are mentioned in the book of Genesis—it remained outside the horizon of the Greek world until Xerxes levied the Armenians for his invasion of Greece. Xenophon and his forces were probably the first Greeks to enter at least the fringes of the region, in the winter of 401–400 BC, by which time it was already famous as a large and prosperous territory.[50]

After Alexander the Great passed to the south in 331 BC,[51] Armenia came under Seleukid control, but as Seleukid power declined, it was divided into two kingdoms, generally called Greater (to the east) and Lesser (to the west) Armenia. Taking advantage of the restrictions placed on the Seleukids in 189 BC, Antiochos III's satrap of Greater Armenia, Artaxias I, declared himself king and founded a new capital city, Artaxata (near modern Aralik). Hannibal was said to have planned and supervised its construction, but this is questionable and may be nothing more than a later Armenian attempt to adopt an anti-Roman posture by indicating closeness to Rome's great enemy.[52] Yet it can be presumed that Artaxias began to have worries about Pharnakes's ambitions, although not directly threatened, and thus he became a signatory to the treaty of 180 BC restraining him.

To the west, between Artaxias's territory and Pontos, was Lesser Armenia, and to its south, Sophene. Both of these had evolved into kingdoms under similar circumstances as Greater Armenia. The ruler of (probably) Lesser Armenia, Mithridates, is only known because he was an ally of Pharnakes; presumably, for the dynast of a small territory that had recently become independent, opposition to the ambitious king of Pontos would not have seemed wise. But nothing more is known about Lesser Armenia until Mithridates V of Pontos, Pharnakes's son, was styled "king of Pontos and Armenia" around 130 BC.[53] This can only refer to Lesser Armenia, since the dynasty of Greater Armenia remained in power and independent, and thus Lesser Armenia had been absorbed into the Pontic kingdom sometime during the previous half century. Yet it is clear that as early as the 180s BC Pharnakes had his designs on all of Armenia.

Not mentioned in the treaty of 180 BC were the Seleukids, once the greatest power in Asia Minor. Since the Apameia agreement they had been constrained to the extreme southeast. Antiochos IV, who came to the throne in 175 BC, turned his efforts against the Ptolemies—with little success—and cultivated relationships with the cities of Greece.[54] Yet the great power of the era was Pergamon, where Eumenes II and his brother Attalos II were already working to bring the kingdom to the peak of its influence and territorial extent, endowing the magnificent artistic and architectural program for which the dynasty came to be known. When Attalos came to the throne in 159 BC, Pergamene territory extended from Thrace in Europe to Cappadocia and the Seleukid frontier at the edge of Cilicia, excepting only some districts in the west and southwest that were under the control of free Greek cities.[55] And even though the Romans did not actually acquire territory in Asia Minor until after the Pergamene legacy of 133 BC, their presence was everywhere, and they had had contacts with most if not all of the cities and states in the region. Such was the world that Pharnakes confronted in the last two decades of his reign.

Having been blocked on all sides, Pharnakes spent his final years in more diplomatic activities. His acquisition of Sinope and the construction of a fleet allowed him to extend his influence across the Black Sea and into the Aegean.[56] Chersonesos was the most remote location cited in the treaty of 180

BC, and it is hardly unexpected that cautiously, and after a number of years, Pharnakes would reach out in its direction. Even though the Romans were probably involved in dictating the terms of the treaty, it might be believed that any interest by Pharnakes in the region north of the Black Sea would attract only nominal Roman interest.

In 155 BC Pharnakes and the city of Chersonesos concluded an agreement.[57] The text, partially preserved on an inscription discovered at Chersonesos, reveals that the city would assist Pharnakes in protecting his kingdom, and that the king would provide aid to Chersonesos if it were attacked by the neighboring barbarians. Pharnakes also swore that he would not make any hostile moves against the city, including stockpiling weapons, which suggests that he may have done so previously. Both sides agreed to continue their friendship with the Romans, demonstrating that Chersonesos and Pontos had already entered into some alliance with them, however limited, and perhaps with each other. The inscription is dated to the month of Daseios in the 157th year as "King Pharnakes reckons time," which would be, according to the Seleukid era generally in use in Asia Minor at that time, spring 155 BC.[58] The date is supported to some extent by archaeological evidence, particularly Rhodian stamped amphoras.[59]

Presumably the friendship between Rome, Pontos, and Chersonesos had been established as a feature of the treaty of 180 BC, and thus it shows the long reach of Roman power even at this date, perhaps into regions that no Roman official had as yet seen.[60] Moreover, the treaty was valid only as long as both participants remained on good terms with Rome. In addition, Pharnakes had some sort of relationship with the city of Odessos (modern Varna in Bulgaria), on the western Black Sea coast, although the inscription recording this is too fragmentary to determine context. Odessos, a Milesian foundation, was a prosperous free city only forty miles north of Mesembria, one of the signatories to the treaty of 180 BC; thus there was some unspecified Pontic interest in this region. Like Chersonesos, Odessos may have looked to Pharnakes for help against the indigenous populations of the interior.[61]

In these attempts to reach out to cities on the western and northern shores of the Black Sea, Pharnakes was continuing a process that had been gestating for some time. As early as the end of the fourth century BC, Eumelos, the dynast of the Bosporos, centered at Pantikapaion, envisioned a coastal confederacy all around the sea. In part this was a counterbalance to the aggressive movements of Alexander's successor Lysimachos. Eumelos's plans came to nothing—he died in a freak accident after only a few years in power—but his concept of the Black

Sea littoral as a unified territory surely influenced Pharnakes and especially his grandson, Mithridates VI.[62]

The northern shore of the Black Sea is an area of unusual topography, where a strait known as the Kimmerian Bosporos (the modern Strait of Kerch), from four to twenty miles wide, divided the continents of Europe and Asia and led from the Black Sea to an interior sea, the Maiotis (the modern Sea of Azov). This strait was called "Kimmerian" to distinguish it from the more famous Bosporos at the other end of the Black Sea. Both names were believed to mean "cow ford" and had been applied because Io, who had been turned into a cow because of the jealousy of Hera, wandered through the region. The Kimmerians (the biblical people of Gomer) had been long known to the Greeks and were eventually localized in the regions north of the Black Sea.[63]

The first Greek settlement in the region was Pantikapaion (at modern Kerch), traditionally founded by a brother of Medea. It may have had an early indigenous history, but by the seventh century BC Greeks from Miletos had established a trading quarter there, and the town gradually became hellenized.[64] It became the most important city in the region; in the 430s BC its ruler, Spartakos, established a dynasty whose members were calling themselves kings of Bosporos by the following century. The independent kingdom lasted until 109 BC when its ruler, Paraisades V, was unable to withstand barbarian pressures and turned over his territory to Mithridates VI of Pontos.[65]

At its Hellenistic peak, the kingdom of Bosporos covered much of the Maiotic shore, especially the southern and western portions, including a large part of the diamond-shaped peninsula to its west, the Chersonesos (modern Crimea). In the western Chersonesos, but within the same economic zone, was the independent Greek city of the same name (near modern Sevastopol, where extensive remains are visible), often called Chersonesos Taurike to distinguish it from the many other localities with this common Greek toponym meaning "peninsula." This was the home of the Taurians, famous in Greek myth for the stories about Iphigeneia, the daughter of Agamemnon, who, in some versions of the story, had escaped sacrifice at Aulis and ended up as a Taurian priestess of Artemis. Outside of mythology, the region had been visited by Greek traders as early as the sixth century BC, with the Greek town probably founded in the following century.[66] This was the city with which Pharnakes sought to establish relations in 155 BC. Other than pure expansionism, there was a solid economic reason for the king to show interest in the northern Black Sea region, especially to connect with the agricultural resources of the territory.

Since the fifth century BC the principal export of the northern Black Sea territories had been grain. When this trade began is a matter of uncertainty, but in 480 BC Xerxes, at the Hellespont, saw ships of grain moving from the sea into the Aegean, and archaeological evidence confirms that the modern Kerch region had numerous agricultural settlements by that time, and even more thereafter, whose major products included cereal grains.[67] The agricultural proclivities of the locals were well known to Greeks by the fifth century BC, and by the following century the northern Black Sea provided more grain to Athens than all other regions combined.[68] Presumably this trade was still flourishing two centuries later when Pharnakes made a treaty with Chersonesos, indirectly gaining his own foothold in the Bosporos and Chersonesos. He probably was well aware of the importance of grain supplies to the economy of the Pontic kingdom, since there had been a grain shortage during the time of his grandfather Mithridates II.[69] In addition to grain, the Bosporanian region was a major wine producer, from perhaps as early as the fifth century BC. There was also *tarichos*, or salted fish (which itself required an extensive salt-producing industry).[70] All these products meant that the Bosporos would be a major economic prize. In the time of Mithridates VI, Bosporos and Chersonesos would become an integral part of the Pontic state.

Pharnakes may also have attempted some sort of arrangement with his traditional enemy of Pergamon. A peculiar statement in Justin's *Epitome*, often ignored, states that Pharnakes was made the successor to Eumenes II.[71] To be sure, the context is suspect: it is from an alleged speech of Pharnakes's grandson Mithridates VI to his troops, and he would have had his own agenda justifying his contemporary expansionism. But the statement may reflect a momentary alliance between Pergamon and Pontos, perhaps in the 170s BC, when Eumenes II had no obvious heir. His son Attalos III was not born until 168 BC, and his brother Attalos II was, with Roman encouragement, considering becoming the ruler of a separate kingdom.[72] It may have seemed to Eumenes that designating Pharnakes as the future king of Pergamon was a sensible move and an attempt to control the aspirations of his own family, but if such an arrangement were made, it did not last long. When Eumenes died in 159 BC, Attalos II became king, to be followed in 138 BC by Attalos III.[73]

Close relations with Athens were also established.[74] The city, noting the historic friendship that they had had with Pharnakes's ancestors—something not specifically documented—accepted a donation from the king despite the fact that the kingdom was still in economic distress (for reasons not mentioned). It seems that the king had requested deferment of an agreed payment to the city, giving only one-third of the promised amount. The Athenians, hoping to receive the remainder, attempted to solicit his goodwill by giving him a golden crown, an event to be announced several times in public. The king's recent marriage to the Seleukid princess Nysa was to be commemorated, and she was also to be crowned. Bronze statues of king and queen were to be set up on Delos, and a certain Philoxenos of Peiraieus was selected to convey the decree and crowns to the royal couple and to persuade them to pay the rest of the promised funds within a year.

Unfortunately, the date of the inscription is far from clear, and suggestions have ranged from 196/195 BC to 160/159 BC.[75] The presiding archon's name must be heavily restored, but his term of office was one those two years. The matter cannot be resolved, but it seems that the later date makes more sense historically, in large part because Delos had been assigned to Athens by the Romans in 167/166 BC, and thus it would be more appropriate after that time for the Athenians to erect statues of their benefactors on the island.

Further support for the later date concerns the construction of the Middle Stoa in the Athenian Agora (fig. 4.3). Its foundations were laid around 183 BC, and it may have been Pharnakes—at the peak of his ambitions, having just conquered Sinope—who financed this construction.[76] He perhaps made the

Figure 4.3 Athens, Middle Stoa. Shutterstock 1184868205.

first payment, for terracing and foundations, but delayed the remainder due to the costs of the war against Pergamon. The Athenians eventually grew tired of waiting and appealed for prompt remitting of the remainder, sweetening the request by honors toward king and queen. Pharnakes did not see the construction through to its completion—he was dead within a few years—and the stoa was finished later by the Athenians at their own expense. Yet the second century BC was certainly a time for eastern monarchs to make dedications and to finance projects in Athens, most notably the great stoas built by Eumenes II and Attalos II of Pergamon. If the Athenian inscription is later rather than earlier, the kingdom suffered for many years after the settlement of the war with Pergamon, unless Pharnakes's refusal to make his payments was merely a posture. But there is no evidence in ancient literature regarding any economic problems Pharnakes faced.

It is difficult, then, to construct the trajectory of the Pontic economy during Pharnakes's reign. But it is certain that his capture of Sinope in 183 BC was to have a lasting effect on the overall welfare of the kingdom. This not only gave Pontos a major port on the Black Sea, thus enhancing the trade opportunities of the kingdom, but it also meant that Pontos now controlled the ancient trade route across Asia Minor from Mesopotamia and the Levant (especially since Seleukid aspirations had been curtailed).[77] The Athenians had relied on Black Sea grain since at least the fifth century BC, and Sinope was one of the major ports for this trade, which may explain why they were anxious to treat Pharnakes gently when he failed to make his payments.[78] The king was probably the one who moved the Pontic capital to Sinope from Amaseia (although it may have been his brother and successor Mithridates IV), an astute move that placed the political and cultural center of the kingdom at a long-established and prosperous Greek port city rather than at inland Amaseia.[79] In addition to the economic results of the move, this emphasized to the world that Pontos was now a truly hellenized state. It was firmly aligned with the international Greek world.

THE FINAL YEARS OF PHARNAKES

Inscriptions provide what little is known about Pharnakes's family. Less than a year before the Athenians made their plea for the king to pay what he had promised, he had married the Seleukid princess Nysa, the daughter of King Antiochos (probably IV) and Queen Laodike (probably XV) (fig. 4.4). One might think

Figure 4.4 Intaglio, perhaps of Nysa. Bibliotheque National Français 1974.1093.

that the marriage between Pharnakes and Nysa occurred earlier, but his failure
to have a son mature enough to succeed him (he was followed by his brother
Mithridates IV, and only thereafter by his own son, Mithridates V) suggests a
late date for the marriage. On this basis it seems best to assume that it was in
161/160 BC and that Nysa was born in the 170s. The marriage was probably
due to the intrigues of Demetrios I, the nephew of Antiochos IV, who had been
a hostage in Rome but escaped (with the help of Polybios) in 162 BC, returning
to Antioch. Despite Roman opposition, he took the Seleukid throne by execut-
ing his cousin Antiochos V.[80] Demetrios attempted to regain some Seleukid
influence in Asia Minor: he understood that crossing the Tauros with an army
would be unwise, but there was always the possibility of marriage alliances. Yet
his first attempt, to arrange that his sister Laodike XII, the widow of Perseus
of Macedonia, marry Ariarathes V of Cappadocia, failed; Ariarathes realized
that any connection with the renegade Demetrios would not be looked upon
favorably by the Romans. Demetrios then may have reasserted the long history

of marriage connections between the Seleukids and Pontos—he himself was a great-grandson of Mithridates II—and arranged the marriage of Nysa (who was probably his aunt) to his remote cousin Pharnakes.[81]

The portrait of Pharnakes on his coinage shows a family resemblance to his father, Mithridates III, presenting a similar physiognomy with a determined expression and the same prominent lips, nose, and type of beard (fig. 4.2).[82] It easily shows a personality that would seek conquest in all directions. On the reverse is the legend "of King Pharnakes" and a male figure with a cornucopia and caduceus in the left hand and a vine branch in the right, with a doe nibbling at the branch. This complex symbolism has not been fully explained, but it may represent a pantheistic divinity seeking peace by joining east and west. It was a concept that had originated with Alexander the Great and which was to grow over the next several centuries, reaching its peak in the ideology of Cleopatra VII and Marcus Antonius. The depiction on the reverse of Pharnakes's coins is visually reminiscent of that of Alexander. If Pharnakes sought to join east and west—perhaps referring to a connection between the Persian heritage and the Greek world or even Rome—this would be a strong expression of dynastic aspirations.[83] The artistic quality of the royal coin portrait is exceedingly high, again demonstrating that Greek die cutters were at the court.

Another example of the hellenism of his kingdom is a silver statue of the king, erected perhaps either by his brother Mithridates IV or his son Mithridates V, probably at Sinope.[84] It may have been part of a dynastic group, since there was also one of Pharnakes's grandson Mithridates VI. The statues were brought to Rome and exhibited in the triumph of Pompey the Great in 61 BC; what happened to them thereafter is unknown. A further artifact from the era of Pharnakes is a bronze shield, now in the Getty Museum in Los Angeles. It is 80 cm in diameter with a six-pointed solar image and the Greek inscription "of King Pharnakes." The nature of the lettering assigns it to Pharnakes I, not his great-grandson Pharnakes II. Its provenience is unknown, but it could have been a dedication at a sanctuary or even something lost by its owner, in the manner so eloquently described by Archilochos and Horace.[85]

The exact date of the death of Pharnakes is not known, but by the winter of 155/154 BC his brother Mithridates IV was on the throne.[86] Pharnakes's tomb had been started at Amaseia, next to that of his father Mithridates III. It was never completed, and in all probability he was buried at Sinope in what would come to be a dynastic mausoleum for him and his successors. Above the unfinished tomb at Amaseia is an inscription reporting that a certain Metrodoros, who was commander of the garrison (*phrourarchos*), dedicated an altar and flower garden to the king, perhaps on a terrace above the tomb accessed by a stairway that is still visible, a memorial probably created when it was decided not to bury him in Amaseia. Metrodoros may have been an ancestor of Metrodoros of Skepsis, the advisor to Mithridates VI.[87]

Pharnakes's wife Nysa is not mentioned after being honored by the Athenians. It was common for Seleukid princesses of the era to return home after their husbands died or were deposed, as was the case with two of her relatives, Laodike (XII), the wife of Perseus of Macedonia, and Antiochis, the wife of Ariarathes IV of Cappadocia, and it is reasonable to assume that Nysa did the same.[88] Early coins of her husband's successor Mithridates IV have been found in Seleukid territory, and these may have been brought by her entourage.[89]

Pharnakes had ruled for over thirty years, leaving a mixed reputation. Polybios had a low opinion of him: according to the excerptor of his *Histories*, "Pharnakes, then, was more lawless than all previous kings."[90] The thought stands alone and is incomplete, presumably the concluding sentence in a lost summary of Pharnakes's faults, but it lacks context or detail. Yet Polybios was a contemporary of the king, and was very much involved in the destiny of the eastern dynasties, and his opinion was certainly based on personal knowledge, although the two probably never met.

Pharnakes's ambitions surpassed his abilities, and he attempted to expand his kingdom in every direction, only achieving success with Sinope and the territories north of the Black Sea. He engaged with the other powers in northern and central Asia Minor—Pergamon, Bithynia, and Cappadocia—but was defeated or rebuked by all of them. Only the Seleukids were a constant ally, probably largely due to the marriages; yet they were banned from activities in the vicinity of Pontos. Like all his contemporaries, Pharnakes underestimated the expanding power and long reach of Rome and that state's ability to dictate the destinies of the eastern kingdoms. Yet, paradoxically, he had some concept of his own limitations: he did not become involved in the events leading to the Apameia treaty, despite the role of his uncle (by marriage) Antiochos III as a protagonist.

His wars caused financial difficulty for the kingdom (or at least the royal court), but acquisition of Sinope and the Chersonesos opened up possibilities that would allow Pharnakes's son and grandson, Mithridates V and VI, to bring Pontos to the peak of its territorial extent, power, and influence in the last brilliant century of the kingdom. His cultivation of the Greek cities, especially Athens, was another policy that would serve his successors well. But Rome was in the ascendancy; a decade after Pharnakes's death the final defeat of Carthage would allow it to turn its attention even more dramatically to the future of the eastern dynasties.

Chapter 5

The Collapse of Pergamon

MITHRIDATES IV AND HIS SISTER-WIFE LAODIKE

When Pharnakes died, probably in the early 150s BC, he left no one who was in a position to succeed to the kingship. His son, the future Mithridates V, only became king a decade later, suggesting that he was merely a few years old when his father died. The kingship of Pontos passed to Pharnakes's brother Mithridates IV; the relationship between the two is shown on an inscription from Rome that refers to Mithridates (IV) the son of Mithridates (who can only be Mithridates III).[1] Nothing is known about the laws of succession in Pontos; one would expect Mithridates IV to have been a regent, not a king, but this was not the case, and there may have been some sort of royal council that acclaimed him as king. This is the only case of horizontal succession in the dynasty.

Mithridates IV also broke with tradition and married his sister Laodike (figs. 5.1, 5.2).[2] Royal incest had existed in the Hellenistic world for over a century, ever since Ptolemy II of Egypt had married his sister Arsinoë II in the 270s BC. This certainly provided a precedent, and the practice became accepted in the Seleukid family, when Antiochos IV married his sister Laodike V (both were grandchildren of Mithridates II), but the reality in Pontos was that there was no suitable marriage candidate from the Seleukid family after Nysa married Pharnakes. The Seleukids had been the traditional source of Pontic queens for three generations, but as the reign of Demetrios I (162–150 BC) became more turbulent and it became apparent that his position would never be recognized by Rome, a further liaison between the Pontic and Seleukid kingdoms may not have seemed wise.[3] Moreover, by this time the Seleukids were in decline and the Mithridatids in the ascendancy. Marriage within the family would have been the best option.

Figure 5.1 Coin of Mithridates IV. American Numismatic Society 1097.152.388. Courtesy American Numismatic Society.

(a)   (b)

Figure 5.2 Coin of Mithridates IV and Laodike. Numismatica Ars Classica NAC AG, Auction 59, Lot 658.

Mithridates IV was the first Pontic king known to have adopted titles: his full name was Mithridates Philopator Philadelphos, documented on both the inscription from Rome and his coinage.[4] These surnames are Ptolemaic in origin. "Philopator" ("Father-loving") is first attributed to Ptolemy IV (reigned 221–204 BC), and "Philadelphos" ("Sibling-loving"), especially relevant because it implied royal incest, had first been used by Ptolemy II and his sister-wife Arsinoë II.[5] Mithridates's sister-wife Laodike also took the epithet.[6] There is no reason to believe that the nomenclature represents any particular Ptolemaic connection (although, to be sure, the contemporary Ptolemies were descendants of Mithridates II): such titles were becoming commonly attached to royalty in the mid-second century BC. Attalos II of Pergamon was Philadelphos,[7] and Ariarathes V of Cappadocia (ruled 163–130 BC) was Philopator.[8] The assumption of these titles by the Pontic monarchs indicates a self-perception that placed them on equal footing with the other Hellenistic dynasties and would serve to stress the legitimacy of Mithridates IV, given his somewhat anomalous succession.

During his reign—probably the briefest of all the Pontic kings—Mithridates IV adopted a less aggressive foreign policy than his brother. The only known military initiative was involvement in a war between Attalos II of Pergamon and Prousias II of Bithynia, which broke out in the summer or autumn of 156 BC and lasted into 154 BC.[9] Both sides appealed to Rome, and Attalos was told not to invade Bithynia but to secure his own territory. Prousias was ordered to stand down, which he refused to do, and the Romans terminated their alliance with him. They forced a truce, whose terms were totally to the advantage of Pergamon: Prousias was ordered to give Attalos twenty cataphracts (armored triremes)[10] and five hundred talents. He never recovered politically, and his subjects demanded his removal. When his son Nikomedes II went to Rome to request an easing of the terms, the Romans and Pergamenes encouraged him to revolt. Nikomedes had his father killed at the altar of Zeus in Nikomedeia and became king (in 149 BC) by this dubious method.[11]

The relevance of the war between Attalos and Prousias to the history of Pontos is that Mithridates IV was somehow involved on the Pergamene side. In the only reference to the king in extant literature, Polybios reported that Mithridates and Ariarathes V of Cappadocia sent a force of cavalry and infantry to Attalos early in the winter of 156/155 BC.[12] The expedition was under the command of a certain Demetrios, an otherwise unknown son of Ariarathes. It was mobilized because of an existing alliance that the two kings had with Pergamon, which shows a change in the political dynamics of northern Asia Minor in the years after the treaty of 180 BC, when the three states had been at odds. All three kings had come to the throne since the treaty (Ariarathes around 163 BC and Attalos in 159 BC), and Ariarathes and Attalos were already closely allied, since the latter had assisted in restoring the former to his throne when he had been expelled during a brief dynastic war in 157 BC.[13] Although Pontos and Cappadocia had long been opposed to one another, Ariarathes was a grandson of Mithridates II, and this may have brought the two kingdoms closer. But the fact remains that with new kings on the thrones alliances were readjusted. Unfortunately nothing further is known about Pontos's involvement in this war between Pergamon and Bithynia, yet it can be assumed that the Pontic-Cappadocian forces briefly invaded Bithynia, and then promptly withdrew when the Romans began to dictate terms.[14]

The most notable achievement during the reign of Mithridates IV was the establishment of strong relations with the Romans, a policy that would survive into the era of his successor and nephew Mithridates V. In 168 BC, the Macedonian kingdom had come to an end with the defeat of Perseus at Pydna, who was sent into retirement in Italy. Although southern Greece was still independent, the Romans could now become more involved in the affairs of Asia, and the eastern dynasts, Mithridates IV included, may have felt that accommodation was the better move, a reaction, perhaps, to the more aggressive policies of Pharnakes.[15] Thus the previously mentioned inscription from Rome, set up on the Capitol, records in both Greek and Latin that King Mithridates Philopator Philadelphos, son of King Mithridates, made a dedication to the people of Rome, with whom he had friendship and alliance. This is one of a group of dedications, not all of the same date, created by a total of sixteen rulers and peoples. The one from the Lykians may be as early as the 160s BC, and one from (probably) Ariobarzanes I of Cappadocia is as late as the 90s BC.[16] Nevertheless, the titles and ancestry provided for Mithridates can mean no one other than Mithridates IV, and his dedication would have been set up during the 150s BC. The inscription is part of a major monument on the Capitol which may have reached its final form during the era of Sulla in the 80s BC.[17] Thus Mithridates IV, differing in his foreign policy from his brother, started no wars and acquired no territory, but, realizing the inevitability of Roman involvement in Asia Minor and the importance of good relations, made an alliance with Rome during his short reign.

Mithridates's sister-wife Laodike had a profile of her own and was honored with a statue on Delos.[18] The inscription was set up by three Rhodians, Agathanax and the brothers Asklepiodoros and Hermogenes (sons of Asklepiodoros). An Asklepiodoros was the father of a certain Helianax, who some years later was in the service of Mithridates VI and dedicated a monument to him, also on Delos,[19] so that family presumably had connections with the Pontic kingdom and may have been their agents on Rhodes. The island had recently—in 164 BC—concluded its own alliance with Rome. Delos had been made a free port (under Athenian supervision) three years earlier and was rapidly becoming the greatest mercantile center in the Aegean.[20] Thus the honors given to Laodike connected the Pontic kingdom with the great island powers of the era—Rhodes and Delos—as well as with Rome and Athens (fig. 5.3).

Figure 5.3 View of Delos. Shutterstock 549487042.

That Mithridates and Laodike were joint rulers is reflected in their coinage (fig. 5.2).[21] For the first time, a Pontic queen appears on coins, both by herself and in a portrait with her husband. The joint coinage has right-facing profiles of the couple, with Mithridates in front of Laodike. On the reverse is the inscription "Of King Mithridates and Queen Laodike, Sibling-Loving." The style of the portraits is similar to those of previous Pontic monarchs and continues to reflect the highly artistic coins common throughout the dynasty.[22] Showing monarchs as a joined pair was another Ptolemaic feature that the Pontic rulers adopted, again originally from the era of Ptolemy II and Arsinoë II. The reverse of the Pontic coins has facing portraits of Zeus and Hera, thus equating the Pontic siblings with the most important of all sibling marriages and placing them firmly within a Greek context, a strong assertion of the hellenic quality of the state and court.

There are also coins of Mithridates alone. On their reverse is Perseus, the Greek hero who was the mythological founder of the Persians, connecting the Persian antecedents of the monarchy with its contemporary Greek outlook (fig. 5.1). The king may also be shown on a cameo now in Geneva. If this represents him, it provides a rare personal name of an artist at the Pontic court of this period, a certain Nikias, who carved the gem.[23] In addition, Laodike had autonomous powers of coinage, the first Pontic queen to be so honored, issues that may have been minted after her husband's death.

Mithridates IV had died by the early 140s BC, since his successor and nephew, Mithridates V, sent aid to the Romans in the Third Punic War (149–146 BC).[24] How long Laodike survived is not known, but her autonomous coinage suggests that she may have briefly ruled as dowager queen before the accession of her nephew. A fine intaglio in pale blue chalcedony from the region of Amisos may show her, and perhaps dates from after her husband's death (fig. 5.4).[25]

Figure 5.4 Intaglio of Laodike (wife of Mithridates IV). Metropolitan Museum 42.11.26. Purchase, Joseph Pulitzer Bequest, 1942.

THE MEDITERRANEAN WORLD AFTER 150 BC

The decade that Mithridates IV ruled, mostly in the 150s BC, was the beginning of profound changes in the political and cultural structure of the Mediterranean world. By the time his nephew Mithridates V ascended the throne, the balance of power was undergoing major shifts: when he was assassinated in 120 BC, the Pergamene and Carthaginian states had ceased to exist, the Seleukids were in irreversible decline, and the Romans possessed territory on all three continents.

Romans had been involved in the Greek and Asian worlds since the late third century BC. Part of this was due to repercussions from their lengthy fight with Carthage for control of the western Mediterranean. Conflict began in 264 BC when their interests collided in Sicily (where there were also Greek cities); when that war ended twenty-three years later the Carthaginians had been removed from the island, and the Romans began an unprecedented period of expansion that was to continue well into the imperial period. A second war (218–201 BC) included an invasion of Africa as well as extensive Roman acquisitions in the Iberian Peninsula. This war was also of particular relevance to the future of Asia Minor and the Pontic world because of the appearance of the instigator of the war, Hannibal, at the Seleukid court of Antiochos III in 195 BC. The Carthaginian spent the remaining decade of his life moving between the Hellenistic courts fomenting anti-Roman sentiment and directing Roman interest toward Asia Minor, thus initiating the Roman involvement in the destinies of the local kingdoms.[26]

Even with the death of Hannibal, matters between Rome and Carthage were not yet settled. By 150 BC, about the time that Mithridates V came to power, Carthage had rearmed and was expanding its influence in northern Africa, which gave the Romans an excuse to start a third war in 149 BC. Mithridates IV sent some assistance—ships and a few troops—to the Romans.[27] The city of Carthage was eventually besieged, and despite its vigorous resistance, it fell to Publius Cornelius Scipio in 146 BC. Polybios was in his entourage and described the uncertain emotions of seeing the city in flames: Scipio was said to have remarked that in time Rome would suffer the same fate.[28] In the settlement after the war, Rome acquired the Carthaginian heartland and organized it as the new province of Africa.

Roman attention had not solely been directed toward the Carthaginians. In the Greek peninsula, the Macedonian empire had been dissolved in 168 BC, with its territories divided into four republics carefully watched by Rome.[29] But the peninsula to the south was dominated by the Achaian Federation, which controlled the Peloponnesos, and although the situation was initially peaceful after 168 BC, the next twenty years saw increasing instability and contention between the federation and the Romans. By early 146 BC they had slipped into open warfare. The conclusion of the war against Carthage allowed the deployment of more Roman troops to Greece, and Corinth, the seat of the federation assembly, was burned and its artworks destroyed or removed to Rome.[30] Almost the entire Greek peninsula was effectively provincialized, including the four Macedonian republics. Essentially simultaneously, the Romans had defeated both Carthage and the Achaian Federation.

THE END OF THE PERGAMENE KINGDOM

The kingdom of Pergamon had become the most powerful state in Asia Minor after the Treaty of Apameia eliminated Seleukid power in the region. Under the reigns of Eumenes II (197–159 BC) and his brother Attalos II (159–138 BC), the kingdom extended inland as far as Cappadocia in the southeast and the Halys River in the northeast, and included parts of the European shore of the Thracian Bosporos. Pergamon became noted for its art and culture, and the kings developed the city itself into a magnificent showplace with outstanding art and also supported intellectual endeavors with the second-best library (after Alexandria) in the Hellenistic world. The Pontic kingdom had varying relations with the Pergamenes, including opposition to their expansionism, outright war for several years around 180 BC, and then attempts at accommodation.

Perhaps because of the increasing power of the Pergamene state, the Romans became more deeply involved in its future, most notably when, in the winter of 168/167 BC, they attempted to persuade Attalos, who was not yet king and in Rome on a diplomatic mission, to depose his brother and take the throne, or acquire at least part of the kingdom.[31] Attalos was tempted, but when the news reached Eumenes, he sent his physician Stratios to Rome in order to reason with his brother. This effort was successful, and Attalos was persuaded to ignore the Roman suggestion. Even though this scheme to sow dissension between the Pergamene brothers came to nothing, it was indicative of the Roman desire to interfere in the dynastic succession of the eastern kingdoms, even when there seemed no major strategic or political reason to do so.

A decade later (in 159 BC), Eumenes died and Attalos did become king, significantly taking the epithet "Philadelphos." Despite his refusal to accede to the ambitions of the Romans while his brother was alive, he now resolved "in no way to do anything without them," specifically citing their suspicion of his late brother as a primary reason for such a policy.[32] Attalos continued the cultural preeminence of Pergamon, both in the city and abroad, most notably with his stoa in the Athenian Agora. Yet the dependence of the kingdom on Roman goodwill was clear, and this became even more apparent when, in 138 BC, he was succeeded by his nephew Attalos III, who was not favorably remembered.[33] Diodoros, writing about a century later, noted that his rule was quite different from that of his predecessors, since he allegedly killed many of the ruling aristocracy, as well as his mother and wife, driving the populace to hopes of revolution.[34] Some of this seems formulaic slander of an unpopular ruler who succeeded a popular one—it is significant that the ever-watchful Romans did not interfere—but Attalos III was more interested in scholarship than rule, specializing in botany and pharmacology and writing treatises that were used by Varro and Pliny.[35] He was especially noted for his agricultural research and an interest in poisons; in this he was a precursor of Mithridates VI half a century later. His preference for scholarship over politics may also have affected his reputation, as would be the case with the Roman emperor Claudius. Nevertheless, he reigned only five years, dying a few days after falling ill from sunstroke.[36] Yet what was to be revealed after his death had major repercussions.

Attalos had written a will which left his kingdom to Rome. Details are lacking as to why he did this and exactly what the legal implications were (at least from his point of view), and the sources are brief and scattered.[37] The only contemporary references are epigraphic: a decree of the Pergamene assembly shortly after Attalos's death that refers to the need for the will to be ratified by the Romans (without stating what was in it) and a slightly later decree of the Roman Senate (preserved in a Greek copy set up at Pergamon), which seems to say that it decided to uphold the will, again without indicating what it contained. The earliest documentation in literature is from a century later. All sources that mention the nature of the will record the bequest to Rome, although Sallust reported an alleged speech by Mithridates VI of Pontos that claimed it was a forgery. This can easily be dismissed, not so much because the speech, like most in ancient literature, is a construct, but because it served the needs of Mithridates at the time—69 BC—to reject the will's validity.[38]

For a king to make a will favoring Rome was a recent idea. The earliest seems to be that of Ptolemy VIII, who in 155 BC when he was king of Kyrene (he did not become Egyptian king until a decade later) announced that he would leave "my proper kingdom to Rome, with whom, from the beginning, I have truly preserved friendship and alliance. "[39]

What is notable is that Ptolemy cited a specific reason for his action:

to take vengeance upon those implicated in the impious plot against me who have undertaken to deprive me not only of my kingdom but of my life.

The will was only valid if he died without heirs. He also set up the document on a public inscription, thus allowing everyone to know his intentions. But the plot he referred to was not successful, and in fact he became king of Egypt and ruled there until 116 BC, at which time he was succeeded by his son Ptolemy IX. So the will was never implemented, and the Romans did not have to decide what to do about it.[40]

Yet this will, published two decades before that of Attalos III, reveals a solid reason for writing such a document. It was a way of restraining usurpers and potential assassins, making it clear that there was nothing to gain from deposing the ruler. This was exactly the situation that Attalos faced, since an alleged son of Eumenes II, Aristonikos, was fomenting rebellion before Attalos died, and upon his death claimed the kingship as Eumenes III.[41] This was no minor revolt: he held on for nearly four years, lasting until 129 BC, when he was captured and sent to Rome, dying shortly thereafter. That he was able to survive for so long is a confirmation of the negative reports of Attalos's reign.

But regardless of Aristonikos's fortunes, there was still the matter of the will. Much like the instance of Ptolemy VIII, is quite possible that Attalos's will reflected more the internal political situation within the kingdom than any recognition of the inevitability of Roman power. Nevertheless, a prompt Roman response was out of the question, since when the news reached Rome in the early summer of 133 BC, the city was embroiled in the land reform legislation of Tiberius Gracchus.[42] Although Gracchus attempted to use any monetary benefits from the will to finance his reforms, there was no possibility that the Roman government would seriously debate its implications, and when Gracchus was assassinated a few weeks later, the will became, for the time being, irrelevant to Roman interests.

Shortly thereafter the Romans learned of the matter of Aristonikos. Again they were in no position to act, and at first the cause against the usurper was undertaken by the Greek cities and the eastern dynasts—perhaps at Roman request—including Mithridates V of Pontos.[43] It was only after the defeat of Aristonikos that the Roman Senate considered the will, as part of a general settlement of the volatile situation in western Asia Minor.

The issue for the Senate was more than the disposition of the Pergamene territories, as demonstrated by the upheaval caused by Aristonikos. Furthermore, when the Romans did pursue the usurper, two Roman officers were killed, Crassus Mucianus and Marcus Peperna (the consuls, respectively, of 131 and 130 BC), enough to make the Romans realize that the Asian problem was a serious one that needed meticulous attention. Basically, the Senate opted to leave parts of the legal structure of the Pergamene kingdom intact, but under close Roman observation. The final Roman commander sent against Aristonikos, Manius Aquillius (the consul of 129 BC), supervised the organization of the Pergamene territories. The city of Pergamon remained autonomous, but much of the interior was ceded to the various dynasts whose coalition had inaugurated the suppression of Aristonikos. A major beneficiary was Mithridates V, who received Greater Phrygia, although bribery of Aquillius was suspected.[44] This accusation—the same charge was made against Nikomedes III of Bithynia—may be pure slander. It was mentioned in a speech of Gaius Gracchus (Tiberius Gracchus's younger brother) during his brief political career in the 120s BC (he was killed in 121 BC), but the context is uncertain.[45] Nevertheless Gracchus reflected increasing Roman suspicion about the pernicious effects of the wealth of the Hellenistic kings.

The Romans exercised indirect control of the Pergamene lands and the surrounding dynasts, as they had for some time. Roman commanders were regularly sent to the region, essentially as observers and policemen, not as administrators of Roman territory. It can be presumed that the Roman state benefitted financially from Attalos's will, but the sources are silent on this. Aquillius was said to have organized the region as a Roman province, yet this seems premature, and the process was probably more evolutionary and lengthy than implied. Roman dithering, always a problem, had been aggravated by the matter of Aristonikos. For the time being, those who profited most from the end of the Pergamene kingdom were the eastern dynasts, particularly Mithridates V of Pontos.

ELSEWHERE IN CONTEMPORARY ASIA MINOR

Although the Pergamene question dominated politics during much of the reign of Mithridates V, other states and dynasts were less affected by the end of the Attalids. In the northwest, the generally disliked Prousias II of Bithynia had been assassinated in 149 BC by his son, Nikomedes II, who remained on the throne until 128 or 127 BC and was a member of the coalition against Aristonikos. Bithynia was increasingly surrounded in its eastern portions by the expanding kingdom of Pontos, and an unspecified dispute between Nikomedes III and Mithridates V, probably in the late 120s BC, may be due to territorial concerns, but this is so faintly documented as to indicate that it may have been brief and minor. What is known is that the Romans seem to have ruled in favor of Mithridates, but the details are not preserved.[46]

Bordering both eastern Bithynia and western Pontos was Phrygia, which was not a coherent state and tended to be appropriated by its neighbors, such as when Mithridates V received portions of it in the Pergamene settlement. The various Galatian tetrarchs were also in possession of part of this district, although they are hardly known during the period in question. Mithridates had some control over this region, since his Phrygian territories would have been isolated from Pontos proper had not some arrangement been made with the tetrarchs. Eventually the king asserted a more direct claim.

Directly west of Pontos was Paphlagonia, a minor state generally at the mercy of the surrounding powers which was eventually incorporated into the Pontic kingdom, although not without difficulty.[47] South was Cappadocia, extending over much of southeastern Asia Minor from the Halys River almost to the Mediterranean. It was ruled by the Ariarathid dynasty, descended from Persian satraps and in power since the early third century BC.[48] The territory had greatly profited by the Peace of Apameia and the removal of Seleukid control, but its relations with Pontos had always been contentious: Pharnakes I had invaded Cappadocia, and Mithridates V was to claim it.[49] Yet Cappadocia retained its independence long after the collapse of the Mithridatic dynasty.

Mithridates V lived in a world that had changed markedly since the establishment of the successor kingdoms of the era after Alexander the Great. The Macedonian kingdom had disappeared in 168 BC, and the Greek peninsula was essentially under direct Roman control by 146 BC. The Treaty of Apameia of 183 BC had ended Seleukid aspirations to most of Asia Minor, although there were faint attempts to reassert this. Nevertheless, by the time of Mithridates V any regional claims of the Seleukids were limited to Cilicia, at the extreme southeast of the territory. Under a series of weak and competitive kings the empire would continue to decline: Cilicia was acquired by the Romans at the end of the second century BC, and the final dissolution of the Seleukids took place in 65 BC. They had once been rivals with Pontos for parts of northern Asia Minor, but after the middle of the second century BC they played no further role in local politics.

The most stable of the successor kingdoms was Ptolemaic Egypt, which at its peak in the third and second centuries BC claimed the eastern part of North Africa, portions of southern Asia Minor, Crete, and some of the Aegean islands, and had designs on the Levant and much of western Asia Minor. Yet it too suffered from loss of territory, largely due to weak monarchs and internal dissension, beginning with Ptolemy VIII—the great-grandson of Mithridates II of Pontos—who came to the Egyptian throne in 145 BC. But intensive Ptolemaic involvement in Asian politics had come to an end, although in the first century BC there were attempts by Mithridates VI to reach out to them as an ally in his wars with Rome, and after his death Cleopatra VII acquired parts of the southern coast of Asia Minor.

The demography of Asia Minor in the second century BC was complex. In addition to the dynasts and regional powers mentioned above, there was an assortment of free Greek cities and independent temple states scattered throughout the territory, which would play varying but minor roles in contemporary politics: seventeen ethnic groups were identified by the late second century BC.[50] And everywhere there was the lengthening shadow of Rome.

THE REIGN OF MITHRIDATES V EUERGETES

At the beginning of 149 BC, Rome again declared war on Carthage; the conflict lasted into 146 BC.[51] At some time during this period, probably close to the beginning of the war, Mithridates V sent aid to the Romans in the form of some ships and a few troops.[52] This is the first event associated with his reign; he was probably on the throne no later than the last months of 150 BC. In sending help he continued the pro-Roman policies of his uncle Mithridates IV. Ships were the best support that he could give, because the Romans, although having developed a fleet a century previously, were never comfortable with sea power, and as early as the third century BC they had begun to rely on the ships of others, primarily the Greek cities and the Phoenicians.[53] There is no evidence how Mithridates's ships were used, but a likely possibility is for troop transports.

Mithridates V followed the pattern of his uncle and adopted a title, in this case Euergetes ("Benefactor"), one used for various reasons by Hellenistic royalty as early as Ptolemy III in the mid-third century BC. Mithridates's title appears on a dedication from Delos and on his coinage, and consistently in the literary sources.[54] It may have been bestowed on him by the Delians. The thirty years that he was on the throne are somewhat better documented than the reigns of his predecessors, despite the loss of Polybios as a source in his early years.[55] But as is often the case, specific dates for events are generally lacking. Moreover, since Mithridates V was the father of Mithridates VI the Great, many of the extant notices are in the context of his son's activities, who often justified his own policies by referring back to those of his predecessors, especially his father.

The next datable event in the career of Mithridates V was his participation in the coalition against Aristonikos, the pretender to the Pergamene throne.[56] The members, in addition to Mithridates, were Nikomedes II of Bithynia, Pylaimenes of Paphlagonia, and Ariarathes V of Cappadocia.[57] All four ruled adjoining territories extending from the Propontis to the Mediterranean, effectively forming a blockade against any attempts by Aristonikos to move into central Asia Minor. In fact, his efforts were mostly directed toward the Greek cities south of the traditional Pergamene territory, such as Phokaia, Kolophon, and Samos.[58] He seems to have had utopian aspirations, calling his followers *heliopolitai* ("citizens of the sun"; the meaning of the term remains enigmatic) and gaining extensive support, which allowed him to hold off the coalition and the Romans for four years. The coalition was not purely defensive, since the kings coveted part or all of the territory of Pergamon.[59] But it seems to have been surprisingly ineffective, lacking the moral edge that Aristonikos had, since the cities of western Asia Minor feared the ambitions of the dynasts more than those of the usurper. Aristonikos was only eliminated when the Romans became involved, and after great difficulty, including the deaths of two proconsuls and King Ariarathes V.

After the end of Aristonikos, the Romans gave various Pergamene territories to the coalition dynasts, with Mithridates receiving Greater Phrygia.[60] There had long been Pontic interest in the territory: Seleukos II allegedly had given it to Mithridates II as a dowry when he married Laodike IV.[61] But after that time, however, the Pergamenes claimed it. Phrygia was not contiguous with Pontos, lying beyond Galatia to its southwest, and this suggests some accommodation with the Galatian tetrarchs. Half a century later Mithridates VI was to claim a strong alliance with them.[62]

Mithridates VI made a number of statements about his father's territorial ambitions in order to legitimize his own expansionism. These need to be considered cautiously. Mithridates V was explicitly said to have invaded Cappadocia.[63] But the evidence is confused, because Appian emphasized that Cappadocia was a foreign entity—something seemingly obvious—yet in 88 BC the official Pontic point of view was that Cappadocia had always been Pontic territory but had been recovered by Mithridates V, a somewhat contradictory statement. Moreover, the daughter of Mithridates V, another Laodike, was married to the king of Cappadocia, Ariarathes VI, who came to the throne in 130 BC after his father's death at the hands of Aristonikos.[64]

It may seem difficult to reconcile these statements, but a plausible explanation is that the "invasion" of Cappadocia has been overemphasized and may have been little more than a gesture on the part of Mithridates V which resolved itself through a diplomatic solution that included a marriage alliance. Mithridates would not have been unaware that his father Pharnakes I had been less than successful in invading Cappadocia[65] and may have rethought his plans. But then Mithridates VI, for his own reasons, stressed his father's claim to the territory, letting it be known that Cappadocia had always been Pontic (manifestly untrue), but giving his assertion the nuance that Mithridates V had "recovered" it.

The situation in Paphlagonia was a little more straightforward, but again the ideology of Mithridates VI causes a certain amount of confusion. Pylaimenes, the local king, had participated in the coalition against Aristonikos but is hardly known otherwise. When Mithridates VI, in 108 BC, invaded Paphlagonia in a joint operation with Nikomedes III of Bithynia, he claimed that it had belonged to his father, who received it as an inheritance, presumably from Pylaimenes.[66] But the Roman Senate ordered that the territory be returned "to its former status," which hardly suggests Pontic control. Whether the obscure Pylaimenes was still on the throne over twenty years after the Aristonikos matter is not known, but this suggests again that Mithridates VI was presenting a revisionist view of history. Even if his father had inherited Paphlagonia from Pylaimenes, Pontic control of the territory was brief or ephemeral, or never implemented.

Any direct control Mithridates V had over Paphlagonia and Cappadocia seems limited or even nonexistent. Perhaps movements in that direction were enough for his son to claim that they previously belonged to Pontos. But the marriage alliance between his daughter Laodike and Ariarathes VI of Cappadocia was an important element of his foreign policy, defining his international posture, and thus he became the ancestor of the remaining two Ariarathid kings (VII and VIII) of Cappadocia.

Pontic acquisition of Phrygia was a major boon and further laid the groundwork for the empire of Mithridates VI. By the time of the death of Mithridates V in 120 BC, the Pontic kingdom occupied a broad swath of territory from the Armenian mountains almost to the Aegean, adjoining on its west Bithynia and the new Roman province of Asia. In the east there was some relationship with Lesser Armenia, since one source, perhaps in exaggeration, called Mithridates V "king of Pontos and Armenia," and Mithridates of Lesser Armenia had been an ally of Pharnakes I during the war with Pergamon in the 180s BC.[67] In all probability, the Pontic kingdom in the later years of Mithridates V was the largest political entity in Asia Minor. It was also the wealthiest, which may explain the accusation of bribery of the Romans in the years after the Pergamene legacy.[68] But ironically the reign of Mithridates V was not as expansionist as that of his father Pharnakes I; to be sure, there was some involvement in the destiny of Paphlagonia and a marriage alliance with Cappadocia, but the only territorial acquisition was Phrygia, which had been donated to him rather than conquered, an attempt to stabilize the political situation of northern Asia Minor after the collapse of the Pergamene dynasty.

Mithridates V also reached out to the Greek states. The strongest relationship seems to have been with Delos. The tiny sacred island had been the birthplace of Apollo and Artemis and a major cultic center since earliest times, but it began to flourish economically after the fall of Corinth in 146 BC. It was famous for its innovative architecture as well as its slave market, which, with the assistance of the piracy that was endemic in the eastern Mediterranean in late Hellenistic times, could process ten thousand a day.[69] The religious immunity of the island also helped in its prosperity. Mithridates's aunt, Laodike the wife of Mithridates IV, had already been honored by the island,[70] and the king early realized that good relations would be to his advantage. An Athenian, Dionysios son of Boethos, may have been his agent there;[71] given the relationship of Pharnakes I with the island, one might expect some of its citizens to migrate to the Pontic court. Another Pontic representative honored at Delos was Panias of Amisos. Two local citizens, Seleukos and Aischylos, dedicated statues of the king; Seleukos's statue, at least, was probably erected while he was gymnasiarch in 129/128 BC.[72] Moreover, coinage of the king also seems to emphasize his connection with Delos. The reverse of one type has the inscription "Of King

Mithridates Euergetes" and a standing male figure, identified as Apollo of Delos, with a bow and holding a small female figure in his outstretched hand, possibly commemorating a restoration of the Temple of Apollo on the island. He may have also rebuilt the local Palaestra on the Lake, a project in evidence after the middle of the second century BC.[73] While these endeavors were not as impressive as the efforts of the Pergamene kings, they show an awareness in Pontos of the role of architecture in asserting royal power.

Another coin has the date 173, which would be 140/139 BC according to the Seleukid era, the most probable one in use in Pontos at the time.[74] This date, and that of Seleukos's gymnasiate, fall well within the reign of Mithridates V, and he may have reached out to the island in the later 140s BC, after it began to flourish. Ironically it would be his son, Mithridates VI, who brought Delos's prosperity to an end by sacking the island in 88 BC.

The king also participated in athletic contests on the island of Chios, winning four equestrian competitions.[75] There was a long tradition of royal involvement in athletics, through either patronage or actual participation. Among the many examples were Hieron of Syracuse, who won the chariot race at Olympia in 476 BC, and Berenike II of Egypt at Nemea, in the 240s BC.[76] The presence of Mithridates V at the games on Chios—which was still a free Greek state—was an additional foothold for the Pontic kingdom in the Greek world.

THE ROYAL COURT AND FAMILY OF MITHRIDATES V

Mithridates V is the first of the Pontic monarchs whose associates are known in some detail. In addition to those who were his contacts on Delos, there was a certain Alkimos, son of Menophilos, to whom the citizens of the city of Abonouteichos gave honors, probably in 137/136 BC.[77] This was an obscure town on the Paphlagonian coast (at modern Inebolu), and Alkimos may have been the local Pontic representative. But of all the royal functionaries of the reign of Mithridates V, the best known is Dorylaos, who was the great-great-grandfather of the historian and geographer Strabo and thus was given a brief biography in his *Geography*.[78] Dorylaos was by profession a military tactician, whom the king commissioned to recruit mercenaries. Like most Hellenistic states, military manpower for Pontos relied not on citizen armies but hired mercenaries, and Greek commanders, such as Leokritos, had already been in the Pontic service.

Dorylaos was a high-ranking officer in the Pontic military. His background and early career are unknown, but eventually he was sent to Thrace and Greece for recruitment purposes. He then went to Crete, a known source of military manpower: both Prousias II of Bithynia and Eumenes II of Pergamon seem to have acquired troops there, and later Mithridates VI continued to recruit from the island.[79] Dorylaos settled in Knossos, and regardless of how he fulfilled his duties, he became assimilated into the Knossian hierarchy, becoming commander in a war between that city and Gortyna. Interurban warfare was endemic in Crete during the second half of the second century BC, and Knossos and Gortyna were the most frequent belligerents. This particular war is not otherwise documented, but it has been dated to the late 120s BC, since Strabo reported that the death of Mithridates V (probably in 120 BC) was "a little later."[80] Dorylaos had married a Macedonian woman named Sterope and had had three children, and when he learned of the assassination of Mithridates V and resultant dynastic disorder, he decided to remain in Knossos with his family and cut all ties with Pontos. But in time at least two of his children—Lagetas (Strabo's great-grandfather) and Stratarchas—moved to Pontos. Lagetas served in the government of Mithridates VI but eventually became caught between Rome and Pontos and "was destroyed." Strabo's biography of Dorylaos is a brief insight into the career of at least one family associated with Mithridates V.

Dionysios, Dorylaos, and others demonstrate the high degree of hellenization that the kingdom had undergone by the time of Mithridates V. This was manifested as early as the first Pontic coin issues, from the late third century BC, which show the presence of Greek die cutters.[81] Coins of Mithridates V are rare but continued this tradition, with the royal portrait somewhat idealized and youthful: he was probably no more than twenty when he came to the throne.[82] Other examples of increasing hellenization are the large number of Greeks who served at the court, although it is possible that some of them were of Persian descent with Greek names (also evidence of hellenization). It is significant that there is no known member of the court with a Persian name; only the monarchs themselves retained that tradition, and even their daughters and wives tended to have Greek names. The official language of the court had long been Greek. Roman ways, on the other hand, had not penetrated into Pontos, since the connection with the Roman Republic was purely political, not cultural, and Mithridates V continued the policy of his uncle and father in being styled "a friend of the Roman people." This was a term with some legal force, but it had not yet been formalized into the "friendly and allied king (or queen)" of the early imperial period.[83] His limited territorial ambitions at a time of increasing Roman power in Asia Minor were also evidence of a pro-Roman attitude. Moreover, it is possible that Mithridates V was one of the kings who reached out to Cornelia, the most prominent Roman matron of the era and the mother of the ill-fated agrarian reformers, Tiberius and Gaius Gracchus.[84] Cornelia held court from her estate at Misenum on the Bay of Naples and made contacts with Greek intellectuals and eastern royalty. Since Ptolemy VIII of Egypt made a marriage proposal (unsuccessfully) to her,[85] his cousin Mithridates V may have been one of the "reigning kings" who interacted with her as an important person to know in the Roman Republic. It is doubtful that Mithridates V actually went to Misenum, but he may have corresponded and exchanged gifts with Cornelia.

Unlike her predecessors, the wife of Mithridates V is not known by name, a particular irony given her prominence in the royal succession after his death. Her name may have been, expectedly, Laodike, but this is pure speculation.[86] Mithridates VI explicitly said that his mother was a Seleukid (as well as a descendant of Alexander the Great).[87] Having Alexander as an ancestor can easily be dismissed—it was a standard claim of Hellenistic royalty—but Seleukid descent is perfectly credible, given the regular intermarriage between the Pontic dynasty and the Seleukids. By the time of the maturity of Mithridates VI, the Seleukids were in such decline that there would have been little advantage in fabricating such an ancestry. It has been suggested that his mother was a daughter of Antiochos IV and Laodike XVIII, themselves both of Pontic descent.[88]

Mithridates V and his wife had at least four children. Laodike, as already noted, married Ariarathes VI of Cappadocia. She became sole ruler of Cappadocia after her husband was assassinated through the orders of her brother Mithridates VI, and she then married Nikomedes III of Bithynia. Eventually he sent her to Rome in order to escape from her brother and to attempt to restore the Cappadocian succession, which she seems to have done.[89] She then drops from the historical record; presumably this was before the death of Nikomedes III in the 90s BC. Her sister, another Laodike, married her brother Mithridates VI and was executed after attempting to poison him in (probably) 115 BC.[90] Three younger sisters, Nyssa, Rhoxane, and Stateira, are also recorded, but their exact parentage is uncertain, and they never married.[91] The two known sons of Mithridates V were Mithridates VI and Mithridates Chrestos, who was killed by his brother.[92]

Around 120 BC, at the Pontic capital of Sinope, Mithridates V was assassinated. The date is dependent on the rule of his son, who died in 63 BC, after having ruled for fifty-six years.[93] There are no details about the plot except Strabo's

statement that he was killed by his "friends," a term in Hellenistic royalty referring to the monarch's inner circle. This seems to rule out his family, although it
is difficult to imagine that they were not involved, given that the event occurred
at the royal capital of Sinope and the turbulent start to the following reign. His
widow became ruler or regent for her son Mithridates VI, who was eleven or
thirteen years old, and who would become the most famous Pontic ruler.

PART II

MITHRIDATES VI THE GREAT

Chapter 6

The Rise of Mithridates VI

INTRODUCTION

Around 120 BC the last and greatest of the Hellenistic kings of Pontos came to the throne (fig. 6.1, 6.2). Mithridates VI Eupator Dionysos would rule for about fifty-seven years, substantially longer than any of his seven predecessors, and even though his kingdom would largely be assimilated by the Romans or broken up into lesser states, his direct descendants would rule part of his realm—under Roman supervision—until at least the third century AD.[1] One of the major dynasts of the late Hellenistic era, Mithridates VI would generate interest among Greeks and Romans alike for hundreds of years after his death. Moreover, he would have a vigorous afterlife in the arts and music into modern times. His accomplishments were not limited to the political and military world; he would create an intellectual and artistic presence at his court, including his own scholarly profile. Like other great opponents of Roman expansionism, his achievements would be preserved by those who defeated him, creating a problematic situation, which nevertheless does not hide his character profile as one of the notable personalities of antiquity.

Over forty ancient literary sources mention Mithridates VI, a totally different situation from the scant documentation of his predecessors. To be sure, as is the case for much of the late Hellenistic world, the primary sources come from a later era. In addition, any account by an ancient biographer, such as Cornelius Nepos or Plutarch, is lost; the sketch surviving in the collection of biographies known today as *De viris illustribus*, of uncertain Roman date, is extreme in its brevity. Probably no extant writers knew the king, although Cicero, who was involved in the Roman actions leading to Mithridates's death, commented frequently on his activities. Poseidonios of Apamea was another contemporary, but he seems to have mentioned him only in passing. Diodoros of Sicily, whose life overlapped

Figure 6.1 Head of Mithridates VI. Louvre MA 2321. Courtesy Musée du Louvre and Art Resource. Photograph by Hervé Lewandowski.

the king's later years, is the earliest extant author to provide any details about his career. His contemporary Sallust treated Mithridates's last years in his *Histories*, but only fragments survive. In the following generation, Livy's account of the king's era exists only in summaries, and while the family of Strabo of Amaseia served at the royal court, his historical work is essentially lost, although it was probably a primary source for the king's reign. Strabo's *Geography* mentions Mithridates over forty times, in a scattered yet revealing fashion.

Thus one must largely rely on later historians to understand Mithridates's rule, most notably Appian and Plutarch, both active around AD 100. Plutarch's biographies of the Roman commanders of the king's era (Sulla, Lucullus, Pompey, and Sertorius) are a major source, as well as the Roman history of Appian, who devoted one of his primary sections to the wars between Rome and Mithridates. In fact, without Appian's *Mithridateios*, knowledge of the entire history of the Pontic kingdom would be far more limited. One of the sources for his account may be Archelaos of Cappadocia, whose lengthy reign began in the 30s BC and

Figure 6.2 Head of Mithridates VI. The State Hermitage Museum, St. Petersburg, П1860-20. Photograph © The State Hermitage Museum. Photography by Vladimir Terebenin.

lasted into the early years of Tiberius.[2] Archelaos was the great-grandson of the Pontic general of the same name and was a scholar of note, with known writings on agriculture, cults, and Alexander the Great.[3] Moreover, he was (briefly) the father-in-law of the historian Juba II of Mauretania, who married his daughter Glaphyra. It is hard to imagine that with such a scholarly presence at the Cappadocian court, attention did not turn toward Archelaos's famous ancestor, the intimate of Mithridates VI, who appears prominently in Appian's account. Other sources, such as Memnon (probably from the second century AD) and his approximate contemporary Justin, are also of value. Moreover, there is a wealth of epigraphic and numismatic evidence. This material is what the modern scholar must rely upon to reconstruct the life and world of Mithridates VI.

Mithridates VI was the only Pontic king whose life was interesting enough to Greek and Roman authors that they recorded details about his personal characteristics. Sources are consistent in reporting that he was a large man, demonstrated by the armor that he dedicated to the sanctuaries of Nemea and Delphi, and which was still on view in the second century AD.[4] He was athletic until nearly the end of his life, able to ride one thousand stadia (about 125 miles) in a day, and may have participated in the chariot races at the Olympic Games.[5] His devotion to physical ability was also revealed, in a bizarre way, when he executed an unfortunate named Alkaios, from Sardis, who was superior to him in horse racing.[6] The king was famous for speaking twenty-two (or twenty-five, or even fifty) languages—more than anyone else—and was able to converse with each of the ethnic groups within his kingdom in their own language, conducting official business without an interpreter.[7] In this talent he was followed by his cultural successor Cleopatra VII.[8] He was also said to be a glutton, although this is probably a slander—analogous to the alleged promiscuity of Cleopatra—because it is not recorded in the major historical sources.[9] Perhaps more accurate is the report that he was moderate in his personal habits.[10] The story that he kept a bull, horse, and stag as bodyguards because he did not trust human ones may be merely an anecdote about the strange and suspicious ways of tyrants.[11]

Like all Hellenistic monarchs, he was conscious of his connection to Alexander the Great, who was improbably said to have been his ancestor.[12] He lost no opportunity to act in ways that reflected the career of his illustrious predecessor, staying where Alexander had stayed, reorganizing the sanctuary at Ephesos, and paying for earthquake relief at Apameia in Mysia.[13] He even recreated an event in Alexander's life: when wounded, he had himself lifted up to be visible to his troops, as the Macedonian king had done in India. Mithridates also somehow possessed a cloak that was said to have belonged to Alexander, which Pompey wore in his triumph after the Pontic king's defeat.[14] The authenticity of the token is difficult to ascertain, but it is demonstrative of his self-image. Mithridates's personal conception as the new Alexander was an astute piece of dynastic propaganda, because it allowed him, as the conqueror from the east, to play a role that paralleled the great conqueror of the east. This heritage was also manifested in Mithridates's epithet of "Dionysos," since Alexander believed that he was connected to the god.[15]

THE YOUNG HEIR

The assassination of Mithridates V, probably in 120 BC, may have been in order to control the succession, since he was killed before any of his children had reached adulthood. Whether his wife was involved remains unknown. She certainly took immediate control, since her eldest son and the presumptive heir, Mithridates VI, was only eleven or thirteen years old, having been born at Sinope in the late 130s BC.[16] Presumably he was the legal heir, and, as with many people of prominence, later traditions reported portents connected with his birth and accession. At the time of his birth, a comet was seen for seventy days, brighter than the sun, and another appeared under similar circumstances when he began to rule in 120 BC.[17] The report of the comets may be little more than the standard tale of the epiphany of a great personality, but, according to Chinese sources, the time of Mithridates's birth was marked by an unusual number of comets, with the most significant reported in 135 or 134 BC.[18] The exact date of the king's birth is not certain in the Greco-Roman writings, but they place his age as between sixty-eight and seventy-two when he died, and since his death was without doubt early in 63 BC, this would mean that he was born between 135 and 131 BC.[19] According to the report in the *Shih-Chi* (*Records of the Grand Historian*), two comets appeared, known as the Banner of Ch'ih-Yu; dates are not precise, but the earlier was between 134 and 129 BC and the later between 122 and 117 BC. These seem to correspond to the birth of Mithridates and his accession about fifteen years later. Other Chinese texts seem to place the first comet in September 135 BC. It perhaps appears on coins issued by the king after 110 BC, when his rule became secure: there is a representation of a star in the form of a flower, with eight rays.[20] This may also be the comet mentioned by Seneca, which was said to be as extensive as the Milky Way and which occurred during the reign of a King Attalos of Pergamon. Since Seneca had just mentioned a previous comet from around 150 BC, the Attalos in question is either Attalos II (reigned 159–138 BC) or, more probably, Attalos III, who died in 133 BC, perhaps further limiting Mithridates's birth date to between 135 and 133 BC. In all probability, Seneca's immense comet is the Banner of Ch'ih-Yu.[21] One should always be suspicious of astronomical portents that mark the birth of someone who later became famous—the "star in the east" at the birth of Jesus of Nazareth comes to mind[22]—but in the case of the birth and accession of Mithridates the independent Chinese evidence provides a credibility unusual with such events.

There is certainly no doubt that after his accession the king exploited the story of the comet, and it continued to evolve even beyond his death, because the report became adjusted to reflect his later career. The seventy days could be seen to refer to his life span, with the eclipsing of the sun a metaphor for his great political power. Moreover, it was said that the future king was struck by lightning as a baby, which burned his clothes but left him unharmed except for a mark on his forehead.[23] The tale may be an etiology for a birth defect, but it connected him with the birth of Dionysos, whose mother, Semele, had been killed by the bolt of Zeus. Yet the king was more favored than the god's mother and survived, taking "Dionysos" as one of his epithets. More importantly, this was another parallel with Alexander the Great, whose mother, Olympias, dreamed that a thunderbolt kindled fire in and around her womb at the time of conception.[24] Although these portents and signs are not documented in extant Greco-Roman literature until well after the time of the king—the earliest is the report of the comet, recorded by Pompeius Trogus and written perhaps two or three generations after the king's death[25]—the tales demonstrate the mythology that began to be generated around him, in contrast to the scant data about his predecessors.

Except for the horizontal succession after the death of Pharnakes I, inheritance in the Pontic monarchy had passed seemingly smoothly from father to son since the dynasty had been established in the early third century BC. But the assassination of Mithridates V and his lack of adult children introduced an element of instability that had not figured previously in the history of the kingdom. In fact, the only succession that was remotely parallel was, in fact, the matter of the heirs of Pharnakes I. In that case the kingship passed to Pharnakes's brother, Mithridates IV, yet there is no evidence that, thirty-five years later, Mithridates V had any siblings to take over the rule. Thus it would seem that the only choice to inherit the kingdom was one of his several children, none of whom was an adult. But some additional arrangement would have to be made.

The obvious solution would be to involve the widow of Mithridates V in some way. Since her oldest child was no more than thirteen, she was probably young herself, perhaps in her thirties. The earliest extant source on the succession is Strabo, who was probably well-informed about the events, since his ancestor Dorylaos (the nephew of the homonymous officer of Mithridates V) was a childhood companion and later the secretary of Mithridates VI.[26] Strabo was explicit: no one was involved in the succession except Mithridates VI. This seems improbable, but it may have been the official point of view at the royal court in later years, when there were no longer any potential rivals to the kingship of Mithridates. By the time of his maturity—and that of his secretary Dorylaos—it may not have been politically correct to refer to any issues or problems regarding the assumption of the kingship, and the actual events may have been conveniently forgotten.

Mithridates's taking of the epithet Eupator ("Noble ancestry" or "Noble father") also fits into this ideology. It is an ancient Greek word, but not a common title in Hellenistic monarchy.[27] The term seems to have been applied first to the Seleukid king Antiochos V (another son of a powerful father), who reigned in the late 160s BC, as a way of establishing his credibility.[28] Given Antiochos's short and unsuccessful reign, this may have been an odd precedent for Mithridates VI, but the unusual term allowed the king to stress his own legitimacy through his father and other ancestors.[29]

It is most probable that Mithridates V named both his eldest son and his wife as joint rulers, as reported by Memnon.[30] Needless to say, if this were the arrangement, the mother of Mithridates VI would have exercised the true power upon the death of her husband. A precedent of sorts had been established thirty years previously with Laodike (the grandmother of Mithridates VI), who may have had some autonomous powers upon the death of her husband Mithridates IV. In late Hellenistic times, the status of royal women was rising. Cleopatra II of Egypt drove her husband into exile and ruled alone for several years after 131 BC; her daughter Cleopatra III would become sole ruler in 116 BC.[31] The women of the Pontic dynasty in Hellenistic times never held the power and independence that Ptolemaic women exercised, but Laodike and the widow of Mithridates V demonstrate that under certain circumstances women would be called upon to provide continuity in difficult times when there was a lack of a suitable male ruler. The widow of Mithridates V and the queens of Egypt were probably remote cousins, and the former may have looked to the latter for inspiration. Whether she came to power due to some official arrangement provided by her late husband or simply assumed the rule as independent queen with a son too young to be effective cannot be determined.

Thus it seems that around 120 BC Pontos was under the control of its first ruling queen, although her legal power may have been as regent for her adolescent son. The later tradition stated that attempts were made from the beginning to do away with the young man, actions attributed to his "guardians."[32] None of these is known by name, and whether they included his mother is not specified. Too little is understood about her character to determine whether she would attempt to have her son killed. The reports are anachronistic, mixing together elements of Mithridates's education with his later knowledge of poisons. Yet given the ultimate fate of his mother, it is difficult to believe that she did not attempt to secure her own position at the expense of her older son, perhaps with the intent of replacing him with his brother Chrestos, who might be more malleable.

According to Justin, Mithridates's perfidious guardians attempted to kill him by forcing him into a dangerous athletic regimen, having him ride an unbroken horse and simultaneously throw a javelin. Yet this seems nothing more than part of the typical training of a Hellenistic dynast: highly skilled horsemanship was certainly a necessity, and it was also a characteristic of Persian monarchs, the purported ancestors of the king. Xenophon in the *Kyropaideia* stressed the riding and hunting skills of Cyrus of Persia and the dangerous nature of such activities. Young Alexander the Great was remembered for taming an unbroken horse, his famous Boukephalos. Such training is hardly evidence of murderous intent, and Mithridates grew up to become a particularly notable horseman.[33]

Nevertheless, after the failure of the alleged attempt to kill Mithridates by especially vigorous horsemanship, his guardians next tried to poison him, but he was able to take an antidote. Attempted poisoning is plausible—although perhaps not the easiest and quickest way of disposing of the young man—but the account has become tangled with Mithridates's known expertise later in life with antidotes. It is improbable that the adolescent king was skilled enough in pharmacology to determine a way to be immune to professional poisoners, and if there were attempts to poison him, they simply failed.

Realizing that his life at court was perilous, Mithridates allegedly went into hiding for seven years. This, too, is disputable, because there is no interval of seven years within the regnal chronology of the young king: by 116/115 BC, five years after the death of his father, he was honored as king by the island of Delos, and his coin sequence does not allow for a multi-year gap.[34] Nevertheless, there were instances of the removal of aristocratic young men from society, such as in the Krypteia at Sparta, forcing them to fend for themselves under harsh conditions in order to strengthen their character and physical capabilities.[35] There were other traditions throughout antiquity of a period of withdrawal from civilization as part of the training of a notable personality, most famously the later case of Jesus of Nazareth.[36] Seven years for such an experience on the part of Mithridates VI is impossible, but there may have been a briefer period, which assisted in his survival.

All the assumed attempts by Mithridates's guardians to kill him shortly after the death of his father can be better explained as part of the typical physical education of a young aristocrat, especially one who believed that he was descended from Persian royalty. Even the poisoning can be seen as some sort of Persian ordeal.[37] Later in his career, the king reconstructed these events in a revisionist history of his youth, picturing himself as the young hero who achieved his position by fighting off numerous plots from the very beginning of his career.

Nothing is known about the intellectual education of Mithridates beyond what can be assumed from his later abilities. He was famous for knowing many languages, and in his maturity he possessed a fine library, which was eventually acquired, catalogued, and partially translated into Latin by Pompeius Lenaeus, a freedman of Pompey the Great, the king's conqueror. The king published treatises, especially on pharmacology.[38] All this is evidence for a solid academic education, whose details are not documented.

DISSENSION AT THE PONTIC COURT

Nevertheless, even if the efforts to do away with Mithridates are exaggerated, there is no doubt that there was dissension at the Pontic court. The king had been assassinated by his inner circle, and there was no adult male successor.[39] The situation was so unstable that Strabo's ancestor Dorylaos, stationed at Knossos on Crete as the king's agent, abandoned all hope of return to Pontos. There probably were at least two hostile factions at the court in 120 BC: those around the family of Mithridates V, and the "friends" who assassinated him, although these groups need not to have been mutually exclusive. Even though the plots against Mithridates VI described by Justin have been anachronistically mixed into his regular education as well as events from his later life, they probably did exist, and there may have been an attempt to hide the young man from the court for a while.[40] The position of his mother in all this cannot be determined: Sallust, writing not long after the death of Mithridates VI, reported that the king ascended the throne only after her death, suggesting that she held power for a while.[41]

A glimpse of the factions at the court may be provided by the status of two sisters of Mithridates VI, Rhoxane and Stateira, who are only known because they were killed at about the age of forty in 71 BC.[42] This means that they were born around 110 BC, a decade after the death of Mithridates V, and thus must have had a different father. If the account is accurate, it means that at this late date Mithridates's mother was not only still alive but had entered into another relationship that lasted for over a year. The evidence is frustratingly incomplete and seemingly contradictory, but it suggests that the mother of Mithridates VI had dynastic ambitions of her own for a number of years after the death of her ruling husband. Plutarch's account is the only one that provides the sisters' names, and these are worth noting, as they are unusual. The original Rhoxane and Stateira were both wives of Alexander the Great: Rhoxane was the Baktrian princess who was the mother of his son Alexander IV, and Stateira was the oldest daughter of Dareios III, the last king of Persia.[43] These are names that had not been used in Hellenistic royalty since the eponyms themselves and suggest the self-image of the court faction around the mother of Mithridates VI, which perhaps looked toward the past and the east more than the one represented by Mithridates V, which was strongly hellenized. If the sisters were in fact not born until around 110 BC, these groups confronted each other for at least a decade.

CLAIMING THE THRONE

In summation, Mithridates VI, born in the late 130s BC, became involved in the same court intrigues that had killed his father around 120 BC. Nevertheless, he received a proper education befitting Hellenistic royalty. After the death of his father he may have been removed from the court environment for a while to insure his own survival, but by 116 BC, when he was probably between fifteen and eighteen years of age, his position was strong enough that the gymnasiarch at Delos—a certain Athenian named Dionysios son of Neon (or Neikon)— erected a statue in his honor.[44] There was also one to his brother, Mithridates Chrestos, indicating that he was still a person of importance in the Pontic royal family, but it was Mithridates VI who was recognized as king; Chrestos was merely cited as his brother. A dedication was also made on their behalf to Zeus Ourios.[45] Their father Mithridates V had had a close relationship with the island—in fact it was his strongest ally in the traditional Greek world—and it is fitting that Delos seems to have been the first state to recognize the new regime.

The inclusion of Mithridates Chrestos on the Delian inscription was perhaps an act of cautiousness by the dedicator, Dionysios, showing that while events were turning in favor of Mithridates VI and it was legitimate to recognize him as king, matters may not quite have been settled in Pontos. Chrestos could have been anywhere between four and sixteen years of age, and these dedications are the last mention of him. The sources are explicit in recording that he was eliminated by his brother, although no date is known.[46]

There was still the matter of their mother. Whether or not she was complicit in any of the plots against Mithridates VI, she was still a power at the royal court, remaining so for several years after the death of her husband. The available information about her later career is vague to nonexistent, but she may have owed her survival to removing herself from the court at Sinope, perhaps to a country estate. At some time she entered into a relationship with a person who remains unknown today, which produced the two daughters. This may have been the catalyst that caused her son—by now firmly established in power—either to imprison her or even to kill her, allegedly by poison, since a new husband for his mother would be a distinct threat to his rule. The daughters survived but were removed from any dynastic plans of their brother, even being denied marriages.[47] Moreover, the historical record was cleansed so that not even the name of the mother is known today.

To be sure, such a late date for her disposal—no earlier than around 110 BC—depends on the age of the daughters forty years later as reported by Plutarch. If they were in fact older and also the children of Mithridates V, the chronology becomes far simpler, allowing their mother to be eliminated earlier, perhaps around 116 BC. But this goes against the explicit statement by Plutarch, who was generally well informed and whose biography of the Roman commander Lucullus—the source for the sisters' ages—used contemporary material.[48] Nevertheless an earlier birthdate solves some major chronological issues.

Mithridates VI had three additional sisters. Nyssa was captured by the Romans at Kabeira when it was taken in 71 BC but may have been released later.[49] Two others, both named Laodike, are more apparent in the historical record. The elder had been married to Ariarathes VI, the king of Cappadocia, for some time, probably since the mid-120s BC. Ariarathes had been too young to rule alone when his father, Ariarathes V, died around 130 BC, and his mother became regent.[50] Mithridates V thus saw his chance to strengthen relations with (and control over) Cappadocia by marrying his daughter to the young king. But as Ariarathes VI matured, he became less susceptible to those around him, and thus he was killed at the instigation of Mithridates VI by a certain Gordios, a member of the Cappadocian aristocracy who would become a close advisor to the Pontic king for many years.[51] The date for the death of Ariarathes VI is not certain but was probably sometime between 116 and 111 BC. His widow was now in a position to advance Pontic interests in Cappadocia through her son, Ariarathes VII, who was still an adolescent. With Mithridates becoming increasingly involved in Cappadocian affairs, he may have taken the epithet Eusebes ("Pious"), previously unknown in Pontos but common among Cappadocian kings. It was especially attached to Ariarathes IV and V, the grandfather and father of Ariarathes VI. Other Ariarathid kings also held the epithet, including Ariarathes IX, a son of Mithridates VI.[52] Thus it is possible that the Pontic king appropriated the epithet to assert the legitimacy of his involvement with Cappadocia, although the evidence for this is scant, and the single citation presumed to be "Eusebes" must be restored on an inscription from Delos where only the first two letters of the word are preserved.

The other full sister of Mithridates VI, also named Laodike, married the king himself. But it was a brief relationship.[53] Early in his reign the king made a secret journey around Asia Minor, gathering information and allegedly plotting his future conquests. When he returned to Sinope after an absence of over a year, he found that his wife had had a son. Playing Klytaimnestra to Mithridates's Agamemnon, she tried to eliminate him, but the king learned of the plot in advance. Laodike herself was killed; the fate of the child is unknown. There are no hard dates for these events, but presumably they were shortly after the king solidified his control around 116 BC, although Justin seems to place them somewhat later. Thus in the early years of his reign, Mithridates eliminated both his mother and his sister-wife Laodike. The other sister named Laodike remained in Cappadocia, acting for the time being as his agent.

Mithridates's secret journey at the beginning of his reign ("all over Asia," as Justin noted), which obviously took at least a year, allowed him to survey the status of the region.[54] What long-range plans the new king had at this time cannot be determined, but the travels certainly acquainted him with many of the regions that he would conquer over the following years. The only place mentioned by Justin was Bithynia, to the west of Pontos, whose ruler Nikomedes III had been on the throne since around 128 BC and was the most powerful regional dynast. Mithridates would wisely see him as his best ally: in time, in a complex turn of events, Nikomedes would eventually marry Mithridates's sister Laodike, the regent of Cappadocia.[55]

Although one can only speculate about Mithridates's itinerary on his journey, some information can be gathered by his future interests. He probably began his travels by heading into Paphlagonia and Galatia, two regions that long had had connections with Pontos. Pharnakes I had attempted unsuccessfully to conquer Paphlagonia, and Mithridates wanted to fulfill his grandfather's plans.[56] The king would have learned that there was no unified Paphlagonian state but a relatively weak confederacy of regional dynasts; this would be his first conquest.

To its south was Galatia, also divided into several regional dynasties that could easily be acquired. Phrygia, farther southwest, was in a similar situation, although the Romans were showing intense interest in the territory and may have annexed it soon after the death of Mithridates V, but the evidence is complex and contradictory.[57] One would expect that these two regions were an important part of Mithridates's travels: whether he went farther into southern Asia Minor cannot be determined. Presumably he had no need to visit Cappadocia, since reliable information would be supplied by his sister and Gordios, but Lykia to the west might have been worth a visit. It was a confederacy of twenty-three independent cities that had existed in its present form since the Seleukid withdrawal earlier in the century. Information about Lykia would have been valuable, but the king does not seem to have shown any specific interest in the territory until the first war with Rome began in 89 BC.[58]

West of Lykia, and extending up the coast and its hinterland to Bithynia, was the Roman province of Asia; there is no evidence that the king entered Roman territory. In southeastern Asia Minor, along the Mediterranean coast, were several small states that had achieved an independent identity with the Seleukid withdrawal. Lykaonia, Pamphylia, and Pisidia eventually became involved in the wars between Mithridates and Rome, but it seems unlikely that he went this far afield at this time. Much the same can be said for Cilicia, farther east. Scattered through this region, and to the east, was the Seleukid territory, where Antiochos IX, Mithridates's cousin, was in the process of establishing himself as the last strong ruler of the dying kingdom. Despite the long-standing connections between the Seleukids and the Pontic dynasty, it does not seem that Mithridates had much concern with their territory at this time, although this would change as conflict with Rome became inevitable.

To the north, Armenia was beginning to emerge as an important regional kingdom. It had come into existence as an independent state due to the Seleukid decline in the late third century BC but was still relatively obscure at the time of the accession of Mithridates VI, under its ruler Tigranes I. Around 95 BC his son Tigranes II would succeed him and become the first great king of the territory, ruling for forty years. He would be a major ally of Mithridates and would marry his daughter Cleopatra.[59]

An incognito king obviously could not make any visits to royal courts or make any political decisions involving other dynasties, and the journey was largely a topographical reconnaissance, laying the groundwork for the military operations that would characterize his reign, although it is impossible to determine his contemporary state of mind and his thoughts regarding the future. In time he returned to Sinope, confronted his unfaithful wife, and began his reign in earnest. Within several years of his father's death, Mithridates had eliminated or neutralized any potential rivals to his rule. He was now ready to embark on his dramatic career, which over the next half century would make him the dominant personality of the eastern Mediterranean world and the second of the three great rivals of the late Roman Republic, after Hannibal and before Cleopatra VII.

Chapter 7

The Early Expansion of the Kingdom of Mithridates VI

ENCIRCLING THE BLACK SEA

His domestic problems settled, Mithridates VI began a program of expansion of his kingdom. Despite his journey through Asia Minor, his first interests were along the coasts of the Black Sea beyond the traditional boundaries of Pontos. No precise detailed chronological outline is available—nor is it possible to determine whether the Asian reconnaissance was before, during, or after his acquisition of the Black Sea territories—but one must assume that his efforts along the coast were within a few years after he gained total control around 116 BC.

Strabo, writing several generations later, suggested that Mithridates had the idea of making war against the Romans in mind from the very beginning of his reign and that he soon planned to go as far as the Adriatic.[1] Such a global reach is unlikely at this early date, but the king certainly had cause for complaint against the Romans, since Phrygia, which had been given to his father in 129 BC, was repossessed by them and added to the province of Asia.[2] Although the Romans were later to claim that they were merely liberating the territory, not annexing it, this was hardly the case, and it came to be believed that this incident was the primary cause of Mithridates's subsequent wars against Rome. To be sure, it would be a quarter century before open warfare began, but Mithridates would devote those years to building a power base that could, in fact, allow him to go to war.

One of his early acquisitions may have been somewhat serendipitous. Around 107 BC the dynast of Lesser Armenia, a certain Antipatros son of Sisis, "yielded" his kingdom to Mithridates.[3] Lesser Armenia, the mountainous region southeast of Pontos, was rich in natural resources, especially minerals. The Pontic kings had had an interest in the region for half a century, and Mithridates V had

actually been styled "king of Pontos and Armenia"—the latter presumably referring only to Lesser Armenia—during the war against Aristonikos the Pergamene
pretender.[4] Now, in the early years of Mithridates VI, Antipatros handed it over
to the Pontic ruler (under exactly what circumstances is not known), and it
would remain an integral part of his kingdom.

To the east of Pontos was Colchis, the territory at the southeastern corner
of the Black Sea, long famous as the destination of Jason and the Argonauts. It
too was a rich region, as the tale of the Golden Fleece implies. There were also
timber and linen resources, both of which were important components of shipbuilding (linen was used for sails) and thus necessary to create the fleet that the
king would need to move against the Romans; in fact, Colchis would become
the primary supplier of these essential items.[5] Moreover, it was a trade outlet
for the interior, located on the Phasis (modern Rioni) River and at the west end
of a major route from the southern Caucasus and Caspian regions. Possession
of Colchis gained Pontos access to a vast area of south central Asia. Its acquisition was linked by Strabo with the annexation of Lesser Armenia, although if
Mithridates did not obtain that region until 107 BC, he may have moved into
Colchis a few years previously.

It is also reported that the king took Colchis peacefully, through inheritance,
but not enough is known about its contemporary organization to understand
the details, or whether any coercion was involved.[6] Colchis was not a unified
state, and remnants of the Persian local administration persisted. The collapse
of this weak government may have been what led the Colchians to request that
Mithridates become their ruler: local invitation or a bequest was a claim that the
king made regularly when acquiring territory. In this era of the Pergamene legacy such means of transferring power were common, although there may have
been some sort of self-justification by the king.[7] In time, Strabo's great-uncle
Moaphernes would be royal governor, and he and other Pontic administrators
gave Colchis the centralized government that it needed.

By all accounts these events were early in the king's reign, certainly by 106
BC.[8] Regardless of his thoughts about the future, he had obtained important
economic resources that would serve him well in any subsequent campaigns.
Included in his new territorial reach was the city of Dioskourias (at modern
Sukhumi in Georgia), the northernmost city in Colchis and the largest Greek
city on the eastern Black Sea coast. Allegedly founded by the Dioskouroi, it
was considered (slightly inaccurately) the most remote sailing point in the
Mediterranean system.[9]

Less is known about his interest in the western Black Sea.[10] The people of Odessos (modern Varna in Bulgaria) had appealed to Pharnakes I for assistance, citing the usual reason—pressures from the populations of the interior—and Mithridates may have continued his grandfather's relationship with that city. At the northwestern corner of the sea was Borysthenes, or Olbia (at modern Parutino in Ukraine), lying near the mouth of the Borysthenes (modern Dnieper) River. It had been founded by Milesians in the sixth century BC and, while prosperous, had a certain notoriety as the farthest north Greek city.[11] In Mithridates's day it was in decline, in part because of barbarian advances, and in fact the Skythian leader Skilouros had occupied it and struck his own coins there.[12] Mithridates, presumedly as part of his general campaign in the northern Black Sea regions, removed the Skythians, but it is not certain whether he took direct control of the city.

Farther along the coast to the west was Tyras, another Milesian settlement.[13] It lay at the mouth of its homonymous river (the modern Dniester); Mithridates may have acquired it at roughly the same time as Borysthenes. Two other cities on the west coast, Istros (in modern Romania south of the mouth of the Danube) and Apollonia (at modern Burgas in Bulgaria) were allied with Pontos at the time of the first war with Rome, but details of their earlier relationship with the king are lacking.[14]

It was also said that Mithridates completely defeated the Skythians. This is problematic, in part because "Skythian" tended to be a generic term for the primitive peoples north and west of the Black Sea, and it is unlikely that any defeat of them was as thorough as Justin's text implies.[15] Moreover, Mithridates's "total defeat" is contextually associated by Justin with the Skythian expedition of Alexander the Great, whose commander Zopyron allegedly lost thirty thousand men in an engagement with the Skythians near the mouth of the Borysthenes.[16] This may provide the approximate location of Mithridates's victory, and it allowed him to succeed where Alexander (or at least those representing him) had failed. Thus it became the royal ideology that all the Skythians had been defeated, whatever actually happened.[17]

THE INVASION OF THE CHERSONESOS

Sometime during the first years of the king's rule, Chersonesos Taurike sent him an urgent message. Mithridates's grandfather Pharnakes I had concluded a treaty with the city in 155 BC, which included among its conditions that he would provide assistance if there were a barbarian invasion.[18] Now, perhaps forty years later, the city had been attacked, and—reluctantly, Strabo implied—it appealed to Mithridates. His commanders were already in the region, somewhere between Dioskourias and the Kimmerian Bosporos, engaging the locals.

Chersonesos, another remote Greek city, had been under almost constant threat from the north. Skilouros, the Skythian dynast, had put together a kingdom whose outposts threatened Chersonesos. He built fortresses north of the city at Palakion, Chabon, and Neapolis. The southern part of the peninsula on which the city of Chersonesos was located (modern Crimea) is precipitous and mountainous, and Skilouros and other local chieftains would harass the Greek cities from refuges on the rugged uplands of Mount Trapezous and Mount Kimmerion, which reach elevations of over five thousand feet within a few miles of the coast. Moreover, presumably as a part of this general policy, Skilouros also seized the Greek city of Olbia, to the west. The Skythians themselves were being forced to the south by population movements to their north, and an actual attack on Chersonesos (and probably the occupation of Neapolis and Olbia) resulted in the appeal to Mithridates.[19]

In response, the king sent his most senior commander, Diophantos son of Asklepiodoros, to Chersonesos.[20] His campaigns are documented better than most of the events of this era because the people of Chersonesos set up a bronze statue of the commander in full armor (now lost), whose surviving dedicatory base contains a detailed account of the events, spread over three years, perhaps 111–109 BC.[21] Upon landing at an unspecified point, Diophantos was immediately attacked by Palakos, Skilouros's son and successor. Although the Skythians had a reputation for being undefeatable, the Pontic army routed them, and it was claimed that this was the first time they had been beaten; this may have been what led Mithridates to assert that they had been totally defeated.[22] Next Diophantos overcame a nearby ethnic group, the Taurians, whom he consolidated into a town. They had been famous in Greek mythology as the protectors of Iphigeneia but in reality had long been a problem for Greek settlers.[23] The town that Diophantos established may have been Eupatorion, named after the king, although, as with so many Hellenistic city foundations, it was both the collection of people from the hinterland and the reestablishment of an existing town.[24]

Having secured a Pontic presence in the Chersonesos, Diophantos then headed east to the kingdom of Bosporos, in order to meet with its king, Paraisades (or Pairisades) V, and to persuade him of the inevitability of Pontic expansion into the region. The kingdom of Bosporos was situated around the narrow strait known as the Kimmerian Bosporos (modern Strait of Kerch). It also extended to the north along the Maiotis (the modern Sea of Azov), as far as the mouth of the Tanais (modern Don) River. Paraisades was being pressed by barbarians from the north, who demanded increasingly large tribute.[25] Diophantos persuaded him either to hand over his kingdom outright or to leave it as a bequest to Mithridates, but there is no report of military action in Bosporos at this time.

The commander then returned to the Chersonesos and moved inland, taking control of two Skythian royal fortresses, Chabaioi (or Chabon) and Neapolis. The former lies near modern Kermen-Kyr and the latter near Simferopol.[26] There may have been a particularly compelling reason to capture Neapolis, since its name indicates that it was originally a Greek city that had been appropriated by the Skythians. The Greek population of the Chersonesos was quite satisfied with Diophantos's achievements, and, his campaign finished, he returned to Sinope.

But in time—how much later is not documented—the Skythians reconstituted their forces. The situation reached a point of urgency, and Diophantos was sent out again, even though winter was approaching. He attempted to move against the Skythian fortresses, presumably well in the interior, but had to retreat because of bad weather and returned to the coast, where the Skythians had taken a number of cities (including, perhaps, Eupatorion). This campaign initially did not go well for the Pontic forces: it was the middle of winter in a region where they were less accustomed to the extreme weather than the locals. Yet after difficulties Diophantos prevailed, even though he was besieged for a while in the vicinity of Ktenous (near modern Sevastopol).[27]

Nevertheless Palakos, the Skythian commander, believed that he had the Pontic forces at a disadvantage, and put together an indigenous coalition, especially including the Roxolanians—whom the Greeks believed were the farthest north population—led by their commander Tasios.[28] The coalition forces allegedly numbered fifty thousand, perhaps an exaggeration, but due to their inferior tactics they were no match for the Greek phalanx, even though Diophantos had only six thousand troops. At the beginning of spring they were defeated, and Diophantos was able to retake some of the fortresses in the Chersonesos.

Issues regarding the arrangement made with Paraisades of Bosporos to hand over his kingdom to Mithridates became urgent when it was learned that he had been killed by a Skythian chieftain, Saumakos, who, ironically, had been raised at the Bosporanian court. The Skythians also attempted to assassinate Diophantos himself, who presumably had gone to Bosporos in order to negotiate with Saumakos, and he was only rescued by a ship sent from Chersonesos. In time he returned to Bosporos with both land and sea forces and captured the major cities, along with Saumakos, who was sent to Sinope and vanished from the historical record. Invoking whatever arrangements Paraisades had made, Mithridates now took possession of the Bosporanian kingdom.

There is evidence for another Pontic expedition to the northern Black Sea region, but it cannot be dated. In command was Neoptolemos, who was best known for fighting two battles on the Kimmerian Bosporos: one in winter when the straits were frozen, and using cavalry, and another in summer with ships, events remembered because of the Greek incredulity at the cold weather of the north.[29] These battles may have occurred shortly after Diophantos's campaigns or much later, perhaps even in the 80s BC, when Neoptolemos was prominent as one of Mithridates's major commanders and the indigenous peoples of the northern Black Sea were again causing difficulty.[30] A Tower of Neoptolemos, which was near modern Primorskoye in Ukraine, may be a memorial to this campaign. It does not survive today, but it is evidence for campaigning well west of the Chersonesos.[31]

With the acquisition of the Bosporanian kingdom, Mithridates VI had now assimilated the most important Greek state on the northern Black Sea. This gave him control of the entire eastern seacoast from Pontos all the way around to the end of Asia at the Kimmerian Bosporos and somewhat beyond, although his presence in the unorganized territory between Dioskourias and the eastern edge of the Bosporanian kingdom was marginal. This was a region of little-known and primitive peoples—the Achaians, Zygians (who gave their name to modern Sochi in Russia), Heniochians, and others—who lived on the northern and western slopes of the Caucasus.[32] Mithridates also had some relationship—presumably more protectorate than outright control—over the region of the Chersonesos and some of the cities beyond to the west.

THE ROMAN RESPONSE

The Romans must have looked askance at the activities of Mithridates. Although it is difficult to credit Strabo's statement that Mithridates's involvement with the northern Black Sea territories was part of a greater campaign that would take him all the way to the Adriatic, the king would have given the Romans cause for worry.[33] They had officially known about Pontos since the time of Pharnakes I, yet their repossession of part of Phrygia, whatever the details, meant that Roman and Pontic territory were coming ever closer to one another.

These were difficult years for Roman Republic. The internal instability that was to last for a century and which would cause its eventual collapse was in its initial stages.[34] The attempted land reforms of the two tribunes, the Gracchi brothers—connected in part to the projected revenue from the Pergamene legacy—had resulted in civil violence, with the elder brother, Tiberius, killed on the Capitol in the late summer of 133 BC and the younger, Gaius, meeting the same fate a decade later on the Aventine. Then there was trouble in North Africa, where a civil war in Numidia resulted in the alleged killing of many Italian merchants in the capital, Cirta. This led to open warfare against the claimant to the Numidian throne (and the assumed instigator of the violence), the Roman-trained Jugurtha, a conflict that lasted from 112 to 104 BC, the very years that Mithridates was encircling the Black Sea.

Peoples in Europe were also on the move. The Cimbrians and Teutonians had been drifting south from the region of Jutland, and the first Roman consul sent against them, Gnaeus Papirius Carbo, suffered a massive defeat at Noreia (probably in modern Austria). He returned home and was prosecuted in 113 BC by Marcus Antonius, grandfather of the triumvir, but committed suicide by ingesting copper sulfate.[35] Then there were problems in Gaul, and the consul of 107 BC, Lucius Cassius Longinus, was defeated by the Volcians; he was killed and his army captured. Two years later, near Arausio (modern Orange in France), the Roman army, in the field against the Cimbrians, was said to have lost eighty thousand men, its greatest defeat since the time of Hannibal.[36]

Although there is no evidence that the Romans had any contact with Mithridates during the first decade of his rule other than the partial acquisition of Phrygia around 120 BC, reports of his activities on the Black Sea certainly reached Rome. The war against Jugurtha broke out in 112 BC, and Diophantos may have been in negotiation with Paraisades of Bosporos at almost exactly the same time. It may even have been the Roman preoccupation with Jugurtha (and the contemporary issues in Europe) that encouraged Mithridates to believe that he could begin his expansionism without Roman interference.[37]

But whatever was heard in Rome about Mithridates, it cannot have been well received. If the rumors included a report that he was moving toward the Adriatic, that would have been worse. In later years, when war had actually started, the king stressed his good relations with the peoples of interior Europe, not only the Skythians and Taurians but also the Bastarnians—who lived on the upper Vistula and along the Danube—and others in the region.[38] He may have been making connections with them as early as the beginning of his reign.

The only report of specific Roman reaction to Mithridates's presence in the northern Black Sea region is difficult to interpret and, as always, may be anachronistic. According to Memnon, the Romans were suspicious of what the king was doing and ordered him to return to the Skythians their hereditary territories, which Mithridates did in as limited a way as possible.[39] The passage is part of Memnon's report on Mithridates's career and his wars against the Romans, and it lacks specific chronological grounding. Moreover, if the Romans did insist on the return of the Skythian acquisitions, there is no other evidence that Mithridates did so. It is more probable that Memnon's report is a garbled account of senatorial concerns about the king's activities in central Asia Minor, perhaps in Phrygia or Cappadocia, close to Roman territory, and a region where the Senate, in time, would become involved.[40] It is improbable that the Romans had any serious interest in the Skythians. But if the king were already reaching out to those in Europe along the Danube, the Romans might have found this a reason for worry, since they already had a presence in northern Thrace and thus might believe that Mithridates would be able to bring to his side some of the European peoples who were already threatening Rome. But for the time being, Rome was occupied elsewhere, especially with Jugurtha and the various pressures north of Italy. Yet a prescient analysis of current conditions might have led some in Rome to wonder if Mithridates would be the next Jugurtha.

THE ECONOMIC BENEFITS

There is the inevitable tendency—put forth since Mithridates's own era—to see the king as primarily an aggressor who conquered other peoples for his own self-aggrandizement. To some extent this is true, but acquisition of the coasts of the Black Sea was of significant economic benefit to the Pontic kingdom. As noted, Colchis was the primary supplier of the timber and linen needed for shipbuilding, and the fleet that this produced was important for trade as well as military purposes. There were also Colchian mineral resources, along with those of Lesser Armenia. The Chersonesos and Bosporos had long been major grain exporters to the Mediterranean world, and the king was able to turn this to his own purposes. Shipments to the Athenians and elsewhere had begun by the fifth century BC, and by Mithridates's day the region of Sindike, in the eastern portion of the Bosporanian region, sent 180,000 *medimnoi* (over 250,000 bushels) of grain and two hundred talents of silver (presumably annually) to the king; the grain could supply a large number of soldiers.[41] Tanais, at the mouth of its river, the most remote city in the Bosporanian territory and the contact point with the nomadic barbarians, would receive "slaves, hides, and other such nomadic things" from the interior, and the nomads in return would obtain "clothing, wine, and other such products of a civilized life."[42]

As Mithridates acquired the Black Sea territories, part of the arrangement was that they would supply manpower for his growing military needs, and the accounts of his battles are replete with the foreign soldiers that he levied. He was said to have obtained his army from Skythia and to have caused the entire east to make war against the Romans.[43] When the first war began, in 89 BC, Pelopidas, his envoy to the Romans before the outbreak of hostilities, reported that Mithridates's empire included troops from the Colchians, Skythians, Taurians, Bastarnians, Thracians, Sarmatians (a particularly remote people from north of the Black Sea), and "all those around the Tanais, Istros [Danube], and the coasts of the Maiotis."[44] It is clear that Mithridates's conquests during the first decade of his reign provided him with a vast amount of human as well as natural resources.

THE INVASIONS OF PAPHLAGONIA AND GALATIA

Mithridates's creation of a greater Pontic kingdom spreading through northern Asia Minor and the Black Sea littoral began when he and Nikomedes III of Bithynia made an agreement to partition Paphlagonia, which lay between their two kingdoms. This probably happened in the early part of the last decade of the second century BC.[45] Weak and unorganized, Paphlagonia was ripe for conquest, but Mithridates realized that any such move might be viewed aggressively by Nikomedes, who had been on the throne longer than him (since the early 120s BC) and who would see a Pontic army heading west as moving toward his kingdom. Mithridates realized that Bithynia was the only other significant Greek state in northern Asia Minor, and probably respected Nikomedes's seniority. Relations between Pontos and Bithynia had more often been contentious than harmonious, but any conquest of Bithynia was probably not on Mithridates's agenda at this time. Yet a closer relationship might help neutralize Roman ambitions in the region, as well as give the king access to the Aegean without going through the Thracian Bosporos. Nikomedes had his own issues with the Romans: a few years later the consul Gaius Marius requested help from Nikomedes in his campaign against the Cimbrians, but the king refused, noting that a significant number of Bithynians had been sold into slavery for failing to pay their taxes.[46] Presumably these were Bithynians living in Roman territory (the province of Asia adjoined Bithynia on the south), and even though Marius's unsuccessful request came several years after the alliance with Pontos, the problem had probably existed for a while. Mithridates himself had his complaints against Rome—although he was somewhat more remote—involving the loss of at least part of Phrygia at the beginning of his reign. The two kings would have seen an alliance as a way of exercising their common antipathy toward Rome, and, moreover, acquisition of Paphlagonia would prevent the Romans from driving a wedge between them.

Thus, with the Romans occupied elsewhere, Mithridates and Nikomedes invaded Paphlagonia, probably around 108 BC. There are no details preserved about the campaign or other activities connected with the conquest: Justin merely reported that the year after Mithridates's incognito travels around Asia Minor he and Nikomedes attacked Paphlagonia and then partitioned it. The campaign was probably brief.[47]

If the kings had thought Rome would not respond, they were mistaken. When the Senate learned about the invasion, they sent ambassadors to both courts, demanding a withdrawal. Mithridates claimed that Paphlagonia was his by right of inheritance, a ploy that he used regularly, taking into account all the real and attempted conquests of his ancestors. In this case he stated that it had belonged to his father Mithridates V, something documented only in Justin's account. Nikomedes, with more authority to dictate Paphlagonia's future, announced that he would return it to its proper ruler, and then placed his own son on the throne, giving him the Paphlagonian dynastic name Pylaimenes, the name of a king at the time of the Pergamene pretender Aristonikos.[48] The Roman ambassadors, realizing that they were in a losing situation, gave up and returned home. To be sure, the kings may not have expected any response to their invasion on the part of the Romans, who were in the midst of the war with Jugurtha, and the actual Roman reaction seems weak and formulaic: clearly there were no troops available to support the Roman demands. Mithridates now believed that he was equal to Rome in power—ultimately a fatal overestimation—and after his initial bluster he may actually have given up Paphlagonia for a time, since in 85 BC the Roman commander Lucius Cornelius Sulla accused the king of seizing the territory while Rome was engaged in the Marsic War of 91–87 BC, an indication that he had not possessed it just previous to that time.[49]

The weak Roman response emboldened Mithridates, and he promptly invaded Galatia, to the southwest of his kingdom.[50] The Pontic relationship with the Galatians had been varied, and their groups (there were twelve tetrarchies in the late first century BC)[51] had vacillated between being Pontic allies and opponents. Pharnakes I had attempted to acquire Galatia in his war with Pergamon of 183–179 BC but had been forced to give it up and, moreover, to cancel all treaties that he had with them. He also was prohibited from invading the territory ever again for any reason.[52] These terms may have led his grandson Mithridates VI to feel that he had an obligation to restore Galatia to Pontic control.

Yet his invasion of Galatia was probably even more minimal than that of Paphlagonia, essentially an assertion of his ancestral rights and his way of rebuking the Roman response to the matter of Paphlagonia. He probably had the approval of Nikomedes III of Bithynia and his son Pylaimenes, now king of Paphlagonia. Mithridates advanced far enough to build a fortress in eastern Galatia, which he named Mithridation (located perhaps at modern Gerdekkaya) and which remained in Pontic hands until Pompey restored it to the Galatians in the 60s BC, perhaps even after the king's death.[53] The fortress was presumably the sole visible manifestation of his occupation of Galatia, and the invasion made little impression on Rome.

The war with Jugurtha came to an end in late 105 BC. The Numidian king was turned over to Sulla and was transferred to Rome, dying in January 104, through either execution or suicide.[54] Two years later, Marius, who had been Sulla's superior in Africa, defeated the Teutonians at Aquae Sextiae (modern Aix-en-Provence), bringing the northern threat to Rome to an end.[55] Mithridates was coming to realize that he could no longer count on Roman disinterest in his activities; little did he realize that Marius and Sulla would become very much involved in his future destiny.

Thus the king, who was also becoming embroiled in the affairs of Cappadocia, would have been naive to continue to expect a weak Roman response to his activities. He therefore resorted to another tactic: bribery of prominent Romans. Presumably he knew enough about Roman history to believe that such an approach would work. As early as the fourth century BC bribery had become an problem in the Roman electoral process, and in subsequent years there had been numerous cases of both the practice and legislation against it.[56] Internal electoral bribery was hardly the same as bribery by a foreign potentate, as Mithridates would learn, but the distinction may have been lost on him, and he saw it as a part of the Roman way of life.

The king sent a well-financed embassy to Rome, probably in 102 or 101 BC; the date is determined by the election of the tribune Lucius Appuleius Saturninus to his second term, which began in 100 BC.[57] Saturninus, a popular leader and protégé of Marius, believed that the attempted bribery, and the Senate's receptiveness to it, could be used in order to attack their vested interests. He insulted the ambassadors, perhaps even resorting to violence. Encouraged by the senators, they pressed charges. Saturninus, in an emotional defense, argued that he was only trying to protect the needs of the people, and thus he was unexpectedly acquitted and reelected tribune. He was elected again for 99 BC, but before he could assume office, he fell victim to the civic violence of the era and was killed by a mob.[58]

Diodoros is the only source for the bribery, and, needless to say, his account is about Saturninus, not Mithridates. Nothing more is known about the king's ambassadors or how successful their bribery attempt was, although it is possible that it may have encouraged the Senate to ignore the invasion of Galatia. But the king had learned that Rome was now in a position to react more strongly to his endeavors, with the end of their problems in Numidia and Gaul, and that a direct approach to Romans of power might have certain advantages.

TROUBLE IN CAPPADOCIA

Cappadocia had essentially been a Pontic protectorate since early in Mithridates's reign, when the king effected the assassination of King Ariarathes VI, leaving the kingdom to his wife Laodike (Mithridates's sister) and her young son Ariarathes VII. But as the new king reached maturity, he became less easy to control, and his mother saw her influence waning. Yet intervention in Cappadocia came not from her brother but from Nikomedes III of Bithynia, who took the initiative and invaded the territory, perhaps around 103 or 102 BC, expelling Ariarathes VII.[59] This may have been at the instigation of the queen, who realized that her role as regent for her son, now an adult, made her vulnerable and that both her son and brother might find her dispensable. To protect herself, she married Nikomedes, but if the couple had any illusions about reigning in Cappadocia, these were futile, since Mithridates promptly expelled them and restored his nephew.

A few months later, Mithridates and Ariarathes had a falling out, and because Mithridates needed a strong presence in the territory, he called upon his trusted advisor Gordios, who was Cappadocian and had been directly responsible for the death of Ariarathes VI a decade or so previously. He would now take control in Cappadocia. Needless to say, this was not acceptable to Ariarathes VII, who put together a large force, ready to oppose a Pontic army of approximately equal size. Mithridates was not certain that he could prevail and so pretended negotiations, at which he killed Ariarathes VII with his own hand. Mithridates then made his eight-year-old son king, giving him the royal name Ariarathes IX, with Gordios as regent. With the death of Ariarathes VII, the Ariarathid dynasty of Cappadocia that had been established in the early third century BC came to an end. The Cappadocians were hardly pleased at these events and attempted unsuccessfully to place the brother of Ariarathes VII on the throne as Ariarathes VIII, but he soon died of natural causes. Nikomedes of Bithynia also put forth his own claimant, allegedly another son of Ariarathes VII.

At this point both Mithridates and Nikomedes sent embassies to the Romans. The former sent Gordios and the latter Laodike the mother of Ariarathes VII, perhaps one of the first examples of a royal woman appealing to the Senate. But the Senate was not impressed by either claimant. They ordered Mithridates to remove his army from Cappadocia, and, to give the appearance of equanimity, they ordered Nikomedes to give up Paphlagonia, which he had held (at least in part) for the previous decade. Further, the Senate declared that both Cappadocia and Paphlagonia would be free and independent states, without a ruling dynasty.

By this time the Romans were becoming seriously worried about the activities of Mithridates, and in 98 or 97 BC Gaius Marius visited Asia Minor, using personal business to make a reconnaissance of the situation in Cappadocia and Galatia.[60] Plutarch reported that as a private citizen after holding an unprecedented six consulships and achieving numerous outstanding military successes, Marius was looking for new adventures and was hoping to capitalize on the wealth of the east, but this is unlikely. Specifically, he went to Asia in order to fulfill a vow at the shrine of the Great Mother in the Galatian city of Pessinous. Some years previously a certain Battakes, priest at the shrine, had appeared in Rome and, among other things, had predicted Marius's victory against the Cimbrians.[61] After defeating them, Marius eventually went to Galatia to give thanks at Pessinous. Whether he had any official commission remains debatable; there is no specific evidence for it, but it seems unlikely that the Senate would not take advantage of the presence of one of their most senior commanders on the borders of Pontos, whose king was becoming a problem. In all likelihood, the Romans were concerned that war with Mithridates was approaching the inevitable and thus sent the experienced Marius to investigate. Marius met with Mithridates (the location is not specified) and advised him either to be stronger than Rome or to submit to it in silence, a bold statement that impressed the king, who would have been aware that Alexander the Great was believed to have said the same thing about the Romans.[62] Although the anecdote is thus somewhat formulaic—fitting into traditions about Roman virtue in the presence of an eastern king—both Marius and Mithridates would have understood the subliminal message. Whether it affected Mithridates's long-term policy cannot be determined, but he probably remembered Marius's (and thus Alexander's) words for the rest of his life.[63]

The Paphlagonian response to the Senate's orders is not recorded, but the Cappadocians, surprisingly, rejected the proposal and asked for a king, feeling that their status deserved one.[64] What was more astonishing was that they chose Gordios for their king; presumably he had some status within the Cappadocian ruling elite that is unknown today. The Senate, however, did not approve of this selection—since Gordios was too connected to Mithridates—and instead appointed another Cappadocian aristocrat, a certain Ariobarzanes (I), who was probably related to the royal family. Despite a career that was tenuous at best—Mithridates kept expelling him—he lasted thirty years, and his descendants ruled until 41 BC.[65] Of the other contemporary participants in Cappadocian affairs, Gordios continued to serve Mithridates for many years, and Nikomedes III of Bithynia reigned until around 94 BC. His new wife Laodike—Mithridates's sister—may have been honored at Delphi (along with her husband) but otherwise drops from the historical record.[66] And Mithridates VI, although now fully within the horizon of Rome, nevertheless turned his interests toward the east.

Chapter 8

The Gathering Storm

TIGRANES II OF ARMENIA

Although Mithridates had exercised a remarkable show of power, the first two decades of his reign had had mixed results. The Black Sea littoral was firmly under his control, despite barbarian incursions into the Bosporos and Chersonesos. But his activities in Asia Minor were problematic: his influence in Cappadocia was diminishing, he may have had to give up Paphlagonia, and his invasion of Galatia was limited. Moreover, he had alienated his closest ally, Nikomedes III of Bithynia, and probably also his own sister Laodike. This may be part of the reason that when it was reported a new king had come to the throne of Greater Armenia, Mithridates responded with interest.

Greater Armenia, the high and rugged territory between Mesopotamia and Colchis and extending east almost to the coastal districts of the Caspian Sea, had emerged as an independent kingdom with the retrenchment of the Seleukids in the early second century BC. The local satrap of Antiochos III, Artaxias, declared himself king and established a dynasty that lasted into the Augustan period.[1] Yet Armenia is hardly known during the second century BC, and the territory probably remained weak and unimportant until the beginning of the following century.

In 95 BC, Tigranes II came to the throne (fig. 8.1).[2] He was not young; many years previously he had been sent east of the Euphrates to the Parthian court as a hostage and had spent much of his youth there.[3] He was recalled to Armenia upon the death of his father; the date of 95 BC is secure, since when he met the Roman legate Appius Clodius Pulcher at Antioch in 70 BC he had been on the throne for twenty-five years.[4] But even when Tigranes returned to Armenia, he remained beholden to the Parthian king, because Parthia had established him on

Figure 8.1 Tigranes II, king of Armenia, vintage engraved illustration. Shutterstock 271069871.

the throne in exchange for parts of Armenia. At some time Tigranes's daughter Automa married Mithridates II of Parthia.[5]

Tigranes would rule Armenia for forty years, extending his kingdom as far as Antioch in Syria and outliving Mithridates VI. Unlike him, he would come to an accommodation with the Romans.[6] He was the only dynast of the era to become equal to Mithridates in power and prestige. How much Mithridates realized Tigranes's potential at the beginning of his reign is uncertain, but he soon saw the Armenian king as a possible ally whose interests might not compete with his own. If the sequence of events preserved by Justin is in correct chronological order, the first arrangement between the two kings was the marriage of Mithridates's daughter Cleopatra and Tigranes. The royal couple would have six children, including the king's successor, Artavasdes II (ruled ca. 55–34 BC) and several daughters who married various Parthian kings.[7]

After the marriage alliance, the next step was to create a political one. Mithridates was allegedly well advanced with his plans for a war against Rome and recognized the value of the Armenian king's support. Given his mixed success in Cappadocia, Mithridates came to believe that Tigranes might be able to act on his behalf there. An Armenian presence in Cappadocia would also suit the plans of the Parthian king. Mithridates's advisor Gordios was sent to the Armenian court to persuade Tigranes to attack Cappadocia, whose ruler, the Cappadocian aristocrat Ariobarzanes I, was already in difficulty with his people.[8] Allegedly Tigranes had no idea that such an action would offend the Romans; although this sounds unlikely, it may be true, since he had spent much of his life in far-off Parthia, and the Parthians and Romans as yet had had no formal contact. Tigranes was ambitious, and one of his first actions was to annex Sophene, just to the west of Armenia, which may have brought him to the notice of Mithridates, since Sophene was only across the Euphrates from Cappadocia.[9]

Thus around 92 BC Tigranes invaded Cappadocia and removed Ariobarzanes, who promptly fled to Rome. In a peculiar but revealing arrangement, Tigranes was to take possession of the captives (presumably soldiers) and their equipment, and any other items that he could acquire, while Mithridates would have the cities and the land. Clearly he wanted to hold the actual territory, and thus he placed Gordios as governor but allowed Tigranes to have anything that was movable. Tigranes promptly returned to Armenia and advanced his interests in other directions. This was yet another Cappadocian adventure that was less than successful for Mithridates, since he was seen as the obvious aggressor, and the Roman response was swift.

Shortly before, Sulla had been sent to Cilicia, the coastal regions located at the northeast corner of the Mediterranean. It was still largely Seleukid territory, but it was also an area where piracy was endemic, which affected the Mediterranean as far as Italy. The Romans had established a foothold in the district in 102 BC in order to combat the pirates.[10] But a Roman provincial command was geographically fluid and broadly interpreted, and thus when Ariobarzanes appeared in Rome, Sulla was detailed to restore him. Moreover, the Senate told Sulla that his primary orders were to watch and restrain Mithridates.[11] This resulted in a military engagement between the Romans and a Cappadocian force led by Archelaos, the brother of Neoptolemos, who enters the historical record at this point. He would become the most important of Mithridates's commanders, leading his forces in the first war with Rome.[12] His descendants would be major personalities in the eastern Mediterranean for many generations. Although Gordios was removed and Ariobarzanes eventually restored, it was not without difficulty on the part of Sulla, who did not comprehend the rough terrain of Cappadocia and had to use a truce in order to withdraw both his forces and Ariobarzanes surreptitiously.

Sulla, having retreated from Cappadocia, met a Parthian embassy on the banks of the Euphrates. The Parthians would have worried about the Romans— if they had ambitions in Cappadocia, the Roman presence there was a matter of concern—and thus they sent a delegation to meet Sulla. The propraetor had already gone as far as the Euphrates and thus could be seen to threaten Parthia directly. Matters did not go well for the Parthians, and the Parthian envoy, Orobazos, was later executed, evidently because the Parthians objected to the presence of Ariobarzanes, whom they had deposed from the Cappadocian throne (through the agency of Tigranes). In the Parthian view, Orobazos should not have been a party to negotiations that involved Ariobarzanes.[13] This contact between Rome and Parthia inaugurated seventy years of contentious relations between the two powers, in which the Pontic kingdom, as long as it lasted, was regularly involved.

During these years Mithridates was repeatedly attempting to form an alliance with Parthia. In one sense, his relationship with Tigranes was part of this, since the Armenian king was to some extent subject to the Parthians. Sulla's meeting on the Euphrates may have been to investigate exactly what the situation was between Parthia, Armenia, and Pontos. Mithridates had reached out to the Parthians and considered them one of his allies; this alliance with the strongest state to the east helped encourage him to make war on Rome a few years later.[14] The Romans cannot have been unaware of the direction in which matters were moving. But when the Parthian king, Mithridates II, died in 88 BC, unstable conditions in the kingdom made it less interested in territory beyond the Euphrates, and further attempts at alliance by Mithridates VI of Pontos came to nothing.[15]

EVENTS IN BITHYNIA

Around 94 BC, Nikomedes III of Bithynia died. The fate of his wife, Mithridates's sister Laodike, if she were still alive, is unknown. His son Nikomedes IV succeeded him: it was reported that he had poisoned his father. Mithridates saw the regime change as an opportunity and attempted to have the new king assassinated.[16] When this failed, he persuaded the king's younger brother, Sokrates Chrestos, to claim the throne and provided him with an army. Sokrates was successful, and Nikomedes IV promptly went to Rome to lodge a complaint. For good measure, Mithridates also had Ariobarzanes expelled again from

Cappadocia, replacing him with his own son Ariarathes IX. In order to do this he employed two Armenians, Mithras and Bagoas, indicating that Tigranes was still of use to him.[17]

Mithridates may have felt that such bold action was possible because Rome was once again otherwise occupied. In 91 BC it became involved in the Social ("Allies"), or Marsic, War. The Marsians, who lived in the uplands of the Apennines, believed that they were not being treated properly by the Roman government, and led a revolt of the Italian allies, which lasted until 87 BC.[18] The headquarters of the rebels was at Corfinum (modern Corfino), which for a few years claimed to be the new capital of Italy, with civic structures to match. Mithridates, therefore, might reasonably think that the Romans would be too distracted to object to his activities in Cappadocia and Bithynia.

MITHRIDATES AND GREECE

During these years, Mithridates cultivated relations with the traditional Greek world, especially the island of Delos, which had had contacts with the Pontic kingdom since the time of Mithridates IV. The island had become prosperous after the Roman sack of Corinth in 146 BC, becoming the major mercantile center of the Aegean, and was especially known for its slave trade, profiting from a commodity increasingly in demand.[19] As early as 115 BC there had been a dedication to Mithridates VI on the island. In 102/101 BC, an Athenian, Helianax, commissioned a memorial in honor of the king, the Mithridateion (fig. 8.2).[20] Helianax was the local priest of both Poseidon Aisios and the Samothrakian divinities of the Kabeiroi and Dioskouroi, and he built his monument to Mithridates at the earlier Samothrakeion, adjoining it on the north side of its front. The building was small (4.30 m by 3.05 m, and 4.65 m high) but innovative architecturally—essentially a porch with two Ionic columns—an example of the monumental heroon that became common in the Hellenistic period.[21] The dedicatory inscription stood on a frieze course above the columns, and above that was a pediment with a bust in a medallion. Inside there was a statue of the king and twelve medallion busts of his presumed associates (perhaps chosen by Helianax), which were later mutilated by the locals, probably after the king sacked the island in the First Mithridatic War.

Figure 8.2 Drawing of Mithridateion on Delos. Courtesy Patric-Alexander Kreuz.

The inscription records that the monument was on behalf of the Athenians and Romans and dedicated to the divinities of Helianax's priesthood, as well as King Mithridates Eupator Dionysos, an early citation of his divine surname. Helianax was a son of Asklepiodoros, and half a century earlier an Asklepiodoros and his brother Hermogenes, who themselves were sons of another Asklepiodoros, had made a dedication on Delos honoring Mithridates IV and his wife Laodike. Moreover, Mithridates's commander Diophantos—who campaigned in the Chersonesos and Bosporos—was a son of an Asklepiodoros. All this may be evidence for a single Athenian family that over several generations had a close relationship with the Pontic monarchy.[22]

The interior statue of the king depicts him in Roman military dress, demonstrating that at the time of the dedication he was still attempting—or believed to be attempting—a favorable relationship with Rome. The medallions inside provide important documentation about his connections and alliances a decade before the first war with Rome.[23] On the long north side, probably the place of honor, two kings are represented, Ariarathes VII of Cappadocia (Mithridates's nephew) and the Seleukid Antiochos VIII (who ruled from the 120s to 96 BC and was a remote cousin). This is a rare indication of contemporary contact between the Pontic and Seleukid dynasties, and since Mithridates's relationship with his nephew was problematic, it is possible that the inclusion of the two kings was Helianax's way of casting a wide net.

Also on the north side were Asklepiodoros the father of Helianax, perhaps demonstrating that he was closely associated with the royal court, and Diophantos the son of Mithares, probably a relative of the Diophantos who had been Mithridates's commander in the Chersonesos and Bosporos. This later Diophantos may have been an officer in the Third Mithridatic War.[24] There was also a bust of an official at the Parthian court, whose name is not preserved, but which shows the extent of relations between Pontos and Parthia several years before the latter had any contact with the Romans.

On the east wall were Papias son of Menophilos, the royal physician, and another Parthian official. The west wall contained Gaius the son of Hermaios, perhaps the companion of Mithridates mentioned by Plutarch, and Dorylaos, the ancestor of Strabo, who would become commander of the army and also priest-king at the great sanctuary of Komana.[25] The three remaining medallions—one on each side—cannot be identified.

A few years later, in 94/93 BC, a certain Dikaios of the Attic deme Ionidai, who was the priest of Sarapis on Delos and a prosperous merchant, made a dedication in the adjoining Sarapieion, also from the Athenians and Romans, in honor of the king.[26] There are several other inscriptions from the island that are fragmentary but mention the king.[27] He also participated in an equestrian competition on the island of Chios (whether in person or simply supplying the horses is not known), as well as one on Rhodes. There was also a statue of him on that island.[28] Neither the statue nor the athletic events can be dated precisely, but they can be assumed to have been when Mithridates's prestige in the Greek world was at its height, before the outbreak of the first war.

THE COMMISSION OF MANIUS AQUILLIUS

If Mithridates believed that there would be no response to the removal of the kings of Bithynia and Cappadocia, he once again had underestimated the

Roman determination to keep the province of Asia secure and to exercise some control over the activities of the eastern kings. In addition, the Roman presence in Cilicia meant that their influence in Asia Minor was more extensive than ever. Both Ariobarzanes of Cappadocia and Nikomedes IV of Bithynia immediately went to Rome after their expulsion; Justin made a point of noting that the former "took his wealth" with him, suggesting that there might be funds available to assist in persuading the Senate to effect his restoration.[29]

Even though the Romans were occupied with the Italians, they were able to appoint Manius Aquillius to see to the matter of the contentious kings. He was probably the son of the opponent of Aristonikos some forty years previously,[30] and an experienced political and military leader, having been consul in 101 BC and then holding a proconsular command the following years in Sicily. He was sent to Asia probably in 90 or early 89 BC. The other commissioners were Mallius Maltinus and a certain Mancinus, perhaps Titus Manlius Mancinus, tribune of the people in 107 BC. Also involved was Gaius Cassius, the proconsul of Asia, who was in the vicinity of Pergamon with a small military force.[31]

They ordered Mithridates to be cooperative, but the king was obstinate and immediately raised the matter of the loss of Phrygia. Yet Aquillius and Cassius were able to restore Ariobarzanes and Nikomedes without incident, urging both to start a war against Mithridates, perhaps hoping that the Pontic problem could be settled without major Roman involvement. Ariobarzanes, territorially more remote, refused to do this, but Nikomedes, heavily in debt to the Romans since he had promised to pay the costs of his restoration, reluctantly invaded Pontos, going as far as Amastris, which lay about twenty miles within Pontos from the Bithynian border. In doing so he collected a large amount of plunder. Moreover, he blockaded the Black Sea outlet at the Thracian Bosporos, which would have been a major economic blow to Pontos and a serious provocation. Mithridates made no military response, but he began to mobilize those allies who could supply troops, mostly from the north. Mentioned are the Cimbrians (probably referring to peoples along the lower Danube), Sarmatians, Bastarnians, and Skythians.[32] His ability to levy forces from these distant regions shows the broad reach of his power as he prepared for war against the Romans. But he made no attack; he wanted as much provocation as possible before going to war.

There was still time for diplomacy, and the king sent an envoy, Pelopidas, to negotiate with the Romans, perhaps at Pergamon. This could also serve as a delaying action. Appian presented in detail his speech to the commissioners, as well as the response of Nikomedes's envoys.[33] Despite the inevitable problematic nature of speeches in Greco-Roman literature, Appian's account is a good summary of the issues between the belligerents at the outbreak of the First Mithridatic War.

Pelopidas spoke first, structuring his comments in such a way as to provide solid causes for a war, should it come. He emphasized that Phrygia and Cappadocia had been unlawfully taken away from the king, stating (rather ingenuously) that Cappadocia had always been a Pontic possession and that Phrygia had been given to Mithridates V in return for his services in the war against the Pergamene pretender Aristonikos. Moreover, the king had paid a large amount for the territory. Pelopidas then complained about the closure of the Black Sea and the plundering of portions of Pontos—noting that Mithridates had shown restraint by not responding to either—in order to demonstrate to the Romans that Nikomedes was the aggressor. He closed his speech by reminding the commissioners that Mithridates was a friendly and allied king, and that by treaty the Romans were obligated to restrain Nikomedes, which suggests that Mithridates had a higher legal status than the Bithynian king.

Then the ambassadors of Nikomedes replied. They referred to Mithridates's history of interference in the Bithynian dynasty—especially the matter of Sokrates—and argued that this was an insult to Rome as well as to Bithynia. They also insisted that the king's taking of the Chersonesos was in violation of the Roman policy that the eastern kings not acquire territory in Europe. The Chersonesos was, to be sure, barely in Europe, but its remoteness and the lack of a Roman response at the time of the seizure made this claim questionable. It was further pointed out that Mithridates had mobilized a massive army, with a large number of allies, and had made a marriage alliance with Armenia (which was presented as a provocation). He had also made contact with Ptolemaic Egypt (quite possible but otherwise undocumented except in this context, although there was a later attempt at a marriage alliance) and with the Seleukids (which was supported by the presence of the medallion of Antiochos VIII in the Delian Mithridateion). Furthermore, the king had put together a large naval force—three hundred cataphracts—with manpower from Phoenicia and Egypt (again presented as a provocation but hardly unexpected since they were the best suppliers of naval forces). The ambassadors quite rightly emphasized Mithridates's anger over the matter of Phrygia and Cappadocia yet urged the Romans to attack before it was too late. Although Nikomedes and his spokesmen certainly had their own agenda, the speech is a remarkable summary of Mithridates's state of mind at the time.

Pelopidas then replied, pointing out that the past history of relations between Pontos and Bithynia was not relevant to current issues (a questionable argument at best), but the present concern was the injustice of Nikomedes's recent activities. He depicted Mithridates as a victim who needed the Romans either to protect him or to leave him alone. This speech put the Roman commissioners in an awkward position, because they had already decided to support Nikomedes (perhaps the large amount of money he owed affected their decision). But they attempted a posture of conciliation, stating that they did not want either side to suffer from the other (not an effective response). They were clearly at a loss, and they adjourned the meeting, not allowing Pelopidas to speak further.

Mithridates was now totally offended and promptly sent his son Ariarathes IX to reclaim Cappadocia and once again to drive out Ariobarzanes. It was a swift and effective operation, and several weeks later Pelopidas addressed the Roman commissioners again, making a final desperate attempt to prevent a full-scale war. He pointed out that Mithridates had been exceedingly patient regarding Phrygia, Cappadocia, and the recent activities of Nikomedes. Yet the Romans had been unresponsive to Mithridates's requests for friendship and alliance; although this seems to contradict what Pelopidas had said in his first speech—that such a relationship existed—he may have meant that the Romans did not respect the existing arrangement. Thus the recent events in Cappadocia were in fact the Romans' fault, a solid piece of sophistry on the part of Pelopidas.

Then Pelopidas announced that Mithridates would appeal directly to the Senate, which suggests it was perceived that Aquillius was acting independently, an early example of what would become so pernicious in the last years of the Roman Republic, when so many field commanders acted solely in their own interests. Mithridates wanted the commissioners themselves to meet with his ambassadors before the Senate, presumably believing that he would have more leverage there than with the commissioners alone. Pelopidas also reiterated the extent and depth of Mithridates's forces and allies—adding Arsakes of Parthia to the list—and put forth the interesting suggestion that if the Romans restrained Nikomedes, Mithridates would offer them help in the Marsic War. Pelopidas ended his speech by encouraging all to settle their differences in Rome.

His subtle suggestion that Aquillius and the commissioners were not in step with Roman policy touched a raw nerve, and the commissioners considered his speech rather arrogant and ordered Mithridates to leave Bithynia and Cappadocia alone. They also said that they would restore Ariobarzanes. Furthermore, they arrested Pelopidas and ordered him to leave the meeting and not to return unless he could report that Mithridates had obeyed their orders.

THE REASONS FOR WAR

It is impossible to determine whether war was inevitable or not. The ancient sources give the impression that Mithridates had planned a war against Rome for many years. Lucius Annaeus Florus, writing in the early second century AD, gave a succinct account of the official Roman view:

> Because of his great ambition, he [Mithridates] burned with a desire to possess all of Asia, and, if possible, Europe.[34]

Allegedly the king had told Tigranes II of Armenia, when the latter came to the throne, that his intent to make war on Rome had existed for many years,[35] and, a decade later, after the first war, Sulla said to Mithridates:

> You kindled the war, and had thought about it for a long time, because you hoped to rule the entire world, if you could conquer the Romans.[36]

Needless to say, such a point of view is a mixture of hindsight and the standard tendency to demonize one's enemies, but if Sulla's comments—very likely based on his own memoirs—are accurate, they show that a belief in Mithridates's desire for world conquest was current even relatively early in his career. Such an obsession on the part of the king may be true and reflects a desire to parallel the career of Alexander the Great. It may have come to be part of his self-image after he conquered the Chersonesos and the Kimmerian Bosporos at the beginning of his reign, coupled with his awareness of the general instability of late Hellenistic Asia Minor and, after 112 BC, Rome's wars elsewhere. The Roman acquisition of western Asia Minor was an event of Mithridates's earliest years (the Pergamene legacy occurred when he was about three years of age, and the Roman establishment of the province of Asia a few years later), and this movement of the

Romans into regions closer to his homeland was part of the received experiences of his youth.

The king may also have felt that Rome's various problems would be an advantage to his own interests, since the years of the war with Jugurtha and the various conflicts with the peoples of Italy might make Rome uninterested in Asian matters. Moreover, he felt that Rome's enemies would come to his side: allegedly representatives of the Italian peoples and the Carthaginians approached him just after the first war started.[37] Since Carthage was essentially a Roman city by this time, the notice of them is enigmatic, but it may refer to interest in northern Africa regarding Mithridates's activities, perhaps from Numidia (just south and west of Carthage), which at the time was ruled by Jugurtha's brother Gauda, who probably still had complaints about the Romans. The king may already have reached out to these peoples before the first war started and, like Hannibal, had come to believe that he could put together a coalition of those opposed to Rome. The Italians even appealed to Mithridates for help in their conflict with the Romans and seem to have struck coins in the Pontic style. Significantly, these showed a warrior stepping off a boat and joining hands with another warrior on land (fig. 8.3).[38] But the Italian request came after the first war started, and the king replied that he could only help after it ended, by which time the issue was moot.[39] So it seems plausible that Mithridates had long thought about war with the Romans—perhaps limited to expelling them from Asia Minor—but such plans only began to solidify in the 90s BC, when his own successes and Roman problems made such a possibility more reasonable.

(a)   (b)

Figure 8.3 Italian coin, possibly of Mithridates VI. British Museum 1860,0328.258. Photograph © The Trustees of the British Museum.

On the Roman side, there were worries about Mithridates's intentions as early as Marius's meeting with the king in 97 BC. Such concern was the alleged reason for Sulla's command in Cilicia in 92 BC, and it was said that the Romans had even looked with suspicion at the king's earlier activities in the Bosporos and Chersonesos.[40] But the real issue that eventually led to war was Mithridates's activity in Bithynia and Cappadocia: this was repeatedly mentioned in the conferences between Pelopidas, the representatives of Nikomedes IV, and the Roman commissioners, and to some extent in the tone of Appian's *Mithridateios*, whose opening sections are a summary of the history of the two regions.[41]

Yet another factor leading to war was the internal situation at Rome and the increasing tendency of Roman commanders to act independently of the Senate. Marius had established a precedent for lengthy commands with his five consecutive consulships (104–100 BC), and within three years of his last one he was meeting with Mithridates. Plutarch, at least, thought this was a subtle way of agitating for a war that he would command. Although Aquillius was experienced, he gave the impression of becoming more intransigent as the negotiations with Pelopidas progressed, twice asking him to leave the conference. Whether or not this was because he wanted to provoke a war in which he would be given the command is speculative, yet Pelopidas's second speech was more conciliatory than Aquillius understood it to be. But he was obviously not about to allow the conference participants to settle matters in Rome, where he would be subject to senatorial supervision. As it happened, he was given the command when the war started, a decision that was fatal for him.[42]

There is no doubt that Mithridates had mobilized a large force by the end of the 90s BC. Appian reported that he had a fleet of three hundred cataphracts and one hundred *dikrotai* (a ship with two banks of oars).[43] In addition there were 250,000 soldiers,[44] 40,000 cavalry, and various allied troops. The Romans had about 120,000 men and cavalry, and a fleet that was guarding the mouth of the Black Sea. Nikomedes contributed 50,000 soldiers and 6,000 cavalry.[45] Despite the regular tendency to exaggerate the size of the enemy, as well as to minimize one's own forces, there is no doubt that massive numbers had collected on both sides. Even if Pelopidas had made a final attempt to avoid war, it was futile, and in the summer of 89 BC hostilities began, without any official decision on the part of the Roman government to sanction their initiation.[46]

Chapter 9

The Eruption of Hostilities

PORTENTS, OMENS, AND PRECONCEPTIONS

The beginning of Mithridates's first war with Rome was accompanied by portents, omens, and an eastern Mediterranean preconception of the goals of the Roman Republic. The predictions and omens could be selectively structured to indicate that Mithridates would achieve a swift victory. Some of these were misinterpreted or were even after the fact, and others were existing oracles that did not necessarily apply to the king but could be used to his advantage. They all seemed to point in one direction: confirmation that the king was held in high esteem throughout the eastern Mediterranean and that there were also serious complaints about the Roman presence in the Greek peninsula and Asia Minor.

Anti-Roman prophecies had been a feature of the Greek world since the early second century BC. It was said that after the Romans defeated the Seleukid king Antiochos III at Thermopylai in 191 BC, one of the Seleukid dead, a cavalryman named Bouplagos, rose up and went to the Roman camp. He told them that Zeus was angry with the Romans and would send avengers who would bring an end to their power.[1] This is the earliest known prophecy to emanate from the Greek world against the Romans, recorded by Antisthenes of Rhodes, of uncertain date but nearly contemporary with the event.[2] After Bouplagos made his prophecy, he immediately died (again) and was properly buried, and the Romans wisely sent to Delphi for advice. But the oracle was not comforting, warning the Romans to act with restraint or Ares would be unleashed against them. Having heard this, they were said to have abandoned any further war with the peoples of Europe; this was hardly true but provides a dramatic end to the prophecy.

The Roman army then withdrew to Naupaktos in the west of Greece, whereupon the proconsul Publius (a person not identified, if he existed at all) became mad and was possessed by a god, announcing (in both poetry and prose) that a king would lead a great army from both Europe and Asia and lay waste to all the Roman territory. Publius then prophesized that his own death would come through being devoured by a red wolf, which promptly happened, but his head remained and continued to speak further prophecies.[3]

Other prophecies included the king who would come from "faraway Asia" and cross the Hellespont. In the early second century BC—the time of the oracle—this may have been more vague than it seemed later, but by the following century it might be thought to apply specifically to the ambitions of Mithridates VI.[4] To be sure, these are formulaic reports and can be considered questionable in detail, but they—and others—reflect a steady stream of anti-Roman sentiments common to the era and the hope that the Romans would in some way be removed from the east. Such feelings developed almost as soon as the Romans set foot on the Greek peninsula.

The traditional Roman antipathy toward kingship was also a factor in stirring up eastern attitudes against them. They had abolished their kingship by the fifth century BC and had a strong distaste for the institution. Cato the Elder—on the occasion of a visit by Eumenes II of Pergamon to Rome—reported that he believed a king to be a carnivorous animal who was not worthy of comparison with the great leaders of classical Greece, Rome, or Carthage.[5] Although there were certainly those among the subjects of eastern kings who might agree with such sentiments, the kings themselves found this attitude threatening and an insight into what they believed was the overall Roman policy. Demetrios of Pharos (the modern Adriatic island of Hvar), one of the first eastern kings to encounter the Romans, in the late third century BC, believed that they acted as if it were a crime to have any king bordering their territory.[6] Perseus, the last king of Macedonia, felt that Roman policy was to eliminate all kings one by one.[7] That kingship was a respected institution and indeed a desired form of government—after all, it provided a connection to the world initiated by Alexander the Great himself—was almost incomprehensible to the Romans. The actions of the Cappadocians in 96 BC can be seen as proof: they demanded that their kingship be restored when the Romans abolished it, feeling that to be deprived of a king was an insult.[8] Yet the Romans could hardly understand why anyone would prefer to be governed by a king.

The prophecies and oracles were more folk wisdom than any analysis of actual events, but they helped to create an attitude toward the Romans that persisted among the dynasties and peoples of the east. The early first century BC was a particularly fertile time for oracles, some of which may have referred to Mithridates

VI, and others which were so interpreted.[9] Regardless of their meaning, the king exploited all that were available, especially the prophecies of forthcoming disaster to the Romans, which he coupled with Roman antagonism toward the established form of government in the eastern Mediterranean. He was able to take the moral high ground, and also to emphasize documented instances of Roman mistreatment of the locals, especially in matters of taxation and litigation.[10] When war broke out in 89 BC, all these concerns came together, and Mithridates was seen as the savior of Greece and the Greek way of life. He was the new Alexander, although this was a strangely mixed image, since the Macedonian had also conquered the east. But in Asia Minor, Alexander was more liberator than conqueror, the one who freed the region from Persian rule. Mithridates adopted a policy of direct imitation of his illustrious predecessor, such as extending the asylum precinct of the Temple of Artemis at Ephesos, claiming that he possessed Alexander's cloak, and staying at an inn in Phrygia also visited by him.

Mithridates might also have remembered another ancestor, the Seleukid king Antiochos III, probably his great-grandfather. Under the terms of the Peace of Apameia a century previously, Antiochos had been forced to withdraw from all of Asia except the extreme southeast. Mithridates could now vindicate his illustrious forebear's failure and take vengeance against the Romans for what they had done to him.[11]

The king was especially astute in interpreting prophecies and portents to his own advantage, using them to predict success for himself or disaster for the Romans. Yet he was not immune to realizing that such signs could work in both directions. An example was an incident at Pergamon, after he had established his headquarters there during the first war, when a bizarre spectacle took place in the theater.[12] The locals had contrived a device that would lower a Nike with a crown in her hand, to be placed on the king's head. At the last moment the mechanism collapsed, and the crown fell away and broke, to the great consternation of the spectators. This caused Mithridates to become despondent despite the success that he was enjoying at the time, in a Herodotean sense that present prosperity can only lead to future disaster.

THE WAR BEGINS

In the late summer of 89 BC the war began.[13] The Roman side was represented by Aquillius, Cassius, and the proconsul of Cilicia, Quintus Oppius.[14] They adopted a defensive posture and sent Nikomedes IV of Bithynia to engage Mithridates. Aquillius placed himself along the low divide west of Krateia (modern Gerede) in Paphlagonia, near the source of the Billaios River, on the main route from Bithynia into the heart of Pontos.[15] Cassius was at the boundary of Bithynia and Galatia, protecting against any movement by Pontic forces south through Ankyra into Phrygia. His position was perhaps around Dorylaion (modern Şarhüyük near Eskişehir) in northern Phrygia. Oppius was at or near the boundaries of Cappadocia, preventing any connection between troops from that territory and Pontic forces. Moreover, a Roman fleet was at the mouth of the Black Sea, isolating Pontos from the Aegean. The overall strategic situation was that the Roman commanders would set up a blockade that prevented Mithridates from moving out of the Pontic region into the rest of Asia Minor, but Nikomedes would make the actual attack on Pontos.

The battle between the two kings took place along the Amnias (modern Göksu) River, which flows from a source in northern Paphlagonia almost due east, emptying into the Halys (modern Kızılırmak) River at the western edge of Pontos. The fighting was around the site of the later city of Pompeioupolis (modern Taşköpru) in northeastern Paphlagonia.[16] Here the Amnias is in a plain several miles across, with the river close to its southern edge; presumably the engagement was north of the stream.

Nikomedes took the field himself; Mithridates's forces were led by Neoptolemos (who had fought in the Kimmerian Bosporos) and his brother Archelaos (who had been involved in Mithridates's attempts to take Cappadocia).[17] Nikomedes was said to have had fifty-six thousand men and cavalry, his entire force, but the Pontic heavy infantry had been delayed, and the commanders had only light-armed troops and a cavalry detachment commanded by a certain Arkathias, one of the king's sons.[18] The battle began when the Pontic forces, vastly outnumbered, attempted to secure a hill in the middle of the plain. They were unsuccessful, however, and the early part of the engagement was marked by a Bithynian advantage. But when the Pontic scythe-bearing chariots went into action, the Bithynians were terrified: Appian described the horrifying result of their charge. Chariot warfare had been essentially obsolete among the Greeks since shortly after the Bronze Age, yet the scythed chariot was an invention of Cyrus the Great of Persia and became a standard weapon in Persian warfare; the Greek world had known about it since the late fifth century BC. Despite their terrors—vividly described by Lucretius—they were largely an ineffective tactical element, unless they were able to surprise the enemy. This is what happened on the Amnias River, where they threw the Bithynians into a panic, and they became so disordered that the Pontic forces were able to surround them.[19] Nikomedes lost most of his men and fled the battlefield, seeking protection at the camp of Aquillius. His own camp and personal resources were captured. When Mithridates arrived with the heavy infantry, he released all the prisoners and gave them supplies for their journey home, which only added to his reputation. The Roman commanders were astonished, and indeed frightened, at how successful Mithridates had been; they realized, at least to some extent, that they had made a bad strategic error in sending out only Nikomedes, even though his forces were much larger in number than those of Pontos.

Mithridates took possession of Mount Skoroba, an unidentified location said to be on the border between Bithynia and Pontos, but which actually was in Paphlagonia. It was perhaps at the western end of Mount Olgassys, the highest range in the region.[20] There followed another minor engagement, toward the west near Krateia, where some Bithynian cavalry were captured. Neoptolemos, accompanied by an Armenian commander, Nemanes, then engaged Aquillius at Protopachion (unlocated, but probably around Krateia). It was reported that ten thousand Roman troops were killed. In both these cases Mithridates released all the prisoners and sent them home, enhancing his popularity even more. He also captured Aquillius's camp, but the Roman commander escaped by night to Pergamon.

Meanwhile Nikomedes and the Romans who were not with Aquillius withdrew to Cassius, who took up a position at a locality called the Lion's Head, on the borders of Phrygia.[21] They tried to fashion a new army out of the locals but found that they were untrainable and gave up. Cassius retreated to Apameia, which placed him near Roman territory and where he might have felt more secure. Aquillius left Pergamon and headed toward Rhodes, which was independent but strongly on the Roman side.[22] Oppius also moved south, taking up a position at Laodikeia (modern Eskihisar) in extreme southwestern Phrygia, an independent city but probably within Roman territory. Nikomedes effectively abandoned his kingdom and went to Pergamon, eventually fleeing to Italy and remaining there until the end of the war.[23] The ships at the mouth of the Black Sea scattered and were captured by Pontic forces.

The Romans and Nikomedes may have been attempting to create a defensive line, essentially from Pergamon toward Cappadocia, that would protect Roman territory from any Pontic advance, but events moved so swiftly that this never happened. Mithridates quickly began to follow up the advantage obtained on the

Amnias River. He promptly occupied Bithynia, seemingly without resistance, and assimilated it into the Pontic state.[24]

In early 88 BC, according to the best chronology, the king moved into Phrygia and on toward the south, sending various forces in the direction of the Roman troops, which did not respond. His first goal was Apameia, where Cassius was located, and he took the city without difficulty. It had recently suffered from an earthquake—the first in many years—which caused significant tectonic changes to the landscape, and the king gave one hundred talents for its reconstruction.[25] Not only was this the expected benevolence on the part of a Hellenistic monarch, but the locals also connected it with Alexander's similar actions in late 334 BC, a point of view that the king encouraged: he had just made his stop at the inn visited by Alexander.

When Mithridates took Apameia, Cassius fled to Rhodes.[26] The Rhodians immediately began strengthening their defenses and preparing for an invasion, and the island became a refuge for those fleeing the Pontic advance. Mithridates moved west from Apameia to Laodikeia, seventy miles away, which was being defended by Oppius with assistance from nearby Aphrodisias.[27] The king promised that Laodikeia would not be harmed if its inhabitants handed over Oppius, which they promptly did. The proconsul was subject to some personal ridicule but was otherwise unharmed, and his army was dispersed; with the Roman presence removed, the city immediately went over to the Pontic side. Oppius entered Mithridates's entourage but was eventually given to Sulla at the end of the war and retired to the island of Kos for rehabilitation.[28]

Laodikeia was the first place to resist Mithridates, largely because of the presence of a Roman force. Generally, the reaction to the king's movement through southwest Asia Minor was mixed. Tralleis (modern Aydın), an ancient city on the Maeander eighty miles west of Laodikeia, easily joined the Pontic cause and received a rich payment from the king for doing so,[29] but Magnesia on the Meander, fifteen miles farther west, resisted vigorously, and Mithridates's commander Archelaos was wounded. Stratonikeia in Karia also opposed him and was garrisoned.[30]

Although there were indeed pockets of opposition—mostly notably in Paphlagonia and Lykia—much of central and southwest Asia Minor was conquered by the middle of 88 BC. Also taken was the Aegean island of Kos, where the king enhanced his treasury by capturing the personal wealth of Cleopatra III of Egypt (which had been deposited on the island) as well as eight hundred talents that Jewish communities in Asia had removed there.[31] Other funds came from various sources: a vague reference to acquisitions from "former kings" suggests that Mithridates obtained the Bithynian treasury and perhaps others that were scattered around Asia Minor. Some of these may have been used for the extensive program of debt relief that he initiated.[32]

The king's greatest disaster early in the war involved the island of Rhodes. It was the most powerful independent state in the region, and both a major sea power and an early ally of Rome. Its empire extended to the mainland and included a number of southern Aegean islands. It was also famous for its high degree of social welfare and its role as an intellectual center. Because of its naval strength and its alliance with Rome, neutralizing Rhodes was an essential part of Mithridates's strategy.[33]

Appian preserved a long and detailed account of the king's attempt to take the island.[34] Rhodes was prepared with elaborate defenses, and the local forces were augmented by allies from the mainland, especially Lykians. Mithridates began with a naval engagement, and then landed at the north end of the island near the city of Rhodes. He constructed a *sambouke* (or *sambuca*), a siege engine that allowed troops to be lifted up so that they could scale walls, so named because it resembled a type of lyre.[35] But everything went wrong: the Pontic troops mistook a Rhodian fire signal for their own and revealed their position, and the *sambouke* collapsed as an apparition of Isis was seen hurling fire onto it.[36] Eventually the Rhodians prevailed, and in time the king gave up and moved into Lykia. Before long he retired from personal involvement in combat and left Pelopidas to carry on the war, devoting himself to strategic concerns, eventually establishing his headquarters at Pergamon.

A final event of the first months of the war was the capture of Aquillius, who had taken refuge at Mytilene on the island of Lesbos, and who was handed over to Mithridates by the locals.[37] Accounts are confused, however, and it is by no means certain when this happened. One report is that he survived to the end of the war, late enough for Sulla to ask for his return. But it is more probable that he was captured when Mytilene received the king in the first year of the war. Up to this point Mithridates had shown clemency to those whom he captured, but Aquillius was a different matter. As the king himself pointed out, he had started the war. He bound Aquillius and put him on a donkey, taking him everywhere and requiring him to state his name and rank, a blatant insult. Eventually, according to Appian, he killed him at Pergamon by pouring molten gold down his throat. On the other hand, Diodoros, the earliest extant report, stated that he committed suicide, and, but the vivid and unusual nature of the molten gold story gives it credibility.[38]

In killing Aquillius in such a way Mithridates was making the particularly dramatic statement that it was Roman avarice that had caused the war. The king also stressed this when addressing his troops early in the war, referring to the greed of the officials and tax collectors, and he further reiterated it to Sulla after the war.[39] Pelopidas, in his speech to the Roman commissioners, had specifically referred to Roman greed as a cause for the Marsic War in Italy.[40] A quarter century after the first war, while the third war was still in progress, Cicero could write:

> It is hard to express how much we are hated among foreign nations because
> of the wantonness and injustice committed by those whom we have recently
> sent to govern them.[41]

The greed and hatred of Rome was real and indeed endemic, and as the first war continued, it would soon have especially tragic consequences.

MITHRIDATES'S VIEW OF THE WAR

Despite problems with Rhodes, in the first year of the war Mithridates was at the peak of his career.[42] His quick victories against the Romans and Bithynians gained him enormous prestige, for both his military abilities and his role as a liberator. His sphere of influence now extended, in theory, from the Aegean to the mountains of Armenia. Whether world conquest as the new Alexander was a fully formed concept at this time cannot be determined, but the hints that he was interested in moving the theater of war to Europe, as well as his alliances with Armenia and, to some extent, Parthia, suggest the genesis of such an idea. Roman ineptitude and the strife in the city of Rome and Italy, although dangerously overestimated by the king, played into his self-conception.

Mithridates was also acutely aware of his descent from the great kings of Persia.[43] Persian culture was still strong in Pontos, and a king whose alleged ancestry included Cyrus, Dareios, and Xerxes—names that he used for some of his sons—would have had even more respect, especially with members of the general population who themselves were of Persian descent. Moreover, the three Persian kings were great conquerors. Cyrus reached the remote country east of the Caspian Sea and was said (although improbably) to have gone as far as India.[44] Dareios and Xerxes, with varying levels of success, brought Persian power to Europe. Since Greek was taught in Pontic schools, the students could read about them in Herodotos's *Histories*. Thus Mithridates had numerous role models to suggest that world conquest was a legitimate theory of rule.

Justin preserved a speech that Mithridates supposedly gave early in the war, either to his general staff or his assembled troops.[45] No location for it has been preserved, but it would have been delivered sometime between the attack on Pontos by Nikomedes IV and the end of the Marsic War some months later, and thus probably late in 89 BC. As noted previously, speeches in ancient historical writing have always been a problematic rhetorical device. Yet they can be more revealing as to the thoughts or attitudes of the speaker, rather than a transcript of what was said. But Justin made a point of noting that his immediate source, the Augustan writer Pompeius Trogus, implied that the speech was a fairly accurate rendition of what the king had actually said.[46] Because Pompeius Trogus was active only about half a century after the death of Mithridates, he thus was chronologically close to the events, and even if he rewrote the speech for rhetorical and political reasons or created a construct from various public statements by the king, nevertheless it is probably a solid representation of his feelings early in the war. Credence to this idea is leant by the various flaws in the king's argumentation that could easily have been corrected if the speech were merely a literary construct. Moreover, he was well known as a skillful orator.[47]

The thrust of Mithridates's agenda was to convince his soldiers that they were fighting Rome, not the Asian peoples. He provided a carefully rendered summary of Roman history, often lacking in accuracy of detail for rhetorical effect. He noted that there was a long history of Rome's enemies doing well despite serious disadvantages (Pyrrhos, Hannibal, and the Gauls were mentioned), avoiding drawing attention to the fact that all of these, in the long run, had failed to defeat Rome. The Roman conquest of Italy, he said, had seen repeated acts of violence, and Rome was still involved in the Marsic War, which had erupted because the Marsians wanted nothing more than basic civil rights. In fact, the continuation of this war meant that it was a good time to attack the Romans, in particular to avenge the insult of the loss of Phrygia, which the king claimed had been Pontic for well over a century.

Mithridates went out of his way to stress his efforts at conciliation with the Romans, such as giving up Phrygia and Cappadocia. There was also a faint attempt to blame Gordios and Tigranes II for unauthorized actions, not one of the king's better arguments. But he said that the Romans had had a long history of offending Pontos, starting with their denial of the kingship of Pergamon to Pharnakes I, Mithridates's grandfather, although this had been his right. In fact, the Romans had a way of turning against their former allies (the Pergamenes and Numidians were specifically mentioned), largely due to their obsessive hatred of kingship, with the suggestion that the Romans' own primitive origins—from wolves, no less—made them incapable of appreciating civilization.[48] By contrast, Mithridates was a descendant of the great kings of Persia, Alexander the Great, and many famous Hellenistic kings. He had even gone farther than Alexander—into Armenia and remote parts of Skythia—conquering peoples who were now a large part of his manpower against the Romans. Having fought in such barbarous and primitive places, the Pontic forces were now moving into the province of Asia, an area noted for its wealth and fertility, which made its people far weaker than the northerners, an allusion to the statement of Cyrus the Great reported by Herodotos regarding the softness of people living in luxury.[49] Yet the locals, whatever their faults, hated the Romans and were demanding Mithridates's intervention. He also emphasized that his territories had never been ruled by foreigners such as Alexander and the Successors. Although there is a certain exaggeration to his statement—the Persians were conveniently ignored—the ideology as he presented it was central to his self-image and stressed the unique quality of his empire.[50] The speech is a rhetorical masterpiece, coupling a revisionist view of Roman history with an exaltation of Mithridates's achievements, a classic campaign speech revealing the king at the peak of his power and prestige. He also astutely brought together all the prejudices against Rome that had been fermenting in western Asia Minor. Mithridates condemned Rome not through the recent actions of specific people but through the nature of their history ever since the time of Romulus and Remus. Ridicule of the role of the wolf in Roman origins was a common device among their enemies in the first century BC.[51] The only Romans mentioned by name are the "Superbi," an allusion to the last king, Tarquinius Superbus, whose removal represented the end of Roman kingship. In choosing to mention—not unfavorably—a king whose very name meant "arrogant," Mithridates created an unusual image that reflects a totally different view of monarchy from that of the Romans. Other Romans were not specified beyond general allusions to tax collectors and other deplorables. As presented in Justin's recension, the speech was an emotional high point for Mithridates and all he represented. Yet matters were to turn bad very quickly.

THE MASSACRE

In 88 BC, Mithridates was stationed at Ephesos, making preparations for his attack on Rhodes. He sent a secret message to his satraps and the governors in the cities that he had conquered, ordering them thirty days later to kill all the Romans and Italians in their jurisdictions, including all freedmen of Italian birth and all their wives and children. They would remain unburied, and their property would be confiscated. He offered rewards to those who informed on ones in hiding, freedom to slaves who turned in their masters, and remission of half the debts to those who reported their creditors. Whatever the reason for such actions, it forever became a blot on Mithridates's reputation and seriously damaged his image as a just and forgiving conqueror. Over a dozen ancient sources mention the event, all in strong condemnation. Obviously many of these reports are Roman and might be expected to react unfavorably, yet Greek sources are equally negative.[52] Cicero, writing thirty years later, gave the first extant account, needless to say from the Roman point of view:

> I would have you remember in your minds the Mithridatic War, and the horror of that cruel slaughter of every Roman citizen in every city simultaneously, the surrender of our praetors, the placing of their legates in chains, and almost the entire obliteration of all the memory of the name of Rome and the removal of any vestige of our rule from the Greek settlements and indeed from their records.[53]

Valerius Maximus recorded the event in his section on cruelty:

> By means of a single communiqué he killed eighty thousand Roman citizens in Asia—the businessmen scattered through the cities—and splattered the gods of hospitality in that great province with unlawful blood.[54]

It even became a case study among Christian scholars, who used it to demonstrate the dangerous inadequacies of paganism. Augustine, describing the suffering of the affected Romans in rhetorical detail, saw it as a failure of their gods, and his contemporary Orosius wrote that the event was impossible to understand or describe.[55]

Allegedly, Mithridates was encouraged to precipitate the massacre by Publius Rutilius Rufus, the consul of 105 BC, who had been living in exile at Smyrna since being convicted of extortion in 92 BC. When Pompey the Great discovered the papers of Mithridates at Kainon in 63 BC, one of the documents was said to be a letter from Rutilius to the king, encouraging him to instigate the massacre.[56] Although Plutarch rejected the account, it is significant that Rutilius happened to survive the massacre, one of the few Italians to do so.

The earliest extant report is that eighty thousand were killed on a single day; by the time of Plutarch the number had grown to 150,000.[57] Some Romans even changed into Greek dress to save themselves.[58] In all likelihood the account originally comes from sources contemporary to the event, including Sulla's memoirs, and such reports are always exaggerated, but there is no doubt that a vast number were killed. To be sure, massacres—especially as a reason for revenge or starting a war—always play a dubious role in human events. In 112 BC, an alleged massacre of Romans in the Numidian city of Cirta had served as the reason for Rome to initiate a campaign against Jugurtha. This assumed event, a mere twenty-four years before the Asian massacre, would have been well remembered in Rome, although there is doubt that it even occurred.[59] Yet it is certain that, probably in the late summer or autumn of 88 BC, Mithridates gave his orders, and an undetermined but large number of Italians resident in western Asia were killed. Appian provided a catalogue—certainly incomplete—of the places affected. Even those seeking refuge in temple sanctuaries were not spared, as happened at Ephesos, Pergamon, and Kaunos in Karia. At Adramyttion in the southern Troad, the Romans futilely tried to escape by swimming out to sea. The citizens of Tralleis in Karia found themselves unable to carry out the orders and hired a Paphlagonian, a certain Theophilos, to perform the deed, who executed the victims in a temple shrine. Appian's list demonstrates that the killings occurred all the way from the southern Troad to the borders of Lykia. As he wrote:

> Such was the fate suffered by the Italians and Romans in Asia—men, as well
> as children and women, and their freedmen and slaves—who were all of the
> Italian race. It was especially clear that it was not only fear of Mithridates but
> also hatred of the Romans that caused the Asians to do such things.[60]

In retrospect, killing all the Italians seems like the worst policy decision that Mithridates ever made. Yet many Italians had flooded into the province of Asia since the Roman presence had been established in the 120s BC, with the businessmen numbering in the tens of thousands.[61] Exploitation of the locals became rampant. In 97 BC, Quintus Mucius Scaevola, the proconsul of Asia, had attempted to restrain the rapaciousness of the tax collectors and others, as well as making a point of not using public funds for his private needs. He was said to be the first provincial official to act in this way, but he became hated by those whom he attempted to restrain.[62] His legate was Rutilius Rufus, the one who was later allegedly implicated in the massacre. He supported his superior and thus was charged with extortion in 92 BC, although evidently innocent, and was forced to flee into exile. The Romans looked askance at Scaevola's honesty, but the Asians created a festival in his honor, which, significantly, Mithridates allowed to continue, an indication that the king was more opposed to Roman practices than to individual Romans.[63] The fact that the careers of these two Roman magistrates are so well documented shows how exceptional they were: the normal order of business in the province of Asia was extortion of the locals, and if the perpetrators were brought to trial in Rome, they were judged by the very people who previously had profited by the same means.

The solution to this problem that Mithridates implemented was elimination of the miscreants.[64] The only other possible option was deportation, which was logistically impossible. Although Roman sources violently condemn Mithridates's decision, hardly unexpectedly, the willingness with which the order to kill was carried out by the locals is demonstrative of support, and Appian blamed them more than the king. Without hindsight, it must be seen as Mithridates's way of eliminating the problematic situation in his new territories and restoring them to the status that they had held before the Romans arrived. Rome had not seriously responded to Mithridates's campaigns so far, and the king had no reason to think that this would change, or that any Roman action would be effective. Moreover, many approved of what he was doing, and eliminating the Italians was financially beneficial to both the king and the cities. In the long run his analysis of the situation was wrong, yet this was impossible to tell in late 88 BC.

Those who escaped removed themselves out of the province, with many going to Rhodes. One of the best-documented examples is that of Chairemon of Nysa (in Karia), perhaps the wealthiest man in the region. When the Roman forces moved into the area after the disaster on the Amnias River, Chairemon supplied them with sixty thousand *modii* of grain (perhaps fifteen thousand bushels), enough to feed the army for a lengthy period. Mithridates put a price on his head, and Chairemon became one of those taking refuge on Rhodes. Later he went to Ephesos, and it is unknown what happened to him thereafter. Yet in one of the most ironic twists in the history of Asia Minor in the first century BC, seventy years later Chairemon's granddaughter (or perhaps great-granddaughter) Pythodoris would become queen of the reconstituted kingdom of Pontos.[65]

One result of the massacre was a collapse of credit, since payments were suspended. Credit was too easily granted in Rome at that time, and the financial system was fragile.[66] This may have been part of Mithridates's overall plan: to weaken Rome by causing an economic panic. Moreover, the elimination of so many Roman citizens in the massacre (and elsewhere through other military actions and public disturbances) led the Roman censors—who were responsible for determining eligibility for citizenship—to make new enrollments, so that Roman citizenship actually increased during these years, but there was a major change in the nature of the citizenry, something that would come to have its demographic effect on the last years of the Republic.[67]

The reaction to the massacre was swift. Ephesos, the king's headquarters when the orders were given, promptly declared war on Pontos and adopted a revisionist history, stating that the Ephesians had never wanted him in their city, conveniently ignoring the fact that he had been welcomed and been given cultic status, and that the local Roman statues had been overthrown.[68] Other cities reacted with varying degrees of horror.

EVENTS IN ATHENS

The Greek peninsula had as yet not been involved in Mithridates's military activities but could not have been unaware of them. Needless to say, the first place to respond to the king's efforts was Athens, which indirectly had been in contact with him ever since its citizen Helianax had commissioned the Mithridateion on Delos in 102/101 BC. When news of Mithridates's successes in Asia Minor reached Athens late in 88 BC, the city decided to send an envoy, a certain Athenion, to the king.

The only source for Athenion's embassy is his contemporary Poseidonios, who was exceedingly hostile toward him, claiming that he was the illegitimate son of a slave girl and a Peripatetic philosopher, whose name he took, and that he had obtained Athenian citizenship illegally.[69] To some extent this is hardly relevant to the events that materialized, but it may lead to questions about some of Poseidonios's details and his overall tone. Led by hindsight, Poseidonios believed that the Athenians were especially foolish to be swayed by Athenion.[70]

It is probable that this episode, not mentioned by Diodoros, Strabo, Plutarch, or Appian—the primary sources for the era—was a closing event in Poseidonios's *History*, portraying a minor tyrant who demonstrated the failures of the political system, as well as looking ahead to the Mithridatic era, which would dominate the east for the next quarter century, and which Poseidonios survived but many not have written about.[71] Nevertheless, whatever Poseidonios's motives were, his account of Athenion provides an insight into the difficulties experienced by Athens at the time of the First Mithridatic War.

Athenion went to Mithridates and began to write letters back to Athens which not only described the king in eulogistic terms but gave the impression that he had become part of his inner circle and that enormous benefits would result from Athenian support. Athenion returned home to great acclaim—almost the entire city turned out to greet him, and numerous honors were bestowed—and made a triumphal progression through the streets. He was especially honored by the festival artists, who, as devotees of Dionysos, were impressed that one of the king's surnames was that of the god.

Athenion then mounted the speaker's stand (the Bema) in front of the Stoa of Attalos in the Agora—its remains are still visible—and spoke about the king in a highly supportive manner, emphasizing his defeat of the Romans and stating that his overall plan was to destroy them. He then catalogued the various instances of Roman mistreatment of Athens: a lack of elections and the closure of the temples and the philosophical schools. Regardless of how true these claims were, it is certain that in the immediately previous years there had been a great amount of instability in the city. A certain Medeios had been elected archon for the three consecutive years of 91/90, 90/89, and 89/88 BC and had become absolute ruler.[72] In the following year the records show no archon (a state of *anarchia*), but it may be that Mithridates himself held the office and was later removed from the lists.

Athenion's words were quite effective, in the long tradition of Athenian demagoguery. Whether or not the Romans had been responsible for the recent problems, it was an easy charge to make, and Mithridates was presented as the city's savior. Current thinking, promoted by the king, was that Rome had overstepped and her power could only decline. The result was that Athenion was elected military commander (*strategos*), and as such was able to put a government of his liking into place.[73] Yet not everyone supported him, Mithridates, or the causes they represented, and (according to Poseidonios's hostile account) civil strife broke out, and many left the city. Athenion and his followers stationed guards to prevent further departures, and instituted a reign of terror, even going into the countryside to track down those who had left.

Athenion also sent Apellikon of Teos—otherwise famous because he owned Aristotle's library[74]—to attack Delos, in part because of its pro-Roman stance but also as a fundraising expedition, since the island was a depository of great wealth. There is no evidence that Apellikon had any previous military experience, and he seems to have hardly taken the campaign seriously. When he arrived on Delos, he failed to set proper guards or watches, with the result that the Roman commander on the island, Orbius, easily killed or captured the Athenian force while they were sleeping or drunk and destroyed their equipment. Apellikon escaped and returned to Athens, dying in 86 BC, just as Sulla attacked the city and confiscated Aristotle's library.[75] Athenion is not heard from again and seems to have played no role when Mithridates's general Archelaos arrived in Greece later in the year. But these events caused a departure of many of the leading intellectuals of Athens—including Philon, the head of the Academy—who dispersed to Alexandria, Rome, and Athenian settlements, spreading contemporary Athenian thought throughout the Greco-Roman world.[76]

THE INVASION OF GREECE

At the end of 88 BC, Mithridates sent an invasion force into the Aegean. In retrospect, such an action seems to be the first clear example of the king overextending himself militarily, since he was leaving the more familiar confines of Asia Minor to carry on a war in the Greek peninsula. He was already in contact with the Italians who were fighting the Romans in the Marsic War, and who had asked the king to bring an army to them so that together they could overthrow Rome. The Saunitians (known as the Samnites to the Romans) were specifically mentioned as having been approached by the king. According to Appian, some sort of agreement was actually concluded, and, moreover, the king had replied that he would help the Italians when Asia was conquered, which was now the case, but no further details are preserved.[77] This was despite the fact that through Pelopidas he had offered, under the proper conditions, to help the Romans against the Italians, perhaps demonstrative of the king's ability to advance his interests in any way possible.[78] Yet this still does not fully address the matter of attacking Greece, but the route to Italy lay in that direction, and the king's role as the new Alexander the Great provided him with a reason to liberate Greece.

He may also have been driven by the memory of Hannibal: near the end of his own life, Mithridates was planning a campaign that would attack Italy by crossing the Alps. Most probably, the king simply believed that invading Greece was a necessary component in his overall plan to continue the war against Rome.[79] For the time being, however, the situation at Athens and Delos required immediate attention. Archelaos was the supreme commander of the invasion force, and Menophanes, who had been on the Amnias River campaign, was detailed to carry out an assault on Delos. He followed existing policy by killing all the resident foreigners—as many as twenty thousand, who would be largely Roman and Italian—and confiscating the treasures stored on the island.[80] Delos was given over to the Athenians and the treasures sent to Athens in the hands of a certain Aristion, who seems to have been a member of the king's entourage but was of Athenian origin.[81] Destruction on the island was widespread, and it never recovered its previous prosperity.[82] Menophanes did not escape divine retribution for attacking the sacred island and was killed when his ship was sunk while leaving the harbor.

The Pontic soldiers sent along with Aristion were to guard the Delian treasure, but when he arrived in Athens, he used them to establish himself as tyrant of the city and carried out another purge of those opposed to Mithridates. There is a suggestion of class warfare in Athens, with the more educated and prosperous favoring Rome and the lower classes—identified as the more troublesome element—on the side of Mithridates.[83] Aristion secured his position and remained in power until Sulla arrived in 86 BC.[84] In due time Archelaos appeared, establishing his headquarters in the Peiraieus—necessary since his logistics were seaborne—and embarked on a conquest of the Greek peninsula. Before long the Pontic forces controlled much of the Peloponnesos, Euboia, and Boiotia.[85] Another Pontic army landed in northern Greece—exactly when cannot be determined—under the command of Arkathias (one of the sons of Mithridates) and Metrophanes.[86] This force subjected Macedonia without difficulty and set up a Pontic government in the region, although Arkathias became sick and died near Tisaion in Thessaly. Some of the northern islands and parts of Thrace also came under Pontic control. Maroneia, noted for its strong wine, suffered a particularly violent destruction of the entire city.[87] Abdera received a Pontic garrison.[88] Quintus Bruttius (or Braetius) Sura, who had been legate to the governor of Macedonia since 93 BC, attacked these Pontic forces, probably in early 87 BC, first taking the island of Skiathos, where Pontic funds and resources had been deposited, and then moving south toward Boiotia.[89] He engaged Archelaos and Aristion at Chaironeia, the western entrance to Boiotia, where Philip II and Alexander the Great had defeated a Greek coalition in 338 BC. Although he was initially successful, he withdrew when he heard that reinforcements from the Peloponnesos were approaching. Bruttius was then told to return to Macedonia by Lucius Licinius Lucullus, who had been sent to Greece by the Senate to investigate the situation in advance of a Roman army of five legions that was on its way from Italy under the command of Sulla.

SULLA ON THE GREEK MAINLAND

Lucius Cornelius Sulla obtained the consulship in 88 BC, after a career that had begun twenty years previously, when he was Marius's quaestor in the Jugurthine War. He had then engaged Mithridates's forces in Cappadocia in 92 BC. Four years later, the king's activities in Asia Minor and Greece finally reached the point where a strong Roman response was needed, and, moreover, the Marsic War had ended in late 89 BC and Rome was free to turn its attention to the east. Many prominent Romans were anxious for the command, including Gaius Julius Caesar Strabo (great-uncle of the dictator), Marius, and Sulla.[90] The contention had reached the point of violence when the position was awarded to Sulla, who was appointed to lead an expeditionary force, beginning in early 87 BC.[91] After a violent dispute with Marius over who would actually have the command, resulting in the killing of many of Sulla's opponents (including Julius Caesar Strabo) and the exiling of others (including Marius), Sulla and five legions set out for Greece.[92] As an indication of the serious financial situation, it was necessary to sell part of the treasures of Numa—the second king of Rome—which he had collected long ago for religious sacrifices; as Appian noted, the Romans were lacking in means but not in ambition.[93] The treasures sold were valued at nine thousand *litras*, but this was not considered a particularly lavish sum to finance the war.

Sulla landed, presumably in Epeiros, and moved toward Athens. Mithridates himself had his headquarters at Pergamon and left the defense of Greece to Archelaos and his subordinates.[94] Sulla, as he progressed south through Greece, received support from many of the areas that he passed through or near: the Aitolians and Thessalians sent troops, money, and provisions. Cities and districts regularly came over to his side, especially in central Greece, including the

Thebans, but only when they saw the Roman army approaching. Sulla placed garrisons in many of the cities on his route.

Eventually he reached the borders of Attika. Part of his army was detached to besiege Athens, and Sulla himself went to the Peiraieus to confront Archelaos.[95] The Peiraieus was easily defended—the walls built by Perikles were still standing—and Sulla laid siege to the city, building engines from wood obtained from the groves of Plato's Academy. He also demolished the parallel Long Walls that created a corridor between the Peiraieus and Athens, so that the two cities would be cut off from one another. There was heavy fighting around the Peiraieus, but Sulla had no fleet, and thus the Pontic forces were able to keep themselves supplied. He sent his legate, Lucullus, in a *keletion*—an especially fast ship[96]—to attempt to obtain naval support from various seafaring powers, such as the Rhodians, and later the Ptolemies and Phoenicians, but Mithridates's control of the seas made this essentially futile.

Fighting around the Peiraieus lasted for months, and in time Sulla abandoned the siege, in part, as Plutarch reported, because he was obsessed with taking Athens, which was still under the control of Aristion. At the end of 87 BC, Sulla established his headquarters at Eleusis, just to the west, and kept up the pressure on the city, with the result that the Athenians endured severe famine. Eventually Athens fell, on the kalends (first) of March 86 BC.[97] Aristion took refuge on the Acropolis but finally gave himself up, and Sulla, although issuing a general pardon, executed him. Sulla then also took the Peiraieus, which Archelaos had abandoned. There had been much destruction in both cities, including Plato's Academy, the Odeion of Perikles, the Tholos, the South Stoa, parts of the Hephaisteion, and the Arsenal of the Peiraieus. In fact, the Sullan destruction level remains a major archaeological datum throughout Athens.[98]

Shortly thereafter two additional Pontic commanders arrived, Dromichaetes and Taxilles, and their troops. The total Pontic force was now reported to be between 60,000 and 120,000 men—a number that is probably exaggerated—and another battle was fought at Chaironeia.[99] Sulla's forces had been augmented by another legion, commanded by Lucius Hortensius. Yet the Romans could have had no more than forty thousand men, and thus were greatly outnumbered by the army of Archelaos. But the victory was total for the Romans, largely due to Archelaos's tactical blunders, including positioning his troops in a rugged location that did not allow for easy movement and failing to use his chariots effectively. Thus he lost all but ten thousand of his troops. Sulla erected a trophy commemorating his victory, whose remains were discovered in 1990 on the promontory known today as Isome, now identified as ancient Thourion, about a mile west of the modern town of Chaironeia. It consisted of an unfluted marble column on a commemorative base. Identification is certain, since the inscription mentions Homoloichos and Anaxidamos, whom Pausanias and Plutarch noted as prominent in the battle.[100]

When Mithridates, at Pergamon, heard of the defeat, astonishingly he was able to raise a new army promptly and send it to Greece under the command of Dorylaos. He joined with Archelaos and engaged Sulla at Orchomenos, a few miles east of Chaironeia.[101] Although the Romans fought badly at first—fear of the Pontic cavalry was the major issue—Sulla's encouragement and his personal heroism rallied the troops. This too was a disaster for the Pontic forces. Archelaos escaped to Chalkis on the island of Euboia, where he was safe for the time being, since Sulla had still heard nothing from Lucullus about a fleet and was unable to cross over to the island. Archelaos took his ships and harried the Peloponnesos, going as far as Zakynthos off its west coast, but was driven away by a Roman detachment that happened to be stationed on the island. By this time he was more pirate than soldier, as Appian put it, and, accomplishing nothing, he returned to Euboia.[102] The engagement at Orchomenos effectively ended the fighting on the Greek peninsula.

THE REACTION IN ASIA

As expected, Mithridates reacted badly to what had happened in Greece. There may have already been a growing opposition to his rule in Asia Minor. Needless to say, precise chronological details are difficult to determine, but there were reports of widespread discontent, which may have developed at the time of the Greek disaster. In fact, a number of the cities in western Asia Minor were ambivalent about which side to support, especially Ephesos, Mytilene, Pergamon, Kyzikos, and, above all, Herakleia Pontika.[103] Much of this was the inevitable failure to realize the impossible: whether Rome or Mithridates represented the future.

The king established absolute rulers (tyrannoi) at Tralleis, Ephesos, and elsewhere.[104] This suggests that due to local instability and a lack of support, he was increasingly bypassing the traditional governments of these cities and placing his own people in power, as with Aristion in Athens. The king began to act more erratically, seeing—perhaps quite justly—growing opposition, to which he retaliated violently. He even singled out suspects who he thought might be disloyal in the future. There was a contingent of Galatian aristocrats residing with him at Pergamon, and when one of them plotted assassination, he killed practically all of them. He then turned to Galatia proper and eliminated most of the tetrarchs and their families, fearing that they were about to support Sulla, and put his own satrap, Eumachos, in power. But some of the surviving tetrarchs promptly evicted him.[105]

At Chios, a local ship collided with the king's royal vessel, which became the stated reason for him to confiscate the property of the locals who were said to be on the side of Sulla. One of his commanders, Zenobios, was on his way to Greece but detoured to take possession of the city of Chios. He asked the inhabitants to give up their arms and their children (as hostages), and then also demanded an indemnity of two thousand talents. When this was paid, Zenobios nevertheless arrested the citizens of Chios and put them on ships, sending them toward Colchis for resettlement as, oddly, slaves of Pontic slaves.[106] Whether they made it to Colchis is not certain; some, at least, were eventually rescued by forces from Herakleia Pontika and restored to Chios, perhaps after the war had ended. Zenobios had sailed to Ephesos, and when the Ephesians invited him into the city, suggesting that he enter unarmed, they killed him. Unrest spread to other cities, and Mithridates retaliated against those who had revolted, but he attempted to strengthen his power base in those that remained loyal by canceling debts, extending the rights of citizenship, and freeing slaves.[107] Yet plots were developing against the king: the murder of the Galatians at Pergamon was because a certain Poredorix, one of the tetrarchs, noted for his bodily strength, had intended to throw the king from the gymnasium (where he was hearing cases) into a ravine. He was foiled when, on the appointed day, the king never came to the gymnasium and the plot became known. Four associates of the king from Smyrna and Lesbos also planned to assassinate him, but this was betrayed by one of the conspirators. Eighty citizens of Pergamon also conspired against him, yet this too was revealed. In panic, the king sent informers throughout western Asia Minor, and as a result 1,600 suspects were killed. He also encouraged piracy along the Aegean coast, not only for naval support but as a revenue-collecting measure.[108] Yet despite all these efforts, Mithridates knew that he was beaten.

THE END OF THE WAR

The Romans now realized that it was necessary to carry the war to Asia Minor. Marius was elected consul for 86 BC and was to lead the expedition, but he died on 13 January, and Lucius Valerius Flaccus was elected in his place. He was not popular with his troops and was killed at Nikomedeia in Bithynia in a mutiny perpetrated by his legate, Gaius Flavius Fimbria, who took over the command.[109] But Fimbria had his own agenda—there had been much plundering as the army crossed Macedonia and Thrace, which he hoped would continue in Asia Minor—and this, in part, led to a falling out with Sulla regarding who held the supreme command against Mithridates. It was believed that Fimbria was causing as much damage to Roman interests as the king.

Meanwhile, Sulla had been negotiating peace terms with Archelaos, who had received instructions to that effect from the king. At the end of 86 BC the two met near Delion on the eastern Boiotian coast. Sulla, who had no ships or money, was in a surprisingly weak position. Archelaos began by mentioning the hereditary friendship that had existed between Rome and the Pontic dynasty, referring to Mithridates V (the father of Mithridates VI).[110] He then offered to finance an invasion of Italy on the part of Sulla, since there was dissent in Rome about how the war should be fought and who was truly in charge. The mere fact of this statement shows how well informed the Pontic command was about events in the city. In return, Sulla suggested that Archelaos depose Mithridates, take over the Pontic empire, and become an allied king of the Romans. With these extreme suggestions out of the way, it was agreed that Mithridates was to give up the province of Asia as well as Paphlagonia, and that Nikomedes IV of Bithynia and Ariobarzanes of Cappadocia be restored. He was also to pay the Romans two thousand talents and give them seventy armed ships (the numbers vary in the sources). Roman prisoners and exiles from the Asian cities would be returned. The king would retain the rest of his kingdom and most of his naval forces and be recognized by the Romans as an allied monarch. Archelaos withdrew his garrisons from Greece and referred the terms to Mithridates.[111]

Although the king did very well by this agreement, he would not yield Paphlagonia or any ships. There was also the matter of Fimbria, who was operating independently from Sulla. He forced Mithridates out of his headquarters at Pergamon to the coast at Pitane, where the king hoped to escape by sea.[112] Lucullus, who had finally acquired some ships and was nearby, was asked to blockade the harbor, but since he was Sulla's legate, he would not take orders from Fimbria, and the king moved to the island of Lesbos, establishing himself at Mytilene. Lucullus let him go and headed north, perhaps intending to enter the Black Sea and attack Pontos directly by sea. At Tenedos he encountered a Pontic fleet under Neoptolemos, which was lying in wait for him, but in the engagement that followed Lucullus was victorious. This may have led Mithridates to realize that his naval superiority was not as great as he thought.[113] Fimbria continued operating in the Troad, and although he had been successful against Mithridates, he also engaged in extensive plunder. He would be most remembered for ravaging Ilion, the presumed side of ancient Troy, reducing it to poverty.[114]

Despite suggestions that if Mithridates surrendered to Fimbria, he would receive better terms than from Sulla, the king decided otherwise. It was probably in late summer or early autumn of 85 BC that he met Sulla at Dardanos on the Asian side of the entrance to the Hellespont.[115] Mithridates began by blaming the Romans and the gods for the war, but Sulla, while complimenting the king's oratorical skills, cut him short and asked directly whether he would agree to the terms that he and Archelaos had outlined. The king had previously told Sulla through ambassadors that he would not give up Paphlagonia or any ships, but he withdrew these conditions and agreed to everything. The two men embraced, and Ariobarzanes of Cappadocia and Nikomedes IV of Bithynia, who were by now in Sulla's entourage, were also welcomed by the king. He gave Sulla the seventy ships and promptly left for Pontos.

Sulla then went to Fimbria and demanded his army, pointing out that it had been obtained illegally. After harsh words, and an attempt to have Sulla assassinated, Fimbria retreated to Pergamon. He attempted to kill himself in the Asklepieion, but a slave had to complete the task.[116] Sulla, having effectively restored the Roman government to Asia, gave freedom to a number of cities but punished the Ephesians for their disobedience. He then returned to Italy, although he stopped for a while at the spa of Aidepsos at the north end of Euboia, where there were hot and cold springs. It was the autumn of 85 BC, and the war was over.

Mithridates had begun the war by exploiting legitimate grievances against Roman rule in Asia Minor but in time had gone far beyond this issue, through attacking Greece, killing many innocent civilians, and letting it be known that an assault on Italy might follow. He failed to recognize that Rome was not as weak or preoccupied as he believed, and when the Romans finally opposed him in the field, his large armies were repeatedly defeated by much smaller Roman ones. The Roman armies were far more experienced and cohesive than the complex military coalition that Mithridates had put together, which relied heavily on peoples from the northern limits of his kingdom. After the failure of the Greek invasion, matters deteriorated quickly, and as the king became more oppressive, plots against him and his rule were more common. His only hope at the end was his navy, but even that suffered defeat at the hands of the Romans, who were able to levy ships from the most experienced seafaring states in the eastern Mediterranean, such as the Ptolemies and the Rhodians.[117] That only the Romans were able to do this is another indication of the ultimate shallowness of Mithridates's support, especially outside of western Asia. The peace terms were quite gentle—Sulla's army grumbled at this[118]—and Mithridates's territories around the Black Sea (Colchis, the Bosporos, and the Chersonesos) were not even discussed. He accepted almost without question what the Romans offered and went home. Yet one should not underestimate the significance of the war, which came close to excluding the Romans from Asia Minor.[119]

Chapter 10

The Aftermath of the First War

PROBLEMS

One of the results of the war was an economic crisis in Rome.[1] As Cicero wrote in the context of Pompey's command of nearly twenty years later, many in Asia had lost large fortunes, and, moreover, payments on loans were not being made.[2] This was aggravated because the Mithridatic War had followed immediately after the Marsic War. Legislation allowing relief was passed, probably in February 86 BC, cutting debt by three-quarters.[3] This may have resulted in deflation, and counterfeited coins became common. There were also problems in the province of Asia and the surrounding areas. Not only was there the cost of the war, in manpower and resources, but there was also the large indemnity required by Sulla.[4] Even in defeat, Mithridates had affected the Roman economy.

Despite this, in a political sense the first war effectively restored the situation to what it had been in 89 BC, before the battle on the Amnias River. But there was now instability in Mithridates's Black Sea territories.[5] The people of Colchis asked that one of Mithridates's sons, also named Mithridates, be made their king. In part this may have been the feeling—as with the Cappadocians—that their status deserved kingship, but at the same time it could be seen as a movement toward independence, or at least some sort of objection to the royal governors who had been in place for a number of years.

The younger Mithridates had fought in the war, but not particularly well: he had been defeated by Fimbria in an engagement on the Rhyndakos River (the modern Koca Dere), which empties into the Propontis.[6] Fimbria had attacked while Mithridates's troops were sleeping, and the Pontic forces had lost six thousand men. Given this, it may be that Mithridates wanted to get as far from Pontos as possible, and there is some evidence that he was in

162

collusion with the Colchians about the appointment as king. His father was probably already dubious about his son's abilities and intentions and would have seen the move to Colchis as a prelude to seizing the kingship of Pontos. Although he was allowed to take up his position in Colchis, before long the king arrested him and returned him to Pontos—as royalty he was allowed to travel in golden chains—and soon executed him. This shows that whatever the younger Mithridates did in Colchis, it was seen as treasonous. Nothing more is heard about a Colchian desire for kingship, and presumably the system of royal governors was reinstated.[7] Colchis remained a stable part of the Pontic empire thereafter. It is not certain whether the Colchian episode was an attempt at revolt or merely a plot by the younger Mithridates (it may have been both), but the situation was indicative of the uncertain conditions in the Pontic world after the first war.

There were also issues in Bosporos, which were somewhat more serious than those in Colchis. Appian's brief report does not indicate whether it was the Greek cities or the indigenous peoples of the hinterland who were rebelling. The situation was serious enough that the king put together extensive land and sea forces,[8] an activity that caused concern among the Romans, for it was generally believed that he had done nothing since the war except to prepare for another one, and the Bosporanian mobilization was proof of this.[9] Moreover, the king was delaying any action on his promise to restore Cappadocia to Ariobarzanes I. By the beginning of 83 BC, it appeared that war would break forth again.

THE DEFECTION OF ARCHELAOS

Archelaos, Mithridates's commander in Greece, was Cappadocian in origin and is first known in 92 BC when he engaged Sulla as Mithridates's agent in that territory. At the end of the Greek campaign he met with Sulla to establish the peace terms. But Mithridates was becoming suspicious of his loyalties, feeling that he had made a private agreement with the proconsul to the king's disadvantage. The ease with which the vastly outnumbered Romans had defeated the Pontic forces at Chaironeia suggested that there had been some kind of treachery. Sulla and Archelaos—who had known each other for several years—were said to be too friendly with one another: Sulla's proposal that Archelaos depose Mithridates, although probably more bargaining point than serious, further heightened the king's worries.[10] After the conference at Delion, Archelaos became exceedingly sick at Larisa in Thessaly, and Sulla, who was heading toward the Hellespont, stopped his march and made certain that he had proper medical care. It was also said that the killing of Aristion, the only Athenian executed among the leaders who had resisted Sulla, was done on the orders of Archelaos and, moreover, that Sulla had given him land on Euboia. These stories—true or not—were such that Sulla felt the need to defend his own actions in his *Memoirs*.[11] It was easy to make the charge that there had been collusion between the two commanders.

Mithridates's suspicions of Archelaos reached the danger point, and the king began to blame him for the loss in the war. Archelaos soon realized that remaining at the Pontic court would be fatal, and thus he sought refuge with Lucius Licinius Murena, who had been one of Sulla's legates in the Greek campaign (and thus was already known to Archelaos). Murena had been given Fimbria's legions and was left in Asia to reestablish Roman control. Archelaos's defection probably occurred late in 84 BC, and he became an important advisor to the Romans in the engagements that followed. He is last known on the staff of Lucullus at the beginning of the third war, around 73 BC. Nothing more is reported about him, and he probably died of natural causes early in the war.[12]

Yet Archelaos's legacy was greater than his own career, since he was the founder of a dynasty that endured at least into the second century AD and which, as was common in Hellenistic times, became royalty. His son, also named Archelaos, was appointed by Pompey the Great to be priest-king at the major Pontic sanctuary of Komana, an office with royal rank which controlled a cult center with a population of thousands. But in 56 BC he became the husband of Berenike IV of Egypt, the sister of Cleopatra VII, who had a brief reign while her father, Ptolemy XII, was in exile. When he was restored, Archelaos and Berenike were promptly killed. The son of this second Archelaos, the third of that name, inherited the Komana priesthood, and his son, the fourth Archelaos, was made king of Cappadocia by the triumvir Marcus Antonius in 41 BC and, ironically, ruled Pontos for a number of years in the Augustan period. His daughter, Glaphyra, married successively two sons of Herod the Great and also King Juba of Mauretania, and her descendants, including two kings of Armenia and a Roman consul, are known for several generations thereafter. The descendants of Archelaos, the commander of Mithridates, demonstrate well how the aristocrats of the Late Hellenistic period would produce the eastern royalty of the Roman period, as well as the future leadership of Rome itself.[13]

THE SECOND MITHRIDATIC WAR

Licinius Murena was ambitious, and he had Archelaos in his entourage, as well as, presumably, other Pontic refugees. He was anxious to start a war that might yield him a triumph, the highest honor in Rome for a returning commander.[14] To this effect he interpreted Mithridates's mobilization in the Bosporanian matter as aggression against Rome and responded by garrisoning Cappadocia and initiating in 83 BC the series of engagements that ancient writers called the second war between the Romans and Mithridates. Murena marched through Cappadocia and attacked the temple town of Komana, killing some Pontic cavalry and appropriating the treasures. Ambassadors from the king were sent to protest, but oddly they spoke against him, giving Murena's actions more credibility. Nevertheless they cited the treaty at Dardanos that had ended the first war, but Murena—whether through ignorance or deceit—denied that it existed, since Sulla had never written it down. Murena then returned to Cappadocia, where he spent the winter of 83–82 BC.

Mithridates then complained to Rome but had not heard any reply when, in the spring of 82 BC, Murena appeared in Pontos again, engaging in extensive plunder. Appian reported that he overran four hundred villages,[15] but this seems impossible—especially at the beginning of the campaigning season—and if not simply an exaggeration it may refer to a toponym, a general term for a region of farmsteads in one of the fertile agricultural plains of Pontos, analogous to the district called the Chiliokomai (the Thousand Villages) northwest of Amaseia, a locality where there could not be a thousand villages.[16] The "four hundred villages" that Murena plundered would be a similar toponym, probably in the vicinity of Zela, on the southern route of access into Pontos and the site of many battles.[17]

As Murena approached, the king did not respond but waited for word from Rome. This eventually came in the person of a certain Calidius, probably Gaius Calidius, who would be a praetor in 79 BC.[18] He publicly told Murena that it was the will of the Senate that he desist in his activities, but he also had a private interview with him, and since Murena promptly invaded again, Mithridates believed that there was a secret plan to continue the war. There were also reports that Murena was preparing to attack Sinope, the Pontic capital, and an appeal by both sides to Herakleia Pontika for negotiation went nowhere.[19]

Eventually Mithridates moved into action, first sending out Gordios, and then taking the field himself with a large army. The two sides engaged at a river crossing, perhaps on the Halys, and the Pontic forces gained a victory described as "brilliant and striking."[20] Many were said now to come to the support of the king, and the garrisons that Murena had established in Cappadocia were eliminated. Mithridates made a large sacrifice to Zeus Stratios, the Zeus of the Armies. It was said that the sacrificial flames were visible a thousand stadia (about 125 miles) out to sea, which suggests a location on the coast, perhaps at Sinope, but there was also a major sanctuary to the god in the heights east of Amaseia, the old Pontic capital.[21] The event was a mixture of Greek and Persian ritual—particularly Persian was the great banquet for those present—showing the dual nature of the heritage of the Pontic kingdom. Moreover, it was perhaps yet another imitation of Alexander the Great, reflecting the great banquet he gave at Opis in Mesopotamia in June 324 BC.[22]

When word of the war reached Sulla in Rome—either through the original embassy sent by the king or later reports—he was not pleased. He was now dictator, with extraordinary powers, and he used them to bring an end to the conflict. He sent a trusted aide, Aulus Gabinius, who had been with him at Chaironeia, to order Murena to stand down.[23] Gabinius arrived in Asia early in 81 BC and delivered his instructions; he also told Mithridates to reconcile with Ariobarzanes on the matter of Cappadocia, which had been festering ever since the end of the first war. To implement this, a marriage alliance was concluded between the son of Ariobarzanes I (Ariobarzanes II) and Mithridates's four-year-old daughter, perhaps the Athenais who, twenty years later, would be involved in a plot to interfere with the Cappadocian succession.[24] The arrangement would give Mithridates continued access to Cappadocia, and he used it to retain control over some parts of the territory.

Murena served out his term as governor and returned to Rome. He was given the triumph that he sought, which was hardly deserved but indicative of the ambivalent attitudes in the city about the entire situation in Pontos, which itself was affected by Rome's own political problems.[25] The second war was over, and Mithridates had not only strengthened his position but redeemed the loss in the first war. He had finally defeated a Roman army and, moreover, had improved his relationship with Cappadocia. One loose end remained: the Dardanos treaty was still not in writing, and in 80 BC the king sent envoys to Rome to attend to the matter.[26] But the Senate never responded because of the internal issues at Rome, and the treaty would never be written down.

THE LAST YEARS OF SULLA

Mithridates was probably well aware that during these years Rome was in an almost permanent state of chaos.[27] He would have had agents in the city, and he had been in contact with the Italian rebels during the Marsic War. For many years Sulla and Marius had quarreled—often with violent and deadly results— over who was truly responsible for ending the war with Jugurtha in 103 BC. The sudden death of Marius at the beginning of 86 BC, while Sulla was bringing the war in Greece to an end, eliminated their personal rivalry, but civil strife in the city of Rome continued, largely under the leadership of Lucius Cornelius Cinna, who was an opponent of Sulla and held the consulship for four successive years beginning in 87 BC.

Sulla was declared a public enemy by Cinna, who made preparations to take an army to Greece in order to prevent Sulla from returning to Italy but was killed by his troops at Ancona early in 84 BC.[28] Yet Sulla had many enemies, and although the Senate had offered him an amnesty, the attempted attack by Cinna and agitation by the surviving consul for 84 BC, Gnaeus Papirius Carbo, put Sulla in an untenable position. In the spring of 83 BC he and his troops landed at Brundisium and headed toward Rome. While on the road he began to gather numerous supporters, including many young aspiring political leaders who would become the dominant personalities in Rome during the last years of the Republic. Pompey the Great, who had fought in the Marsic War, was living without political office on his estates in Picenum, on the Adriatic coast northeast of Rome. He raised a private army from his retainers (an unfortunate harbinger of the future) and hastened to Sulla's side.[29] Marcus Licinius Crassus, who had escaped from Cinna and sought refuge in Spain, was also able to raise a private army and join Sulla.[30] Pompey and Crassus would become consuls in 70 BC, and then two of the members of the unofficial triumvirate of 59 BC that was formed to determine the future destiny of Rome. Crassus would die in 53 BC during an ill-advised invasion of Parthia, but Pompey would become the most powerful man in Rome until his death in Egypt in 48 BC.

Two other young aspirants, not directly associated with Sulla but highly influential in later years, also appear in the historical record at about this time. Gaius Julius Caesar was a nephew of Marius and thus unlikely to be well-disposed to Sulla, but later he would be the third member of the triumvirate of 59 BC and would continue his well-known career. He is first noted on the staff of Marcus

Municius Thermus, the governor of Asia, and was sent in 81 BC to Nikomedes IV of Bithynia as his naval advisor.[31] And Marcus Tullius Cicero first appears as quaestor to the governor of western Sicily in 75 BC.[32] These men, all of whom emerged in the years around 80 BC, would determine the future of Rome and control the final years of the Republic.

Sulla arrived at Rome late in 83 BC, after a long progress north that saw many battles, especially as he neared the city. Although there was still opposition in the provinces, especially from Quintus Sertorius in Nearer Hispania, Sulla was now in control of Italy. He no longer had any legal power—under Roman law, his proconsular command in the Mithridatic campaign ended when he returned to the city of Rome—but he was named dictator for 82 BC and redesignated for 81, 80, and 79 BC.[33] The dictatorship was an extraordinary magistracy, an office given to someone to meet an immediate danger to the Republic. It had been a regular feature of the early and perilous years of the Roman state but had not been invoked for over a century until Sulla reestablished the practice. Later it would be famously used by Julius Caesar.

Sulla initiated a vicious purge of his opposition and confiscation of their property. He then used his dictatorships for a series of reforms, which are generally not relevant to the issues concerning Asia Minor or Mithridates, although the Sullan legislation did include some regulation of provincial magistrates, whose ability to act without proper authorization had precipitated both Mithridatic wars. Also under his powers as dictator, he was able to bring the second war to an end, sending out Gabinius to order Murena to cease his aggression. In the same year, 81 BC, Sulla celebrated his triumph over Mithridates, one of the most extravagant that Rome had ever seen.[34]

In 79 BC, after over three full years as dictator and many reforms, and after the election of the consuls for 78 BC, Sulla resigned his office, one of the few cases ever of someone voluntarily giving up absolute power. As Appian put it, "He had become tired of the city and enamored of country life." He retired to his estate at Cumae in Campania and died the following year. Despite attempts to block it, he was given a public funeral unexcelled in its splendor.[35]

Sulla was dead, but Mithridates VI still remained. It was during Sulla's dictatorship that the king had attempted to get the terms of the Dardanos treaty in writing, without success.[36] Moreover, it was probably during 80 BC that Ariobarzanes I of Cappadocia sent his own embassy to Rome to complain that Mithridates still occupied his territory, whereupon Sulla told Mithridates to withdraw from it. In addition, one of the consuls of 79 BC, Publius Servilius

Vatia, would be sent the following year to Cilicia, placing a consular army on the borders of Cappadocia, a possible threat to Mithridates.[37] There were also problems in the coastal regions of the northeastern Black Sea. The Bosporanians had been subdued, with Mithridates's son Machares placed as "king" (essentially royal governor) over them, probably in late 81 or early 80 BC. Yet those living between Bosporos and Colchis, the Achaians, a primitive warlike group, resisted a Pontic invasion, and due to both military action and the weather Mithridates lost two-thirds of his army.[38] These issues may have made the king believe that with Sulla in absolute power in Rome, a gesture of conciliation was in order, and he gave up the parts of Cappadocia that he still controlled, without objection. He then sent another embassy to Rome to inquire again about the matter of the Dardanos treaty which had ended the first war. But when the envoys arrived, Sulla had just died, and the Senate was so preoccupied it did not even receive them.

The king, who had tried to be agreeable, would have seen the treatment of his ambassadors as nothing other than an insult. Rather than retake Cappadocia himself, he once again persuaded his son-in-law Tigranes II of Armenia to invade the territory, as he had done in 92 BC. This would also fit into the grandiose plans that Tigranes himself was developing, for he was establishing a new capital, Tigranokerta, in the southern part of his kingdom at the place that he had become king. It was planned to be a great multicultural city—three hundred thousand Cappadocians were allegedly removed to be part of its population—but it was never completed, and what existed was destroyed by Lucullus in 69 BC as part of the Third Mithridatic War.[39]

MITHRIDATES AND SERTORIUS

But the Romans were not fooled regarding Cappadocia and well knew what the king was up to. Not long after Sulla's death, there was already talk about another war. And it was about this time that Mithridates reached all the way to the opposite end of the Mediterranean for a new alliance. Quintus Sertorius had served under Marius against the Cimbrians, and then in the Marsic War.[40] He was elected praetor for 83 BC, but as a protégé of Marius he opposed Sulla. Sertorius felt that it was in his best interest to go to his assigned province, Nearer Hispania, as soon as possible, and he established himself there late in the year. But Sulla, when he became dictator, sent a force to take control of the Iberian Peninsula. Sertorius then abandoned his province and crossed over to Mauretania, the vast territory of northwest Africa, establishing himself at Tingis (modern Tangier) and becoming effective ruler of the region.[41] Eventually, probably early in 80 BC, he answered a call from the Lusitanians (the population on the Atlantic coast of the Iberian Peninsula) to be their commander against Rome. Sertorius devoted great effort to organizing the locals and teaching them Roman and Greek ways, and even created his own Senate, becoming a highly popular leader; like Mithridates, he became a focal point of anti-Roman concerns.[42] But the situation quickly degenerated into warfare. Sulla and his successors sent out a number of commanders against him, and Sertorius's fortunes began to fade when Pompey arrived in the peninsula as proconsul in 76 BC.[43] At first he was not successful against Sertorius, but he eventually gained the upper hand. After a series of defeats, Sertorius was assassinated by members of his own staff at the end of 73 BC.

Around 76 or 75 BC Mithridates and Sertorius made contact. Two Romans, Lucius Magius and Lucius Fannius, resident in Miletos, allegedly made a proposal to the king that he ally with Sertorius. Magius and Fannius, generally mentioned in tandem, seem to have had unusual careers. They had served in the army of Fimbria and, after his death in the autumn of 85 BC, ended up at the court of Mithridates.[44] In 79 BC the two purchased a ship in Miletos from Gaius Verres, who at the time was legate to the governor of Cilicia but would become infamous later for his mismanagement of Sicily. Verres had commandeered the ship for a journey from Miletos to Myndos, some thirty miles away in Karia, and then sold it to Magius and Fannius.[45] The account of the activities of Magius and Fannius is enigmatic, but it seems that sometime after their arrival at Mithridates's court they used the ship to make regular voyages between Sinope and Dianium, the latter an ancient sanctuary to Artemis (and then Diana) at a prominent location on the southeastern Iberian coast. In some way they connected with Sertorius and became his adherents, and it was allegedly in this context that they persuaded Mithridates to make contact. Yet some of their activities seem rather close to piracy—an institution that was endemic in the Mediterranean at that time— especially since the ship was a *myoparon*, a type favored by pirates. This may be one of the reasons that the Senate eventually declared them public enemies.[46]

In whatever way Mithridates conceived of the idea to reach out to Sertorius, he was fully aware of its advantages: he could play Pyrrhos to Sertorius's Hannibal, and Italy would be simultaneously attacked by the greatest military commander and the greatest king of the era. The alliance would also be a way of linking the External Ocean at the Atlantic to Pontos.[47] Mithridates sent ambassadors to Sertorius, offering him money and ships in return for the province of Asia. Sertorius convened his Senate and received the envoys but well knew that the disposition of Asia was not in his power. The king was astonished at this and may have misunderstood the limits of Sertorius's legal position in Rome.[48] Yet a treaty was signed between the two leaders, and Sertorius sent a certain Marcus Marius (not the consul and opponent of Sulla) with soldiers to Pontos, and in return Sertorius was to receive three thousand talents and forty ships. He allegedly offered to give Mithridates Bithynia, Cappadocia, and Galatia; none of these was Roman territory, and how he was going to do this is not specified, but the offer is indicative of Sertorius's own grandiose plans to be ruler of all of the Roman world. In fact, Mithridates believed that in time Sertorius would take up residence on the Palatine in Rome, a suggestion of kingship. Sertorius's ulterior motive was revealed when Marcus Marius captured some cities in Asia (where there were resurgent problems with tax collectors and occupying troops) and did so in the name of Sertorius, not Mithridates.

The treaty between the two was finalized in the summer of 74 BC, before the Third Mithridatic War started the following spring. But by the end of 73 BC Sertorius was dead, and nothing further came of the arrangements. Marius continued to serve in the Pontic army, presumably with his own forces, until in 72 BC he was defeated and executed by Lucullus in an engagement off the island of Lemnos. Magius and Fannius were declared public enemies by the Senate after Sertorius's death but were reconciled and served in the army of Lucullus.[49]

At roughly the same time, the Romans were establishing a presence in the interior of Thrace and had gone as far as the Danube, and perhaps across it. The proconsul of Macedonia, Lucius Scribonius Curio, reached the river probably in 75 BC.[50] The Romans had legitimate interests in the area, since the Dardanians, who lived in the region south of Belgrade, were causing difficulty. But, knowing about Mithridates's alliance with Sertorius and the suggestion of an attack on Italy via the Danube, it may be that the Romans wanted to assert their presence along a possible line of Pontic advance.[51] Needless to say, any Roman efforts to this end were unnecessary, and Curio returned to Rome in 72 BC and celebrated a triumph.

PREPARATIONS FOR WAR

It had been realized for some time in Rome that a further war with Mithridates was inevitable. As early as 77 BC, Lucius Marcius Philippus, a senior senator, told the Senate that Mithridates was looking for an opportunity to start another war. In the summer of 75 BC, the consul Lucius Aurelius Cotta noted that Roman armies were being maintained in Asia and Cilicia as a check on the ambitions of the king.[52] Mithridates's alliance with Sertorius was at about the same time as Cotta's report, and it could not have been comforting to the Romans. In 74 BC the balance of power in western Asia changed significantly with the death of Nikomedes IV of Bithynia. He seems to have had no legitimate heir, although an alleged son did come forward, perhaps even promoted by Mithridates, but he was quickly discredited.[53] Nikomedes willed his kingdom to Rome, and Bithynia was annexed. The governor of Asia, Marcus Juncus, was charged with organizing the new province.[54] This certainly would have caused Mithridates great concern.

During these years the king was building up his support throughout the eastern Mediterranean, as well as creating a sophisticated military force. His defeats had in part been due to the inferiority of his troops, who were large in number but recruited from barbarians and no match for the disciplined Roman army. The king's previous soldiers had been more ostentatious than capable, wearing armor inlaid with gold and precious stones. To reform his forces he dismissed many of the barbarian contingents and trained the remainder in Roman fashion; by now he had several Romans in his entourage. His ships were stripped of their luxuries, and the elaborate cabins were converted into storerooms for weaponry. Swords and shields were forged in the Roman manner. All in all, it was said that he mobilized 120,000 (or 140,000) infantry, 16,000 cavalry, and 400 ships.[55]

He also reached out to others for support. His arrangement with Sertorius was the most prominent of these efforts. In addition, he planned a number of marriage alliances, although they may never have been implemented. Yet the king seems to have had a large supply of daughters for this purpose. Some were to be sent to various Skythian chieftains; Mithridatis was betrothed to Ptolemy XII of Egypt and Nyssa to his brother Ptolemy, king of Cyprus. The two kings may have spent time at the Pontic court in their youth.[56]

Mithridates also went outside of the established royal or aristocratic families. The Cretans had provided forces to his father, and this may have continued.[57] The various piratical groups centered on Cilicia may also have given support, and he seems to have encouraged piracy at the end of the first war, since he lacked the sea power to hold the Aegean coast. The pirates remained a resource into the later wars.[58] Pirates could be dangerous, since they had their own agenda, but they could also be useful: a pirate ship rescued the king in 73 BC, when his own ship foundered in a storm somewhere between Kyzikos and Sinope.[59]

But his advisors told him, quite rightly, that any contact with the pirates was questionable—the king could be held for ransom—and there is no evidence of any formalized agreement between him and the piratical groups.[60]

How long Mithridates was preparing for war is uncertain, but clearly the death of Nikomedes and the Roman annexation of Bithynia in 74 BC intensified his actions. Not only did the new province of Bithynia bring Roman territory close to the boundaries of Pontos, but it meant that the Romans now had effective control of the route from the Black Sea to the Aegean, through the Thracian Bosporos, Propontis, and Hellespont. Moreover, much of the local instability that had been a factor in the first war had returned to Asia: the excesses of the tax collectors and moneylenders were such that children were being sold into slavery to pay debts.[61] This gave the king a moral cause for war.

His preparations complete, Mithridates made an address to his soldiers in the spring of 73 BC.[62] Part of it was familiar material about his royal lineage and his own accomplishments. He could no longer say that his army had never been defeated by the Romans, so he added that this had never happened while he was present. Once again, Roman greed was stressed, greed which had resulted in the enslavement of Italy, an allusion to the fact that the Marsic War had ended in the Romans' favor. He also noted that the failure to record the Dardanos treaty was because they were waiting for an opportunity to violate it. As before, he emphasized that the Romans were otherwise occupied (this time with Sertorius), and there was continuing civil disorder in Italy and in the city. Piracy was rampant on the seas, which the Romans had been unable to control. The king ended his speech by pointing out that even Romans had come to his side, citing by name Magius, Fannius, and Marius. Then he invaded Bithynia, initiating the third war with Rome.

Chapter 11

Lucullus and Mithridates VI

EVENTS AT ROME

In his speech to his troops in 73 BC, just before his invasion of Bithynia, Mithridates emphasized the disorder that was a continuing feature of Roman politics and society, causing "civil dissent throughout Italy." Regardless of the king's perspective and agenda, and how much this speech is a construct, it is certainly an accurate assessment of the situation.[1] After the funeral of Sulla in early 78 BC, the two consuls, Quintus Lutatius Catulus and Marcus Aemilius Lepidus, began to quarrel bitterly over the future direction of the Roman state. Conflict broke out—the details of which are not particularly germane to the situation with Mithridates, other than providing him support for his view of a Rome in chaos—and only ended when Lepidus died of natural causes on Sardinia the following year. His supporters fled to Sertorius.[2] Catulus continued his career for another twenty years, and in 66 BC would oppose giving the command against Mithridates to his former protégé, Pompey.[3] With the retreat and convenient death of Lepidus, who had seen himself as a new Sulla, Rome had been spared another round of civil war, although a battle had actually been fought at the northern edge of the city. That a dispute between two consuls could so easily yield to physical violence must have pleased Mithridates.

Civil instability was a feature of life in the city of Rome during these years. In June of 75 BC the consuls, Lucius Octavius and Gaius Aurelius Cotta, were attacked by a mob because of food shortages. A few days later Cotta gave a speech to the Roman people. Although the extant text is a construct of several decades later by the historian Sallust, it is an excellent summary of the state of affairs in the mid-70s BC.[4] Cotta allegedly emphasized that the republic faced the greatest of obstacles both at home and in war. Things were not going well in the Iberian Peninsula due to Sertorius and the constant defection of Roman

allies to his side. Because of the threat of Mithridates, it was necessary to main-
tain standing armies in both Cilicia and Asia. Macedonia was unstable, since
the Thracians to its north were pressuring the province, and piracy plagued the
coasts everywhere, so much so that in the following year Marcus Antonius, the
father of the triumvir, was given an extraordinary command valid anywhere in
the Mediterranean where the issue was a problem.[5] Moreover, Cotta continued,
Rome's expenses were outstripping its revenue, which meant a reduction in
available military resources.

The war with Sertorius was a major effort on the part of the Roman military. The adventurer was at the peak of his power when Cotta spoke and would
conclude his treaty with Mithridates the following year. Moreover, in 73 BC, the
Romans were afflicted by a new problem: the revolt of Spartacus.[6] He had been
in the Roman army but for unknown reasons had ended up in the gladiatorial
school of Lentulus Batiatus in Capua. With about eighty companions, he escaped
and hid on the slopes of Mount Vesuvius. Soon their force was joined by many
of the disaffected, and the two Roman armies sent against him were defeated.
Eventually Spartacus was said to have seventy thousand followers. His primary
interest was to return to his Thracian home by retreating to the north, but many
of his supporters were more interested in plundering southern Italy—this may
be part of the continuing civil disorder in Italy that Mithridates mentioned in his
contemporary speech—and in 71 BC Spartacus was trapped in Lucania by the
proconsul Marcus Licinius Crassus and killed in battle.

Whether Mithridates's invasion of Bithynia was after he learned about
Spartacus cannot be determined—the revolt and invasion were almost
contemporary—but it would have pleased the king to know that the Romans
had yet another insurgent on their hands. They were effectively at war on three
fronts (in Iberia, against the pirates, and now in southern Italy), and Mithridates's
agreement with Sertorius further complicated the issues. The king would have
felt that it was time to open up a fourth line of attack, and the contemporary
death of Nikomedes IV of Bithynia and the provincialization of his kingdom
would have given Mithridates both a reason for worry and an opportunity.

LUCULLUS AND POMPEY

The Roman response to Mithridates in the third war was dominated by
two of the powerful personalities whose careers embody the world of the

collapse of the Roman Republic. Lucius Licinius Lucullus (117–57/56 BC) was a protégé of Sulla's, serving under him in the Marsic War and joining him in his march on Rome in 88 BC.[7] He was Sulla's legate in the First Mithridatic War, and after various commands in the eastern Mediterranean reached the consulship in 74 BC, with Marcus Aurelius Cotta as his colleague, the brother of the Cotta who was consul the previous year. The following year Lucullus was assigned Asia and Cilicia as his provinces, positioning him to take command of the third war against Mithridates, which started early in 73 BC. He prosecuted the war for the next seven years, but defeats as well as dissensions among his soldiers meant that beginning in 68 BC the extent of his command was steady reduced, and in 66 BC he was replaced by Pompey.

Gaius Pompey (106–48 BC) had also begun his career during the Marsic War, serving at a young age, and then also joined Sulla in his march on Rome.[8] His prominence rose rapidly, and he took the surname Magnus (the Great) early in his career. He received a triumph in 81 BC for campaigns in Africa and another in 70 BC for defeating Sertorius and the remnants of the followers of Spartacus. In that year he attained the consulship (with Crassus as colleague). Thereafter he succeeded Antonius in the command against the pirates, and in 66 BC was given an extraordinary command to replace Lucullus. He prosecuted the war against Mithridates during its final years.

THE INVASION OF BITHYNIA

Whether or not he knew about Spartacus, in the spring of 73 BC Mithridates invaded Bithynia, while Roman organization of the kingdom as a province was still largely unformed. He began the campaign with another sacrifice to Zeus Stratios and one to Poseidon, driving a chariot led by white horses into the sea. This was probably at Sinope, a demonstration of his new emphasis on naval power.[9] Both the exact years and sequence of events of the war remain disputed, although there is no doubt that it involved the years 73–63 BC.[10] The consuls of 74 BC, Lucullus and the younger Cotta, were sent to Asia near the end of their terms, probably in reaction to the treaty between Mithridates and Sertorius.[11] With this arrangement in hand, the king devoted the rest of 74 BC and the first months of the following year to war preparations. The Romans would have had two strong hints that war was imminent: not only the treaty with Sertorius but also the death of Nikomedes IV, which changed the balance of power in north-western Asia Minor.[12]

The Romans were not as distracted as Mithridates had hoped. Lucullus had originally been assigned Cisalpine Gaul as his consular province, but the procon-sul of Cilicia, Lucius Octavius (the consul of 75 BC), died early in 74 BC. There were many applicants to replace him, but Lucullus exerted great pressure to have Cilicia assigned to himself, knowing full well that this would give him the command against the king.[13] He raised his own army and went to Asia—whether he even made it as far as Cilicia is not certain—where he found Roman forces in disarray, with the effect of the depredations of Fimbria still noticeable. He spent several weeks if not more turning them into an effective army.

Like Lucullus, Cotta had originally been assigned another province—which one is not known—but he persuaded the Senate to send him to Bithynia. The previous governor, Juncus, who had been given the task of organizing the region upon the death of Nikomedes, seems to have been removed from office, perhaps due to local complaints. He was prosecuted in Rome by Julius Caesar, but noth-ing further is known about him, and he may have died about this time.[14] Thus Bithynia was available, and so by early in 73 BC the Romans had two consular officers in the field, whatever Mithridates might do.

The king must have questioned his assessment that the Romans were in general disarray when he learned that two armies were in position to oppose him even before he made any definite action. Lucullus seems to have been mov-ing his forces around western Asia Minor and was reported in Phrygia.[15] Yet Mithridates might have been pleased to know that the two commanders were not on the best of terms—as seemed inevitable in the Roman world of the era—with Cotta believing that a quick victory would give him a triumph and Lucullus, influenced by Mithridates's former commander Archelaos, who was now on his staff, open to suggestions that he attack Pontos directly.

Mithridates, concerned about where the Romans might position their armies, sent his commander Diophantos son of Mithares—one of those who had been commemorated on the Mithridateion on Delos—to protect his southern frontier by garrisoning Cappadocia, with orders to attack Lucullus if he moved toward Pontos.[16] The king had laid his plans well, and the time that it took Lucullus to bring the Roman soldiers into shape was also to his advantage. The king's knowledge of Bithynia—he probably had long had agents at the Bithynian court and in Bithynian cities—meant that he under-stood the local situation better than the Romans. The problems with Juncus, the first governor of Bithynia, demonstrate that the Roman organization of the new province was not going well, another point of advantage for the king. He moved swiftly in the spring of 73 BC and, passing through Paphlagonia and Galatia, arrived in Bithynia in nine days; even if this were just the eastern edge of the territory on the Billaios River, it meant he had marched his massive army—allegedly 150,000 infantry—at a rate of twenty miles or more a day. The king was well received by the inhabitants of the Bithynian cities, because of the usual heavy-handed tactics on the part of Roman moneylenders and tax collectors.[17] Evidently in recent years the western parts of Asia Minor had returned to their normal disaffected state.

At the same time the king sent a fleet out from Sinope, with its objective coastal Bithynia on the Propontis, and perhaps the Aegean, under the command of a certain Aristonikos, as a part of his strategy to keep the war away from Pontos.[18] But when the fleet arrived at Herakleia Pontika, it was not allowed to enter the harbor, although the city did provide supplies. At the time Herakleia was a free city that had survived and even prospered for years by balancing its interests against the surrounding powers and, more recently, the Romans. Presumably their first reaction was to avoid involvement with the developing war. But eventually the ships were allowed to land, and Aristonikos promptly arrested two leading citizens, Silenos and Satyros, and held them hostage until the Herakleians agreed to supply five triremes for the war effort. Although the only detailed account, by Memnon, is confused, it seems that after initial hostility Aristonikos earned the gratitude of the Herakleians by a general slaughter of the tax collectors.[19] Herakleia was now on the Pontic side and the fleet continued and entered the Thracian Bosporos.

Meanwhile, Mithridates's land forces advanced into Bithynia. Cotta, who had established himself at Nikomedeia, the Bithynian capital, retreated in the face of the Pontic army and took up quarters at Chalkedon (modern Kadıköy), at the mouth of the Bosporos on the Asian side, leaving the heartland of Bithynia open to the king. Cotta had relatively few troops, and was described by Appian as "completely weak in warfare" and "inexperienced." Mithridates probably knew about Cotta's lack of a military career and thought that if he could promptly neutralize the proconsul, he would then be free to concern himself with the far more experienced Lucullus.[20]

Cotta sent out his naval commander, Publius Rutilius Nudus, with a land force to occupy a position near Chalkedon.[21] The king drove him back toward the city, but Cotta, in panic, sealed the gates. Nudus and his officers abandoned their soldiers—most of whom were then killed—and allowed themselves to be drawn up into the city by ropes. The king's troops were led by his Bastarnian infantry, said to be among the best of fighters, and whose home territory was north of the mouth of the Danube, indicative of the broad extent of his allies.

On the same day, Mithridates's fleet arrived at Chalkedon, having passed through the Bosporos. Cutting the chain blocking the harbor, they took possession and burned four Roman ships, towing the remaining sixty away. Cotta and Nudus, barricaded in the city, offered no resistance: Nudus is not heard from again, and one source reports that he was killed in the engagement, which seems unlikely but may indicate that he died shortly thereafter. The Romans were said to have lost thousands on land—reports vary between 3,000 and 5,300—and as many as 8,000 in the naval engagement.[22] These numbers are certainly exaggerated, but there is no doubt that in this first battle of the war the Romans had been badly defeated. The Pontic fleet, now augmented by Cotta's ships, sailed across the Propontis to the Hellespont, capturing Parion (on the south side of the Propontis) and Lampsakos (at the entrance to the Hellespont), thereby assuring access to the Aegean.[23]

Mithridates realized that Cotta was no threat and that any siege of Chalkedon would have been a poor use of manpower with minimal results, and thus he began to organize Bithynia as the latest acquisition to his territories. The major Bithynian cities went over to his side, either forcibly or willingly, including Prousa, Nikaia, Nikomedeia, Prousias, and Apameia.[24] At this time the king was also joined by the representative from Sertorius, Marcus Marius, who brought a military force from Spain. Marius used his senatorial rank and his position as Sertorius's quaestor to assert himself as a legitimate representative of the Roman government, appearing in public with Roman badges of office (fasces and axes) to demonstrate Roman approval of the king's actions.[25] This posture would be especially valuable when the king entered Roman territory late in 73 BC: it was even reported that on occasion, when it was politically expedient to do so, Mithridates would subordinate himself to Marius, who would then act as any Roman magistrate, giving cities their freedom and reforming tax policy.

It was probably at this time that Mithridates fulfilled his pledge to Sertorius by sending him forty ships, perhaps supplied from those captured at Chalkedon. Nothing is known about their route or how far they got before it was learned that Sertorius was dead. This occurred in the winter of 73/72 BC, and the ships either never reached Spain or headed back shortly after their arrival: the following summer Lucius Valerius Triarius, one of Lucullus's legates, was dispatched to the Hellespont to intercept them upon their return.[26]

By the summer of 73 BC Mithridates was again at a peak of his career and power. He had quickly subjugated Bithynia and brought Herakleia Pontika to his side. He had neutralized one of the consuls sent against him: Cotta seems to have remained in Chalkedon for quite some time, uncertain of what to do next. The king's ships had access to the Mediterranean, something especially frightening to the Romans.[27] As the king entered the last decade of his life, he had every reason to be confident.

THE WAR SPREADS

The later months of 73 BC were marked by a number of engagements, as Roman detachments spread across central Asia Minor battling various Pontic forces, often successfully. Fannius, the renegade Roman who had defected to Mithridates some years earlier and had been noted by the king as a good example of Roman support for his policies, joined with Metrophanes, who had commanded Pontic forces since the first war, but both were defeated at an unknown location somewhere near the volcanic territory of the Lydian-Karian borderlands.[28] Their opponent was Mamercus, otherwise unknown but presumably one of Lucullus's legates.[29] A Pontic attack on Mysia and the nearby portions of Phrygia was repelled by Gaius Salluvius Naso.[30] The Pontic commander Eumachos invaded Phrygia and killed many Romans—presumably traders and merchants—and then moved south into Pisidia, Isauria, and Cilicia, but was pursued and neutralized by Deiotaros, one of the Galatian tetrarchs.[31] Most interesting, perhaps, was the brief involvement of Julius Caesar, who had been studying on Rhodes with the famous Apollonios Molon of Alabanda, who also taught Cicero. After an interlude when he was captured by pirates and only released after forty days and a payment of fifty talents, he crossed over on his own initiative to the province of Asia (where he had previously served and probably had connections) and raised a private army, using it to expel one of the king's officers from the province, thus demonstrating to the ambivalent locals that there was a reason to be loyal to Rome.[32] As always, it is impossible to place these various incidents in sequence, but it is clear that as the autumn of 73 BC approached, things were no longer going well for Mithridates.

KYZIKOS

The city of Kyzikos lies at modern Balkıs in an impressive location on a coastal island in the Propontis, connected to the mainland by a causeway. It had been founded by Milesians perhaps as early as the seventh century BC and was the most important Greek city in the region, greatly involved in the politics of Greek history.[33] It was noted for its shipping industry and the attractiveness of its public buildings. By the first century BC it was a free city within Roman territory and would be a major prize for Mithridates, as well as an excellent staging point for an invasion of the Roman territories of western Asia Minor.[34]

In the late summer or autumn of 73 BC, the king decided to mount a total attack on the city, in hindsight a major strategic blunder. He may have been overly optimistic because of the weak Roman response at Chalkedon and had high hopes due to his alliance with Sertorius. Moreover, a Kyzikene force, part of the Roman troops at Chalkedon, had lost three thousand men and ten ships, and Mithridates may have wanted to make an example of those who opposed him.

Despite committing his entire army against Kyzikos, the king embarked on an impossible campaign.[35] Lucullus quickly moved into position on the landward side of the city. He realized that it was unwise to engage the massive Pontic army and thus settled into a siege, which lasted well into the early part of 72 BC. North of Kyzikos was the mountain known as Arktonesos, and here Mithridates besieged the city from the other side. The major ancient sources—Plutarch and Appian—describe in detail the activities of both armies in maintaining the sieges, including the complex works of the king.[36] These included a double wall and a trench, as well as a tower one hundred *pecheis* (about two hundred feet) high, which served as a platform for sending forth projectiles. There were also other towers and even ships on the seaward side of the city that could serve as troop platforms. He attempted to use his Kyzikene prisoners from Chalkedon as a bargaining chip, but the local commander, Peisistratos, refused to accept this and considered them part of the enemy. Thus the engagement settled into a peculiar three-way operation, with the Kyzikenes trapped between the two opposing armies and attempting to provide for their own defense, at one point almost capturing the king as he inspected his works.

As winter began, the supply ships that Mithridates depended upon became less frequent and reliable, and eventually ceased to arrive altogether. His troops began to suffer famine, and in time the cavalry—useless in this situation—was sent away, moving east along the coast toward Bithynia, with some troops and the baggage animals. These included camels, still a rare sight for the Romans. Lucullus sent out a detachment and largely eliminated them at the crossing of the Rhyndakos River, about thirty-five miles east of the city.[37]

In early 72 BC, word came that Sertorius had been killed, a severe blow to Mithridates's aspirations. Moreover, there were various secret negotiations developing at Kyzikos, which came to nothing but were another indication of the increasingly futile situation. In an attempt to retake the initiative, Mithridates prepared to send Aristonikos, his fleet commander, into the Aegean with money to bribe the Romans and presumably to attempt to draw their forces away from Kyzikos, but Lucullus learned of the plan and captured Aristonikos even before he set forth. The loss of one of his most senior commanders—who is not heard from again and was probably executed by Lucullus—was the final blow for Mithridates. He took his fleet and sailed to Parion, at the west end of the Propontis, which he had taken some months previously. The land army, under the command of Hermaios and Marius, also headed west, but Lucullus intercepted them at the Granikos River (where Alexander the Great had first defeated the Persians over 250 years previously) and killed many. Others made it as far as Lampsakos on the Hellespont. Mithridates rescued as many as he could and, after a futile attack on Perinthos, on the European side of the Propontis, retreated to Nikomedeia by sea in a perilous winter voyage that resulted in many more casualties. Lucullus, on the other hand, was welcomed into Kyzikos as a liberator and honored with games that were still celebrated in the second century AD.

Mithridates had lost vast numbers of men: an estimate is that the whole campaign resulted in three hundred thousand killed, including supply forces and camp followers. Most of what remained was his naval contingent, which itself was diminished because of the squadron sent to Sertorius, whose location was unknown. Some ships returned with the king to Nikomedeia, but many were lost on the way. The remainder, fifty ships, were placed under the command of four officers (Marius, Alexander, Dionysios, and Isodoros, who, except for Marius, are otherwise unknown) and moved into the Aegean.

Lucullus pursued them, equipping a fleet at the Hellespont. He caught up with Isodoros's squadron at the Harbor of the Achaians, where the forces were said to have landed to besiege Troy, and executed the commander. The citizens of Ilion—the village believed to be at the site of ancient Troy—reported that the other ships were seen heading for Lemnos, fifty miles to the west. Lucullus found them at a barren island just off its coast and, after a difficult engagement, prevailed. Marius was killed and Dionysios took poison. Alexander survived to appear in Lucullus's triumph a decade later. The proconsul sent a report (and probably also Alexander) to Rome and then went after Mithridates, who was now on the defensive. The optimism of the first year of the war had evaporated.

THE KING IN RETREAT

Mithridates seems to have had about one hundred ships left at Nikomedeia. His prime interest at this point was to return to Pontos and protect it while reconstituting his forces. He may have believed that removing himself from territory claimed by the Romans would bring the war to an end, and he would thus be able to salvage his historic kingdom. Lucullus sent one of his legates, Voconius (otherwise unknown), to blockade the king and to prevent him from moving into the Black Sea, but the legate was being initiated into the mysteries on the island of Samothrace and got too late a start, allowing the king to escape with his ships.[38] At some point during the retreat, perhaps between the Bosporos and Herakleia Pontika, another winter storm destroyed most of them (sixty to eighty ships were reported lost); this was when the king himself had to be rescued by a nearby pirate vessel commanded by a certain Seleukos, who may have been an ally.[39] He eventually landed at Herakleia and installed a garrison of mercenaries and bestowed gifts on the locals, then continued to Sinope and on to Amisos, seeking support and organizing the protection of his kingdom.[40]

This was the effective end of any Pontic attempt to be a naval power. At its peak the fleet may have had about four hundred ships, but only a fraction of these remained, and except for the matter of those sent to Sertorius, which were still unreported, sea power would play no further significant role in Mithridates's career.[41] The Romans also had no large fleet of their own but depended on ships provided by their eastern allies. Lucullus had even refused senatorial funding for a fleet, well knowing that the war would be won on land, where the Roman military excelled.

The collapse of Pontic naval aspirations and the quick victories of the various Roman detachments led some in Rome to believe that the war should be terminated. Yet Lucullus, whose experience with Mithridates went back fifteen years to the first war, knew better, and realized that the only long-term solution was an invasion of Pontos. But first he had to return Bithynia to the Romans.[42] One by one the Bithynian cities fell to Roman forces, with many of these welcoming the Roman return. The Roman success was so great that even Cotta decided it was possible to leave Chalkedon and become involved in the war. He moved to Nikomedeia, but he remained safely 150 stadia (about twenty miles) from the city while it was being retaken. By the early summer of 72 BC Bithynia was back under Roman control, and the Roman command made its headquarters at Nikomedeia.

Meanwhile Mithridates was attempting to find the means to continue the war: Lucullus was prescient in recognizing that the king would do nothing else, although he could hardly realize that it would be another nine years before he was eliminated. Mithridates turned his attention toward the east and north, where he might find allies who were not beholden to the Romans.[43] An obvious choice was his son-in-law Tigranes II of Armenia, who had been on the throne for over twenty years and had long been married to Mithridates's daughter Cleopatra. In the Kimmerian Bosporos, Mithridates's son Machares had been governor for a number of years and presumably had access to the vast resources of that region. But there seems to have been no immediate response from either. A request for aid from the Parthian king was rejected.[44] An envoy, a certain Diokles, was sent to the Skythians with gold and presents, but he promptly deserted to Lucullus.

But the king was not to give up easily. He withdrew to Kabeira, lying inland on the Lykos River. Here he had constructed a palace with a hunting park and the first known water mill.[45] Mithridates probably realized that given the collapse of his naval power, any position on the coast was vulnerable, but interior Pontos was believed to be relatively safe. He spent the winter of 72/71 BC at Kabeira, showing once again his ability to raise an army, and by spring he claimed to have forty thousand infantry and four thousand cavalry.

THE ROMAN CONQUEST OF PONTOS

In the summer of 72 BC the three senior Roman commanders met at their new headquarters, Nikomedeia. These were Lucullus, Cotta, and Lucius Valerius Triarius, not previously documented in the war. He had been a praetor in 78 BC and then was sent to Sardinia the following year in pursuit of Lepidus. Triarius was Lucullus's naval commander.[46]

It was decided to undertake an invasion of Pontos. But there was still the matter of the ships that had been sent to Sertorius, which could assist in rebuilding Mithridates's fleet, and which had been reported somewhere around Crete, perhaps obtaining reinforcements. Triarius was assigned the task of keeping them out of the Black Sea and thus blockaded the entrance to the Hellespont. Eventually—probably during the autumn of 72 BC or even as late as the following spring—the ships appeared. In an engagement off the island of Tenedos, just south of the Hellespont, they were destroyed, marking the final end of Pontic sea power.[47]

Cotta was to retake Herakleia Pontika. This was basically a punitive expedition, and it was probably thought that it would be a relatively easy task for the weakest of the Roman commanders. But Cotta once again demonstrated his inability to perform his duties.[48] He was not able to capture the city by siege—Memnon, a local, described the events in detail—and a stalemate dragged on for two years. The city became isolated except for what it could receive from the sea, until the Roman fleet under Triarius arrived and cut off this access, causing increasing distress. Eventually, the royal governor, Konnakorex, negotiated a surrender with Triarius, which offended Cotta, who had been marginalized, and the two Romans almost came to blows. To settle the matter, Cotta was allowed to plunder the city, which he did before burning it. He stole many of its famous works of art, including the monumental statue of Herakles from the agora, taking so much booty that some of his heavily laden ships sank while leaving the harbor.

This was the end of the one of the less distinguished careers of the era. Cotta returned to Rome with his surviving acquisitions. He was eagerly welcomed as a conqueror and given the title Ponticus. But then reports began to arrive of what had actually happened, and he was put on trial and expelled from the Senate, not to be heard of again.[49] Herakleia was restored to its free status.

Meanwhile, Lucullus had moved into Pontos, passing through Galatia, where he obtained supplies from the locals.[50] Although his soldiers complained about the desultory nature of the campaign, lacking opportunities for plunder, the proconsul realized that to force Mithridates out of Pontos and to seek the aid of his son-in-law Tigranes was dangerous. This would create a formidable alliance against the Romans, since Tigranes controlled territory from Armenia to the Levant. It was believed that Tigranes, who had taken advantage of Seleukid weakness and advanced as far as the Mediterranean a decade previously, was looking for an excuse to attack Rome.

Thus Lucullus spent the winter of 72/71 BC in a siege of Amisos, on the coast eighty miles southeast of Sinope, not pressing matters greatly and allowing the king, still at Kabeira, to rearm. By springtime Lucullus was ready to move against him. There was a series of engagements, which began with victories on the part of the king, but the advantage gradually turned in favor of Lucullus. The king's losses steadily mounted, including one of his senior commanders, Dorylaos, the ancestor of Strabo. Eventually the king retreated to Komana, the great Pontic temple town, lying about twenty miles south of Kabeira. On the way he was almost captured, but Lucullus's soldiers were diverted by plundering his baggage train, and he made it to the sanctuary. Then he headed toward Tigranes, having nowhere else to go. Lucullus pursued him for several days, as far as Talaura, on the border of Lesser Armenia (probably at modern Sivas), about a hundred miles south of Komana, and then let him go, now that he was out of Pontos.[51]

Lucullus then spent some time in subduing Lesser Armenia and two regional ethnic groups that had been allied with the king, the Chaldaians and the Tibarenians, both of whom lived in the mountainous region east of Kabeira. His expedition may have been little more than a demonstration of a Roman presence in the region, since before long he was back at Amisos, where the siege was continuing under his legate Murena, who had been with Sulla in Greece.[52] Over the next few months, probably into the beginning of 70 BC, Pontos steadily fell to the Romans, although it was premature to attempt any organization of the territory as a province, since Mithridates might return at any time. Yet matters soon were stable enough that Lucullus returned to the province of Asia, which was still in economic difficulty and needed his attention.[53]

MITHRIDATES AND TIGRANES

Mithridates was desperate. After half a century on the throne, the king saw his world collapsing around him. His effort to contain Roman power, which had occupied him for twenty years, had repeatedly been unsuccessful. Western Asia Minor was closed to him, and hopes for his survival lay to the east and north. The historian Sallust has preserved the letter that Mithridates allegedly wrote to the Parthian king Phraates III, outlining his complaints against Rome.[54] To be sure, Sallust had his own agenda, and similar indictments of Roman imperialism appear in the speech that he attributed to Jugurtha, whose dramatic date is nearly half a century previously.[55] In fact, the letter falls into the genre of the condemnation of Roman policy by its most vigorous opponents: in addition to Jugurtha, other examples include the speech of the Arvernian chieftain Critognatus (from about twenty years after that of Mithridates) and, a century later, that of the Caledonian leader Calgacus.[56] Like these, Mithridates's letter is certainly a literary construct and was presented in Latin rather than the original Greek or Persian. But it is probably based to some extent on actual documents, presumably those eventually discovered by Pompey at Kainon.[57]

In the letter, Mithridates outlined his view of the current situation, much as he had done several years earlier in a speech to his troops.[58] He accused the Romans of warmongering toward the eastern Mediterranean world ever since they had engaged Philip V of Macedonia a century earlier. They always betrayed their friends, and most recently had taken Phrygia away from its rightful ruler, the son of Nikomedes IV. Roman expansionism had reached a necessary end in the west because of the Atlantic (this was a theme of the era, but perhaps more Sallust's than Mithridates's), and thus they had no choice except to turn east.[59] Mithridates had to take the initiative and begin a new war. He pointed out that a Roman attack on Parthia was inevitable, and he repeated his view that the Romans had contempt for monarchy.

The letter set out the king's well-established view of Roman expansionism, but despite its dire predictions, it had no effect, and Phraates III refused his request for help. An attempted marriage alliance with Ptolemy XII of Egypt was not implemented.[60] The Seleukids were moribund, and much of their remaining territory was occupied by the Armenians. Only Tigranes might be of assistance, being at the peak of his power and also the son-in-law of Mithridates. Tigranes had helped his father-in-law previously when he had twice invaded Cappadocia, but so far had remained neutral in the most recent conflict with Rome.

But as he fled east to Armenia, Mithridates paused long enough to give orders that eliminated many members of his family. The reason for this is not obvious (unless he was beginning to demonstrate personal instability), but it may reflect the fact that his son Machares, the ruler of the Kimmerian Bosporos, had defected, asking to be considered a friend and ally of Rome, which may have led the king to see major threats within his own family.[61] Several of his family members had been sequestered at Pharnakeia, at the eastern edge of Pontos.[62] There were two wives, Berenike, from Chios, and Monime, from Miletos. The latter, at least, had not been happy at the Pontic court, seeing herself in exile in a barbarian land, even though she had the title of *basilissa*, or queen, and had exchanged erotic letters at some time with the king.[63] The king sent one of his eunuchs, Bakchides (or Bakchos) to carry out his order. Both wives attempted suicide but were actually killed by Bakchides. Berenike's mother, also in residence at Pharnakeia, was successful in her suicide. Two unmarried half-sisters of the king, Rhoxane and Stateira, committed suicide.[64] Other unnamed women of the royal court were also killed.

After these orders were given, Mithridates continued on his way to his son-in-law. But Tigranes was ambivalent about receiving him. In fact Mithridates was kept away from the court for nearly two years; Plutarch reported that he was almost a prisoner, living on royal estates in remote areas of Armenia.[65] In effect, Tigranes was providing refuge while carefully avoiding any personal contact, since he had reason to worry about a possible Roman invasion of his territory. At about this time the historian Metrodoros of Skepsis, Mithridates's ambassador to the Armenian court, advised Tigranes—against his instructions—not to become involved with the Romans. Mithridates's reaction was to have Metrodoros executed, although later he regretted his decision and gave the scholar a magnificent funeral.[66] Tigranes's interests were more to the south of Armenia than the west: he had moved into upper Mesopotamia (where he was building Tigranokerta) and had annexed much of the remnants of the Seleukid empire and parts of adjoining Cilicia. Although the latter action had brought him close to Roman territory, there seemed to be no conflict of interest.[67]

Lucullus, however, realized the danger of any alliance between the two kings, and almost as soon as Mithridates fled Pontos, he was in contact with Tigranes. He sent one of his legates, Appius Clodius Pulcher, to the Armenian king. Clodius was at the beginning of a dubious career that would last until the early 40s BC and become increasingly scandalous, reaching its peak with a proconsulate in Cilicia in 53–51 BC that, according to his successor Cicero, "permanently ruined the province."[68] But this was still in the future when in late 71 BC he went to Antioch on the Orontes for a meeting with Tigranes. Clodius bluntly told the king that he had come to obtain Mithridates (who was still being excluded from the Armenian court) so that he could appear in Lucullus's triumph. Moreover, if Mithridates were not produced, Rome would declare war on Armenia. Tigranes, who must have been rather astounded at this ultimatum, found the legate excessively arrogant in the face of royalty and replied that he would not hand over Mithridates and, moreover, he would defend his kingdom against the Romans.

Lucullus, when he received Tigranes's reply (a letter was sent, in addition to Clodius's report), promptly invaded Armenia. He reported that this was because he had received information that the two kings were about to attack Roman Asia, a questionable assertion at best that may have been Lucullus's fabricated justification for war.[69] In Rome there was extensive opposition to the invasion, the beginning of the decline of Lucullus's fortunes, since it was believed that he was warmongering and seeking both a perpetual command and personal enrich-ment.[70] Nevertheless, in the winter of 70/69 BC the expedition was underway, marked by a difficult crossing of the flooded Euphrates. Lucullus unknow-ingly had played into Mithridates's hands, forcing Tigranes to make war against Rome. The proconsul quickly captured Tigranokerta in early 69 BC; the city was never finished and was reduced to a village.[71] But Tigranes had finally admitted Mithridates to his presence, and the two began to mobilize against Rome, a pro-cess that began in the autumn of 69 BC and continued into the following spring. Mithridates was given the senior command, since Tigranes believed that he must have learned from his previous disasters.[72] Mithridates also reached out to the king of Parthia, and Lucullus did the same.

THE RETURN TO PONTOS

In late 68 BC Mithridates returned to Pontos. The Romans had made no attempt to organize the territory but had left six thousand men under three of Lucullus's legates, Fabius Hadrianus, Sornatius, and Triarius. All had been on the procon-sul's staff for a number of years; Triarius seems to have given up his naval com-mand and was in charge of a detachment of infantry.[73] The locals had seen the effects of Roman occupation for three years and were excited at the king's return. In a series of swift battles that lasted into the spring of 67 BC, he easily reestab-lished his position. He first engaged Fabius, who was able to avoid total defeat only because the king was wounded, both in the knee and near his eye. Among his troops was a detachment of Agarians, who came from somewhere north of the Black Sea and who used the venom of snakes as a curative and were always in the king's service. At this time they were able to cure him of his wounds. Because of his injuries, there was a lull in the fighting, and Fabius was able to retreat to Kabeira and was essentially besieged there until he was rescued by Triarius, to whom he gave his command. Triarius did no better against the king and was decisively defeated at Zela, losing seven thousand men and more officers than in almost any previous Roman battle. But the king had been wounded again—a cen-turion stabbed him in the thigh—and he was withdrawn from the engagement and attended by his physician Timotheus, who ensured he was raised up so that his troops could see that he was still alive, in imitation of a similar event involv-ing Alexander the Great in India.[74] When the king returned to the battlefield, the Romans had fled. Mithridates did not pursue them, because it was reported that Tigranes was approaching with a large force. He withdrew to the east and waited, knowing that the Romans were in no position to reengage. Triarius's soldiers mutinied, and Lucullus, who had opportunely arrived from Armenia, had to hide the commander from his men. Nothing more is known about Triarius, who had been one of Lucullus's legates for many years, but a number of his naval officers and men made dedications to him on Delos. Interestingly, these provide the name of two of his ships, the *Athena* (perhaps his flagship, whose first officer made the dedication) and the *Parthenos*.[75]

THE DISMISSAL OF LUCULLUS

For some time questions had been raised about Lucullus's competence as a commander. He had made significant efforts in restoring confidence in Roman rule in the province of Asia, and from the beginning of his command he had moved against those who were exploiting the province financially, winning local respect for doing so. But his handling of military issues was causing him difficulty. The invasion of Armenia had seemed unnecessary to some, and now the recent disasters in Pontos conflicted with the optimistic reports that the proconsul had been sending to Rome stating that Mithridates had been neutralized. At the end of 68 BC his command in Asia had not been renewed, and shortly thereafter he lost his legal position in Cilicia.[76] In both cases he was accused of unreasonably prolonging the war and making unreliable reports about his progress. Lucullus made a last attempt at success by going after Tigranes, who was ravaging Cappadocia. But his soldiers began to mutiny and would not enter the territory.

Then commissioners arrived from Rome to organize the new province of Pontos. Needless to say, they were astonished to discover that the district was not even in Roman hands. In the summer of 67 BC Lucullus was stripped of his remaining commands, and the war against Mithridates was handed over to Manlius Acilius Glabrio. But he was unwilling to engage the king; Cicero saw him as not adequately equipped for the campaign.[77]

The Roman withdrawal from any activities against Mithridates in 67 BC allowed the king to secure his kingdom and, once again, to rearm, something that he never seems to have had difficulty doing. But old age was beginning to affect him; whether this played a role in the slaughter of the women of his court cannot be proven, but he had been wounded three times in the recent campaign. Moreover, his position as king of Pontos was weakening even with his reacquisition of the territory. His son Machares had gone over to the Romans, as had a large number of his officers and supporters. There were also conspiracies: the king suspected that a Roman fugitive of senatorial rank, Attidius, who had been in his service for many years, was plotting against him and thus had him executed.[78]

Lucullus stayed in Asia Minor into 66 BC, meeting with his successor, and then returned to Rome. He was not allowed to have his edicts validated or to reward his followers; one of those so affected was Moaphernes, the king's governor of Colchis and the great-uncle of Strabo, who had defected to the Romans (handing over fifteen fortresses) and who was promised great honors, which were denied when Lucullus lost his command. Thus opposition to Lucullus continued after his return home, and his triumph was repeatedly postponed and not celebrated until 63 BC.[79] When it did occur, it was one of the most impressive spectacles of the era, including scythe-bearing chariots, sixty members of the king's court, 110 ships, a life-sized gold statue of the king, and bearers and wagons with vast amounts of precious stones, gold, and silver. Lucullus also gave a great feast to the people of the city and the surrounding villages. He then left politics and became famed as one of the richest men in Rome and a connoisseur of the arts, although there were repeated and futile calls for him to intervene in the increasingly authoritarian world of contemporary Rome.[80] He owned several estates; the one at Rome, known familiarly as the Gardens of Lucullus and located on the Pincian Hill—where some remains have been identified—included his vast library, one of the most extensive in the city.[81] His parties were so elaborate that the adjective "Lucullan" is still used today to mean lavish luxury. In his final years, however, he deteriorated mentally and physically, allegedly from drug overdoses, and he died in 57 or 56 BC, to be buried on his estate in Tusculum, despite attempts to have his tomb located in the Campus Martius near to that of Sulla.[82]

In later years, Lucullus's luxurious lifestyle was seen as symptomatic of Roman decline: he was said to have adopted the rich tastes of both Mithridates and Tigranes and exploited them for his own benefit.[83] There were complaints about postwar inflation, with a new need for fancy foods and an ever increasing number of slaves. In many ways such reports are more moral paradigms than historical reality, a standard complaint about Roman attitudes toward eastern luxury that had existed ever since the days of Cato the Elder a century previously.[84] Yet there is no doubt that the intensive exposure to the world of the east in the first half of the first century BC changed Roman ways forever.

Chapter 12

The Royal Court

The emphasis by ancient authors on the military activities of the Mithridatic dynasty means that it is easy to forget that the monarchs functioned within the expected parameters of Hellenistic kingship in many matters other than warfare. The royal court was extensive, especially in its later years, with a large family whose numbers were bolstered by the polygamy common in many eastern dynasties. In the case of Pontos, this was one of the vestiges of its Persian origins. There were also numerous court members who provided the intellectual environment typical of the Hellenistic royal world. Most of the evidence, as usual, comes from the era of Mithridates VI, but it can be assumed that his immediate predecessors had many of the same values.

THE ROYAL FAMILY

Many of the family relationships of the Mithridatic kings have already been discussed in previous chapters. But the family of Mithridates VI is unusual in that it was especially large, since the king had eight known wives or partners, fifteen sons, and eight daughters. There were probably others not documented. Yet the information remains vague: the mothers of particular children are usually not identified.

The king's first marriage, and the one that conformed the most to the historic practices of his dynasty, did not last long. This was to his sister Laodike, who was eliminated in the early years of his reign.[1] Her most prominent successor was Monime, daughter of Philopoimen, who was Mithridates's governor of Ephesos in the 80s BC. Monime and her father came from Stratonikeia (whether the Karian or Mysian city cannot be determined).[2] She was said to be the king's favorite, and she is the only one after Laodike to be documented with the title of *basilissa* ("queen"). As such she may have been the mother of one or more of his prominent sons. But she was not happy at court, feeling that she was living a life of exile among barbarians. As conditions deteriorated in the war with Lucullus, the king ordered her execution when she was sequestered at Pharnakeia. She attempted to hang herself with her royal diadem, but this failed, and she was killed by the king's eunuch Bakchides (or Bakchos).

Another prominent wife was Stratonike. Her father was a musician who was given an estate when the king took her as his partner. She was important enough to be left in charge of the fortress of Sympharion,[3] but when the king fled his kingdom for the last time, she was not pleased at being left behind and surrendered to Pompey, handing over the royal treasures. He accepted some of them— what he could use in his triumph—but allowed her to keep the remainder. She then joined Mithridates in the Bosporos, but he killed her son Xiphares in her presence as retaliation for her treachery.[4]

Other wives and partners of the king were less prominent. Berenike of Chios was among those killed at Pharnakeia. Hypsikrateia had Amazonian qualities and was noted for her horsemanship and military skills; the king called her by the masculine form of her name, Hypsikrates. A woman with such characteristics might be expected at the Pontic court, since this was the land of the Amazons. She joined the king in his flight north, and a memorial to her, using the masculine Hypsikrates but identifying her as a wife of the king, was recently found at the Bosporan city of Phanagoreia.[5] A certain Adobogiana was also said to have been a partner of the king, yet her connection with the dynasty is dubious. She was a daughter of one of the Galatian tetrarchs and used an assumed relationship with the king to advance the fortunes of her son, conveniently named Mithridates, whose father was actually a Pergamene aristocrat.[6] Mithridates of Pergamon became a close associate of Julius Caesar, assisting him in Alexandria at the time Cleopatra VII was placed on the throne. He was then made king of Bosporos in early 47 BC but was not well received locally and was soon eliminated.[7]

Between them the king's partners had over twenty children, many of whom are obscure. The most important daughter was Cleopatra, who married Tigranes II of Armenia. She seems to have advanced her father's interests there, much to the annoyance of her husband, and had six known children, who ruled or married into various eastern dynasties.[8] Another daughter, Athenais, was betrothed to Ariobarzanes II of Cappadocia (ruled ca. 63–51 BC) at the age of four and was the mother of the last two kings of that dynasty, Ariobarzanes III and Ariarathes X. She also became heavily involved in the politics of the kingdom: Cicero found her a destabilizing influence.[9] Two other daughters, Orsabaris and Eupatra, are known because they were in Pompey's triumphal procession. The former was probably the woman of the same name who was the mother of the Queen Mousa who appears on the coinage of the Bithynian city of Prousias.[10] And there was also Drypetina, who either fled north with Mithridates or stayed at Sinoria, where she was killed by the eunuch Monophilos.[11]

The sons of Mithridates VI are also scantily documented in most cases, often only when they assisted their father on campaign. Of interest is the onomastic progression of their names. The oldest had local dynastic names (Mithridates, Pharnakes), and the next group had regional dynastic ones (Artaphernes, Xiphares), reflecting the movement of the kingdom from Pontos into the surrounding areas. The names of the youngest reverted to the peak years of the Persian empire (Cyrus, Dareios, Xerxes), demonstrative of the expansiveness of Mithridates's ideology in his later years, and perhaps an emotional connection to the greatness of the past.[12]

Four sons, however, were particularly prominent and may have been among the eldest. Ariarathes became (as Ariarathes IX) king of Cappadocia (ruled ca. 100–88 BC, with interruptions) but had no known descendants.[13] A son named Mithridates was "king"—probably royal governor—of Colchis but displayed too much independence and was removed and executed.[14] Two others were conspicuous in the politics of the last years of Mithridates VI: Machares, his governor of Bosporos, who defected to the Romans but eventually was killed or committed suicide when the king moved into the region, and Pharnakes II, the designated successor, who became king of Bosporos.[15]

THE CLOSE ASSOCIATES OF MITHRIDATES VI

As with most Hellenistic monarchs, Mithridates VI presided over a court that included a variety of intellectual personalities: philosophers, chroniclers, poets, artists, and physicians were all in his circle. About eighty names are known from the entire history of the dynasty,[16] but almost all are associated with Mithridates VI, and, needless to say, given the king's sixty-year reign, not all were in residence at the same time. Most were military personnel. His senior commanders were Greek, and some—especially Dorylaos and the brothers Neoptolemos and Archelaos—served the king for many years. The most prominent naval commanders were Alexander, Dionysios, Leonippos, Seleukos, and Klearchos, active during the brief period of Pontic naval power in the early years of the third war.[17]

In addition to the military officers, about thirty other followers of Mithridates VI are recorded. Many of these are the types of people that one would find at any Hellenistic court, and some, inevitably, were of dubious character, such as Dionysos, a drinking companion of the king, so named because of his prodigious capacity, or Kalomadrys of Kyzikos, an athlete also known for his eating and drinking abilities. Lucius Lutatius Paccius was the royal perfumer.[18] All courts had their religious characters, and in the case of Mithridates VI this role was primarily filled by a certain Sosipatros, described as a "sorcerer," who made his reputation by flattering the king.[19] Numerous Roman refugees and deserters drifted to the side of the king—the best known was Marcus Marius, the former officer of Sertorius—and these became so numerous that Mithridates's failure to return them became a reason for the collapse of the negotiations offered by Pompey in 66 BC.[20] In addition to Persians, Greeks, and Romans, other ethnicities represented at the court included Cappadocians, Thracians, Armenians, Macedonians, Paphlagonians, Celts, Parthians, and Skythians.

The king's secretaries included Dorylaos, who was also one of his most prominent military commanders, as well as a certain Kallistratos, who had many of the king's private papers but was executed when it was discovered that he had absconded with one of the royal treasuries.[21] There was also Paphios, a royal physician, whose likeness appeared on one of the medallions at the Mithridateion on Delos and thus was active early in the king's reign. Another physician, Timotheus, attended the king when he was wounded late in the third war.[22] An unusual member of the court, at least briefly, was the son of Ptolemy X of Egypt, who had ended up on the island of Kos to escape the chaos at home. When Kos was taken by Mithridates in 88 BC, he joined the king's entourage but eventually fled to Sulla, who made him king of Egypt as Ptolemy XI in 80 BC.[23]

The most important literary personality was Metrodoros of Skepsis (in the Troad).[24] He also served as an ambassador to Tigranes II of Armenia, writing a biography of that king. His writings were especially wide-ranging, including treatises on pharmacology, metallurgy, minerology, mythology, natural history, human physiology, cultural history, and art history. He also invented a widely used mnemonic system. Perhaps most interesting are his extensive geographical writings, which reveal that he had researched material about Italy, Liguria, northwestern Europe, Africa, and India, perhaps laying the groundwork for future expansion of the Pontic empire. Significantly, he seems to have been particularly interested in the geography of Italy. He was said to have hated even the name of Rome, especially the Roman tendency to acquire Greek art by dubious means. Nevertheless, before he came to Pontos, he had lectured in Athens to prominent Romans of the early first century BC, including Marcus Antonius, the consul of 99 BC and the grandfather of the triumvir, and Lucius Licinius Crassus, the consul of 95 BC.

Regardless of the various friends, military personnel, and others attached to the Pontic court, its structure was hierarchic, with the king in absolute control, although delegating some activities to his "friends," or his inner circle. One way in which the court retained its eastern heritage was the prominence of eunuchs, not only Bakchides and Monophilos, remembered for their role in killing the royal women, but a number of others, who even served as military officers. The presence of so many eunuchs in positions of power created tension between them and the Greek and Roman members of the court.[25]

THE KING AS SCHOLAR

Mithridates VI was educated in Greek learning and was especially interested in cultic matters and music. He wrote on the interpretation of dreams, both his own and those of members of his family.[26] But the most important scholarly activity for both the king and members of his court was medical research. The king himself took the lead, even being a practicing physician, although this may have been more a political activity than a medical one.[27] Prominent at the court was the herbalist Krateuas, known as the "root cutter," who wrote an alphabetized herbal, noted for its colored representations of plants. He also wrote extensively on botany.[28] Zopyros, most of whose career was in Alexandria at the court of Ptolemy XII (he may have been a teacher of Cleopatra VII) was an empiricist physician (empiricists believed that careful observation was the basis of all medical knowledge) who exchanged information with the king about antidotes for poison and may have visited Pontos.[29] The king had an extensive medical library, and he collected specimens and information from his territories and corresponded with physicians throughout the Mediterranean world.[30] He urged Asklepiades of Bithynia, who lived in Rome, to come to the court, but their contact was limited to exchanging treatises.[31] Since Asklepiades was dead by 91 BC, this demonstrates that the king's medical interests began early in life.

Interest in pharmacology was a particular concern of Hellenistic royalty: the danger of poisoning by one's intimates was always present and could be success-ful.[32] Attalos III of Pergamon (reigned 138–133 BC) was a noted agriculturalist—so much so that it was said he neglected his royal duties and hastened the end of his kingdom—who wrote on medicine and pharmacology.[33] The Seleukid king Antiochos VIII (reigned ca. 125–96 BC) created a compound effective against venoms as well as other remedies.[34] Nikomedes IV of Bithynia (reigned ca. 94–74 BC) was also a practicing pharmacologist.[35] Thus Mithridates's interest in poisons and their antidotes was hardly unique, but reflected the attitudes of his era. His entourage included Agarians, who were Skythians noted for their ability to use snake venom as a remedy.[36]

The king created a number of antidotes, generally based on herbs and other botanical materials.[37] The most simple used walnuts, figs, and rue; others had dozens of ingredients. It was said that he successfully tested an antidote on a prisoner condemned to death. Although a similar story was told about Cleopatra VII (merely involving the poison, not the antidote), in Mithridates's case the story was probably true.[38] Eventually the name *mithridatios* (or mithridatum) was attached to one or more of these, a word (as "mithridate") still used today to mean a remedy against poison and disease.[39] The Mithridatic antidotes became popular in Rome, especially among the Roman elite, although in time they evolved away from the originals. In the Renaissance, antidotes called mithrida-tum were used against the plague, and a fine gilded terracotta drug jar, created to hold such compounds and with a representation of the death of the king, is attributed to Annibale Fontana and is on display in the Getty Museum (fig. 12.1).[40]

Mithridates also experimented with scientific gardening, especially during his final exile in the Bosporos, attempting (unsuccessfully) to bring Mediterranean plants into that northern region.[41] His name became attached to a number of plants that he identified, including one that Krateuas named *mithridatia*, with rosy flowers whose leaves were similar to an acanthus. There was another called *scordotis* or *scordion*, about a cubit in height with downy leaves like those of the oak, which was indigenous to Pontos. Neither of these can be certainly identi-fied today. There was a third, *eupatoria* (probably *Agrimonia eupatoria*); its seeds could relieve dysentery.[42] Mithridates also developed some remedies for sore throats.[43] Many of the king's writings were discovered by Pompey at the collapse of the kingdom, including notebooks and other material in his own hand. He wrote in Greek, and some of his treatises and notes were translated into Latin

Figure 12.1 Mithridatum Vase. Getty Museum 90.SC.42.1. Digital image courtesy of the Getty's Open Content Program.

by Pompeius Lenaeus, one of Pompey's freedmen and a medical authority in his own right.[44]

Ironically, the reputation of the king as a master gardener would have an impact after his death on his two conquerors, Lucullus and Pompey. Even over a century later, Lucullus's gardens on the Pincian Hill in Rome and near Naples were famed for their opulence and eastern quality. He imported plants from Pontos, especially the cherry tree.[45] Pompey dedicated his theater and portico in the Campus Martius in Rome a few years after his triumph, one of the most

Figure 12.2 Wall painting of garden of Livia in Villa of Prima Porta. Museo Nationale Romano. Courtesy Wikimedia Commons. Photograph by Carole Raddato.

innovative architectural complexes of the era. It included an elaborate garden with trees from Asia, a visible remnant of Pompey's overseas career. The complex may also have had a statue of Mithridates brought from Pontos.[46] The famous garden paintings from the dining room of the villa of Livia at Prima Porta (just north of Rome), now visible in the Museo Nazionale Romano, are perhaps the best extant example of the type of garden that aristocratic Romans cultivated, and perhaps even that of Mithridates himself (fig. 12.2). The spirit of the king was visible in Rome long after his death.[47]

CITY FOUNDATIONS, ARCHITECTURE, AND TECHNOLOGY

City foundation and architectural renewal were features of Hellenistic monarchy. Often the new cities were merely the renaming of existing towns or reflected the shifting populations of the Hellenistic world. A fine example of this process is Soloi in Cilicia (at modern Viranşehir), a Greek settlement that had existed since the seventh century BC. When Tigranes II was creating Tigranokerta in the 70s BC, the inhabitants of Soloi were among those collected for the new city. Soloi remained abandoned for a decade until Pompey reestablished it in 67 BC as a refuge for the pirates that he had gathered, renaming it Pompeiopolis.[48] Such details are not available for any of the Mithridatic foundations, but they demonstrate the manner in which new and renamed cities were established.

The first city foundation associated with the Mithridatic dynasty was Pharnakeia, in eastern Pontos at modern Giresun, created by Pharnakes I in the early second century BC.[49] Its location at the eastern edge of Pontic territory demonstrates another function of Hellenistic city foundation: to define the limits of a kingdom and to serve as a staging point for further conquests. Pharnakeia, positioned between two harbors that provided shelter regardless of the wind direction, was well situated for this purpose.

Needless to say, it was Mithridates VI who was most involved in the creation of new cities.[50] A large number of these were in fact fortresses: Strabo knew of seventy-five, most if not all of which were outside Pontos, especially in coastal Armenia and Colchis.[51] Their function was not only as refuges but as depositories for the royal treasuries. Many were destroyed by Pompey, and most cannot be identified today. Those still visible, such as Dazimonitis (modern Tokat) and Gazioura (modern Turhal), are notable for their secure water supply, and in fact water tunnels were a common feature of contemporary Pontos, with dozens identified.[52] The best known fortress was Sinoria (near modern Baybürt), the last place the king resided before his retreat north.[53] In Galatia was Mithridation, one of the king's earliest foundations.[54] Another fortress was Dasteira, in Lesser Armenia on the upper Lykos River (near modern Yeşilyayla); when Pompey defeated the king he founded his victory city, Nikopolis, nearby, presumably merely transferring the population to a new settlement a few miles away.[55] Kainon (near modern Akgün, just northwest of Kabeira) was where Pompey discovered Mithridates's papers.[56]

The name most favored by Mithridates for his foundations was Eupatoria or Eupatorion, based on his first surname. Three such places are known. The earliest was probably Eupatorion on the Chersonesos peninsula, founded by Diophantos during his expedition to the north shore of the Black Sea at the end of the second century BC. Although the toponym Eupatoria still exists in the area, the exact location of the ancient site is not known.[57] Another Eupatoria was at the junction of the Lykos and Iris Rivers. It was never finished, and Pompey destroyed it in 68 BC, shortly thereafter refounding it as Magnopolis, after his surname of Magnus. Just to the northwest of Amisos in Pontos was the third Eupatoria, a royal residence, which only lasted until 71 BC, when Lucullus destroyed it.[58] When the king established this Eupatoria, he also expanded nearby Amisos and provided it with new temples.[59] He also had a number of palaces, of which the most important were those at Sinope, Eupatoria near Amisos, Kabeira, and Pantikapaion in Bosporos, where he spent his last days in botanical research.[60] The palace at Kabeira had a menagerie and a hunting park.

City and fortress foundation requires architectural talent. Two of the king's royal engineers are known by name: Nikomedes of Thessaly built the elaborate defenses at Kyzikos, and Kallimachos was responsible for works at Nisibis in northern Mesopotamia (commissioned by Tigranes II) and at Amisos.[61] Although both are remembered for their military constructions, they may also have directed some civil projects.

Actual building outside the Pontic kingdom seems to have been limited. Mithridates V may have rebuilt the Palaestra on the Lake on Delos, and Mithridates VI was remembered for the Mithridateion on the same island. It has been suggested that a sculpture group from the Sanctuary of Athena at Pergamon, showing Herakles rescuing Prometheus, was erected by the king when that city was his headquarters during the first war. Such a group would fit into royal ideology, but association with the king remains highly speculative.[62]

If Pharnakes I commissioned the Middle Stoa in Athens, this would be the most extensive extant structure outside Pontos attributed to the dynasty, but it seems that due to his financial difficulties he did not see the project through to its end.[63] There is evidence that after Mithridates VI captured Chios in the first war and caused some damage, he did some rebuilding on the island, importing Pontic settlers and renaming Chios city Berenike, after one of his wives (who was a local). The name did not last long, and seventy years later Herod the Great found the Mithridatic destruction still evident and did more rebuilding.[64] And when Mithridates visited Apameia in southern Phrygia and saw the effects of a recent earthquake, he gave one hundred talents for its reconstruction.[65]

The most important and longest-lasting engineering effort in the world of Mithridates VI was the invention of the water mill, first documented at Kabeira. A casual statement by Strabo is the earliest specific reference to such a device. There is also a generic description, without citing a location but slightly earlier, by Vitruvius.[66] The mill in antiquity was essentially the same as the type familiar today, with toothed wheels driven by water power causing grindstones to interact, producing the flour. The king, or one of his engineers, may have realized the potential of water power, more suitable in Asia Minor than the traditional

Greek world, which is generally lacking in abundantly flowing rivers. Kabeira lay on the Lykos River, one of the major streams of Pontos, in a lush and abundant region that retains this character today. The water mill at Kabeira may not have been the first, but the technology was almost certainly invented in northern Asia Minor and most probably in the environment of the Pontic court. A new Greek word, *hydrauletes*, first documented by Vitruvius and Strabo, was the name for the water mill.[67]

ART AND COINAGE

The king was a collector of fine art and historical artifacts. In the city of Talaura (probably at modern Sivas) he had a vast storehouse of valuable objects, which were confiscated by Pompey.[68] The material included two thousand drinking cups of onyx soldered with gold, a large amount of furniture, and horse tackle decorated with precious stones and gold. Some of this was as old as the era of Dareios I of Persia and had ended up in Ptolemaic Egypt, and then was part of the material deposited by Cleopatra III on Kos, in time given by the locals to Mithridates. The alleged cloak of Alexander the Great also came to the king by this route and may have been a legitimate Ptolemaic heirloom, perhaps part of Alexander's funeral effects when he was buried in Alexandria. A bronze ribbed krater, now in the Capitoline Museum in Rome and inscribed with the name of the king, may be a survival of this booty, or from one of the Roman triumphs. It is a rare extant example of a type of luxury item of Persian inspiration and a fine example of the king's patronage of the arts. The krater was found in the eighteenth century in Nero's villa at Antium (modern Anzio).[69]

A family tomb discovered in the Amisos necropolis in 1995 is a visual demonstration of the artistic wealth and antiquarianism of the Pontic elite in the time of Mithridates VI. The tomb yielded numerous pieces of fine jewelry, dating from as early as the fourth century BC. There were also glass objects of high quality. Although the occupants of the tomb are not known, it is probable that they had some association with the royal court.[70]

The Roman triumphs included artistic representations of the king and his family, but little is extant, and none is certainly attributed. That there was a genre of portrait statues of the king is apparent from the accounts of both Pompey's triumph and that of Lucullus.[71] In the latter there was a golden statue of the king, and in the former a silver one, as well as one of Tigranes II of Armenia. There was also a statue of Mithridates VI on Rhodes, which was respected and not demolished even during his attack,[72] and in the Mithridateion on Delos and elsewhere on that island there were dedications to the king and also to his father Mithridates V. Some of these probably included portraits.[73] A statue base found in the Asklepieion at Nymphaion in Bosporos indicates that the king was commemorated there, perhaps honoring his medical expertise.[74]

Yet extant portraits believed to be of the king are limited and have been attributed through art historical analysis rather than epigraphic evidence. The most generally accepted is one in the Louvre that shows the king as Herakles (fig. 6.1).[75] This is not a role documented elsewhere, but it may refer to his connections with Colchis and the Caucasus, regions associated with the hero. There is also a head in the Hermitage (fig. 6.2), from the Bosporos, and another now in the Odessa museum.[76] Similar heads are in Athens and Frascati (from Ostia). These are probably all that can be identified as the king with any degree of certainty, and even some of them remain disputed.[77] All the portraits are similar, vaguely reminiscent of Alexander the Great, and, as might be expected, all show the king in relative youth.[78]

Athenion, the Athenian agent of Mithridates at the time of the first war, had a gold ring with a cameo of the king set in it; this may have been an official recognition of his authority to speak for him.[79] There were certainly other cameos, and some of those which are extant have speculatively been identified as portraits of the king, but none is certain.[80] He also had a numerous gemstones; Pliny described them as a *dactyliotheca*, a rare Greek term for such a collection. Some of his gems were acquired by Pompey and displayed on the Capitol in Rome.[81] Although Pliny's notice is the sole specific comment on them and does not provide any details, a few may survive today, such as a blue chalcedony portrait of a Pontic queen, perhaps Laodike the wife of Mithridates IV (fig. 5.4), or a red jasper intaglio of Tigranes II of Armenia (fig. 8.1).[82] Chalcedony, at least, is a stone found in northern Asia Minor,[83] and the presumed Laodike portrait is one of the highest quality engraved gems of any period. There are also a number of intaglios of Mithridates VI in the Hermitage in St. Petersburg, which may have originated in the king's collection. Some of these are stylistically remindful of representations of Alexander the Great.[84]

As is often the case with famous personalities from antiquity, only their coinage provides certain portraits. In the Mithridatic dynasty, coinage began during the reign of Mithridates II or III. From the very first issues Pontic coins were noted for their artistic excellence and high-quality engraving—presumably from a local school of engravers that also produced the gems—a hallmark of the Pontic artistic presence.[85] Before the time of Mithridates VI, the quantity of coins struck was small, and except for a few of Laodike the sister-wife of Mithridates IV, they were limited to the kings themselves. The circulation of Pontic coinage was probably originally only within Pontos and the immediately surrounding areas, but by the time of Mithridates VI the number had increased, and Pontic coins could be found as far west as Italy (Poggio Picenze) and east toward the Caspian Sea (at modern Khinisly in Azerbaijan). How much they were actually accepted in regions remote from Pontos is not truly known, and they probably reached these locales when transported by mercenaries who had served in the Pontic army.[86]

There are two different coin portrait types of Mithridates VI, an earlier one that is somewhat more realistic and a later one that has become idealized.[87] The change between type seems to have occurred around 85 BC. A visual imitation of Alexander the Great is apparent, especially in the later type, struck after the first war with Rome, when the king was assuming a posture of liberation that, he hoped, would be remindful of his predecessor. The earliest coins date from around 106 BC and have on their reverse the mythical horse Pegasos, who could be seen as ideologically connecting east and west, an iconography originally adopted by Mithridates IV (fig. 12.3). Pegasos was born out of the remains of the Gorgon Medusa, killed by Perseus (the eponymous ancestor of the Persians) and was given to the Corinthian hero Bellerophon, assisting him on a number of adventures, some of which occurred in territories that would later become the Pontic kingdom. Thus Pegasos was the perfect symbol for the young king: a Greek myth that related both to his homeland and his Persian ancestry.

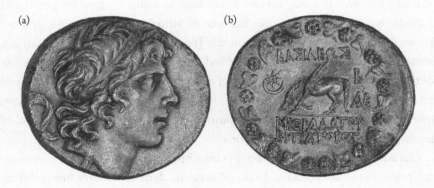

(a) (b)

Figure 12.3 Coin of Mithridates VI with Pegasos: obverse and reverse. American Numismatic Society 1967.152.392. Courtesy American Numismatic Society.

The reverse of the later coin type has a grazing stag, the sacred animal of Artemis, another iconography that linked east and west: Artemis was a Greek goddess with eastern connections but tilted more toward the west than the Pegasos story. Her great cult center was at Ephesos, a locale of particular interest to the king not only for this reason but because it was the administrative center of Roman Asia and thus a focal point for his ambitions. The king enlarged the asylum at the Artemis sanctuary by shooting an arrow for slightly more than a stadion, one of his several imitations of Alexander the Great, who had set its limits at merely a stadion (about 220 yards).[88]

Chapter 13

The End of the Mithridatic Kingdom

THE *LEX MANILIA*

At the beginning of 66 BC, the tribune Gaius Manilius proposed legislation that would assign Pompey the provinces of Cilicia and Bithynia (now, rather optimistically, renamed "Bithynia et Pontus"), allowing him to continue the war against Mithridates.[1] The *lex Manilia* was the Roman reaction to Lucullus's recent failures and the inability of Acilius Glabrio to take any initiative. It was a wide-ranging law, one of the broadest pieces of legislation as yet passed by the Roman Republic, a foreshadowing of the centralized imperial system that was to be established forty years later. As Plutarch wrote, "Thus Roman power was given to a single man."[2] The law also gave Pompey authority to wage war against Tigranes and commands in all the provinces of Asia Minor. It did not pass easily, since there was great opposition to handing so much power to a single person, but both Cicero and Julius Caesar supported the proposal. It was said, perhaps anachronistically, that Caesar's support was because he saw it as a precedent for his own future plans.[3] Cicero's eloquent defense of the legislation provides a detailed account of the views of those who supported it.[4]

Pompey had been active during the immediately previous years. He had defeated Sertorius and his followers, had been involved in eliminating the last supporters of Spartacus, and then had become consul in 70 BC even though underage.[5] Subsequently he had received a command against the pirates, which he handled with great ability, effectively ending piracy in the Mediterranean. When the Manilian law passed, the proconsul was in Cilicia, making final arrangements regarding the disposition of the pirates. Although he pretended to see the law as yet another burden in his life, he was in fact quite pleased, since it catered not only to his sense of ambition but also to his long-standing dislike of Lucullus.[6]

POMPEY IN COMMAND

One of Pompey's first actions was to countermand everything Lucullus had done, including his edicts and the provisions for his supporters. The two commanders had a testy meeting in Galatia before Lucullus returned to Italy, and then Pompey was in full control.[7] He immediately sent Metrophanes—probably the former Pontic commander who had been one of many senior officers to defect to the Romans—to the king, offering friendship and, presumably, to make a general reconnaissance. Yet the king was disdainful of Pompey's overtures and knew that it would be fatal to present himself to the proconsul.[8] Moreover, he expected help from the king of Parthia, Phraates III, who had recently come to the throne and was seen as pliable. But Pompey had already contacted Phraates, who entered into a state of friendship with him and in fact, at Pompey's suggestion, initiated an invasion of Armenia. Mithridates realized that now he had few options and attempted to arrange a truce with Pompey, who asked for both total surrender and the return of the many Roman deserters in the entourage of the king. These were conditions that he found totally unacceptable, and any negotiations failed.

The king felt that if he could draw Pompey into Pontos, his advance would falter for lack of supplies. But the proconsul had had lengthy experience in military logistics, and such was not to be the case. There were several skirmishes, and then a major battle somewhere on the upper Euphrates, in which the king suffered a thorough defeat. Mithridates's vaunted ability to raise manpower was at last having diminishing returns: he could now only acquire untrained soldiers. These attacked without orders, and his cavalry rushed into battle without their horses. The various detachments collided with one another and panicked, eventually being put to flight or becoming captives.[9] Mithridates fled with only his best troops, and those who were sick or unable to travel he had killed. He went to one of his many fortresses, Sinoria, which served as an important treasury, and gathered resources for the journey he was now forced to make.[10] Pompey established himself at Amisos, and numerous regional dynasts came to him, as many as twelve kings, although their names are not recorded. This was another indication of Mithridates's deteriorating fortunes. In fact, Pompey was acting as if he were already governor of a Roman province of Pontos.[11]

Moreover, the local economy was weakening, as Pontos and the Black Sea littoral became more isolated from the Mediterranean.[12] The Roman naval blockade meant that coastal Pontos had less communication and trade with the Aegean, and when Pompey took command, he placed ships along the entire coast from Phoenicia to the Thracian Bosporos, thereby denying Mithridates access to the Mediterranean by any means. Furthermore, he ordered the death penalty for any merchant caught sailing toward the Black Sea.[13] This led to a collapsing economy in Pontos and may have been one of the reasons that the king decided abandonment of his homeland was his only option.

Thus Mithridates was in full retreat. As before, he sought refuge with his son-in-law Tigranes. But the Armenian king was even less willing than before to receive him, since his circumstances had been severely reduced with the loss of Tigranokerta and his Syrian possessions, and he realized that any contact was unwise. Thus he forbade Mithridates entry into Armenia.[14] Tigranes believed, perhaps wrongly, that the king was attempting to have him deposed, and, moreover, he did not want to face the Roman army again. He even offered a reward of one hundred talents for anyone who would capture his father-in-law. In fact, Pompey did invade Armenia, but in a benign manner, and Tigranes agreed to receive a Roman garrison.[15] Then the proconsul set off in pursuit of Mithridates.

THE RETREAT NORTH

It was now late in 66 BC. Mithridates had abandoned Sinoria and was heading toward Colchis. He had few troops beyond his own bodyguard but was well equipped with six thousand talents.[16] The status of Colchis at this time is unknown; the royal governor, Moaphernes, had defected to the Romans in the last years of Lucullus's command, and there is no evidence as to whether he had been replaced.[17] Mithridates's retreat to Colchis was more an act of desperation than any hope of assistance, since he had no other direction in which to go. He eventually reached Dioskourias, located at the northern edge of the territory, where he spent the winter of 66–65 BC. He then decided to continue to the Kimmerian Bosporos and establish himself there, expelling his treacherous son Machares.

Meanwhile Pompey, although theoretically in pursuit of the king, was becoming more interested in the wild and strange country that he was traversing, as well as asserting his own imitation of Alexander the Great rather than continuing to be concerned about the fortunes of Mithridates.[18] This was the world of the Amazons and Jason and the Argonauts, leading up to the high country of the Caucasus. Few if any Romans had ever been in this region, and Pompey was caught by the winter weather. His chronicler, Theophanes of Mytilene, reported on some of the first Roman experiences with high-altitude snows.[19] Eventually Pompey extricated himself with difficulty from the Caucasus and called off any pursuit of Mithridates, returning to the south. He became involved in settling affairs in Syria, which included dissolving the Seleukid empire and creating a Roman province from its final remnants. Moreover, as the latest imitator of Alexander the Great, he wanted to reach the Red Sea and thus see the External Ocean that surrounded the inhabited world, as Alexander had done in India.[20]

In the spring of 65 BC, the king continued to the Kimmerian Bosporos. His journey was not without difficulty, and north of Dioskourias the country became more remote, inhabited by "warlike and strange Skythian peoples." Some of these received him, but others, especially the troublesome Achaians, gave battle, although unsuccessfully.[21] There was also a major earthquake; no details are preserved, but it seems to have impeded Mithridates's passage. A second earthquake occurred after the king arrived in the Bosporos, while he was celebrating the rites of Demeter. This quake caused great damage in both the cities and the countryside and was seen as a portent of the king's coming death as well as a parallel to the signs at his birth and accession.[22]

Eventually he reached the vicinity of the Maiotis (modern Sea of Azov), having passed through the feature known as the Skythian Keyhole, a route that allegedly no one had taken previously. This toponym is impossible to identify but was probably a place on or near the coast where there was a narrow passage, most likely northwest of Dioskourias, where the coastal plain is minimal to non-existent. But it is also probable that the memory of Mithridates's passage was enhanced and a parallel created to Pompey's contemporary exploration of the Caucasus passes, or even Alexander's difficult movement through Cilicia.[23] There is no reason to believe that the Skythian Keyhole is one of the Caucasus passes; the king would have stayed near the coast.

Despite the difficulties with the Achaians, the journey was seen as a heroic progression—another imitation of Alexander—and the king's prestige was still so high that many turned out to greet him and offer support. When he arrived at the Kimmerian Bosporos, he confronted his wayward son.[24] Machares retreated west into the Pontic Chersonesos and eventually was killed or committed suicide. Mithridates established himself at Pantikapaion, the ancient Greek trading center that was now the Bosporanian capital (fig. 13.1). He began to create his last great plan for bringing the Romans to account: he was going to head

Figure 13.1 Pantikapaion. Shutterstock 365774894.

up the Danube and from there invade Italy, cultivating alliances with the Celtic peoples of central Europe and becoming a second Hannibal, fulfilling his never-implemented ideas about European conquest that had begun with Sertorius a decade previously. In conceiving such an expedition Mithridates was influenced by the Hellenistic belief that the Argonauts had returned this way.[25]

Yet those around him were disdainful and even frightened of the plan, but they realized that it was the last effort of someone who wanted to end his life as a man of action. It may be that at this time he also reached out to unspecified "Skythian queens." Appian recorded that they were in Pompey's triumph of 61 BC, along with Colchian, Iberian, and Albanian dynasts (these last two located on the Caspian Sea).[26] No further information was provided, and because "Skythian" had long been a generic term for the peoples at the northern edge of the inhabited world, it is impossible to be precise. Yet the regions on the north shore of the Black Sea are famous for their burials of wealthy royal women, some of which are near Pantikapaion.[27] The Skythian queens who allied with Mithridates and appeared in the triumph are a tantalizing glimpse into the long history of royal women in the Bosporanian region.

Mithridates remained at Pantikapaion for nearly two years, out of the reach of the Romans (Pompey was occupied elsewhere), yet he was a king without a kingdom. He devoted his efforts to gardening, scholarship, and planning his Italian adventure. By late 64 BC, however, he was deteriorating physically, yet this did not temper his resolve to carry out his latest endeavor of invading Italy. His associates became more concerned, realizing that disaster would result, and eventually his son Pharnakes (II), who had often been mentioned as his successor, formed a conspiracy to eliminate his father and become king. A revolt seems to have broken out in Phanagoreia, on the eastern side of the Kimmerian Bosporos, which caused widespread destruction, with the burning of buildings and the hoarding of coins.[28]

In Pantikapaion, about twenty miles away on the European side of the strait, where the king was in residence, matters seemed calmer, but one day in early 63 BC he looked out from the portico of his palace and saw Pharnakes being proclaimed king in the courtyard below. Mithridates was afraid that he would be handed over to the Romans and appear in a triumph. He had poison available, and first gave it to two of his daughters, Mithridatis and Nyssa, who had once been betrothed, respectively, to Ptolemy XII of Egypt and his brother Ptolemy of Cyprus. Both died immediately. But the poison was said to have had no effect on the king, who for many years had been constantly testing antidotes to protect himself. He thus asked a Celtic officer in his entourage, a certain Bituitus, to kill him, who complied. A less dramatic, and probably less reliable, tradition is that he was the victim of a rebellion in his army, a reaction against the planned European expedition.

The story of the poison is suspicious. To be sure, it is commonly reported, with the most complete account by Galen, writing at least two centuries later.[29] Galen's report is introduced by "they say," a way in Greek to indicate something that the author has reservations about. The most obvious concern is that the king, who was an expert on antidotes, would have been unlikely to take a poison that he had every reason to believe would not work. It is more probable that the tale was a created romantic version of the king's death, similar to that of Cleopatra VII and the asp,[30] which glossed over the fact that at the last moment, physically weak and politically destroyed, he was unable to do away with himself and, like Marcus Antonius thirty years later, had to call upon a slave.

Pompey was on the outskirts of Nabataean Petra when he heard the news.[31] He was somewhat annoyed that he had not been present at the end, and he also realized that the death of the king meant that one of the major commissions of the lex Manilia had expired and his legal status in the east could be called into question. He immediately went to Pontos and at either Amisos or Sinope received the embalmed body of the king, which Pharnakes had sent. A bizarre sight greeted Pompey, because there were additionally "many bodies of the royal family," those who had also died in the king's last days. The king had been poorly embalmed and was hardly recognizable. At his own expense Pompey gave Mithridates a royal funeral and buried him in the royal tombs at Sinope. In doing so, he was again imitating Alexander the Great, who buried Dareios III, the last king of Persia. Thus Pompey added to his own long list of emulations of Alexander, especially obvious in his desire to call off the pursuit of Mithridates and mount an expedition deep into the Caucasus. Such an honorable burial of one's opponents would continue: Marcus Antonius would assure it for the Ptolemaic queen Berenike IV and her husband Archelaos (the grandson of Mithridates's general) in 55 BC, and Octavian would do the same for Cleopatra VII twenty-five years later.[32]

Mithridates's personal lands were sold.[33] Pharnakes was officially recognized as a friend and ally of the Romans and was proclaimed (as Pharnakes II) king of Bosporos. The theoretical provincialization of Pontos, assumed under the *lex Manilia*, was now a reality. Pompey returned to Rome and in early 61 BC celebrated a triumph unlike anything Rome had previously seen.[34] It lasted for two days and commemorated his defeat of Mithridates as well as his activities in Syria and Cilicia. Insofar as the Pontic portion was concerned, it included Mithridates's grandson Tigranes (the son of Tigranes II) and five sons and two daughters of the king, as well as the Skythian queens. Various images of Mithridates and Tigranes II were presented, with a tableau of the former's death. As noted, Pompey wore the cloak that had allegedly belonged to Alexander the Great and which had been found in Mithridates's effects.

In the years that followed Pompey made a major reorganization of the eastern Mediterranean in the new environment after the death of the king (and with the simultaneous collapse of the Seleukids). He became the most powerful man in Rome, until 48 BC when he lost out to one even more powerful and capable, Julius Caesar, and was killed in Egypt on 28 September of that year.

THE AFTERMATH

There was yet another attempt to create a kingdom of Pontos, but under a different dynasty. During his actions in the east under his triumviral authority after the death of Julius Caesar, Marcus Antonius returned Pontos to the Mithridatic line, placing on the throne a certain Dareios, a son of Pharnakes II and thus a grandson of Mithridates VI.[35] Little is known about him, and he did not last long, probably from around 39 to 37 BC. He was not satisfactory as king, and when he died or was removed, Antonius could not find a suitable member of the Mithridatic family to succeed him. As was becoming common in the era, he reached outside of royalty for the new king of Pontos, choosing Polemon of Laodikeia, whose father had been of service to the Romans. Eventually he married Pythodoris of Nysa, also from a family known to the triumvir.[36] Under the newly royal couple and their descendants, Pontos remained an allied kingdom until the 60s AD, when it was reprovincialized. But no descendant of the Mithridatids ever ruled there again.

In Bosporos, Pharnakes II proved to be an unreliable ally. He began an expansionist policy, attempting to reconstitute his father's kingdom and calling himself "great king." Within a few years of his accession, he attacked Pontos. He had left one of his officers, Asandros, in charge of Bosporos, who revolted in 47 BC. Julius Caesar confronted Pharnakes in Pontos and drove him back to Bosporos, where he was killed by Asandros.[37] Asandros was allowed a kingship by the Romans, and he astutely married Dynamis, Pharnakes's daughter (and thus a granddaughter of Mithridates VI). The two shared power in Bosporos for thirty years, and then Dynamis ruled alone, conscious of her notable descent, for twenty more.[38] She was the matriarch of a royal line that continued into at least the third century AD; thus the dynasty established by Mithridates I the Founder in the early third century BC lasted for six hundred years, probably the longest such survival in antiquity.

THE LEGACY IN ANTIQUITY

Two decades after his death, Cicero called Mithridates VI "the greatest king since Alexander."[39] Although Cleopatra VII is often seen as the last great opponent of the Roman Republic, her opposition only occupied the last period of her life, yet Mithridates contended with it for nearly thirty years. As the Republic evolved into an empire, the kings and queens around its fringes, such as Herod the Great of Judaea, Archelaos of Cappadocia (the great-grandson of Mithridates's commander), Dynamis of Bosporos, and Juba II and Cleopatra

Selene of Mauretania, sought accommodation with Rome as allied monarchs rather than confrontation.

The history of the Hellenistic period in the eastern Mediterranean was repeatedly one of tension between east and west, or Europe and Asia. In fact, this began with the Trojan War (or, at least, the received interpretation of it in later Greek times), continued in the Persian Wars of the early fifth century BC, and culminated with Alexander the Great, who, when he landed in Asia in 334 BC, immediately went to offer sacrifice at Troy.[40] The Mithridatic dynasty came into being during the aftermath of Alexander's expedition but was actually Persian in origin: Mithridates I the Founder was descended from Persian officers in northwest Asia Minor.[41] But the dynasty would steadily become hellenized, eventually claiming ancestry from both Persian royalty and Alexander.[42] Thus the tension between east and west evolved into a blending, much as the Romans were to adopt a Trojan, Aeneas, as their founder. Yet, as the career of Mithridates VI shows, antagonism between Europe and Asia remained even as their cultures were assimilated. The Persian heritage survived in the dynasty until its final days, with Persian divinities continuing to be worshipped.[43]

With their Persian origins, the Mithridatids were, in theory, more connected historically to the Armenians and Parthians than to the Greek world, and it is no accident that Mithridates VI reached out to both in his final days. But their gradual hellenization gave them a western orientation that those dynasties never had. As the power of Rome increased, the Mithridatids became the champion of Greek ways against the invasive Romans, and when Mithridates VI took the surname Dionysos, who was an ancestor of Alexander the Great, he placed himself firmly in the Greek tradition.

When the dynasty in Pontos ended in 63 BC, the only Hellenistic kingdom left was that of the Ptolemies, which survived another thirty-three years. Members of Mithridates's circle were connected with Alexandria; Zopyros, a correspondent of the king and a physician at the court of Ptolemy XII, is probably the best example.[44] The last Ptolemaic monarch, Cleopatra VII, who came to the throne twelve years after the death of Mithridates, carried on the tradition of the Mithridatic dynasty, with a similar vision of how eastern culture might survive in a Roman world.[45] Cleopatra also shared personality traits with the king: she was an accomplished linguist and a student of medicine.

For 250 years the Mithridatic dynasty was a powerful force in the world between the time of Alexander the Great and the Roman Empire. It collapsed for the same reason that all the Hellenistic dynasties did: an inability to reconcile its needs with those of an ever-expanding Roman Republic, and a failure to understand the complexities of the Roman state. Tension between Pontos and Rome began at the time of Pharnakes I in the early second century BC and eventually overwhelmed the kingdom. Like Hannibal and Cleopatra, the Mithridatic kings could not understand the Romans, and they failed to realize the limited effect that internal dissension at Rome would have on the Republic's long-term foreign needs. Yet, even though the kingdom of Pontos as established by Mithridates I in the early third century BC was gone by 63 BC, the descendants of the Mithridatids would continue to rule in various territories, far outlasting those of any other Hellenistic dynasty and surviving even longer than the family of the emperor Augustus himself.[46]

THE AFTERLIFE

The legend of Mithridates VI began almost at the moment of his death. Pompey's elaborate triumph of 61 BC helped to create a mythic image of the king, and within the year the poet Archias had written an account of his wars with Rome, with a focus on the role of Lucullus.[47] He had already written about Gaius Marius, and his works were an early example of the historical-poetic genre best known from the *Civil War* of Lucan. Lucan's contemporary the emperor Nero also wrote a poem about the king.[48] The earlier history of the Mithridatic dynasty never entered popular imagination and was largely forgotten as the career of Mithridates VI came to dominate the tradition, treated in detail by ancient writers such as Sallust, Strabo, and Appian.

A few months after the death of Mithridates VI, Gaius Octavius was born in a house on the Palatine in Rome.[49] As the emperor Augustus, he would in time create a new Roman state that adopted many of the features of Hellenistic monarchy. Even in antiquity, the connection between the world of Mithridates and that of Augustan Rome was apparent. Rome, in encircling the Mediterranean, fulfilled the stillborn plans of the last Hellenistic king of Pontos.[50]

The career of Mithridates VI still resonated in late antiquity. In the fifth century AD, at the fortified estate of Burgus in Aquitania (located just north of Bordeaux at modern Bourg-sur-Gironde), wall paintings depicted elements of the king's career. They were commissioned by a prominent local, Pontius Leontinus, and were described poetically by his friend the poet and political leader Sidonius Apollinaris.[51] The paintings were a vast cycle of historical and mythological subjects, with one section showing Mithridates's sacrifices of white horses to Poseidon at Sinope and the siege of Kyzikos, in which Lucullus was also represented. Sidonius's description is doubtless condensed, and there is no indication as to why events from the life of Mithridates were chosen or why there was a desire to depict such topics in late antique Aquitania. Yet, if nothing else, the paintings demonstrated the still-mythic nature of the career of the king at such a late date, and far from Pontos.

Interest in Mithridates VI continued in the post-antique world, where the king was praised for his opposition to Rome. The manner of his death became romanticized, especially the conflict between him and his son Pharnakes II.[52] Giovanni Boccaccio in his De casibus virorum illustrium (On the Fall of Famous Men), written in the mid-fourteenth century, described the death of the king, creating a parallel with other famous personalities of the era, including Pompey, Caesar, Antonius, and Cleopatra VII. By the fifteenth century editions of Boccaccio's work included illustrations showing the death of the king. The mithridatum jar attributed to Annibale Fontana has a representation of the same event.[53] In the seventeenth century this was a popular dramatic subject, most notably in Jean Racine's Mithridate (1673), which emphasized the tension between Mithridates and Pharnakes but also introduced a romantic attachment between the latter and his stepmother Monime. The play was popular at the court of Louis XIV, who also commissioned a portrait of Mithridates, now at Versailles.

Racine's play was the inspiration for numerous operatic treatments of the death of the king. The first of note is Alessandro Scarlatti's Mithridate Eupatore (Venice 1707). The most famous is Mozart's Mithridate, re di Ponto (Milan 1770). Both focus on the death of the king and the situation with Pharnakes but, as was typical in opera seria of the eighteenth century, incorporate numerous details from elsewhere in Greco-Roman culture. Scarlatti's work has a revenge motif taken from the tale of Elektra, and Mozart's has some of the elements from the Oedipus story that appeared in Racine's play.

The linguistic abilities of the king were also considered notable in early modern times. Conrad Gesner's Mithridates, sive de differentis linguarum (1555) used the king's name as the title for a linguistic encyclopedia, and Johann Christoff Adelung did the same in his Mithridates, oder allgemeine Sprachenkunde (1806). The diversity of the king's reputation was thus of great interest in a variety of disciplines, and it survives into modern times, where fictionalized accounts of his career continue to appear.

ABBREVIATIONS

ABSA	*Annual of the British School at Athens*
AHB	*Ancient History Bulletin*
AJA	*American Journal of Archaeology*
AJAH	*American Journal of Ancient History*
AJP	*American Journal of Philology*
AK	*Antike Kunst*
ANRW	*Aufstieg und Niedergang der Römischen Welt*
AncSoc	*Ancient Society*
AR	*Archaeological Reports*
BAI	*Bulletin of the Asia Institute*
BAR-IS	British Archaeological Reports, International Series
BCH	*Bulletin de correspondance hellénique*
BMC	*British Museum Catalogue of Coins*
BNJ	*Brill's New Jacoby*
BNP	*Brill's New Pauly*
CAH	*Cambridge Ancient History*
CB	*Classical Bulletin*
CÉA	*Cahiers des études anciennes*
CP	*Classical Philology*
DHA	*Dialogues d'histoire ancienne*
EA	*Epigraphica Anatolica*
EANS	*Encyclopedia of Ancient Natural Scientists* (ed. Paul T. Keyser and Georgia L. Irby-Massie, New York 2008)
ESM	*Early Science and Medicine*

FGrHist	*Fragmente der griechischen Historiker*
G&R	*Greece and Rome*
GH	*Geographica Historica*
GNS	*Gazette numismatique suisse*
HBA	*Hamburger Beiträge zur Archäologie*
HSCP	*Harvard Studies in Classical Philology*
IDélos	*Inscriptions de Délos*
IG	*Inscriptiones Graecae*
IGBulg	*Inscriptiones Graecae in Bulgaria repertae*
IstMitt	*Istanbuler Mitteilungen*
JHS	*Journal of Hellenic Studies*
JÖAI	*Jahreshefte des Österreichischen Archäologischen Institutes in Wien*
JRS	*Journal of Roman Studies*
JSav	*Journal des savants*
JWAG	*Journal of the Walters Art Gallery*
OGIS	*Orientis Graeci Inscriptiones Selectae* (ed. Wilhelm Dittenberger, Leipzig 1905)
ORom	*Opuscula Romana*
OT	*Orbis Terrarum*
PECS	*Princeton Encyclopedia of Classical Sites*
RE	*Paulys Real-Encyclopädie der Classichen Altertumswissenschaft* (Pauly-Wissowa)
RÉA	*Revue des études anciennes*
REArm	*Révue des études armeniennes*
RFIC	*Rivista di filologia e di istruzione classica, Torino*
RhM	*Rheinisches Museum für Philologie*
RömMitt	*Römische Mitteilungen*
SCI	*Scripta Classical Israelica*
SEG	*Supplementum Epigraphicum Graecum*
SIG	*Sylloge inscriptionum graecarum*
VDI	*Vestnik drevnei istorii*
ZPE	*Zeitschrift für Papyrologie und Epigraphik*

NOTES

Preface

1. Duane W. Roller, *Cleopatra's Daughter and Other Royal Women of the Augustan Era* (Oxford 2018) 79–120.

Introduction

1. Cicero, *Academica* 2.3.
2. Herodotos 1.110.
3. Rüdiger Schmitt, "Iranische Personennamen auf griechischen Inschriften," in *Actes du VIIe Congrès International d'Épigraphie Grecque et Latine* (ed. D. M. Pippidi, Paris 1979) 138–52; Richard Bodeüs, "Le premier nom propre iranien du groupe *Mitra*- dans les sources grecques," in *Archeologie et philologie dans l'étude des civilisations orientales* (ed. A. Theodorides et al., Leuven 1986) 213–16.
4. Stephen Mitchell, "In Search of the Pontic Community," in *Representations of Empire: Rome and the Mediterranean World* (ed. Alan K. Bowman, Oxford 2002) 50–52.
5. It did not appear until late antiquity (Orosius 1.26).

Chapter 1

1. Homer, *Iliad* 1.350.
2. Stephanie West, "'The Most Marvellous of All Seas': The Greek Encounter With the Euxine," *G&R* 50 (2003) 158.
3. John Boardman, *The Greeks Overseas: Their Early Colonies and Trade* (4th ed., London 1999) 240.
4. See, for example, the list at Strabo, *Geography* 2.5.19; Mitchell, "In Search" 38–39.
5. Xenophon, *Anabasis* 5.6.15, 19, 25; 6.2.4.
6. Herodotos 3.94, 7.78.
7. *BNP Historical Atlas* 86–87.
8. Xenophon, *Anabasis* 4.8.22–28.
9. Strabo, *Geography* 11.2.18.
10. Herodotos 1.6, 75; Strabo, *Geography* 12.1.3.

11. Foundation dates for Greek cities along the Black Sea littoral remain unclear and vary greatly, as do the actual founders, although there is no doubt that Miletos was heavily involved throughout the region and that most of these cities existed before the rise of the Pontic kingdom. See Brian C. McGing, *The Foreign Policy of Mithridates VI Eupator, King of Pontus* (Leiden 1986) 3–4; Boardman, *Greeks Overseas* 254–55.

12. Herodotos 1.72, 2.34; Strabo, *Geography* 12.2.10.

13. Xenophon, *Anabasis* 5.5.10, 6.1.15; Strabo, *Geography* 7.4.3, 12.3.11.

14. *BMC Pontus, Paphlagonia, Bithynia and the Kingdom of Bosporus*, p. 96, nos. 8–10.

15. Cornelius Nepos, *Datames* 1.11; Polyainos, *Stratagems* 7.29.

16. Waldemar Heckel, *Who's Who in the Age of Alexander the Great* (Oxford 2006) 44.

17. *BMC Pontus*, p. 96–7, nos. 11–25.

18. Strabo, *Geography* 12.3.11.

19. Strabo, *Geography* 12.3.14–15; Memnon 16.2.

20. Strabo, *Geography* 12.3.28.

21. Strabo, *Geography* 11.2.18; David Braund, *Georgia in Antiquity* (Oxford 1994) 153–55.

22. Memnon 9.4; Heckel, *Who's Who* 21.

23. Ismail Kaygusuz, "Zwei Neue Inschriften aus Ilgaz (Olgassys) und Kimiatene," *EA* 1 (1983) 59–60; Mitchell, "In Search" 53–54.

24. Strabo, *Geography* 12.3.41; Strabo, *Géographie* 9 (ed. François Lasserre, Paris 2003) 200.

25. Strabo, *Geography* 12.3.39; D. R. Wilson, "Amaseia," *PECS* 47.

26. Robert Fleischer, "The Rock-Tombs of the Pontic Kings in Amaseia (Amasya)," in *Mithridates VI and the Pontic Kingdom* (ed. Jakob Munk Høtje, Aarhus 2009) 109–20; Fleischer, *Der Felsgräber der Könige von Pontos in Amasya* (Tübingen 2017).

27. Emine Sökmen, "Characteristics of the Temple States in Pontos," in *Mithridates VI and the Pontic Kingdom* (ed. Jakob Munk Højte, Aarhus 2009) 277–87.

28. Roller, *Cleopatra's Daughter* 121–23.

29. Diodoros 31.19.1; Strabo, *Geography* 12.3.31; D. R. Wilson, "Neocaesarea," *PECS* 620.

30. Strabo, *Geography* 12.3.32–36; Strabo, *Géographie* 9 (ed. Lasserre) 99.

31. *OGIS* 372; Plutarch, *Lucullus* 17.

32. Plutarch, *Antonius* 3; Dio 39.57–58.

33. *BNP Chronologies* 111–12.

34. D. R. Wilson, "Comana Pontica," *PECS* 234. A recent archaeological survey has illuminated some of the site and its environs, but evidence remains sparse for the period of the Pontic kingdom. See Deniz Burlu Erciyas, "Komana Pontike: A City or a Sanctuary?" in *Mithridates VI and the Pontic Kingdom* (ed. Jakob Munk Højte, Aarhus 2009) 298–312.

35. Strabo, *Geography* 11.8.4; 12.3.37; D. R. Wilson, "Zela," *PECS* 999.

36. Christian Marek, "Hellenisation and Romanisation in Pontos-Bithynia: An Overview," in *Mithridates VI and the Pontic Kingdom* (ed. Jakob Munk Højte, Aarhus 2009) 36–37.

37. Homer, *Iliad* 2.851–77, 3.187–89; Strabo, *Geography* 12.3.24; R. Hope Simpson and J. F. Lazenby, *The Catalogue of The Ships in Homer's* Iliad (Oxford 1970) 176–83.

38. Duane W. Roller, *A Historical and Topographical Guide to the Geography of Strabo* (Cambridge 2018) 707.

39. Strabo, *Geography* 11.5.1–4.

40. Diodoros 17.77.

41. Appian, *Mithridateios* 117.

42. McGing, *Foreign Policy* 11.

43. Pindar F173; Strabo, *Geography* 16.1.2; see also 12.3.9.

44. Strabo, *Geography* 12.3.37.

45. Herodotos 3.94, 7.78; Strabo, *Geography* 11.2.18.

46. Strabo, *Geography* 11.2.18.
47. Arrian, *Periplous of the Euxine Sea* 1.
48. Aeschylus, *Prometheus Bound* 723–25; Herodotos 4.110; Strabo, *Geography* 12.3.15, 30; Apollonios, *Bibliotheke* 2.5.9.
49. Xenophon, *Anabasis* 6.1.15.
50. Theophrastos, *Research on Plants* 4.5.5; Strabo, *Geography* 12.3.12.
51. Strabo, *Geography* 12.3.13–15.
52. Strabo, *Geography* 12.3.38.
53. Strabo, *Geography* 7.6.2, 12.3.19; Athenaios 6.274f–275a.
54. Strabo, *Geography* 12.3.40; Vitruvius 7.7.5; Pliny, *Natural History* 33.79; Roller, *Historical and Topographical Guide* 717.
55. Homer, *Iliad* 2.856–57; Strabo, *Geography* 12.3.22; M. Rostovtzeff, *Social and Economic History of the Hellenistic World* (Oxford 1941) 572–73.
56. Strabo, *Geography* 12.3.19.
57. Strabo, *Geography* 12.2.10; Dioskourides 5.94–5; Pliny, *Natural History* 33.111–22.
58. Strabo, *Geography* 16.1.24; Dioskourides 1.15; Pliny, *Natural History* 12.48–49; Andrew Dalby, *Food in the Ancient World From A to Z* (London 2003) 8.
59. Christian Habicht, *Athens From Alexander to Antony* (tr. Deborah Lucas Schneider, Cambridge, Mass. 1997) 226–27.
60. *SIG* 40.
61. Strabo, *Geography* 12.3.28.

Chapter 2

1. Strabo, *Geography* 12.3.41.
2. Polybios 5.43.2; Diodoros 19.40.2; Sallust, *Histories* 2.59; Appian, *Mithridateios* 112; *de viris illustribus* 76; Justin, *Epitome* 38.7.1; Charlotte Lerouge-Cohen, "Persianism in the Kingdom of Pontic Kappadokia: The Genealogical Claims of the Mithridatids," in *Persianism in Antiquity* (ed. Rolf Strootman and Miguel John Versluys, Stuttgart 2017) 223–33.
3. McGing, *Foreign Policy* 13; A. B. Bosworth and P. V. Wheatley, "The Origins of the Pontic House," *JHS* 118 (1998) 155–64.
4. Herodotos 7.72.
5. Diodoros 16.90.2, 20.111.4.
6. Brian C. McGing, "The Kings of Pontus: Some Problems of Identity and Date," *RhM* 129 (1986) 249–50. See also Plutarch, *Demetrios* 4.1.
7. Sallust, *Histories* 2.59; Herodotos 7.66; Thucydides 1.129; Jack Martin Balcer, *A Prosopographical Study of the Ancient Persians Royal and Noble c. 550–450 BC* (Lewiston, N.Y. 1993) 83–85; Luís Ballesteros-Pastor, "Los herederos de Artabazo. La satrapía de Dascilio en la tradición de la dinastía Mitridátida," *Klio* 94 (2012) 366–79.
8. Diodoros 20.111.4.
9. The idea that the ancestral seat of the Founder was Kios is still promoted, despite the flaws in such an assumption: see Peter Panitschek, "Zu den Genealogischen Konstruction der Dynastien von Pontos," *RSA* 17/18 (1987–88) 73–95; A. Billows, *Antigonos the One-Eyed and the Creation of the Hellenistic State* (Berkeley 1997) 403–5. For the most compelling argument against Kios, see Bosworth and Wheatley, "Origins" 155–56.
10. Herodotos 5.122; Polybios 15.23; Pliny, *Natural History* 5.144; Getzel M. Cohen, *The Hellenistic Settlements in Europe, the Islands, and Asia Minor* (Berkeley 1995) 405–6.
11. Strabo, *Geography* 12.3.41.

12. Diodoros (14.20.2) recorded that Cyrus the Great moved west "to Tarsos, the greatest city in Cilicia, and quickly became master of it." Diodoros's context makes it clear that Cyrus conquered Cilicia, not Tarsos.

13. Appian, *Mithridateios* 77.

14. For a good summary of the generation after the death of Alexander, see David Braund, "After Alexander: The Emergence of the Hellenistic World 323–281," in *A Companion to the Hellenistic World* (ed. Andrew Erskine, Oxford 2003) 19–34.

15. Heckel, *Who's Who* 32–34.

16. Heckel, *Who's Who* 109. The primary ancient source for Demetrios is Plutarch's biography.

17. Diodoros 20.53; Plutarch, *Demetrios* 10; Claire Préaux, *Le monde hellénistique* (Paris 1978), vol. 1, pp. 183–84; Erich S. Gruen, "The Coronation of the Diadochoi," in *The Craft of the Ancient Historian* (ed. John William Eadie and Josiah Ober, Lanham, Md. 1985) 253–71.

18. Diodoros 18.39.7, 19.63–64; Heckel, *Who's Who* 79–81; Braund, "After Alexander" 29–30.

19. Heckel, *Who's Who* 246–48.

20. Heckel, *Who's Who* 153–55; Braund, "After Alexander" 54–46; Bosworth and Wheatley, "Origins" 164.

21. Billows, *Antigonos* 404–5.

22. Diodoros 20.111.4.

23. See, for example, Pliny, *Natural History* 6.8–9; Josephus, *Jewish Antiquities* 13.286.

24. Hieronymos of Kardia (*FGrHist* no. 154) F7; Heckel, *Who's Who* 139–40.

25. Diodoros 19.69; Appian, *Syriaka* 54; Plutarch, *Demetrios* 4, 5.2; P. V. Wheatley, "The Lifespan of Demetrius Poliorcetes," *Historia* 46 (1997) 19–20.

26. Diodoros 19.40.2.

27. Cornelius Nepos, *Eumenes* 1–13; Plutarch, *Eumenes* 19; Heckel, *Who's Who* 120–21.

28. Diodoros 19.40.2.

29. Plutarch, *Demetrios* 4; Plutarch, *Sayings of Kings and Commanders* 183a; Appian, *Mithridateios* 9.

30. Herodotos 1.108–13. Hundreds of years later the Christian scholar Tertullian used Antigonos's dream as an example of the veracity of such prophecies (*De anima* 46).

31. Diodoros 19.69.1; Plutarch, *Demetrios* 5.2; Appian, *Syriaka* 54.

32. Bosworth and Wheatley, "Origins" 183–84.

33. Strabo, *Geography* 12.3.41.

34. Appian, *Mithridateios* 9.

35. Diodoros 20.111.4.

36. Diodoros 20.107–9.

37. Braund, "After Alexander" 31–32.

38. Strabo, *Geography* 13.4.1.

39. Appian, *Mithridateios* 9. For Hellenistic Cappadocia, see Oleg L. Gabelko, "Bithynia and Cappadocia: Royal Courts and Ruling Society in Minor Hellenistic Monarchies," in *The Hellenistic Court: Monarchic Power and Elite Society From Alexander to Cleopatra* (ed. Andrew Erskine et al., Swansea 2017) 319–42. See also Appian, *Histoire romaine* 12: *la guerre de Mithridate* (tr. and ed. Paul Goukowsky, Paris 2003) 132.

40. Justin, *Epitome* 38.5.3.

41. Christian Habicht, "Zipoites [I]," *RE* 2. ser. 10 (1972) 451–52; F. W. Walbank, "Monarchies and Monarchic Ideas," *CAH* 7.1 (2nd ed. 1984) 63.

42. Synkellos, *Ekloga Chronographia* 332 (Georgios Synkellos, *The Chronography of George Synkellos* [tr. William Adler and Paul Tuffin, Oxford 2002]).

43. Plutarch, *Demetrios* 4.4; Appian, *Mithridateios* 9, 112; McGing, "Kings" 250–51; *BNP Chronologies* 110.

44. Gerhard Perl, "Zur Chronologie der Königreiche Bithynia, Pontos und Bosporos," in *Studien zur Geschichte und Philosophie des Altertums* (ed. J. Harmatta, Amsterdam 1968) 299–306.
45. Fleischer, "Rock-Tombs" 109–19.
46. Barclay V. Head, *Historia Numorum* (Oxford 1911) 499–503.
47. Cohen, *Hellenistic Settlements in Europe* 383–84.
48. Memnon 9.4; McGing, *Foreign Policy* 18.
49. Strabo, *Geography* 13.4.1; Pausanias 1.8.1, 1.10.4; Memnon 7.1–2.
50. Pompeius Trogus, *Prologue* 17; McGing, *Foreign Policy* 17–20.
51. Memnon 8.1–3; Justin, *Epitome* 17.2; Appian, *Syriaka* 62.
52. Justin, *Epitome* 25.1–2.
53. Stephen Mitchell, "The Galatians: Representation and Reality," in *A Companion to the Hellenistic World* (ed. Andrew Erskine, London 2005) 280–93.
54. Apollonios (*FGrHist* no. 740) F14.
55. Günther Hölbl, *A History of the Ptolemaic Empire* (tr. Tina Saavedra, London 2001) 40.
56. Arrian, *Anabasis* 2.4.1; Pausanias 1.4.5; Stephanos of Byzantion, "Ankyra"; A. B. Bosworth, *A Historical Commentary on Arrian's History of Alexander* (Oxford 1980–1995), vol. 1, p. 188.
57. Stephen Mitchell, "Tavium," *PECS* 887.

Chapter 3

1. Xenophon, *Hellenika* 1.4.7; Demosthenes, *Against Aristokrates* 141.
2. Memnon 16.1.
3. Memnon 14.16.
4. Nymphis (*FGrHist* no. 432) T4.
5. Polybios 5.88–90; F. W. Walbank, *A Historical Commentary on Polybius* (Oxford 1970–1979), vol. 1, pp. 616–22.
6. *BNP Historical Atlas of the Ancient World* 116–17.
7. Laodike is one of the most common Hellenistic royal names. Most of those so named were Seleukids, either by birth or marriage, and a list appears in John D. Grainger, *A Seleukid Prosopography* (Leiden 1997) 47–51. Grainger's numbering of the various people named Laodike—which is not strictly chronological—is followed herein. In a few cases, there are personalities called Laodike who were not Seleukid; these are not given numbers, but are described merely in terms of their family relationships.
8. Homer, *Iliad* 3.122–24.
9. Heckel, *Who's Who* 145–46.
10. Eusebios, *Chronicle* 1.251.
11. Oleg L. Galbelko, "The Dynastic History of the Hellenistic Monarchies of Asia Minor According to the *Chronography* of George Synkellos," in *Mithridates VI and the Pontic Kingdom* (ed. Jakob Munk Højte, Aarhus 2009) 50–51.
12. See p. 65 of this volume.
13. Heinz Heinen, "The Syrian-Egyptian Wars and the New Kingdoms of Asia Minor," *CAH* 7.1 (2nd ed. 1984) 412–45.
14. Justin, *Epitome* 38.5.3.
15. Polybios 4.48, 5.57, 5.74.4–5, 8.14–21; Walbank, *Historical Commentary*, vol. 1, p. 501–2, 600.
16. W. W. Tarn, *The Greeks in Bactria and India* (3rd ed., Chicago 1985) 196–97.
17. Polybios 5.43.1–4; Getzel M. Cohen, *The Hellenistic Settlements in Syria, the Red Sea Basin, and North Africa* (Berkeley 2006) 190–97; McGing, *Foreign Policy* 22–23.

18. On Laodike XI, see John Ma, *Antiochos III and the Cities of Western Asia Minor* (Oxford 1999) 222–25, and Gillian Ramsay, "The Queen and The City: Royal Female Intervention and Patronage in Hellenistic Civic Communities," in *Gender and the City before Modernity* (ed. Lin Foxhall and Gabriele Neher, Oxford 2013) 20–37 (both of whom considered this Laodike the third of that name).

19. C. Bradford Welles, *Royal Correspondence in the Hellenistic Period* (New Haven 1934) 156–65. The priestess appointed by Antiochos was a certain Berenike, a minor member of the Ptolemaic family. The letter, set up on an inscription found at modern Durdurkar, near the ancient town of Eriza in Karia, is not dated, but Anaximbrotos passed it on to a certain Dionytas, a local official, and dated his note to the equivalent of May 9, 204 BC.

20. Stanley M. Burstein (ed.), *The Hellenistic Age from the Battle of Ipsos to the Death of Kleopatra VII* (Cambridge 1985), no. 33.

21. Burstein, *Hellenistic Age*, no. 36.

22. Polybios 11.34.8–9; Walbank, *Historical Commentary*, vol. 2, p. 313.

23. Strabo, *Geography* 11.11.1; Justin, *Epitome* 41.6.4; Roller, *Historical and Topographical Guide* 664.

24. Livy 42.19.

25. Polybios 31.7.2; Diodoros 31.19.7; Appian, *Syriaka* 5; Walbank, *Historical Commentary*, vol. 3, pp. 171–72.

26. *OGIS* 251–52; Welles, Royal Correspondence 159–60; Grainger, *Seleukid Prosopography* 48; Georges Le Rider, "L'enfant-roi Antiochos et la reine Laodice," *BCH* 110 (1986) 409–17.

27. Heckel, *Who's Who* 90.

28. Erich S. Gruen, *The Hellenistic World and the Coming of Rome* (Berkeley 1984) 678–92.

29. Livy 35.13.4; Porphyrios F47; Appian, *Syriaka* 5.

30. Žarko Petković, "Mithridates II and Antiochos Hierax," *Klio* 91 (2009) 378–83.

31. Polybios 5.74.5; Edwyn Robert Bevan, *The House of Seleucus* (London 1902), vol. 1, p. 327.

32. Pompeius Trogus, *Prologue* 27; Plutarch, *Sayings of Kings and Commanders* 183f–184a; Plutarch, *On Brotherly Love* 18.489a; Justin, *Epitome* 27.6–12; Eusebios, *Chronicle* 1.251.

33. David Magie, *Roman Rule in Asia Minor* (Princeton 1950) 736–39.

34. Justin, *Epitome* 38.5.3.

35. Polybios 4.56.

36. Walbank, *Historical Commentary*, vol. 1, pp. 511–13.

37. Polybios 4.47–52.

38. *BMC Pontus*, p. xxii–xxiii; Head, *Historia Numorum* 500; McGing, *Foreign Policy* 20; François de Callataÿ, "The First Royal Coinages of Pontos (from Mithridates III to Mithridates V)," in *Mithridates VI and the Pontic Kingdom* (ed. Jacob Munk Højte, Aarhus 2009) 63–94.

Chapter 4

1. Pompeius Trogus, *Prologue* 32; Mario Segre, "Due nuovi testi storici," *RFIC* 60 (1932) 446–52; Christian Habicht, "Über die Kriege zwischen Pergamon und Bithynien," *Hermes* 84 (1956) 90–96; McGing, *Foreign Policy* 25–26.

2. Plutarch, *Demetrios* 4.4; Appian, *Mithridateios* 9, 112; *BNP Chronologies* 110. Mithridates III is cited in *OGIS* 375.

3. Magie, *Roman Rule* 1088.

4. Fleischer, "Rock-Tombs" 115.

5. de Callataÿ, "First Royal Coinage" 66–69; Dimitris Plantzos, *Hellenistic Engraved Gems* (Oxford 1999) plate 94, no. 13.

6. McGing, *Foreign Policy* 97; Lâtife Summerer, "Das pontische Wappen: Zur Astralsymbolik auf den pontischen Münzen," *Chiron* 25 (1995) 305–14. These coins have also been attributed to Mithridates II: *BMC Pontus*, p. 42.

7. For a good summary of·these years, see Peter Derow, "The Arrival of Rome: From the Illyrian Wars to the Fall of Macedon," in *A Companion to the Hellenistic World* (ed. Andrew Erskine, Oxford 2003) 51–70.

8. Polybios 21.43–46; Livy 38.38–39; Appian, *Syriaka* 37–39; Walbank, *Historical Commentary*, vol. 3, pp. 156–75.

9. Livy 33.49.5–8; Justin, *Epitome* 31.1–7; Cornelius Nepos, *Hannibal* 7–8.

10. Plutarch, *Lucullus* 31.3–4. The extant remnants of Hannibal's writings are collected as *FGrHist* no. 181; see also Livy 39.51; Cornelius Nepos, *Hannibal* 12–13; Plutarch, *Flamininus* 20; Appian, *Syriaka* 11.

11. Polybios 23.9.1–14.

12. Erich Diehl, "Pharnakes [1]," *RE* 19 (1938) 1849–51.

13. See pp. 000–000 of this volume.

14. Polybios 33.12.1; Walbank, *Historical Commentary*, vol. 3, p. 555; Théodore Reinach, "Note sur une inscription de Délos en l'honneur de Laodice (Philadelphe), princesse du Pont," *BCH* 34 (1910) 429–31.

15. Josef Wiesehöfer, *Ancient Persia from 550 BC to 650 AD* (tr. Azizeh Azodi, London 1996) 68–72; Balcer, *Prosopographical Study* 83–84.

16. Polybios 21.45.8–10; Livy 38.39.14–17; Justin, *Epitome* 38.5.3.

17. Pompeius Trogus, *Prologue* 32; Justin, *Epitome* 32.4; Cornelius Nepos, *Hannibal* 10–12.

18. The name "Pontos," to be sure, is topographically vague and may merely refer to the Black Sea region (Žarko Petković, "The Aftermath of the Apamean Settlement: Early Challenges to the New Order in Asia Minor," *Klio* 94 [2012] 359).

19. Polybios later met Ortiagon's widow, Chiomara, who may have been the source for certain aspects of his career and the eulogistic assessment of his character: Polybios 21.38, 22.21; Walbank, *Historical Commentary*, vol. 3, pp. 151–52.

20. Polybios 22.21, 23.1.4; Livy 39.46.9; Walbank, *Historical Commentary*, vol. 3, p. 212.

21. *OGIS* 298; Peter Thonemann, "The Attalid State, 188–133 BC," in *Attalid Asia Minor* (ed. Peter Thonemann, Oxford 2013) 35–36.

22. Polybios 23.1.4; Livy 39.46.6–9.

23. Polybios 23.8–9.

24. Stanley M. Burstein, "The Aftermath of the Peace of Apamea," *AJAH* 5 (1980) 2.

25. Polybios 23.9.2–3, 24.1.3; Livy 40.2.6; Strabo, *Geography* 12.3.11.

26. Strabo, *Geography* 12.3.17, 28; McGing, *Foreign Policy* 26.

27. Strabo, *Geography* 12.3.17; Arrian, *Periplous of the Euxine Sea* 16; Cohen, *Hellenistic Settlements in Europe* 387–88.

28. Magie, *Roman Rule* 184–85.

29. Strabo, *Geography* 12.3.11.

30. Polybios 25.2.3–4; Justin, *Epitome* 38.5.3; Burstein, "Aftermath" 2.

31. Polybios 24.1, 14–15; Christian Habicht, "The Seleucids and Their Rivals," *CAH* 8 (2nd ed., 1989) 328–30 Altay Coşkun, "The War of Brothers, The Third Syrian War, and the Battle of Ankyra (246–241 BC): A Reappraisal," in *The Seleukid Empire 281–222 BC* (ed. Kyle Erickson, Swansea 2018) 197–252.

32. Pausanias 1.26.2; Habicht, *Athens* 95–96.

33. Livy 42.57.7–9; Walbank, *Historical Commentary*, vol. 3, pp. 267–68.

34. Polybios 25.2.9; Livy 38.26.4; Strabo, *Geography* 12.3.41.

35. Diodoros 29.23; Strabo, *Geography* 13.4.1.

36. Polybios 27.7.5.
37. Diodoros 29.24; Polybios F96 = *Souda*, "Akeraios."
38. Polybios 23.5.1.
39. Polybios 36.15; Justin, *Epitome* 34.4.1; Appian, *Mithridateios* 4–7.
40. Polybios 25.2.3–13; Habicht, "Seleucids" 329–30.
41. Walbank, "Historical Commentary," vol. 3, pp. 272–73. It can also be argued that the Mithridates listed in the treaty was dynast of Sophene, a small district lying southeast of Pontos in the great westward bend of the Euphrates and somewhat closer to the areas affected by the treaty than Lesser Armenia. See further Lee Patterson, "Rome's Relationship with Artaxias I of Armenia," *AHB* 15 (2001) 156.
42. *OGIS* 771, lines 16–20.
43. Walbank, *Historical Commentary*, vol. 3, p. 273–74.
44. McGing, *Foreign Policy* 29–30.
45. Polyainos, *Stratagems* 8.56.
46. Burstein, "Aftermath" 5–7.
47. Justin, *Epitome* 38.6.2.
48. Livy 39.51.
49. Livy 40.56.
50. Genesis 2:14, 8:4; Herodotos 7.73; Xenophon, *Anabasis* 3.5.17.
51. Arrian, *Anabasis* 3.8.
52. Diodoros 31.27a; Strabo, *Geography* 11.14.6; Plutarch, *Lucullus* 31.4.
53. Polybios 25.2; Orosius 5.10.2.
54. Bevan, *House of Seleukos*, vol, 2, pp. 126–47.
55. *BNP Historical Atlas* 124–25.
56. Magie, *Roman Rule* 192–93.
57. Burstein, "Aftermath" 4–7; Burstein, *Hellenistic Age* 101–2.
58. The idea that the date represents an otherwise unknown Pontic era has been convincingly rejected; see, however, Heinz Heinen, "Die Anfänge der Beziehungen Roms zum nördlichen Schwarzmeerraum," in *Roms auswärtige Freunde in der späten Republik und im frühen Prinzipat* (ed. Altay Coşkun, Göttingen 2005) 37–42, and for an earlier dating of the inscription, see B. H. McLean, *An Introduction to Greek Epigraphy of the Hellenistic and Roman Periods from Alexander the Great Down to the Reign of Constantine (323 B.C.—A.D. 337)* (Ann Arbor 2002) 171–76.
59. Jacob Munk Højte, "The Date of the Alliance Between Chersonesos and Pharnakes (*IOSPE* 1², 402) and its Implications," in *Chronologies of the Black Sea in the Period c. 400–100 BC* (ed. Vladimir F. Stolba and Lise Hannestad, Aarhus 2005) 137–52.
60. McGing, *Foreign Policy* 31; Robert Malcolm Errington, "Rom und das Schwarze Meer im 2. Jh. v. Chr," in *Die Außenbeziehungen pontischer und kleinasiatischer Städte in hellenistischer und römischer Zeit* (ed. Victor Cojocaru and Christof Schuler, Stuttgart 2014) 37–44.
61. *IGBulg* 1, part 2, no. 40; McGing, *Foreign Policy* 32.
62. Diodoros 20.25; D. B. Shelov, "The Ancient Idea of a Unified Pontic State," *VDI* for 1986, pp. 36–42.
63. Homer, *Odyssey* 11.14; Aeschylus, *Prometheus Bound* 732–35; Herodotos 4.11–13; Ezekiel 38:6.
64. Stephanos of Byzantion, "Pantikapaion"; Boardman, *Greeks Overseas* 253; Braund, *Georgia* 68–69; Gocha R. Tsetskhladze, "A Survey of the Major Urban Settlements in the Kimmerian Bosporos (with a Discussion of Their Status as *Poleis*)," in *Yet More Studies in the Ancient Greek Polis* (ed. Thomas Heine Nielsen, Stuttgart 1997) 44–49.
65. Strabo, *Geography* 7.4.4; *BNP Chronologies* 112–13.
66. Boardman, *Greeks Overseas* 251–52.

67. Herodotos 7.47; Thomas S. Noonan, "The Grain Trade of the Northern Black Sea in Antiquity," *AJP* 94 (1973) 231–42.

68. Herodotos 4.17; Demosthenes, *Against Leptines* 31–33. The grain trade from the Chersonesos continued to flourish throughout the era of the Mithridatic dynasty: Mithridates VI received vast amounts from the region (Strabo, *Geography* 7.4.6).

69. See p. 40 of this book.

70. Aleksandra Wasowicz, "Vin, salaison et guerre dans le Bospore aux confins des ères," in *Structures rurales et sociétés antiques* (ed. Panagiotes N. Doukellis and Lina G. Mendoni, Paris 1994) 227–35.

71. Justin, *Epitome* 38.6.2.

72. Polybios 30.1.6–10.

73. Luis Ballesteros-Pastor, "Pharnaces I of Pontus and the Kingdom of Pergamum," *Talanta* 32–3 (2000–2001) 63–64.

74. *IDélos* 1497bis.

75. Habicht, *Athens* 226–27; Cristian Emilian Ghiţă, "Nysa—A Seleucid Princess in Anatolian Context," in *Seleucid Dissolution: The Sinking of the Anchor* (ed. Kyle Erickson and Gillian Ramsay, Wiesbaden 2011) 107–16.

76. Virginia Grace, "The Middle Stoa Dated by Amphora Stamps," *Hesperia* 54 (1985) 1–54.

77. Rostovtzeff, *Social and Economic History* 663–65, 830–31.

78. David Braund, "Black Sea Grain for Athens? From Herodotus to Demosthenes," in *The Black Sea in Antiquity* (ed. Vincent Gabrielsen and John Lund, Aarhus 2007) 39–68.

79. Strabo, *Geography* 12.3.11.

80. Polybios 31.11–15; Habicht, "Seleucids" 357.

81. Diodoros 31.28; Justin, *Epitome* 35.1.2. Nysa may be represented on a sardonyx cameo now in Paris (fig. 7; Marie-Louise Vollenweider, "Deux portraits inconnus de la dynastie du Pont et les graveurs Nikias, Zoïlos et Apollonios," *AK* 23 [1980] 148–50), although this attribution is speculative.

82. Head, *Historia Numorum* 500; *BMC Pontus* 43; Plantzos, *Hellenistic Engraved Gems*, plate 94, no. 14.

83. McGing, *Foreign Policy* 32–33.

84. Pliny, *Natural History* 33.151.

85. Archilochos F5; Horace, *Odes* 2.7; Getty Museum 80.AC.60; Paul Bernard, "Bouclier inscrit du J. Paul Getty Museum au nom de Pharnace I, roi du Pont," *BAI* 7 (1993) 11–19.

86. Polybios 33.12.1.

87. *OGIS* 365; Fleischer, "Rock-Tombs" 117–18; see also p. 197 in this volume.

88. Polybios 31.7.1–4; Diodoros 31.28; Justin, *Epitome* 35.1.2.

89. Harold Mattingly, "The Coinage of Mithradates III, Pharnakes and Mithradates IV of Pontos," in *Studies in Greek Numismatics in Honor of Martin Jessop Price* (ed. Richard Ashton and Silvia Hurter, London 1998) 255–58.

90. Polybios 27.17.

Chapter 5

1. *OGIS* 375; Mithridates VI was the grandson of Pharnakes and the son of Mithridates V, so Mithridates IV would have been his uncle.

2. *IDélos* 1555. Because this Laodike, the daughter of Mithridates III, had no connection with the Seleukids, she does not appear in Grainger's *Prosopography* and is thus unnumbered herein, as are all other holders of the name who did not have Seleukid connections.

3. Polybios 31.1.2; Walbank, *Historical Commentary*, vol. 3, p. 517.
4. *OGIS* 375; Head, *Historia Numorum* 501.
5. Elizabeth Donnelly Carney, *Arsinoë of Egypt and Macedon* (Oxford 2103) 78–79.
6. Head, *Historia Numorum* 501.
7. *OGIS* 329, lines 38–39; for a translation, see M. M. Austin, *The Hellenistic World From Alexander to the Roman Conquest* (2nd ed., Cambridge 2006), no. 245.
8. *OGIS* 352.
9. Polybios 33.12–13; Habicht, "Über die Kriege" 101–10.
10. Lionel Casson, *Ships and Seamanship in the Ancient World* (Princeton 1971) 87–88.
11. Diodoros 32.21; Justin, *Epitome* 34.4; Appian, *Mithridateios* 7.
12. Polybios 33.12.1.
13. Polybios 32.12; Diodoros 31.32–32a.
14. Gruen, *Hellenistic World* 589.
15. Gruen, *Hellenistic World* 47, 186–87.
16. J. A. O. Larsen, "The Araxa Inscription and the Lycian Confederacy," *CP* 51 (1956) 157–59.
17. Ronald Mellor, "The Dedications on the Capitoline Hill," *Chiron* 8 (1978) 319–30.
18. *IDélos* 1555–56.
19. See pp. 129–31 of this volume; McGing, *Foreign Policy* 90; Philippe Bruneau and Jean Ducat, *Guide de Délos* (2nd ed., Paris 1966) 140.
20. Polybios 30.20.8–9, 30.31.10.
21. McGing, *Foreign Policy* 35–36; Head, *Historia Numorum* 501.
22. Leonard Forrer, *Portraits of Royal Ladies on Greek Coins* (Chicago 1969) 55; Plantzos, *Hellenistic Engraved Gems*, plate 94, no. 16.
23. Geneva, Musée d'Art et d'Histoire 22008; Jeffrey Spier, "A Group of Ptolemaic Engraved Garnets," *JWAG* 47 (1989) 29.
24. Appian, *Mithridateios* 10.
25. New York, Metropolitan Museum 42.11.26; see also p. 205 of this volume. The author would like to thank Lisbet Thoresen for her assessment of this piece.
26. Cornelius Nepos, *Hannibal* 10; Scullard, "Carthage and Rome," *CAH* 7, part 2 (2nd ed., 1989) 537–72.
27. Appian, *Mithridateios* 10.
28. Polybios 38.21–22; Strabo, *Geography* 17.3.15.
29. P. S. Derow, "Rome, the Fall of Macedon and the Sack of Corinth," *CAH* 8 (2nd ed., 1989) 319–23.
30. Polybios 38.13.6, 39.2; Strabo, *Geography* 8.6.23.
31. Polybios 30.1–3; Livy 45.19–20.
32. *OGIS* 329, lines 38–39; Welles, *Royal Correspondence* no. 61.
33. An ambiguous statement by Polybios (30.2.6) suggests that Attalos III may have been the son, not nephew, of Attalos II, but this is not supported by other sources. See further Walbank, *Historical Commentary*, vol. 3, pp. 417–18.
34. Diodoros 34/35.3; Justin, *Epitome* 36.4.
35. Varro, *On Agriculture* 1.1.8; Pliny, *Natural History* 1.33, 18.22; Plutarch, *Demetrios* 20.2; Philip Thibodeau, "Attalos III of Pergamon, Philometor," *EANS* 179–80.
36. Justin, *Epitome* 36.4.5; but see Strabo, *Geography* 13.4.2, who reported more prosaically that he died of disease.
37. *OGIS* 338, 435 (Austin, *Hellenistic World* no. 248, 251); Sallust, *Histories* 4.60.8; Livy, *Summary* 58–59; Strabo, *Geography* 13.4.2; Appian, *Mithridateios* 62; Gruen, *Hellenistic World* 592–600.

38. The speech has affinities with that of the Kerkyrians regarding events of 438 BC, reported by Thucydides (1.32–36).
39. Austin, *Hellenistic World*, no. 289.
40. Hölbl, *History* 187.
41. Livy, *Summary* 59; Strabo, *Geography* 14.1.38; Velleius 2.4.1; Justin, *Epitome* 36.4.6; Plutarch, *Flamininus* 21.6.
42. Livy, *Summary* 58; Plutarch, *Tiberius Gracchus* 14; *De viris illustribus* 64; Orosius 5.8.4.
43. Orosius 5.10.2; Brian C. McGing, "Subjection and Resistance: to the Death of Mithridates," in *A Companion to the Hellenistic World* (ed. Andrew Erskine, Oxford 2003) 83–84; Magie, *Roman Rule* 150.
44. Justin, *Epitome* 37.1.2; Appian, *Mithridateios* 57; Magie, *Roman Rule* 1043–44; Appian, *Histoire romaine* 180.
45. Aulus Gellius 11.10; Magie, *Roman Rule* 1049.
46. Aulus Gellius 11.10; McGing, *Foreign Policy* 67–68.
47. Justin, *Epitome* 37.4.4–5.
48. *BNP Chronologies* 106.
49. Appian, *Mithridateios* 12.
50. Strabo, *Geography* 14.5.23.
51. Polybios 36.1–3, 38.19–22; Appian, *Libyka* 74–5, 127–32.
52. Appian, *Mithridateios* 10.
53. Lionel Casson, *The Ancient Mariners* (2nd ed., Princeton 1991) 151, 182.
54. *OGIS* 366; Strabo, *Geography* 10.4.10; Appian, *Mithridateios* 10; McGing, *Foreign Policy* 40–41.
55. Polybios's history ended in 146 BC with the aftermath of the destruction of Carthage and Corinth and the death of Ptolemy VI the following year (39.1–8), although there are some scattered later details.
56. See p. 83 of this volume.
57. Justin, *Epitome* 37.1.2; Eutropius 4.20; Orosius 5.10.2.
58. Strabo, *Geography* 14.1.38; Justin, *Epitome* 36.4.7.
59. Gruen, *Hellenistic World* 518–19.
60. Justin, *Epitome* 37.1.2; Appian, *Mithridateios* 57. Justin reported that he received "Greater Syria," but this seems an outright error.
61. Justin, *Epitome* 38.5.3; see p. 48 of this volume.
62. Justin, *Epitome* 38.4.9.
63. Appian, *Mithridateios* 10, 12.
64. Justin, *Epitome* 38.1.1; Memnon 22.1.
65. See p. 59 of this volume.
66. Justin, *Epitome* 37.3.4–9.
67. Orosius 5.10.2; see p. 61 of this volume.
68. Rostovtzeff, *Social and Economic History* 833.
69. Strabo, *Geography* 14.5.2.
70. See p. 77 of this volume.
71. *IDélos* 1557–59; Louis Robert, "Monnaies et textes grecs," *JSav* for 1978, p. 152.
72. *OGIS* 366.
73. Robert, "Monnaies" 153–63; Habicht, *Athens* 253.
74. At times Pontos also used the Bithynian era, which would yield a date of 125/124 BC. See McGing, "Kings" 253–59; E. J. Bickerman, *Chronology of the Ancient World* (2nd ed., Ithaca 1980) 72.
75. Robert, "Monnaies" 159–65; Rostovtzeff, *Social and Economic History* 1531.

76. Pindar, *Olympian* 1; Dee L. Clayman, *Berenice and the Golden Age of Ptolemaic Egypt* (Oxford 2014) 145–58.
77. Robert, *Monnaies* 153.
78. Strabo, *Geography* 10.4.10.
79. Appian, *On Sicily and the Islands* 6.1; McGing, *Foreign Policy* 39.
80. Angelos Chaniotis, *Die Verträge zwischen kretischen Poleis in der hellenistischen Zeit* (Stuttgart 1996) 49–56.
81. See p. 49 of this volume.
82. McGing, *Foreign Policy* 40–41.
83. *OGIS* 375; Appian, *Mithridateios* 10; Gruen, *Hellenistic World* 47. This is the concept that today is commonly but erroneously called "client kingship": Duane W. Roller, *The World of Juba II and Kleopatra Selene* (London 2003) 267–75.
84. Plutarch, *Gaius Gracchus* 19.
85. Plutarch, *Tiberius Gracchus* 1.4.
86. John G. F. Hind, "Mithridates," *CAH* 9 (2nd ed., 1994) 132.
87. Justin, *Epitome* 38.7.1.
88. Bevan, *House of Seleucus*, vol. 2, p. 210; Richard D. Sullivan, *Near Eastern Royalty and Rome, 100–30 BC* (Toronto 1990) 66.
89. Justin, *Epitome* 38.1–2; see p. 123 of this volume.
90. See p. 107 of this volume.
91. Plutarch, *Lucullus* 18.
92. Sallust, *Histories* 2.62.
93. Strabo, *Geography* 10.4.10; Pliny, *Natural History* 25.6; Appian, *Mithridateios* 112; Dio 37.10.

Chapter 6

1. The modern bibliography on Mithridates VI is enormous, and continues to be augmented. Of particular note are Reinach, *Mithridates Eupator*; Meyer, *Geschichte*; F. Geyer, "Mithridates VI. Eupator Dionysos," *RE* 15 (1932) 2163–2205; Eckhart Olshausen, "Mithridates VI. und Rom," *ANRW* 1.1 (1972) 806–15; McGing, *Foreign Policy*; Luís Ballesteros-Pastor, *Mitrídates Eupátor, rey del Ponto* (Granada 1996); and Karl Strobel, "Mithridates VI. Eupator von Pontos," *Ktema* 21 (1996) 55–94.
2. Luis Ballesteros-Pastor, "Troy: Between Mithridates and Rome," in *Mithridates VI and the Pontic Kingdom* (ed. Jakob Munk Højte, Aarhus 2009) 222–24.
3. Duane W. Roller, *Scholarly Kings: The Writings of Juba II of Mauretania, Archelaos of Kappadokia, Herod the Great, and the Emperor Claudius* (Chicago 2004) 170–76; Roller, *Cleopatra's Daughter* 49–58.
4. Sallust, *Histories* 2.63; Appian, *Mithridateios* 112.
5. Sallust, *Histories* 5.5; Suetonius, *Nero* 24.2.
6. The memorandum ordering his death was found among the king's papers by Pompey the Great (Plutarch, *Pompeius* 37).
7. Pliny, *Natural History* 7.88; Quintilian 11.2.50; Aulus Gellius 17.17; *De viris illustribus* 76. One can only guess at what these languages were, other than Greek, Latin, Persian, and the indigenous languages of his territories. Whether his linguistic ability extended to prominent languages beyond his kingdom, such as Egyptian, Hebrew, or Aramaic, is purely speculative.
8. Plutarch, *Antonius* 27.3–4.
9. Plutarch, *Symposiakon* 1.624; Aelian, *Historical Miscellany* 1.27; Athenaios 10.415e.
10. Appian, *Mithridateios* 112.

11. Aelian, *Characteristics of Animals* 7.46.
12. Justin, *Epitome* 38.7.1.
13. Strabo, *Geography* 14.1.23; Appian, *Mithridateios* 20.
14. Appian, *Mithridateios* 89, 117.
15. The epithet is first documented in connection with the Mithridateion on Delos, dated to 102/101 BC (*IDélos* 1562); see further p. 130 of this volume; A. B. Bosworth, *Alexander and the East: The Tragedy of Triumph* (Oxford 1996) 119–23.
16. Strabo, *Geography* 10.4.10, 12.3.11; Memnon 22.2; McGing, *Foreign Policy* 43.
17. Justin, *Epitome* 37.2.
18. Five were recorded during the period 135–119 BC: John Williams, *Observations of Comets* (London 1871) 6; John T. Ramsey, "Mithridates, the Banner of Ch'ih-Yu, and the Comet Coin," *HSCP* 99 (1999) 197–253.
19. Appian, *Mithridateios* 112; Eutropius 6.12.3; Orosius 6.5.7.
20. Ramsay, "Mithridates" 213–19.
21. Seneca, *Natural Questions* 7.15.2.
22. Matthew 2:2.
23. Plutarch, *Symposiakon* 1.6.624b.
24. Plutarch, *Alexander* 2.2.
25. Justin, *Epitome* 37.2.
26. Strabo, *Geography* 10.4.10; Duane W. Roller, *The Geography of Strabo* (Cambridge 2014) 4.
27. Aeschylus, *Persians* 970.
28. 1 Maccabees 6:17; Josephus, *Jewish Antiquities* 12.361; Appian, *Syriaka* 46; Federicomaria Muccioli, "Εὐπάτωρ nella titolatura ellenistica," *Historia* 45 (1996) 21–35.
29. The epithet seems to have been limited to cases where there might be a question of status, such as with Ptolemy Eupator, the son of Ptolemy VI and Cleopatra II (and thus a remote cousin of Mithridates VI) who was the Ptolemaic heir apparent but died before he could rule (Hölbl, *History* 192).
30. Memnon 22.2.
31. Roller, *Cleopatra's Daughter* 22–23.
32. Justin, *Epitome* 37.2.4–8.
33. Xenophon, *Kyropaideia* 1.4.5–10; Plutarch, *Alexander* 6; Appian, *Mithridateios* 112.
34. Hesso Pfeiler, "Die frühesten Porträts des Mithridates Eupator und die Bronzeprägung seiner Vorgänger," *GNS* 18–22 (1968–72) 75–80.
35. Plato, *Laws* 1.633b.
36. Matthew 4:1–11; Mark 1:12–13; Luke 4:1–13.
37. Luis Ballesteros-Pastor, "Eupator's Unmarried Sisters: An Approach to the Dynastic Struggles in Pontus After the Death of Mithridates V Euergetes," *Anabasis* 4 (2013) 68.
38. Pliny, *Natural History* 25.5–7; Paul T. Keyser, "Mithradates VI, King Of Pontos," *EANS* 557–58.
39. Strabo, *Geography* 10.4.10; Walbank, "Monarchies" 68–71.
40. Justin, *Epitome* 37.2.5–9.
41. Sallust, *Histories* 2.61.
42. Plutarch, *Lucullus* 18; see also Appian, *Mithridateios* 82; Memnon 30.1.
43. Heckel, *Who's Who* 241–42, 255–56; Ballesteros-Pastor, "Eupator's Unmarried Sisters," 65.
44. *IDélos* 1560.
45. *IDélos* 1561.
46. Sallust, *Histories* 2.62; Appian, *Mithridateios* 112.
47. Sallust, *Histories* 2.61; Justin 38.1; Appian, *Mithridateios* 112; Memnon 22.2; Plutarch, *Lucullus* 18.2.

48. Ballesteros-Pastor, "Eupator's Unmarried Sisters" 64–65.
49. Plutarch, *Lucúllus* 18.
50. Memnon 22.1.
51. Justin, *Epitome* 38.1.1.
52. Luis Ballesteros-Pastor, "A Neglected Epithet of Mithridates Eupator (*IDélos* 1560)," *Epigraphica* 76 (2014) 81–85.
53. Sallust, *Histories* 2.62; Justin, *Epitome* 37.3.4–8.
54. Justin, *Epitome* 37.3.4–5.
55. See p. 123 of this volume.
56. Polybios 25.2; Strabo, *Geography* 12.3.41; p. 59 of this volume.
57. Thomas Drew-Bear, "Three Senatus Consulta Concerning the Province of Asia," *Historia* 21 (1972) 75–87; Franz K. Ryan, "Die Zurücknahme Großphrygiens und die Unmündigkeit des Mithridates VI. Eupator," *OT* 7 (2001) 99–106.
58. Strabo, *Geography* 14.3.3; Appian, *Mithridateios* 20.
59. Strabo, *Geography* 11.14.5; Appian, *Syriaka* 48.

Chapter 7

1. Strabo, *Geography* 7.4.3.
2. Justin, Epitome 38.5.3; Appian, *Mithridateios* 11–12, 15, 56–57; Magie, *Roman Rule* 168–69.
3. Strabo, *Geography* 12.3.28.
4. Orosius 5.10.2.
5. Strabo, *Geography* 11.2.17–18.
6. Strabo, *Geography* 11.2.18; Appian, *Mithridateios* 15.
7. Justin, *Epitome* 38.7.10; Braund, *Georgia* 154–55.
8. Hind, "Mithridates" 137–39.
9. Strabo, *Geography* 11.2.16.
10. Alexandra Avram and Octavian Bounegru, "Mithridates VI. Eupator und die griechischen Städte an der Westküste des Pontos Euxeinos," in *Pontos Euxeinos: Beiträge zur Archäologie und Geschichte des antiken Schwarzmeer- und Balkanraumes* (ed. Sven Conrad et al., Langenweißbach 2006) 397–413.
11. Herodotos 4.24–25.
12. McGing, *Foreign Policy* 47.
13. Boardman, *Greeks Overseas* 242, 250.
14. Krzysztof Nawotka, *Boule and Demos in Miletus and Its Pontic Colonies From Classical Age Until Third Century A. D.* (Wrocław 1999) 59, 129, 181.
15. Justin, *Epitome* 37.3.2; Strabo, *Geography* 1.2.28.
16. Justin, *Epitome* 2.3.4, 12.2.16–17; Heckel, *Who's Who* 273.
17. Heinz Heinen, "Mithradates VI. Eupator und die Völker des nördlichen Schwarzmeerraums," *HBA* 18 (1991) 151–65.
18. Strabo, *Geography* 7.4.3, 7; p. 65 of this volume.
19. McGing, *Foreign Policy* 47.
20. Strabo, *Geography* 7.3.17.
21. Basilius Latyschev, *Inscriptiones antiquae orae septentrionalis Ponti Euxini* 1 (Petersburg 1906) 297–307; Zeev Wolfgang Rubinsohn, "Saumakos: Ancient History, Modern Politics," *Historia* 29 (1980) 50–70, with English translation; A. K. Gavrilov, "Das Diophantosdekret und Strabon," *Hyperboreus* 2 (1996) 151–68.

22. Justin, *Epitome* 37.3.2, 38.7.3.
23. Herodotos 4.103.
24. Strabo, *Geography* 7.4.7; Cohen, *Hellenistic Settlements in Europe* 385–86.
25. Strabo, *Geography* 7.4.4.
26. J. G. F. Hind, "Archaeology of the Greeks and Barbarian Peoples around the Black Sea (1982–92)," *AR* 39 (1992–93) 97.
27. Strabo, *Geography* 7.4.7. The harsh climate of the northern Black Sea regions was almost proverbial to Mediterranean peoples; see Strabo, *Geography* 7.3.18.
28. Strabo, *Geography* 2.5.7, 7.3.17.
29. Strabo, *Geography* 2.1.16, 7.3.18.
30. Appian, *Mithridateios* 67.
31. Strabo, *Geography* 7.3.16; Roller, *Historical and Topographical Guide* 359.
32. Strabo, *Geography* 11.2.14.
33. Strabo, *Geography* 7.4.3.
34. Andrew Lintott, "The Roman Empire and Its Problems in the Late Second Century," *CAH* 9 (2nd ed., 1994) 16–39.
35. Cicero, *Letters to His Friends* 9.21.
36. The best concise summary of this era remains H. H. Scullard, *From the Gracchi to Nero* (4th ed., London 1976) 23–62.
37. McGing, *Foreign Policy* 66.
38. Strabo, *Geography* 2.1.41; Pliny, *Natural History* 4.81; Appian, *Mithridateios* 15.
39. Memnon 22.3–4.
40. Appian, *Mithridateios* 10.
41. Strabo, *Geography* 7.4.6; Noonan, "Grain Trade" 231–42.
42. Strabo, *Geography* 11.2.3.
43. Justin, *Epitome* 38.3.7.
44. Appian, *Mithridateios* 15.
45. McGing, *Foreign Policy* 66.
46. Diodoros 36.3.
47. Justin, *Epitome* 37.4.3–9.
48. Orosius 5.10.2.
49. Appian, *Mithridateios* 58. The war is commonly, but inaccurately, known today as the Social War, a somewhat misleading translation of the Latin *socius*, meaning "ally."
50. Justin, *Epitome* 37.4.6.
51. Strabo, *Geography* 12.5.1.
52. Polybios 25.2.
53. Strabo, *Geography* 12.5.2.
54. Sallust, *Jugurtha* 113; Livy, Epitome 66; Velleius 2.12.1; Plutarch, *Sulla* 3.
55. Plutarch, *Marius* 18–21.
56. Livy 7.15.12–13; Christian Gizewski, "Ambitus," *BNP* 1 (2002) 568–69.
57. Diodoros 36.15; T. Robert S. Broughton, *The Magistrates of the Roman Republic* (New York 1951–52) vol. 2, p. 532.
58. Appian, *Civil War* 1.32.
59. Justin, *Epitome* 38.1–2.
60. Plutarch, *Marius* 31; Robert Morstein Kallet-Marx, *Hegemony to Empire: The Development of the Roman Imperium in the East from 148 to 62 B. C.* (Berkeley 1996) 244–47.
61. Diodoros 36.13; Plutarch, *Marius* 17.5–6.
62. Memnon 18.2; Luis Ballesteros-Pastor, "The Meeting Between Marius and Mithridates and the Pontic Policy in Cappadocia," *Cedrus* 2 (2014) 225–39.

63. Although there may have been some after-the-fact rationalization of the account of the meeting, it seems unlikely that the anecdote was merely made up by one of Marius's enemies, but this has been suggested: see Richard J. Evans, *Gaius Marius: A Political Biography* (Pretoria 1994) 127.
64. Strabo, *Geography* 12.2.11; Justin, *Epitome* 38.2.8, 38.5.9.
65. Appian, *Mithridateios* 10; Appian, *Histoire romaine* 134.
66. *OGIS* 345.

Chapter 8

1. Strabo, *Geography* 11.14.5.
2. Because the father of Tigranes II, Tigranes I, is only known through a single brief reference by Appian (*Syriaka* 48), some modern historians, rather confusingly, have called his son Tigranes I, which is not only inaccurate but affects the regnal numbers of the four successor kings named Tigranes. Other modern sources, including this one, consider the son Tigranes II. See further *BNP Chronologies* 96.
3. Justin, *Epitome* 38.3.1. This was around 110 BC: see Lee Patterson, "Mithridates II' Invasion of Armenia: A Reassessment," *REArm* 39 (2020) 161–72.
4. Plutarch, *Lucullus* 21; Broughton, *Magistrates*, vol. 2, p. 125.
5. Strabo, *Geography* 11.14.15; Marek Jan Olbrycht, "Mithridates VI Eupator and Iran," in *Mithridates VI and the Pontic Kingdom* (ed. Jakob Munk Højte, Aarhus 2009) 168–70.
6. Sullivan, *Near Eastern Royalty* 97–105, 280–84.
7. Justin, *Epitome* 38.3; Sullivan, *Near Eastern Royalty*, Stemma 9.
8. Richard D. Sullivan, "The Dynasty of Cappadocia," *ANRW* 7.2 (1980) 1127–36.
9. Strabo, *Geography* 11.14.15.
10. Strabo, *Geography* 14.5.2; Livy, *Summary* 70; Appian, *Mithridateios* 57; *De viris illustribus* 75; Philip de Souza, *Piracy in the Graeco-Roman World* (Cambridge 1999) 97–148.
11. Plutarch, *Sulla* 9.
12. Frontinus, *Stratagems* 1.5.18.
13. Olbrycht, "Mithridates VI" 174–75.
14. Memnon 22.4–5; Appian, *Mithridateios* 15.
15. Marek Jan Olbrycht, "Subjects and Allies: The Black Sea Empire of Mithradates VI Eupator (120–63 BC) Reconsidered," in *Pontika 2008: Recent Research on the Northern and Eastern Black Sea in Ancient Times* (ed. Ewdoksia Papuci-Władyka et al., BAR-IS 2240, Oxford 2011) 275–81.
16. Granius Licinianus 35.29; Appian, *Mithridateios* 10–11, 57.
17. The date for this event is uncertain: Ariarathes IX may have originally been placed on the throne as early as 100 BC, and he, Ariarathes VIII, and Gordios were essentially rival monarchs during the 90s BC: see *BNP Chronologies* 106; Sviatoslav Dmitriev, "Cappadocian Dynastic Rearrangements on the Eve of the First Mithridatic War," *Historia* 55 (2006) 285–97; Paolo Desideri, "Poseidonio e la guerra mithridatica," *Athenaeum* 51 (1973) 3–5.
18. Diodoros 37.1; Livy, *Summary* 72–76; Strabo, *Geography* 5.4.2; Emilio Gabba, "Rome and Italy: the Social War," *CAH* 9 (2nd ed., 1994) 104–28.
19. Strabo, *Geography* 10.5.4; 14.5.2.
20. Fernand Chapouthier, *Le Sanctuaire des dieux de Samothrace* (Exploration Archéologique de Délos 16, Paris 1935) 13–42; Bruneau and Ducat, *Guide* 140; Deniz Burlu Erciyas, *Wealth, Aristocracy and Royal Propaganda under the Hellenistic Kingdom of the Mithradatids in the Central Black Sea Region of Turkey* (Leiden 2006) 134–46.

21. A. W. Lawrence, *Greek Architecture* (4th ed., revised by R. A. Tomlinson, Harmondsworth 1983) 284.
22. As a matter of curiosity, part of the dedicatory inscription (*IDélos* 1562) ended up on the island of Melos, eighty miles to the southwest of Delos, at some unknown date before the end of the sixteenth century (G. D. R. Sanders and R. W. V. Catling, "A New Fragment of *I Delos* 1562," *ABSA* 85 [1990] 327–32).
23. Felix Dürrbach, *Choix d'inscriptions de Délos* (Chicago 1977), no. 136.
24. Memnon 27.2.
25. Strabo, *Geography* 12.3.33; Plutarch, *Pompeius* 42.
26. *IDélos* 2039–40; Javier Verdejo Manchado and Borja Antela-Bernárdez, "Pro-Mithridatic and Pro-Roman Tendencies on Delos in the Early First Century BC: The Case of Dikaios of Ionidai (ID 2039 and 2040)," *DHA* 41 (2015) 117–26.
27. *IDélos* 1564–68.
28. Cicero, *Against Verres* 2.2.159; McGing, *Foreign Policy* 92.
29. Justin, *Epitome* 38.3.3.
30. See p. 84 of this volume.
31. Appian, *Mithridateios* 11–12; Broughton, *Magistrates*, vol. 2, pp. 2, 39.
32. Justin, *Epitome* 38.3.6–7. Some Galatians were also mobilized.
33. Appian, *Mithridateios* 11–17.
34. Florus 1.40.3.
35. Justin, *Epitome* 38.3.1.
36. Appian, *Mithridateios* 57; Appian, *Histoire romaine* 181.
37. Athenaios 5.213c.
38. Isaías Arrayás Morales, "Las guerras mitridáticas en la geopolítica mediterránea: Sobre los contactos entre Mitrídates Eupátor y los Itálicos," *Aevum* 90 (2016) 155–87; C. H. V. Sutherland, *Roman Coins* (New York 1974), pp. 73–74, no. 100.
39. Diodoros 37.2.11.
40. Plutarch, *Marius* 31; Plutarch, *Sulla* 5.3; Memnon 22.4.
41. Appian, *Mithridateios* 1–9; Brian C. McGing, "Appian's 'Mithridateios,'" *ANRW* 34 (1993) 496–522.
42. Appian, *Mithridateios* 16.
43. Casson, *Ships* 132–34.
44. Memnon (22.6) reported merely 150,000.
45. Appian, *Mithridateios* 17.
46. Hind, "Mithridates" 144.

Chapter 9

1. Antisthenes of Rhodes (*FGrHist* no. 508) F2.
2. Craige B. Champion, *Commentary to BNJ* no. 508.
3. Phlegon of Tralleis (*FGrHist* no. 257) F36.3.
4. Peter Herz, "'Aus die Osten wird ein Retter kommen ...': Die Widerstand der Griechen gegen die römische Heerschaft," in *Zur Erschließung von Zukunft in den Religionen: Zukunftserwartung und Gegenwartsbewältigung in der Religionsgeschichte* (ed. Hans Wissmann et al., Würzburg 1991) 67–88.
5. Plutarch, *Marcus Cato* 8.7–8.
6. Justin, *Epitome* 29.2.2.
7. Livy 44.24.1–6.

8. Strabo, *Geography* 12.2.11; Justin, *Epitome* 38.2.6, 38.5.9.
9. Marie-Astrid Buelens, "A Matter of Names: King Mithridates VI and the Oracle of Hystaspes," in *Interconnectivity in the Mediterranean and Pontic World during the Hellenistic and Roman Periods* (ed. Victor Cojocaru et al., Cluj-Napoca 2014) 397–411.
10. Justin, *Epitome* 38.7.8.
11. Glenn R. Bugh, "Mithridates the Great and the Freedom of the Greeks," in *Interconnectivity in the Mediterranean and Pontic World During the Hellenistic and Roman Periods* (ed. Victor Cojocaru et al., Cluj-Napoca 2014) 383–95.
12. Plutarch, *Sulla* 11.1.
13. It is difficult to arrange the events of the war in their proper sequence: although it is clear that it ran from late 89 BC into 85 BC, the ancient sources are not in agreement regarding the order in which events occurred. What follows is perhaps the best reconstruction of the chronology. For a concise and topographically astute summary of the war, see Timothy Bruce Mitford, *East of Asia Minor: Rome's Hidden Frontier* (Oxford 2018), vol. 1, pp. 21–25.
14. Broughton, *Magistrates*, vol. 2, p. 42.
15. Appian, *Mithridateios* 17–19; Magie, *Roman Rule* 1101; Appian, *Histoire romaine* 136–37.
16. Strabo, *Geography* 12.3.40.
17. Frontinus, *Stratagems* 1.5.18.
18. Appian, *Mithridateios* 35.
19. Xenophon, *Kyropaideia* 6.1.27–30; Xenophon, *Anabasis* 1.7.10; Lucretius 2.643–56; R. F. Glover, "Some Curiosities of Ancient Warfare," *G&R* 19 (1950) 5–8.
20. Magie, *Roman Rule* 1083–85.
21. For the location, see Magie, *Roman Rule* 1101.
22. Livy, *Summary* 78; Memnon 22.8.
23. Strabo, *Geography* 12.3.40.
24. Appian, *Mithridateios* 20.
25. Athenaios 8.332–33; Strabo, *Geography* 12.8.18.
26. Appian, *Mithridateios* 24.
27. Joyce Reynolds, *Aphrodisias and Rome* (London 1982) 16–20.
28. Strabo, *Geography* 12.8.16; Appian, *Mithridateios* 112; McGing, *Foreign Policy* 110.
29. Cicero, *Pro Flacco* 59.
30. Appian, *Mithridateios* 21; Pausanias 1.20.5; Tacitus, *Annals* 3.62.
31. Strabo, *Histories* (*FGrHist* no. 91) F6; Josephus, *Jewish* Antiquities 13.349, 14.113; Appian, *Mithridateios* 23.
32. Justin, *Epitome* 38.3.9.
33. Polybios 4.47.1; 30.5.6–8; Strabo, *Geography* 14.2.5, 13; A. N. Sherwin-White, *Roman Foreign Policy in the East, 186 B.C. to A.D. 1* (Norman 1983) 130.
34. Appian, *Mithridateios* 24–27.
35. Polybios (8.4) described the machine in detail as it was used at Syracuse in the Second Punic War; see also J. G. Landels, "Ship-Shape and *Sambuca*-Fashion," *JHS* 86 (1966) 69–77 (with diagram).
36. Appian, *Mithridateios* 27; Julius Obsequens 56.
37. Diodoros 37.27; Velleius 2.18.3; Appian, *Mithridateios* 21; Granius Licinianus 35.27.
38. Valerius Maximus 9.13.1; see also Pliny, *Natural History* 33.48.
39. Justin, *Epitome* 38.7.8; Appian, *Mithridateios* 56; see also Sallust, *Histories* 4.60.5, 17.
40. Appian, *Mithridateios* 16.
41. Cicero, *On the Imperium of Pompeius* 65.

42. Jesper Majbom Masden, "The Ambitions of Mithridates VI: Hellenistic Kingship and Modern Interpretations," in *Mithridates VI and the Pontic Kingdom* (ed. Jakob Munk Højte, Aarhus 2009) 191–201.

43. Appian, *Mithridateios* 108, 117; Brian C. McGing, "Mithridates VI Eupator: Victim or Aggressor," in *Mithridates VI and the Pontic Kingdom* (ed. Jakob Munk Højte, Aarhus 2009) 205.

44. Herodotos 1.205–16; Strabo, *Geography* 15.1.6.

45. Justin, *Epitome* 38.4–7.

46. Justin, *Epitome* 38.3.11.

47. Plutarch, *Sulla* 24.2.

48. For the perceived Roman hostility to kingship, see Elizabeth Rawson, "Caesar's Heritage: Hellenistic Kings and Their Roman Equals," *JRS* 65 (1975) 150–52.

49. Herodotos 9.122.

50. Luís Ballesteros-Pastor, "*Nullis umquam nisi domesticis regibus*: Cappadocia, Pontus and the Resistance to the Diadochi in Asia Minor," in *After Alexander: the Time of the Diadochi* (ed. Victor Alonso Troncoso and Edward M. Anson, Oxford 2013) 183–98.

51. Kurt A. Raaflaub, "Between Myth and History: Rome's Rise from Village to Empire (the Eighth Century to 264)," in *A Companion to the Roman Republic* (ed. Nathan Rosenstein and Robert Morstein-Marx, Malden, Mass. 2010) 143.

52. The most complete account is by Appian (*Mithridateios* 22–23. In addition to the sources listed below, the massacre was mentioned by Livy (*Summary* 78), Velleius (2.18), Florus (1.40.6–7), and Dio (31.101).

53. Cicero, *Pro Flacco* 60; see also his *On the Imperium of Pompeius* 7.

54. Valerius Maximus 9.2.ext.3.

55. Augustine, *City of God* 3.22; Orosius 6.2.2–3.

56. Theophanes of Mytilene (*FGrHist* no. 188), F1 (= Plutarch, *Pompeius* 37); Anthony Kaldellis, *Commentary to BNJ* no. 188.

57. Valerius Maximus 9.2.ext.3; see also Memnon 22.9; Plutarch, *Sulla* 24.4.

58. Cicero, *Pro Rabirio Postumo* 27. On the differences between Greek and Roman dress at this time, see J. P. V. D. Balsdon, *Romans and Aliens* (Chapel Hill 1979) 219–22.

59. Sallust, *Jugurtha* 20–27; Robert Morstein-Marx, "The Alleged 'Massacre' at Cirta and Its Consequences (Sallust *Bellum Iugurthinum* 26–27)," *CP* 95 (2000) 468–76.

60. Appian, *Mithridateios* 23.

61. Robin Waterfield, *Taken at the Flood: The Roman Conquest of Greece* (Oxford 2014) 228–29.

62. Diodoros 37.5. For the career of Scaevola, see Broughton, *Magistrates*, vol. 2, p. 71.

63. Cicero, *Against Verres* 2.2.51.

64. Magie, *Roman Rule* 216–17.

65. *SIG* 741; Robert K. Sherk, *Rome and the Greek East to the Death of Augustus* (Cambridge 1984), no. 60; Roller, *Cleopatra's Daughter* 100–101.

66. Cicero, *On the Imperium of Pompeius* 19; Erich S. Gruen, *The Last Generation of the Roman Republic* (Berkeley 1974) 426–27.

67. Edward Bispham, "The Civil Wars and the Triumvirate," in *A Companion to Roman Italy* (ed. Alison E. Cooley, Oxford 2016) 91–102.

68. Appian, *Mithridateios* 21; *SIG* 742; for a translation of the Ephesian decree declaring war, see Sherk, *Rome and the Greek East*, no. 61; also Christian Mileta, "Mithridates der Große von Pontos—Gott auf Zeit oder: Einmal zur Unsterblickeit und zuruck," in *Lebendige Hoffnung—ewiger Tod?!: Jenseitsvorstellungen im Hellenismus, Judentum und Christentum* (ed. Michael Labahn and Manfred Lang, Leipzig 2007) 359–78.

69. Poseidonios F253 = Athenaios 5.211d–215b; I. G. Kidd, *Posidonius 2: The Commentary* (Cambridge 1988) 863–87.
70. Habicht, *Athens* 300–304.
71. Klaus Bringmann, "Poseidonios and Athenion: A Study in Hellenistic Historiography," in *Hellenistic Constructs: Essays in Culture, History, and Historiography* (ed. Paul Cartledge et al., Berkeley 1997) 145–58.
72. *IG* 2/3.2.1713.
73. *IG* 2.2.1334; Javier Verdejo Manchado and Borja Antela-Bernárdez, "A Crown for Onaso and the Archon Athenion," *ZPE* 177 (2011) 91–96.
74. Strabo, *Geography* 13.1.54.
75. Plutarch, *Sulla* 26.
76. Cicero, *Brutus* 306; P. M. Fraser, *Ptolemaic Alexandria* (Oxford 1972), vol. 1, p. 485.
77. Appian, *Mithridateios* 112; Poseidonios F253 = Athenaios 5.213c; Diodoros 37.2.11; Isaías Arrayás Morales, "Conectividad mediterránea en el marco del conflicto mitidático," *Klio* 98 (2016) 161–81.
78. Appian, *Mithridateios* 16; Arrayás Morales, "Las guerras mithridáticas" 168–81.
79. McGing, *Foreign Policy* 121–23.
80. Appian, *Mithridateios* 28; Pausanias 3.23.3–6.
81. The similarity of the names Aristion and Athenion has provoked comment, leading to the suggestion that they may be the same person, but there is no way of being certain. In one sense it makes no difference to the overall trajectory of contemporary events. See E. Badian, "Rome, Athens and Mithridates," *AJAH* 1 (1976) 105–28.
82. Strabo, *Geography* 10.5.4.
83. Pausanias 1.20.5.
84. Strabo, *Geography* 9.1.20.
85. Appian, *Mithridateios* 28–29; Memnon 22.10.
86. Poseidonios F253 (= Athenaios 5.213c); Appian, *Mithridateios* 35, 41.
87. Kevin Clinton, "Maroneia and Rome: Two Decrees of Maroneia from Samothrace," *Chiron* 33 (2003) 379–417.
88. Granius Licinianus 35.70.
89. Plutarch, *Sulla* 11; Broughton, *Magistrates*, vol. 2, pp. 15, 50.
90. Diodoros 37.2.12–13; Herbert Heftner, "Der Streit um das Kommando im Krieg gegen Mithridates (Diodorus Siculus 37,2,12) und die versuchte Konsulskandidatur des C. Iulius Caesar Strabo," *Tyche* 23 (2008) 79–100.
91. Appian, *Mithridates* 30; Arthur Keaveney, *Sulla: The Last Republican* (2nd ed., London 2005) 64–90.
92. Plutarch, *Sulla* 6–10; Plutarch, *Marius* 34–35. The size of a legion varied but was normally between four and six thousand men: J. Brian Campbell, "Legio," *BNP* 7 (2005) 356–57.
93. Appian, *Mithridateios* 22.
94. Plutarch, *Sulla* 11.1.
95. Appian, *Mithridateios* 30–40; Plutarch, *Sulla*, 12–15.
96. Casson, *Ships* 160–62.
97. Plutarch, *Sulla* 14.6, 23.2, from Sulla's own memoirs.
98. American School of Classical Studies at Athens, *The Athenian Agora: A Guide to the Excavations and Museum* (3rd ed., Athens 1976) 29–30.
99. Memnon 22.13; Appian, *Mithridateios* 41–45; Plutarch, *Sulla* 16–21.
100. Plutarch, *Sulla* 19.5; Pausanias 9.40.7; John Camp et al., "A Trophy from the Battle of Chaironeia of 86 B. C.," *AJA* 96 (1992) 443–55.
101. Appian, *Mithridateios* 49–51; Plutarch, *Sulla* 21.

102. Appian, *Mithridateios* 45.
103. Isaías Arrayás Morales, "Sobre la fluctuación en las alianzas en el marco de las guerras mitridáticas: algonos casos significativos en Anatolia," *RÉA* 118 (2016) 79–98.
104. Strabo, *Geography* 14.1.42; Appian, *Mithridateios* 46–48.
105. Appian, *Mithridateios* 46; Plutarch, *Virtues of Women* 23.259.
106. Poseidonios F51; Nikolaos of Damascus F95 (= Athenaios 6.266de); Memnon 23.1; Egilia Occhipinti, "Athenaeus's Sixth Book on Greek and Roman Slavery," *SCI* 34 (2015) 115–27.
107. Appian, *Mithridateios* 48; Orosius 6.2.8.
108. Appian, *Mithridateios* 48, 63.
109. Appian, *Mithridateios* 51–60; Broughton, *Magistrates*, vol. 2, pp. 53, 56.
110. Plutarch, *Sulla* 22; Appian, *Mithriateios* 54; Lee A. Reams, "The 'Friends' of Mithridates VI: A Case of Mistaken Identity," *CB* 64 (1988) 21–23.
111. Plutarch, *Sulla* 22; Memnon 25.2; Appian, *Mithridateios* 55.
112. Plutarch, *Lucullus* 3.
113. McGing, *Foreign Policy* 130–31.
114. Strabo, *Geography* 13.1.27; Charles Brian Rose, *The Archaeology of Greek and Roman Troy* (Cambridge 2014) 219–21.
115. The primary source is Sulla's memoirs, used extensively by Plutarch (*Sulla* 22); see also Appian, *Mithridateios* 56–58, and Magie, *Roman Rule* 230.
116. Appian, *Mithridateios* 59–60; Plutarch, *Sulla* 25–26.
117. Plutarch, *Lucullus* 3.1–3.
118. Plutarch, *Sulla* 34.4.
119. Kallet-Marx, *Hegemony to Empire* 289–90.

Chapter 10

1. Andrew Collins and John Walsh, "Debt Deflationary Crisis in the Late Roman Republic," *AncSoc* 45 (2015) 149–53.
2. Cicero, *On the Imperium of Pompeius* 19.
3. Sallust, *Bellum Catilinae* 33.2; Velleius 2.23.2.
4. Katherine Clarke, *Between Geography and History: Hellenistic Constructions of the Roman World* (Oxford 1999) 230.
5. Appian, *Mithridateios* 64.
6. Memnon 24.4; Frontinus, *Stratagems* 3.17.5; Appian, *Mithridateios* 52, 64; Orosius 6.2.10.
7. Strabo, *Geography* 11.2.18.
8. Appian, *Mithridateios* 64.
9. Cicero, *On the Imperium of Pompeius* 9.
10. Plutarch, *Sulla* 22.3; Appian, *Mithridateios* 55.
11. Plutarch, *Sulla* 23.1–2.
12. Sallust, *Histories* 4.60.12; Plutarch, *Lucullus* 8.4; Appian, *Mithridateios* 32, 43, 64.
13. Roller, *Cleopatra's Daughter* 49–58.
14. Appian, *Mithridateios* 64–66; Memnon 26.
15. Appian, *Mithridateios* 65.
16. Strabo, *Geography* 12.3.39.
17. Dennis G. Glew, "400 Villages? A Note on Appian, *Mith*. 65, 271," *EA* 32 (2000) 155–62.
18. Broughton, *Magistrates*, vol. 2, p. 83.
19. Memnon 26.2.

20. Appian, *Mithridateios* 65–66.
21. Magie, *Roman Rule* 1072.
22. Arrian, *Anabasis* 7.11.8–9; Shane Wallace, "Court, Kingship and Royal Style in the Early Hellenistic Period," in *The Hellenistic Court: Monarchic Power and Elite Society from Alexander to Cleopatra* (ed. Andrew Erskine et al., Swansea 2017) 10.
23. Plutarch, *Sulla* 16–17.
24. Cicero, *Letters to His Friends* 15.4.6; Magie, *Roman Rule* 395.
25. Cicero, *Pro Murena* 11, 15; Cicero, *On the Imperium of Pompeius* 8.
26. Appian, *Mithridateios* 67.
27. Scullard, *From the Gracchi* 71–79.
28. Appian, *Mithridateios* 51.
29. Plutarch, *Pompeius* 6–8.
30. Plutarch, *Crassus* 6.
31. Suetonius, *Divine Julius* 2.
32. Broughton, *Magistrates*, vol. 2, p. 90.
33. Appian, *Civil War* 1.98–99.
34. Plutarch, *Sulla* 34; Appian, *Civil War* 1.101.
35. Plutarch, *Sulla* 34.3, 38; Appian, *Civil War* 1.3, 103–4.
36. Appian, *Mithridateios* 67.
37. Broughton, *Magistrates*, vol. 2, p. 87.
38. Strabo, *Geography* 11.2.12; Appian, *Mithridateios* 67.
39. Strabo, *Geography* 11.14.15; Plutarch, *Lucullus* 25–28. Its site has not been located with certainty: Getzel M. Cohen, *The Hellenistic Settlements in the East from Armenia and Mesopotamia to Bactria and India* (Berkeley 2013) 50–51.
40. The principal source for his career is Plutarch's biography, supplemented by Appian, *Civil War* 1.108–15.
41. Roller, *World of Juba* 51–54.
42. Appian, *Mithridateios* 68.
43. Plutarch, *Sertorius* 18–26; Plutarch, *Pompeius* 17–21.
44. Orosius 6.2.12.
45. Cicero, *Against Verres* 2.1.86–87; Strabo, *Geography* 3.4.6. Dianium is at modern Denia.
46. Cicero, *Against Verres* 2.1.87; C. F. Konrad, *Plutarch's Sertorius* (Chapel Hill, N. C. 1994) 191–92; Casson, *Ships* 132.
47. Cicero, *Pro Murena* 32; Plutarch, *Sertorius* 23–24; Philip D. Spann, *Quintus Sertorius* (Fayetteville, Ark. 1987) 99–104.
48. Appian (*Mithridateios* 68) reported that Sertorius was willing to cede the province, but this may reflect an anti-Sertorian view that pervades his narrative. Yet Sertorius's position regarding Asia remains a puzzle: see Ronald Syme, *Sallust* (Berkeley 1964) 204–5; Appian, *Histoire romaine* 193.
49. Plutarch, *Lucullus* 12.5; Appian, *Mithridateios* 72; Dio 36.8.2.
50. Florus 1.39.6; Broughton, *Magistrates*, vol. 2, p. 99.
51. Žarko Petković, "The *Bellum Dardanicum* and the Third Mithridatic War," *Historia* 63 (2014) 189–93.
52. Sallust, *Histories* 1.67.8, 2.43.7.
53. Sallust, *Histories* 2.57, 4.60.9; Sullivan, *Near Eastern Royalty* 34–35.
54. Velleius 2.57; Appian, *Mithridateios* 71; Broughton, *Magistrates*, vol. 2, p. 98.
55. Plutarch, *Lucullus* 7; Appian, *Mithridateios* 69, 119.
56. Appian, *Mithridateios* 102, 111; Hölbl, *History* 212–13.

57. Strabo, *Geography* 10.4.10.
58. Appian, *Mithridateios* 63.
59. Appian, *Mithridateios* 78.
60. de Souza, *Piracy* 125–28; Isaías Arrayás Morales, "Más piratas que corsarios: Mitrídates Eupátor y Sertorio ante el fenónemo pirático," *Latomus* 72 (2013) 96–121.
61. Plutarch, *Lucullus* 20.
62. Appian, *Mithridateios* 70.

Chapter 11

1. Appian, *Mithridateios* 70; Robin Seager, "The Rise of Pompey," *CAH* 9 (2nd ed., 1994) 210–152.
2. Appian, *Civil War* 1.107.
3. Cicero, *On the Imperium of Pompeius* 51, 59–60; Plutarch, *Pompeius* 30.
4. Sallust, *Histories* 2.41, 43.
5. Cicero, *Against Verres* 2.2.8; Sallust, *Histories* 3.1–7, 46–54; Velleius 2.31.
6. Appian, *Civil War* 1.116–20; Plutarch, *Crassus* 8.11.
7. The major ancient source is Plutarch's biography; see also Arthur Keaveney, *Lucullus: A Life* (London 1992), especially 75–98.
8. The major ancient source for Pompey's career is Plutarch's biography; see also Robin Seager, *Pompey the Great: A Political Biography* (2nd ed., Oxford 2002).
9. Appian, *Mithridateios* 70.
10. For a discussion of the chronological issues, but not necessarily a resolution of them, see Broughton, *Magistrates*, vol. 2, pp. 106–9.
11. Appian, *Mithridateios* 69–71.
12. Brian C. McGing, "The Date of the Outbreak of the Third Mithridatic War," *Phoenix* 38 (1984) 12–18.
13. Plutarch, *Lucullus* 6–7; Broughton, *Magistrates*, vol. 2, p. 101.
14. Aulus Gellius 5.13.6; Magie, *Roman Rule* 1205–6.
15. Plutarch, *Lucullus* 8; Magie, *Roman Rule* 324.
16. Memnon 27.
17. Plutarch, *Lucullus* 7.5.
18. Plutarch, *Lucullus* 11.5; Memnon 28 (who calls him "Archelaos," certainly an error, since Mithridates's former commander was now an advisor to Lucullus); Sherwin-White, *Foreign Policy* 166.
19. Magie, *Roman Rule* 325.
20. Plutarch, *Lucullus* 8; Appian, *Mithridateios* 71; McGing, *Foreign Policy* 146.
21. For problems with his name, see Magie, *Roman Rule* 1206; Broughton, *Magistrates, Supplement* 54.
22. Plutarch, *Lucullus* 8; Appian, *Mithridateios* 71; Memnon 27; Orosius 6.2.13.
23. Appian, *Mithridateios* 76.
24. Appian, *Mithridateios* 76–77; Memnon 28; Orosius 6.2.23; Magie, *Roman Rule* 1206–7.
25. Plutarch, *Sertorius* 24; Broughton, *Magistrates*, vol. 2, p. 93.
26. Memnon 29.5.
27. Cicero, *Pro Murena* 33; Cicero, *On the Imperium of Pompeius* 21.
28. Appian, *Mithridateios* 29, 70; Orosius 6.2.16–18.
29. Broughton, *Magistrates*, vol. 2, p. 105.

30. Magie, *Roman Rule* 327. A bilingual inscription honoring Salluvius for his bravery in the war was erected at the Temple of Diana at Lake Nemi southeast of Rome, perhaps his home region: *OGIS* 445; Sherk, *Rome and the Greek East* no. 69.
31. Appian, *Mithridateios* 75.
32. Plutarch, *Cicero* 4.4; Plutarch, *Caesar* 3.1; Suetonius, *Divine Julius* 4.
33. Strabo 12.8.11, 14.1.6; Pliny, *Natural History* 5.142; Boardman, *Greeks Overseas* 245–46.
34. Cicero, *Pro Murena* 33.
35. Strabo 12.8.11; Plutarch, *Lucullus* 9–12; Appian, *Mithridateios* 72–77; Memnon 28.
36. For the numerous minor sources, see Magie, *Roman Rule* 1208.
37. Sallust, *Histories* 3.36.
38. Plutarch, *Lucullus* 13.
39. Appian, *Mithridateios* 78; Orosius 6.2.24.
40. Memnon 29.3–5.
41. Sherwin-White, *Roman Foreign Policy* 169–70.
42. *Plutarch, Lucullus* 14; Appian, *Mithridateios* 77; Memnon 28–29.
43. Appian, *Mithridateios* 78.
44. Memnon 29.6.
45. Strabo, *Geography* 12.3.30; Roller, *Historical and Topographical Guide* 711.
46. Memnon 29.5; Broughton, *Magistrates*, vol. 2, pp. 113, 120.
47. Cicero, *On the Imperium of Pompeius* 21; Cicero, *Pro Murena* 33; Memnon 33; Magie, *Roman Rule* 334. It was later claimed that these ships had been on their way to attack Italy, which is unlikely but a measure of the nervousness felt in Rome about the Pontic fleet.
48. Memnon 34–36.
49. Memnon 39; Jerzy Linderski, "A Missing Ponticus," *AJAH* 12 (1987) 148–66.
50. Plutarch, *Lucullus* 14–17; Appian, *Mithridateios* 79–83.
51. Plutarch, *Lucullus* 19.
52. Plutarch, *Lucullus* 15, 19; Appian, *Mithridateios* 82, 83.
53. Plutarch, *Lucullus* 20; Magie, *Roman Rule* 337–38.
54. Sallust, *Histories* 4.60; for a literary analysis of the speech, see Eric Adler, *Valorizing the Barbarians* (Austin 2011) 17–58; also Gerhard Perl, "Kontroverse Stellen in den "Historiae" Sallusts," *Hermes* 133 (2005) 189–95.
55. Sallust, Jugurtha 81; Ellen O'Gorman, "The Politics of Sallustian Style," in *A Companion to Greek and Roman Historiography* (ed. John Marioncola, Malden, Mass. 2007) 383–84.
56. Caesar, *Gallic War* 7.77; Tacitus, *Agricola* 30–32; Friedrich Maier, "Kritik am Imperium Romanum: Die Stimme des Ostens," *Anregung* 40 (1994) 82–88.
57. Plutarch, *Pompeius* 37.
58. Appian, *Mithridateios* 70.
59. Clarke, *Between Geography and History* 308.
60. Appian, *Mithridateios* 111; the date of the arrangement is not certain.
61. Plutarch, *Lucullus* 24; Appian, *Mithridateios* 83; Memnon 37.6.
62. Plutarch, *Lucullus* 18; Appian, *Mithridateios* 82.
63. These were among the documents discovered by Pompey at Kainon a few years later: Plutarch, *Pompeius* 37.
64. See p. 105 of this volume.
65. Plutarch, *Lucullus* 22; Memnon 38.
66. Strabo, *Geography* 13.1.55; see also *FGrHist* no. 184 (Metrodoros).
67. Strabo 11.14.15; Plutarch, *Lucullus* 25; Ronald Syme, *Anatolica: Studies in Strabo* (ed. Anthony Birley, Oxford 1995) 58–65.
68. Cicero, *Letters to Atticus* no. 109; Plutarch, *Lucullus* 21–22; Appian, *Mithridateios* 84.

69. Plutarch, *Lucullus* 23.7; Appian, *Mithridateios* 85; Magie, *Roman Rule* 1215.
70. Plutarch, *Lucullus* 24.
71. Plutarch, *Lucullus* 25–26.
72. Appian, *Mithridateios* 87.
73. Plutarch, *Lucullus* 24, 35; Appian, *Mithridateios* 88; Dio 36.9–10.
74. Appian, *Mithridateios* 89.
75. Sherk, *Rome and the Greek East* no. 71.
76. Plutarch, *Lucullus* 7.6, 20, 23, 35; Dio 36.2.
77. Cicero, *On the Imperium of Pompeius* 5; Broughton, *Magistrates*, vol. 2, pp 142–43.
78. Appian, *Mithridateios* 90.
79. Strabo, *Geography* 12.3.33; Plutarch, *Lucullus* 36–38; Magie, *Roman Rule* 350.
80. Diodoros 4.21.4; Pliny, *Natural History* 9.170, 15.102; Plutarch, *Lucullus* 39–41.
81. L. Richardson, Jr., *A New Topographical Dictionary of Ancient Rome* (Baltimore 1992) 200.
82. Plutarch, *Lucullus* 43.
83. Athenaios 6.274f–275ab.
84. Kidd, *Posidonius*, vol. 2, pp. 910–16.

Chapter 12

1. See p. 108 of this volume.
2. Appian, *Mithridates* 21, 48, 82. Plutarch (*Lucullus* 18) reported that she was Milesian.
3. This was probably the Sinoria recorded by Strabo (*Geography* 12.3.38).
4. Appian, *Mithridateios* 107; Plutarch, *Pompeius* 36; Dio 37.7.5.
5. Valerius Maximus 4.6.ext. 2; Plutarch, *Pompeius* 32.7–9; Mikhail Abramzon and Vladimir Kuznetsov, "The Phanagorian Revolt Against Mithridates VI Eupator," in *Phanagoreia und Seine Historische Umwelt* (ed. Nikolai Povalahev and Vladimir Kuznetsov, Göttingen 2011), p. 15, fig. 2.
6. Strabo, *Geography* 13.4.3.
7. Sullivan, *Near Eastern Royalty* 158–59; Stephen Mitchell, *Anatolia: Land, Men and Gods in Asia Minor* (Oxford 1995), vol. 1, pp. 28–29.
8. Justin, *Epitome* 38.3.2; Appian, *Mithridateios* 108 (perhaps actually a second daughter also named Cleopatra); Memnon 29.6; Sullivan, *Near Eastern Royalty* 280–90.
9. *OGIS* 356; Cicero, *Letters to His Friends* 15.4.6; Appian, *Mithridateios* 66; Sullivan, *Near Eastern Royalty* 52–54, 176.
10. Appian, *Mithridateios* 117; Head, *Historia Numorum* 513; Gabelko, "Dynastic History" 47–61.
11. Valerius Maximus 1.8.ext.13; Ammianus Marcellius 16.7.9–10.
12. Luís Ballesteros-Pastor, "Los príncipes del Ponto: La política onomástica de Mitrídates Eupátor como factor de propaganda dinástica," *RÉA* 117 (2015) 425–45, with a list of the sons on 445.
13. Sullivan, *Near Eastern Royalty* 52–54.
14. See p. 163 of this volume.
15. See p. 215 of this volume.
16. Orosius 6.4.6; Eckart Olshausen, "Zum Hellenisierungsprozess am Pontischen Königshof," *AncSoc* 5 (1974) 153–70.
17. Appian, *Mithridateios* 77; Memnon 37.1.
18. Plutarch, *Symposiakon* 1.624a; Athenaios 10.415e; Olshausen, "Hellenisierungsprozess" 169.
19. Athenaios 6.252e.

20. Appian, *Mithridateios* 98.
21. *OGIS* 377; Plutarch, *Lucullus* 17.7.
22. See p. 191 of this volume; Appian, *Mithridateios* 89.
23. Josephus, *Jewish Antiquities* 13.349; Appian, *Civil War* 1.102; Fraser, *Ptolemaic Alexandria*, vol. 1, p. 124.
24. Metrodoros (*FGrHist* no. 184) F1; Pliny, *Natural History* 34.34; Cicero, *Orator* 1.45, 2.360.
25. Jakob Munk Højte, "The Administrative Organisation of the Pontic Kingdom," in *Mithridates VI and the Pontic Kingdom* (ed. Jakob Munk Højte, Aarhus 2009) 101–2.
26. Appian, *Mithridateios* 112; Plutarch, *Pompeius* 37.
27. Plutarch, *How to Distinguish a Flatterer from a Friend* 14.58a.
28. Dioskourides 1, *Preface* 1; Pliny, *Natural History* 25.8; Jean-Marie Jacques, "Krateuas," *EANS* 491.
29. Galen, *Antidotes* 2.8; Scribonius Largus 169; Stok, "Zopuros of Alexandria" 851; Duane W. Roller, *Cleopatra: A Biography* (Oxford 2010) 44, 50.
30. Pliny, *Natural History* 25.7; Rebecca Flemming, "Empires of Knowledge: Medicine and Health in the Hellenistic World," in *A Companion to the Hellenistic World* (ed. Andrew Erskine, Malden, Mass. 2003) 458.
31. Cicero, *De Oratore* 1.62; Pliny, *Natural History* 25.7; John Scarborough, "Asklepediades of Bithunia," *EANS* 170–71.
32. Stephanie J. Winder, "'The Hands of Gods': Poison in the Hellenistic Court," in *The Hellenistic Court: Monarchic Power and Elite Society from Alexander to Cleopatra* (ed. Andrew Erskine et al., Swansea 2017) 373–407.
33. Pliny, *Natural History* 1.28, 31; Galen, *Antidotes* 1.1; Thibodeau, "Attalos III," *EANS* 179–80).
34. Pliny, *Natural History* 20.264; Jean-Marie Jacques, "Antiokhos VIII Philometor," *EANS* 95–96. Pliny called him "Magnus Antiochus," which would suggest Antiochos III (reigned 212–187 BC), but the other citations (listed in *EANS*) demonstrate that Antiochos VIII is meant. Nevertheless, Antiochos III may also have developed compounds, which were passed down to his descendant.
35. Paul T. Keyser, "Nikomedes IV of Bithunia," *EANS* 581.
36. Appian, *Mithridateios* 88.
37. For a list, see Totelin, "Antidote" 18–19.
38. Galen, *Antidotes* 2.8; for a translation of Galen's account, including the recipe for the antidote, see Laurence M. V. Totelin, "The World In a Pill: Local Specialties and Global Remedies in the Graeco-Roman World," in *The Routledge Handbook of Identity and the Environment in the Classical and Medieval Worlds* (ed. Rebecca Futo Kennedy and Molly Jones-Lewis, London 2016) 166. For the case of Cleopatra VII, see Roller, *Cleopatra* 143.
39. Aulus Gellius 17.16; Sabine Vogt, "Drugs and Pharmacology," in *The Cambridge Companion to Galen* (ed. R. J. Hankinson, Cambridge 2008) 312–14.
40. Getty Museum 90.SC.41.1.
41. Pliny, *Natural History* 16.137.
42. Dioskourides 4.41; Pliny, *Natural History* 25.62–65, 127.
43. Keyser, "Mithridates VI," *EANS* 558.
44. Pliny, *Natural History* 23.149; Philip Thibodeau, "Pompeius Lenaeus," *EANS* 684.
45. Pliny, *Natural History* 15.102; Plutarch, *Lucullus* 39.
46. Propertius 2.31/2.11–16; Bernard Andreae, "Telephos-Mithridates in Museo Chiaramonti des Vatikan," *RömMitt* 104 (1997) 395–416.
47. Laurence M. V. Totelin, "Botanizing Rulers and Their Herbal Subjects: Plants and Political Power in Greek and Roman Literature," *Phoenix* 66 (2012) 134–35.

48. Plutarch, *Pompeius* 28.4; Appian, *Mithridateios* 67; Boardman, *Greeks Overseas* 50.

49. Strabo, *Geography* 12.3.17; Cohen, *Hellenistic Settlements in Europe* 387–88; D. R. Wilson, "Pharnakeia Kerasous," *PES* 699.

50. Deniz Burcu Erciyas, "Studies in the Archaeology of Hellenistic Pontus: The Settlements, Monuments, and Coinage of Mithridates VI and His Predecessors" (Ph. D. dissertation, University of Cincinnati 2001) 128–56.

51. Strabo, *Geography* 12.3.28.

52. Højte, "Administrative Organisation" 103.

53. Plutarch, *Pompeius* 32; Appian, *Mithridateios* 101 (as Sinorax).

54. Strabo, *Geography* 12.5.2; it was perhaps located at modern Gerdekkaya.

55. Appian, *Mithridateios* 105.

56. Plutarch, *Pompeius* 37.

57. Strabo, *Geography* 7.4.7; Cohen, *Hellenistic Settlements in Europe* 385–86. The Eupatoria mentioned by Ptolemy the geographer (*Geographical Guide* 3.6.2) may be another site, but it would also have been founded under the authority of Mithridates VI.

58. Appian, *Mithridateios* 78; Cohen, *Hellenistic Settlements in Europe* 384.

59. Strabo, *Geography* 12.3.14, 12.3.30; Appian, *Mithridateios* 115; Cohen, *Hellenistic Settlements in Europe* 384–85.

60. Strabo, Geography 12.3.30; Pliny, *Natural History* 16.137; Appian, *Mithridateios* 110.

61. Plutarch, *Lucullus* 10.2, 32.4.

62. Patric-Alexander Kreuz, "Monuments for the King: Royal Presence in the Late Hellenistic World of Mithridates VI," in *Mithridates VI and the Pontic Kingdom* (ed. Jakob Munk Højte, Aarhus 2009) 133–34.

63. See p. 68 of this volume.

64. Stephanos of Byzantion, "Berenikai"; Plutarch, *Lucullus* 18; Josephus, *Jewish Antiquities* 16.17–19; Appian, *Mithridateios* 46; Memnon 23; Cohen, *Hellenistic Settlements in Europe* 141.

65. Strabo, *Geography* 12.8.15, 18.

66. Strabo, *Geography* 12.3.30; Vitruvius 10.5.2.

67. Paavo Roos, "Strabo and the Water-Mill at Cabeira: Some Considerations," *ORom* 20 (1996) 99–102. There are no surviving examples of water mills before the first century AD: see Örjan Wikander, "Sources of Energy and Exploitation of Power," in *The Oxford Handbook of Engineering and Technology in the Classical World* (ed. John Peter Oleson, Oxford 2008) 141–43.

68. Appian, *Mithridateios* 115–17.

69. Capitoline Museum MC1068.

70. Monica M. Jackson, "The Amisos Treasure: A Hellenistic Tomb from the Age of Mithridates Eupator," in *The Black Sea, Paphlagonia, Pontus and Phrygia in Antiquity* (BAR-IS 2432, Oxford 2012) 109–116.

71. Plutarch, *Lucullus* 37; Plutarch, *Pompeius* 45; Appian, *Mithridateios* 116–17; Jakob Munk Højte, "Portraits and Statues of Mithridates VI," in *Mithridates VI and the Pontic Kingdom* (ed. Jacob Munk Højte, Aarhus 2009) 145–61; Anna A. Trofimova, "The Sculpted Portrait in the Bosporus," in *Greeks on the Black Sea* (ed. Anna A. Trofimova, Los Angeles 2007) 50–51.

72. Cicero, *Against Verres* 2.2.65.

73. See p. 129 of this volume; *IDélos* 1557, 1560, 1565, 1568; *OGIS* 3166.

74. *SEG* 37.668.

75. Louvre MA 2321; Andrew Stewart, *Greek Sculpture: An Exploration* (New Haven 1990), vol. 1, p. 223 (no. 800); J. M. C. Toynbee, *Roman Historical Portraits* (London 1978) 115–16.

76. Kerch Lapidarium, no. 1900; Højte, *Portraits* 153; Trofimova, "Sculpted Portrait" 50–51.

77. McGing, *Foreign Policy* 99–102.
78. Thuri Lorenz, "Von Alexander dem Großen zu Mithridates," *JÖAI* 70 (2001) 65–79. A Pergamene portrait of Herakles in the Prometheus group in Berlin was long thought to represent the king but is perhaps one of the Attalids (Christiane Vorster, "Mythos in der dritten Dimension—Zu Komposition und Interpretation der Herakles-Prometheus-Gruppe," in *Pergamon: Panorama der antiken Metropole* [ed. Ralf Grüssinger et al., Berlin 2011] 131–37; Stefan E. A. Wagner, "Die Herakles-Prometheus-Gruppe aus Pergamon und ihre Bedeutung im Kontext der attalidischen Herrscherrepräsentation," *IstMitt* 65 [2015] 129–49).
79. Poseidonios F253 (= Athenaios 5.212d).
80. Højte, *Portraits* 157–58.
81. Pliny, *Natural History* 37.11, 169. Zachalias of Babylon may have been the curator. Appian, *Mithridateios* 115, may be an indirect comment on the collection.
82. Metropolitan Museum 42.11.26; Museum of Fine Arts 01.7595. These gems carved for royalty are the environment expressed in the *Lithika* of Poseidippos, probably of the mid-third century BC (Ann Kuttner, "Cabinet Fit for a Queen: The Λιθικά as Posidippus' Gem Museum," in *The New Posidippus* [ed. Kathryn Gutzwiller, Oxford 2005] 141–63).
83. Pliny, *Natural History* 37.115.
84. Jeffrey Spier, *Ancient Gems and Finger Rings* (Malibu 1992), p. 92, no. 218.
85. François de Callataÿ, "The First Royal Coinages of Pontos (from Mithridates III to Mithridates V)," in *Mithridates VI and the Pontic Kingdom* (ed. Jacob Munk Højte, Aarhus 2009) 63–94; see also W. H. Waddington, *Recueil général des monnaies grecques d'Asie Mineure* (Paris 1925) 10–20; Head, *Historia Numorum* 499–502.
86. Erciyas, *Wealth* 171–73.
87. Højte, *Portraits* 148–50.
88. Strabo, *Geography* 14.1.23.

Chapter 13

1. The extensive sources are in Broughton, *Magistrates*, vol. 2, p. 153; see also Magie, *Roman Rule* 351–52; Seager, *Pompey the Great* 40–62.
2. Plutarch, *Pompeius* 30.
3. Dio 36.43.
4. Cicero, *On the Imperium of Pompeius*.
5. Broughton, *Magistrates*, vol. 2, pp. 118–126, 146.
6. Plutarch, *Pompeius* 30.5–6; Dio 36.45.1–2.
7. Plutarch, *Pompeius* 30–32.
8. Appian, *Mithridateios* 107; Dio 36.45.2–5; Seager, *Pompey* 58.
9. Plutarch, *Pompeius* 32; Appian, *Mithridateios* 100; Dio 47–49.
10. The name appears as Sinoria, Sinora, or Sinorex in the sources. It probably was at modern Bayburt. Plutarch, *Pompeius* 32.8–9; Appian, *Mithridateios* 101.
11. Plutarch, *Pompeius* 38.
12. Sergey Vnukov, "Overseas Trade," in *The Northern Black Sea in Antiquity* (ed. Valeriya Kozlovskaya, Cambridge 2010) 138.
13. Plutarch, *Pompeius* 32, 39.
14. Dio 36.50.
15. Plutarch, *Pompeius* 33–34.
16. Appian, *Mithridateios* 101.

NOTES

17. Strabo, *Geography* 12.3.33.
18. Plutarch, *Pompeius* 34–36; Appian, *Mithridateios* 103.
19. Theophanes' report (*FGrHist* no. 188) is not extant, but there are many excerpts in Book 11 of the *Geography* of Strabo.
20. Plutarch, *Pompeius* 38.
21. Appian, *Mithridateios* 102.
22. Dio 37.11.4; Orosius 6.5.1; Sergei Saprykin, "Naturkastrophen und Naturerscheinungen in die Ideologie des Mithridates Eupator," *GH* 10 (1998) 396–403.
23. Strabo, *Geography* 11.3.5; Pliny, *Natural History* 5.99; Tacitus, *Annals* 6.33.
24. Appian, *Mithridateios* 102; Dio 36.50.
25. Appian, *Mithridateios* 109; Dio 37.11; Holger Sonnabend, "Ein Hannibal aus dem Osten? Die 'letzen Pläne' des Mithradates VI. von Pontos," in *Alte Geschichte: Wege—Einsichten—Horizonte* (ed. Ulrich Fellmeth and Holder Sonnabend, Hildesheim 1998) 191–206. Tributaries of the Danube come within a few miles of the Adriatic north of Trieste, and by the third century BC this was seen as the return route of the Argonauts (Eratosthenes, *Geography* F16 = Strabo, *Geography* 1.3.15).
26. Appian, *Mithridateios* 117; Plutarch (*Pompeius* 45) mentioned only "Skythian women"; Strabo, *Geography* 1.2.28.
27. *Greeks on the Black Sea: Ancient Art from the Hermitage* (ed. Anna A. Trofimova, Los Angeles 2007) 237–89.
28. Appian, *Mithridateios* 108–11; Dio 37.13; Abramzon and Kuznetsov, "Phanagorian Revolt" 15–89.
29. Galen, *On Theriac to Piso* 16; Laurence M. V. Totelin, "Mithridates' Antidote—A Pharmacological Ghost," *ESM* 9 (2004) 1–19.
30. Plutarch, *Antonius* 86.
31. Plutarch, *Pompeius* 41–42; Appian, *Mithridateios* 113; Jakob Munk Højte, "The Death and Burial of Mithridates VI," in *Mithridates VI and the Pontic Kingdom* (ed. Jakob Munk Højte, Aarhus 2009) 121–22.
32. Plutarch, *Antonius* 3.5–6, 86.4.
33. Cicero, *De lege agraria* 1.6.
34. Plutarch, *Pompeius* 45; Appian, Mithridateios 116.
35. Appian, *Civil War* 5.75; Sullivan, *Near Eastern Royalty* 160–61.
36. Roller, *Cleopatra's Daughter* 108–9, 119–20.
37. Strabo, *Geography* 13.4.3; Appian, Mithridateios 120; Dio 42.46.
38. Roller, *Cleopatra's Daughter* 82–97.
39. "Rex post Alexandrum maxumus," Cicero, *Academica* 2.3.
40. Arrian, *Anabasis* 1.12.1; Plutarch, *Alexander* 15.4–5.
41. Diodoros 15.90.2; McGing, *Foreign Policy* 13–14.
42. Sallust, *Histories* 2.59; Justin, *Epitome* 38.7.1; Appian, *Mithridateios* 112.
43. Strabo, *Geography* 11.8.4, 12.3.37.
44. Fabio Stok, "Zopuros of Alexandria," *EANS* 851.
45. Roller, *Cleopatra* 49–50.
46. The last Seleukids and Ptolemies were the children of Juba II and Cleopatra Selene of Mauretania, who did not survive beyond the middle of the first century AD. Macedonian royalty died out in the second century BC. The last descendant of Augustus was the emperor Nero, killed in AD 68.
47. Cicero, *Pro Archia Poeta* 19–21.
48. Suetonius, *Nero* 24.2.
49. Suetonius, *Divine Augustus* 5.

50. Appian, *Mithridateios* 121.
51. Sidonius Apollinaris, *Poem* 22; Sidonius Apollonaris, *Apollonaris Sidonius, Carm. 22: Burgus Pontii Leontii* (ed. Norbert Delhey, Berlin 1993).
52. Lâtife Summerer, "The Search for Mithridates: Reception of Mithridates VI Between the 15th and the 20th Centuries," in *Mithridates VI and the Pontic* Kingdom (ed. Jacob Munk Højte, Aarhus 2009) 15–34; Ute Jung-Kaiser, "Mithridates," *BNP Supplement* 7 (2016) 291–95.
53. See p. 199 of this volume.

BIBLIOGRAPHY

Abramzon, Mikhail, and Vladimir Kuznetsov. "The Phanagorian Revolt against Mithridates VI Eupator," in *Phanagoreia und seine historische Umwelt* (ed. Nikolai Povalahev and Vladimir Kuznetsov, Göttingen 2011) 15–89.

Adler, Eric. *Valorizing the Barbarians* (Austin 2011).

American School of Classical Studies at Athens. *The Athenian Agora: A Guide to the Excavations and Museum* (3rd ed., Athens 1976).

Andreae, Bernard. "Telephos-Mithridates in Museo Chiaramonti des Vatikan," *RömMitt* 104 (1997) 395–416.

Appian. *Histoire romaine* 12: *La guerre de Mithridate* (tr. and ed. Paul Goukowsky, Paris 2003).

Arrayás Morales, Isaías. "Conectividad mediterránea en el marco del conflicto mitidático," *Klio* 98 (2016) 158–83.

Arrayás Morales, Isaías. "Las guerras mitridáticas en la geopolítica mediterránea: Sobre los contactos entre Mitrídates Eupátor y los Itálicos," *Aevum* 90 (2016) 155–87.

Arrayás Morales, Isaías. "Más piratas que corsarios: Mitrídates Eupátor y Sertorio ante el fenónemo pirático," *Latomus* 72 (2013) 96–121.

Arrayás Morales, Isaías. "Sobre la fluctuación en las alianzas en el marco de las guerras mitridáticas: Algonos casos significativos en Anatolia," *RÉA* 118 (2016) 79–98.

Austin, M. M. *The Hellenistic World from Alexander to the Roman Conquest* (2nd ed., Cambridge 2006).

Avram, Alexandra, and Octavian Bounegru. "Mithridates VI. Eupator und die griechischen Städte an der Westküste des Pontos Euxeinos," in *Pontos Euxeinos: Beiträge zür Archäologie und Geschichte des antiken Schwarzmeer- und Balkanraumes* (ed. Sven Conrad et al., Langenweißbach 2006) 397–413.

Badian, E. "Rome, Athens and Mithridates," *AJAH* 1 (1976) 105–28.

Balcer, Jack Martin. *A Prosopographical Study of the Ancient Persians Royal and Noble c. 550–450 BC* (Lewiston, N. Y. 1993).

Ballesteros-Pastor, Luis. "Eupator's Unmarried Sisters: An Approach to the Dynastic Struggles in Pontus after the Death of Mithridates V Euergetes," *Anabasis* 4 (2013) 61–72.

Ballesteros-Pastor, Luis. "Los herederos de Artabazo: La satrapía de Dascilio en la tradición de la dinastía Mitridátida," *Klio* 94 (2012) 366–79.

Ballesteros-Pastor, Luis. "Los príncipes del Ponto: La política onomástica de Mitrídates Eupátor como factor de propaganda dinástica," *RÉA* 117 (2015) 425–45.

Ballesteros-Pastor, Luis. "Marius' Words to Mithridates Eupator (Plut. Mar. 31.3)," *Historia* 48 (1999) 506–8.

Ballesteros-Pastor, Luis. "The Meeting Between Marius and Mithridates and the Pontic Policy in Cappadocia," *Cedrus* 2 (2014) 225–39.

Ballesteros-Pastor, Luis. *Mitrídates Eupátor, rey del Ponto* (Granada 1996).

Ballesteros-Pastor, Luis. "A Neglected Epithet of Mithridates Eupator (*IDélos* 1560)," *Epigraphica* 76 (2014) 81–85.

Ballesteros-Pastor, Luis. "*Nullis umquam nisi domesticis regibus*: Cappadocia, Pontus and the Resistance to the Diadochi in Asia Minor," in *After Alexander: The Time of the Diadochi* (ed. Victor Alonso Troncoso and Edward M. Anson, Oxford 2013) 183–98.

Ballesteros-Pastor, Luis. "Pharnaces I of Pontus and the Kingdom of Pergamum," *Talanta* 32–33 (2000–2001) 61–66.

Ballesteros-Pastor, Luis. "Troy, Between Mithridates and Rome," in *Mithridates VI and the Pontic Kingdom* (ed. Jakob Munk Højte, Aarhus 2009) 217–31.

Balsdon, J. P. V. D. *Romans and Aliens* (Chapel Hill 1979).

Bernard, Paul. "Bouclier inscrit du J. Paul Getty Museum au nom de Pharnace I, roi du Pont," *BAI* 7 (1993) 11–19.

Bevan, Edwyn Robert. *The House of Seleucus* (London 1902).

Bickerman, E. J. *Chronology of the Ancient World* (2nd ed., Ithaca 1980).

Billows, Richard A. *Antigonos the One-Eyed and the Creation of the Hellenistic State* (Berkeley 1997).

Bispham, Edward. "The Civil Wars and the Triumvirate," in *A Companion to Roman Italy* (ed. Alison E. Cooley, Oxford 2016) 91–102.

Boardman, John. *The Greeks Overseas: Their Early Colonies and Trade* (4th ed., London 1999).

Bodeüs, Richard. "Le premier nom propre iranien du groupe *Mitra-* dans les sources grecques," in *Archeologie et philologie dans l'étude des civilisations orientales* (ed. A. Theodorides et al., Leuven 1986) 213–16.

Bosworth, A. B. *Alexander and the East: The Tragedy of Triumph* (Oxford 1996).

Bosworth, A. B. *A Historical Commentary on Arrian's History of Alexander* (Oxford 1980–1995).

Bosworth, A. B., and P. V. Wheatley. "The Origins of the Pontic House," *JHS* 118 (1998) 155–64.

Braund, David. "After Alexander: The Emergence of the Hellenistic World, 323–281" in *A Companion to the Hellenistic World* (ed. Andrew Erskine, Oxford 2003) 19–34.

Braund, David. "Black Sea Grain for Athens? From Herodotus to Demosthenes," in *The Black Sea in Antiquity* (ed. Vincent Gabrielsen and John Lund, Aarhus, 2007) 39–68.

Braund, David. *Georgia in Antiquity* (Oxford 1994).

Bredow, Iris von. "Regnum Bosporanum," *BNP* 12 (2008) 443–50.

Bringmann, Klaus. "Poseidonios and Athenion: A Study in Hellenistic Historiography," in *Hellenistic Constructs: Essays in Culture, History, and Historiography* (ed. Paul Cartledge et al., Berkeley 1997) 145–58.

Broughton, T. Robert S. *The Magistrates of the Roman Republic* (New York 1951–52).

Bruneau, Philippe and Jean Ducat. *Guide de Délos* (2nd ed., Paris 1966).

Buelens, Marie-Astrid. "A Matter of Names: King Mithridates VI and the Oracle of Hystaspes," in *Interconnectivity in the Mediterranean and Pontic World during the Hellenistic and Roman Periods* (ed. Victor Cojocaru et al., Cluj-Napoca 2014) 397–411.

Bugh, Glenn R. "Mithridates the Great and the Freedom of the Greeks," in *Interconnectivity in the Mediterranean and Pontic World during the Hellenistic and Roman Periods* (ed. Victor Cojocaru et al., Cluj-Napoca 2014) 383–95.

Burstein, Stanley M. "The Aftermath of the Peace of Apamea," *AJAH* 5 (1980) 1–12.

Burstein, Stanley M. *The Hellenistic Age from the Battle of Ipsos to the Death of Kleopatra VII* (Cambridge 1985).

Camp, John et al. "A Trophy from the Battle of Chaironeia of 86 B.C.," *AJA* 96 (1992) 443–55.

Campbell, J. Brian. "Legio," *BNP* 7 (2005) 356–71.

Carney, Elizabeth Donnelly. *Arsinoë of Egypt and Macedon* (Oxford 2103).

Casson, Lionel. *The Ancient Mariners* (2nd ed., Princeton 1991).

Casson, Lionel. *Ships and Seamanship in the Ancient World* (Princeton 1971).

Champion, Craige B. *Commentary to BNJ* no. 508.

Chaniotis, Angelos. *Die Verträge zwischen kretischen Poleis in der hellenistischen Zeit* (Stuttgart 1996).

Chapouthier, Fernand. *Le Sanctuaire des dieux de Samothrace* (Exploration Archéologique de Délos 16, Paris 1935).

Clarke, Katherine. *Between Geography and History: Hellenistic Constructions of the Roman World* (Oxford 1999).

Clayman, Dee L. *Berenice and the Golden Age of Ptolemaic Egypt* (Oxford 2014).

Clinton, Kevin. "Maroneia and Rome: Two Decrees of Maroneia from Samothrace," *Chiron* 33 (2003) 379–417.

Cohen, Getzel M. *The Hellenistic Settlements in the East from Armenia and Mesopotamia to Bactria and India* (Berkeley 2013).

Cohen, Getzel M. *The Hellenistic Settlements in Europe, the Islands, and Asia Minor* (Berkeley 1995).

Cohen, Getzel M. *The Hellenistic Settlements in Syria, the Red Sea Basin, and North Africa* (Berkeley 2006).

Collins, Andrew and John Walsh. "Debt Deflationary Crisis in the Late Roman Republic," *AncSoc* 45 (2015) 125–70.

Coşkun, Altay. "The War of Brothers, the Third Syrian War, and the Battle of Ankyra (246–241 BC): A Reappraisal," in *The Seleukid Empire 281–222 BC* (ed. Kyle Erickson, Swansea 2018) 197–252.

Dalby, Andrew. *Food in the Ancient World from A to Z* (London 2003).

de Callataÿ, François. "The First Royal Coinages of Pontos (from Mithridates III to Mithridates V)," in *Mithridates VI and the Pontic Kingdom* (ed. Jacob Munk Højte, Aarhus 2009) 63–94.

de Souza, Philip. *Piracy in the Graeco-Roman World* (Cambridge 1999).

Derow, Peter S. "The Arrival of Rome: From the Illyrian Wars to the Fall of Macedon," in *A Companion to the Hellenistic World* (ed. Andrew Erskine, Oxford 2003) 51–70.

Derow, Peter S. "Rome, the Fall of Macedon and the Sack of Corinth," *CAH* 8 (2nd ed., 1989) 290–323.

Desideri, Paolo. "Poseidonio e la guerra mithridatica," *Athenaeum* 51 (1973) 3–29, 237–69.

Diehl, Erich. "Pharnakes [1]," *RE* 19 (1938) 1849–51.

Dmitriev, Sviatoslav. "Cappadocian Dynastic Rearrangements on the Eve of the First Mithridatic War," *Historia* 55 (2006) 285–97.

Drew-Bear, Thomas. "Three Senatus Consulta Concerning the Province of Asia," *Historia* 21 (1972) 75–87.

Dürrbach, Felix. *Choix d'inscriptions de Délos* (Chicago 1977).

Erciyas, Deniz Burlu. "Komana Pontike: A City or a Sanctuary?" in *Mithridates VI and the Pontic Kingdom* (ed. Jacob Munk Højte, Aarhus 2009) 289–312.

Erciyas, Deniz Burlu. "Studies in the Archaeology of Hellenistic Pontus: The Settlements, Monuments, and Coinage of Mithridates VI and His Predecessors" (Ph.D. dissertation, University of Cincinnati 2001).

Erciyas, Deniz Burlu. *Wealth, Aristocracy and Royal Propaganda under the Hellenistic Kingdom of the Mithradatids in the Central Black Sea Region of Turkey* (Leiden 2006).

Errington, Robert Malcolm. "Rom und das Schwarze Meer im 2. Jh. v. Chr," in *Die Außenbeziehungen pontischer und kleinasiatisher Städte in hellenistischer und römischer Zeit* (ed. Victor Cojocaru and Christof Schuler, Stuttgart 2014) 37–44.

Evans, Richard J. *Gaius Marius: A Political Biography* (Pretoria 1994).

Fleischer, Robert. *Der Felsgräber der Könige von Pontos in Amasya* (Tübingen 2017).

Fleischer, Robert. "The Rock-Tombs of the Pontic Kings in Amaseia (Amasya)," in *Mithridates VI and the Pontic Kingdom* (ed. J. M. Højte, Aarhus 2009) 109–19.

Flemming, Rebecca. "Empires of Knowledge: Medicine and Health in the Hellenistic World," in *A Companion to the Hellenistic World* (ed. Andrew Erskine, Malden, Mass. 2003) 449–63.

Forrer, Leonard. *Portraits of Royal Ladies on Greek Coins* (Chicago 1969).

Fraser, P. M. *Ptolemaic Alexandria* (Oxford 1972).

Gabba, Emilio. "Rome and Italy: The Social War," *CAH* 9 (2nd ed., 1994) 104–28.

Gabelko, Oleg L. "Bithynia and Cappadocia: Royal Courts and Ruling Society in Minor Hellenistic Monarchies," in *The Hellenistic Court: Monarchic Power and Elite Society from Alexander to Cleopatra* (ed. Andrew Erskine et al., Swansea 2017) 319–42.

Gabelko, Oleg L. "The Dynastic History of the Hellenistic Monarchies of Asia Minor According to the *Chronography* of George Synkellos," in *Mithridates VI and the Pontic Kingdom* (ed. Jakob Munk Højte, Aarhus 2009) 47–61.

Gavrilov, A. K. "Das Diophantosdekret und Strabon," *Hyperboreus* 2 (1996) 151–68.

Geyer, F. "Mithridates VI. Eupator Dionysos," *RE* 15 (1932) 2163–2205.

Ghiţă, Cristian Emilian. "Nysa—A Seleucid Princess in Anatolian Context," in *Seleucid Dissolution: The Sinking of the Anchor* (ed. Kyle Erickson and Gillian Ramsay, Wiesbaden 2011) 107–16.

Gizewski, Christian. "Ambitus," *BNP* 1 (2002) 568–69.

Glew, Dennis G. "400 Villages? A Note on Appian, *Mith.* 65, 172," *EA* 32 (2000) 155–62.

Glover, R. F. "Some Curiosities of Ancient Warfare," *G&R* 19 (1950) 1–9.

Grace, Virginia. "The Middle Stoa Dated by Amphora Stamps," *Hesperia* 54 (1985) 1–54.

Grainger, John D. *A Seleukid Prosopography* (Leiden 1997).

Gruen, Erich S. "The Coronation of the Diadochoi," in *The Craft of the Ancient Historian* (ed. John William Eadie and Josiah Ober, Lanham, Md. 1985) 253–71.

Gruen, Erich S. *The Hellenistic World and the Coming of Rome* (Berkeley 1984).

Gruen, Erich S. *The Last Generation of the Roman Republic* (Berkeley 1974).

Habicht, Christian. *Athens from Alexander to Antony* (tr. Deborah Lucas Schneider, Cambridge, Mass. 1997).

Habicht, Christian. "The Seleucids and Their Rivals," *CAH* 8 (2nd ed., 1989) 324–87.

Habicht, Christian. "Über die Kriege Zwischen Pergamon und Bithynien," *Hermes* 84 (1956) 90–110.

Habicht, Christian. "Zipoites [I]," *RE* 2. ser. 10 (1972) 448–59.

Head, Barclay V. *Historia Numorum* (Oxford 1911).

Heckel, Waldemar. *Who's Who in the Age of Alexander the Great* (Oxford 2006).

Heftner, Herbert. "Der Streit um das Kommando im Krieg gegen Mithridates (Diodorus Siculus 37,2,12) und die versuchte Konsulskandidatur des C. Iulius Caesar Strabo," *Tyche* 23 (2008) 79–100.

Heinen, Heinz. "Die Anfänge der Beziehungen Roms zum nördlichen Schwarzmeerraum," in *Roms auswärtige Freunde in der späten Republik und im frühen Prinzipat* (ed. Altay Coşkun, Göttingen 2005) 31–54.

Heinen, Heinz. "Mithradates VI. Eupator und die Völker des nördlichen Schwarzmeerraums," *HBA* 18 (1991) 151–65.

Heinen, Heinz. *Pontische Studien* (Mainz 1997).

Heinen, Heinz. "The Syrian-Egyptian Wars and the New Kingdoms of Asia Minor," *CAH* 7.1 (2nd ed., 1984) 412–15.

Herz, Peter. "'Aus die Osten wird ein Retter kommen . . .' Die Widerstand der Griechen gegen die römische Heerschaft," in *Zur Erschließung von Zukunft in den Religionen: Zukunftserwartung und Gegenwartsbewältigung in der Religionsgeschichte* (ed. Hans Wissmann et al., Würzburg 1991) 67–88.

Hind, John G. F. "Archaeology of the Greeks and Barbarian Peoples around the Black Sea (1982–92)," *AR* 39 (1992–93) 82–112.

Hind, John G. F. "Mithridates," *CAH* 9 (2nd ed., 1994) 129–64.

Højte, Jakob Munk. "The Administrative Organisation of the Pontic Kingdom," in *Mithridates VI and the Pontic Kingdom* (ed. Jakob Munk Højte, Aarhus 2009) 95–107.

Højte, Jakob Munk. "The Date of the Alliance Between Chersonesos and Pharnakes (*IOSPE* 1², 402) and Its Implications," in *Chronologies of the Black Sea in the Period c. 400–100 BC* (ed. Vladimir F. Stolba and Lise Hannestad, Aarhus 2005) 137–52.

Højte, Jakob Munk. "The Death and Burial of Mithridates VI," in *Mithridates VI and the Pontic Kingdom* (ed. Jakob Munk Højte, Aarhus 2009) 121–30.

Højte, Jakob Munk. "Portraits and Statues of Mithridates VI," in *Mithridates VI and the Pontic Kingdom* (ed. Jacob Munk Højte, Aarhus 2009) 145–61.

Hölbl, Günther. *A History of the Ptolemaic Empire* (tr. Tina Saavedra, London 2001).

Hope Simpson, R., and J. F. Lazenby. *The Catalogue of the Ships in Homer's* Iliad (Oxford 1970).

Jackson, Monica M. "The Amisos Treasure: A Hellenistic Tomb from the Age of Mithridates Eupator," in *The Black Sea, Paphlagonia, Pontus and Phrygia in Antiquity* (BAR-IS 2432, Oxford 2012) 109–116.

Jacques, Jean-Marie. "Antiokhos VIII Philometor," *EANS* 95–96.

Jacques, Jean-Marie. "Krateuas," *EANS* 491.

Jung-Kaiser, Ute. "Mithridates," *BNP Supplement* 7 (2016) 291–95.

Kaldellis, Anthony. *Commentary to BNJ* no. 188.

Kallet-Marx, Robert. *Hegemony to Empire: The Development of the Roman Imperium in the East from 148 to 62 B.C.* (Berkeley 1996).

Kaygusuz, Ismail. "Zwei neue Inschriften aus Ilgaz (Olgassys) und Kimiatene," *EA* 1 (1983) 59–60.

Keaveney, Arthur. *Lucullus: A Life* (London 1992).

Keaveney, Arthur. *Sulla: The Last Republican* (2nd ed., London 2005).

Keyser, Paul T. "Mithradates VI, King of Pontos," *EANS* 557–58.

Keyser, Paul T. "Nikomedes IV of Bithunia," *EANS* 581.

Kidd, I. G. *Posidonius 2: The Commentary* (Cambridge 1988).

Konrad, C. F. *Plutarch's Sertorius* (Chapel Hill, N. C. 1994).

Kreuz, Patric-Alexander. "Monuments for the King: Royal Presence in the Late Hellenistic World of Mithridates VI," in *Mithridates VI and the Pontic Kingdom* (ed. Jakob Munk Højte, Aarhus 2009) 131–44.

Kuttner, Ann. "Cabinet Fit for a Queen: The Λιθικά as Posidippus' Gem Museum," in *The New Posidippus: A Hellenistic Poetry Book* (ed. Kathryn Gutzwiller, Oxford 2005) 141–563.

Landels, J. G. "Ship-Shape and *Sambuca*-Fashion," *JHS* 86 (1966) 69–77.

Larsen, J. A. O. "The Araxa Inscription and the Lycian Confederacy," *CP* 51 (1956) 151–69.

Latyschev, Basilius. *Inscriptiones antiquae orae septentrionalis Ponti Euxini* 1 (Petersburg 1906).

Lawrence, A. W. *Greek Architecture* (4th ed., revised by R. A. Tomlinson, Harmondsworth 1983).

Le Rider, Georges. "L'enfant-roi Antiochos et la reine Laodice," *BCH* 110 (1986) 409–17.

Lerouge-Cohen, Charlotte. "Persianism in the Kingdom of Pontic Kappadokia: The Genealogical Claims of the Mithridatids," in *Persianism in Antiquity* (ed. Rolf Strootman and Miguel John Versluys, Stuttgart 2017) 223–33.

Linderski, Jerzy. "A Missing Ponticus," *AJAH* 12 (1987) 148–66.

Lintott, Andrew. "The Roman Empire and Its Problems in the Late Second Century," *CAH* 9 (2nd ed., 1994) 16–39.

Lorenz, Thuri. "Von Alexander dem Großen zu Mithridates," *JÖAI* 70 (2001) 65–79.

Ma, John. *Antiochos III and the Cities of Western Asia Minor* (Oxford 1999).

McGing, Brian C. "Appian's 'Mithridateios,'" *ANRW* 34 (1993) 496–522.

McGing, Brian C. "The Date of the Outbreak of the Third Mithridatic War," *Phoenix* 38 (1984) 12–18.

McGing, Brian C. *The Foreign Policy of Mithridates VI Eupator, King of Pontus* (Leiden 1986).

McGing, Brian C. "The Kings of Pontus: Some Problems of Identity and Date," *RhM* 129 (1986) 248–59.

McGing, Brian C. "Mithridates VI Eupator: Victim or Aggressor," in *Mithridates VI and the Pontic Kingdom* (ed. Jakob Munk Højte, Aarhus 2009) 203–16.

McGing, Brian C. "Subjection and Resistance: To the Death of Mithridates," in *A Companion to the Hellenistic World* (ed. Andrew Erskine, Oxford 2003) 71–89.

McLean, B. H. *An Introduction to Greek Epigraphy of the Hellenistic and Roman Periods from Alexander the Great Down to the Reign of Constantine (323 B.C.—A.D. 337)* (Ann Arbor 2002).

Magie, David. *Roman Rule in Asia Minor* (Princeton 1950).

Maier, Friedrich. "Kritik am Imperium Romanum: Die Stimme des Ostens," *Anregung* 40 (1994) 82–88.

Manchado, Javier Verdejo, and Borja Antela-Bernárdez. "A Crown for Onaso and the Archon Athenion," *ZPE* 177 (2011) 91–96.

Manchado, Javier Verdejo, and Borja Antela-Bernárdez. "Pro-Mithridatic and Pro-Roman Tendencies on Delos in the Early First Century BC: The Case of Dikaios of Ionidai (ID 2039 and 2040)," *DHA* 41 (2015) 117–26.

Marek, Christian. "Hellenisation and Romanisation in Pontos-Bithynia: An Overview," in *Mithridates VI and the Pontic Kingdom* (ed. Jakob Munk Højte, Aarhus 2009) 35–46.

Masden, Jesper Majbom. "The Ambitions of Mithridates VI: Hellenistic Kingship and Modern Interpretations," in *Mithridates VI and the Pontic Kingdom* (ed. Jakob Munk Højte, Aarhus 2009) 191–201.

Mattingly, Harold. "The Coinage of Mithradates III, Pharnakes and Mithradates IV of Pontos," in *Studies in Greek Numismatics in Honor of Martin Jessop Price* (ed. Richard Ashton and Silvia Hurter, London 1998) 255–58.

Mellor, Ronald. "The Dedications on the Capitol Hill," *Chiron* 8 (1978) 319–30.

Meyer, Eduard. *Geschichte des Königreiches Pontos* (Leipzig 1879).

Mileta, Christian. "Mithridates der Große von Pontos—Gott auf Zeit oder: Einmal zur Unsterblickeit und zurück," in *Lebendige Hoffnung—ewiger Tod?!: Jenseitsvorstellungen im Hellenismus, Judentum und Christentum* (ed. Michael Labahn and Manfred Lang, Leipzig 2007) 359–78.

Mitchell, Stephen. *Anatolia: Land, Men, and Gods in Asia Minor* (Oxford 1995).

Mitchell, Stephen. "The Galatians: Representation and Reality," in *A Companion to the Hellenistic World* (ed. Andrew Erskine, London 2005) 280–93.

Mitchell, Stephen. "In Search of the Pontic Community," in *Representations of Empire: Rome and the Mediterranean World* (ed. Alan K. Bowman, Oxford 2002) 35–64.

Mitchell, Stephen. "Tavium," *PECS* 887.

Mitford, Timothy Bruce. *East of Asia Minor: Rome's Hidden Frontier* (Oxford 2018).

Morstein-Marx, Robert. "The Alleged 'Massacre' at Cirta and Its Consequences (Sallust *Bellum Iugurthinum* 26–27," *CP* 95 (2000) 468–76.

Muccioli, Federicomaria. "Εὐπάτωρ nella titolatura ellenistica," *Historia* 45 (1996) 21–35.

Nawotka, Krzysztof. *Boule and Demos in Miletus and Its Pontic Colonies from Classical Age until Third Century A.D.* (Wrocław 1999).

Noonan, Thomas S. "The Grain Trade of the Northern Black Sea in Antiquity," *AJP* 94 (1973) 231–42.

Occhipinti, Egilia. "Athenaeus's Sixth Book on Greek and Roman Slavery," *SCI* 34 (2015) 115–27.

O'Gorman, Ellen. "The Politics of Sallustian Style," in *A Companion to Greek and Roman Historiography* (ed. John Marioncola, Malden, Mass. 2007) 379–84.

Olbrycht, Marek Jan. "Mithridates VI Eupator and Iran," in *Mithridates VI and the Pontic Kingdom* (ed. Jakob Munk Højte, Aarhus 2009) 163–90.

Olbrycht, Marek Jan. "Subjects and Allies: The Black Sea Empire of Mithradates VI Eupator (120–63 BC) Reconsidered," in *Pontika 2008: Recent Research on the Northern and Eastern Black Sea in Ancient Times* (ed. Ewdoksia Papuci-Władyka et al., BAR-IS 2240, Oxford 2011) 275–81.

Olshausen, Eckart. "Mithridates VI. und Rom," *ANRW* 1.1 (1972) 806–15.

Olshausen, Eckart. "Zum Hellenisierungsprozess am Pontischen Königshof," *AncSoc* 5 (1974) 153–70.

Panitschek, Peter. "Zu den genealogischen Konstruction der Dynastien von Pontos," *RSA* 17/18 (1987–88) 73–95.

Patacı, Sami, and Ergün Laflı. "Archaeology of the Southern Black Sea Area during the Period of Mithridates VI Eupator," in *Recent Studies on the Archaeology of Anatolia* (BAR-IS 2750, Oxford 2015) 313–25.

Patterson, Lee. "Mithridates II' Invasion of Armenia: A Reassessment," *REArm* 39 (2020) 161–72.

Patterson, Lee. "Rome's Relationship with Artaxias I of Armenia," *AHB* 15 (2001) 156.

Perl, Gerhard. "Kontroverse Stellen in den "Historiae" Sallusts," *Hermes* 133 (2005) 178–95.

Perl, Gerhard. "Zur Chronologie der Königreiche Bithynia, Pontos und Bosporos," in *Studien zur Geschichte und Philosophie des Altertums* (ed. J. Harmatta, Amsterdam 1968) 299–330.

Petković, Žarko. "The Aftermath of the Apamean Settlement: Early Challenges to the New Order in Asia Minor," *Klio* 94 (2012) 357–65.

Petković, Žarko. The *Bellum Dardanicum* and the Third Mithridatic War," *Historia* 63 (2014) 187–93.

Petković, Žarko. "Mithridates II and Antiochos Hierax," *Klio* 91 (2009) 378–83.

Pfeiler, Hesso. "Die Frühesten Porträts des Mithridates Eupator und die Bronzeprägung seiner Vorgänger," *GNS* 18–22 (1968–72) 75–80.

Plantzos, Dimitris. *Hellenistic Engraved Gems* (Oxford 1999).

Préaux, Claire. *Le monde hellénistique* (Paris 1978).

Raaflaub, Kurt A. "Between Myth and History: Rome's Rise from Village to Empire (the Eighth Century to 264)," in *A Companion to the Roman Republic* (ed. Nathan Rosenstein and Robert Morstein-Marx, Malden, Mass. 2010) 125–46.

Ramsay, Gillian. "The Queen and the City: Royal Female Intervention and Patronage in Hellenistic Civic Communities," in *Gender and the City Before Modernity* (ed. Lin Foxhall and Gabriele Neher, Oxford 2013) 20–37.

Ramsey, John T. "Mithridates, the Banner of Ch'ih-Yu, and the Comet Coin," *HSCP* 99 (1999) 197–253.

Rawson, Elizabeth. "Caesar's Heritage: Hellenistic Kings and Their Roman Equals," *JRS* 65 (1975) 148–59.

Reams, Lee A. "The 'Friends' of Mithridates VI: A Case of Mistaken Identity," *CB* 64 (1988) 21–23.

Reinach, Théodore. *Mithridate Eupator, Roi de Pont* (Paris 1890).

Reinach, Théodore. "Note sur une inscription de Délos en l'honneur de Laodice (Philadelphe), princesse du Pont," *BCH* 34 (1910) 429–31.

Reynolds, Joyce. *Aphrodisias and Rome* (London 1982).

Richardson, L., Jr. *A New Topographical Dictionary of Ancient Rome* (Baltimore 1992).

Robert, Louis. "Monnaies et textes grecs," *JSav* for 1978, pp. 145–64.

Roller, Duane W. *Cleopatra: A Biography* (Oxford 2010).

Roller, Duane W. *Cleopatra's Daughter and Other Royal Women of the Augustan Era* (Oxford 2018).

Roller, Duane W. *A Historical and Topographical Guide to the Geography of Strabo* (Cambridge 2018).

Roller, Duane W. *Scholarly Kings: The Writings of Juba II of Mauretania, Archelaos of Kappadokia, Herod the Great and the Emperor Claudius* (Chicago 2004).

Roller, Duane W. *The World of Juba II and Kleopatra Selene* (London 2003).

Roos, Paavo. "Strabo and the Water-Mill at Cabeira: Some Considerations," *OpRom* 20 (1996) 99–102.

Rose, Charles Brian. *The Archaeology of Greek and Roman Troy* (Cambridge 2014).

Rostovtzeff, M. *Social and Economic History of the Hellenistic World* (Oxford 1941).

Rubinsohn, Zeev Wolfgang. "Saumakos: Ancient History, Modern Politics," *Historia* 29 (1980) 50–70.

Ryan, Franz X. "Die Zurücknahme Großphrygiens und die Unmündigkeit des Mithridates VI. Eupator," *OT* 7 (2001) 99–106.

Sanders, G. D. R., and R. W. V. Catling. "A New Fragment of *I Delos* 1562," *ABSA* 85 (1990) 327–32.

Saprykin, Sergei. "Naturkastrophen und Naturerscheinungen in die Ideologie des Mithridates Eupator," *GH* 10 (1998) 396–403.

Saprykin, Sergei. "The Religion and Cults of the Pontic Kingdom: Political Aspects," in *Mithridates VI and the Pontic Kingdom* (ed. Jakob Munk Højte, Aarhus 2009) 249–75.

Scarborough, John. "Asklepiades of Bithunia," *EANS* 170–71.

Schmitt, Rüdiger. "Iranische Personennamen auf griechischen Inschriften," in *Actes du VIIe Congrès International d'Épigraphie Grecque et Latine* (ed. D. M. Pippidi, Paris 1979) 138–52.

Scullard, H. H. "Carthage and Rome," *CAH* 7.2 (2nd ed., 1989) 486–572.

Scullard, H. H. *From the Gracchi to Nero* (4th ed., London 1976).

Seager, Robin. *Pompey the Great: A Political Biography* (2nd ed., Oxford 2002).

Seager, Robin. "The Rise of Pompey," *CAH* 9 (1994) 208–28.

Segre, Mario. "Due nuovi testi storici," *RFIC* 60 (1932) 446–61.

Shelov, D. B. "The Ancient Idea of a Unified Pontic State," *VDI* for 1986, pp. 36–42.

Sherk, Robert K. *Rome and the Greek East to the Death of Augustus* (Cambridge 1984).

Sherwin-White, A. N. *Roman Foreign Policy in the East, 186 B.C. to A.D. 1* (Norman 1983).

Sherwin-White, A. N. "Roman Involvement in Anatolia, 167–88 B.C.," *JRS* 67 (1977) 62–75.

Sidonius Apollonaris. *Apollonaris Sidonius, Carm. 22: Burgus Pontii Leontii* (ed. Norbert Delhey, Berlin 1993).

Sökmen, Emine. "Characteristics of the Temple States in Pontos," in *Mithridates VI and the Pontic Kingdom* (ed. Jakob Munk Højte, Aarhus 2009) 277–87.

Sonnabend, Holger. "Ein Hannibal aus dem Osten? Die 'letzen Pläne' des Mithradates VI. von Pontos," in *Alte Geschichte: Wege—Einsichten—Horizonte* (ed. Ulrich Fellmeth and Holder Sonnabend, Hildesheim 1998) 191–206.

Spann, Philip D. *Quintus Sertorius* (Fayetteville, Ark. 1987).

Spier, Jeffrey. *Ancient Gems and Finger Rings* (Malibu 1992).

Spier, Jeffrey. "A Group of Ptolemaic Engraved Garnets," *JWAG* 47 (1989) 21–38,

Stewart, Andrew. *Greek Sculpture: An Exploration* (New Haven 1990).

Stok, Fabio. "Zopuros of Alexandria," *EANS* 851.

Strabo, *Géographie* 9 (ed. François Lasserre, Paris 2003).

Strobel, Karl. "Mithridates VI. Eupator von Pontos," *Ktema* 21 (1996) 55–94.

Sullivan, Richard D. "The Dynasty of Cappadocia," *ANRW* 7.2 (1980) 1125–68.

Sullivan, Richard D. *Near Eastern Royalty and Rome, 100–30 BC* (Toronto 1990).

Summerer, Lâtife. "Das pontische Wappen: Zur Astralsymbolik auf den pontischen Münzen," *Chiron* 25 (1995) 305–14.

Summerer, Lâtife. "The Search for Mithridates: Reception of Mithridates VI Between the 15th and the 20th Centuries," in *Mithridates VI and the Pontic Kingdom* (ed. Jacob Munk Højte, Aarhus 2009) 15–34.

Sutherland, C. H. V. *Roman Coins* (New York 1974).

Syme, Ronald. *Anatolica: Studies in Strabo* (ed. Anthony Birley, Oxford 1995).

Syme, Ronald. *Sallust* (Berkeley 1964).

Synkellos, Georgios. *The Chronography of George Synkellos* (tr. William Adler and Paul Tuffin, Oxford 2002).

Tarn, W. W. *The Greeks in Bactria and India* (3rd ed., Chicago 1985).

Thibodeau, Philip. "Attalos III of Pergamon, Philometor," *EANS* 179–80.

Thibodeau, Philip. "Pompeius Lenaeus," *EANS* 684.

Thompson, Homer A. *The Tholos of Athens and Its Predecessors* (Hesperia Supplement 4, 1940).

Thonemann, Peter. "The Attalid State, 188–133 BC," in *Attalid Asia Minor* (ed. Peter Thonemann, Oxford 2013) 1–47.

Totelin, Laurence M. V. "Botanizing Rulers and Their Herbal Subjects: Plants and Political Power in Greek and Roman Literature," *Phoenix* 66 (2012) 122–44.

Totelin, Laurence M. V. "Mithridates' Antidote—A Pharmacological Ghost," *ESM* 9 (2004) 1–19.

Totelin, Laurence M. V. "The World in a Pill: Local Specialities and Global Remedies in the Graeco-Roman World," in *The Routledge Handbook of Identity and the Environment in the Classical and Medieval Worlds* (ed. Rebecca Futo Kennedy and Molly Jones-Lewis, Oxford 2016) 151–70.

Toynbee, J. M. C. *Roman Historical Portraits* (London 1978).

Trofimova, Anna A., ed. *Greeks on the Black Sea: Ancient Art from the Hermitage* (Los Angeles 2007).

Trofimova, Anna. "The Sculpted Portrait in the Bosporus," in *Greeks on the Black Sea* (ed. Anna A. Trofimova, Los Angeles 2007) 46–55.

Tsetskhladze, Gocha R. "A Survey of the Major Urban Settlements in the Kimmerian Bosporos (with a Discussion of Their Status as *Poleis*)," in *Yet More Studies in the Ancient Greek Polis* (ed. Thomas Heine Nielsen, Stuttgart 1997) 39–81.

Vinogradov, Jurij G. *Pontische Studien* (Mainz 1997).

Vnukov, Sergey. "Overseas Trade," in *The Northern Black Sea in Antiquity* (ed. Valeriya Kozlovskaya, Cambridge 2010) 100–138.

Vogt, Sabine. "Drugs and Pharmacology," in *The Cambridge Companion to Galen* (ed. R. J. Hankinson, Cambridge 2008) 304–22.

Vollenweider, Marie-Louise. "Deux portraits inconnus de la dynastie du Pont et les graveurs Nikias, Zoïlos et Apollonios," *AK* 23 (1980) 146–53.

Vorster, Christiane. "Mythos in der dritten Dimension—Zu Komposition und Interpretation der Herakles-Prometheus-Gruppe," in *Pergamon: Panorama der antiken Metropole* (ed. Ralf Grüssinger et al., Berlin 2011) 131–37.

Waddington, W. H. *Recueil général des monnaies grecques d'Asie Mineure* (Paris 1925).

Wagner, Stefan E. A. "Die Herakles-Prometheus-Gruppe aus Pergamon und ihre Bedeutung im Kontext der attalidischen Herrscherrepräsentation," *IstMitt* 65 (2015) 129–49.

Walbank, F. W. *A Historical Commentary on Polybius* (Oxford 1970–1979).

Walbank, F. W. "Monarchies and Monarchic Ideas," *CAH* 7.1 (2nd ed., 1984) 62–100.

Wallace, Shane. "Court, Kingship and Royal Style in the Early Hellenistic Period," in *The Hellenistic Court: Monarchic Power and Elite Society from Alexander to Cleopatra* (ed. Andrew Erskine et al., Swansea 2017) 1–30.

Wasowicz, Aleksandra. "Vin, salaison et guerre dans le Bospore aux confins des ères," in *Structures rurales et sociétés antiques* (ed. Panagiotes N. Doukellis and Lina G. Mendoni, Paris 1994) 227–35.

Waterfield, Robin. *Taken at the Flood: The Roman Conquest of Greece* (Oxford 2014).

Welles, C. Bradford. *Royal Correspondence in the Hellenistic Period* (New Haven 1934).

West, Stephanie. "'The Most Marvellous of All Seas': The Greek Encounter with the Euxine," *G&R* 50 (2003) 151–67.

Wheatley, P. V. "The Lifespan of Demetrius Poliorcetes," *Historia* 46 (1997) 19–27.

Wiesehöfer, Josef. *Ancient Persia from 550 BC to 650 AD* (tr. Azizeh Azodi, London 1996).

Wikander, Örjan. "Sources of Energy and Exploitation of Power," in *The Oxford Handbook of Engineering and Technology in the Classical World* (ed. John Peter Oleson, Oxford 2008) 136–57.

Williams, John. *Observations of Comets* (London 1871).

Wilson, D. R. "Amaseia," *PECS* 47.

Wilson, D. R. "Comana Pontica," *PECS* 234.

Wilson, D. R. "Neocaesarea," *PECS* 620.

Wilson, D. R. "Pharnakeia Kerasous," *PECS* 699.

Wilson, D. R. "Zela," *PECS* 999.

Winder, Stephanie J. "'The Hands of Gods': Poison in the Hellenistic Court," in *The Hellenistic Court: Monarchic Power and Elite Society from Alexander to Cleopatra* (ed. Andrew Erskine et al., Swansea 2017) 373–407.

LIST OF PASSAGES CITED

For the benefit of digital users, indexed terms that span two pages (e.g., 52–53) may, on occasion, appear on only one of those pages.

Italicized numbers are citations in ancient sources; romanized numbers are pages in this volume.

Greek and Latin Literary Sources

Aelian
  On the Characteristics of Animals 7.46, 231n11
  Historical Miscellany 1.27, 230n9
Aeschylus
  Persians 970, 231n27
  Prometheus Bound 723–5, 221n48; *732–5*, 226n63
Ammianus Marcellinus *16.7.9–10*, 243n11
Antisthenes of Rhodes *F2*, 235n1
Apollonios, *Bibliotheke 2.5.9*, 221n48
Apollonios of Aphrodisias *F14*, 223n54
Appian
  Civil War
    Book 1: *3*, 240n35; *32*, 233n58; *98–9*, 240n33; *101*, 240n34; *102*, 244n23; *103–4*, 240n35; *107*, 241n2; *108–15*, 240n40; *116–20*, 241n6
    Book 5: *75*, 247n35
  Libyka 74–5, 229n51; *127–32*, 229n51
  Mithridateios 1–9, 235n41; *4–7*, 226n39; *7*, 228n11; *9*, 222n29, 222n34, 222n39, 222n43, 224n2; *10*, 228n24, 228n27, 229n52, 229n54, 229n63, 230n83, 233n40, 234n65; *10–11*, 234n16; *11–12*, 232n2, 235n31; *11–17*, 235n33; *12*, 229n49, 229n63; *15*, 232n2, 232n6, 233n38, 233n44, 234n14; *16*, 235n42, 236n40, 238n78;

17, 235n45; *17–19*, 236n15; *20*, 231n13, 232n58, 236n24; *21*, 236n30, 236n37, 237n68; *22*, 238n93; *22–3*, 237n52; *23*, 236n31; *24*, 236n26; *27*, 236n36; *28*, 238n80; *28–9*, 238n85; *29*, 241n28; *30*, 238n91; *30–40*, 238n95; *32*, 239n12; *35*, 236n18, 238n86; *41*, 238n86; *41–5*, 238n99; *43*, 239n12; *45*, 239n102; *46*, 239n105, 245n64; *46–8*, 239n104; *48*, 239n107, 239n108, 243n2; *49–51*, 238n101; *51*, 240n28; *51–60*, 239n109; *52*, 239n6; *54*, 239n110; *55*, 239n111, 239n10; *56*, 236n39; *56–7*, 232n2; *56–8*, 239n115; *57*, 229n44, 229n60, 234n10, 234n16, 235n36; *58*, 233n49; *59–60*, 239n116; *62*, 228n37; *63*, 239n108, 241n58; *64*, 239n5, 239n6, 239n8, 239n12; *64–6*, 239n14; *65*, 239n15; *65–6*, 240n20; *66*, 243n9; *67*, 233n30, 240n26, 240n36, 240n38, 245n48; *68*, 240n42, 240n48; *69*, 240n55; *69–71*, 241n11; *70*, 241n62, 241n1, 241n9, 241n28, 242n58; *71*, 240n54, 241n20, 241n22; *72*, 240n49; *72–7*, 242n35; *75*, 242n31; *76*, 241n23; *76–7*, 241n24; *77*, 222n13, 242n42, 243n17; *78*, 241n58, 242n43, 245n28, 245n58; *79–83*, 242n50; *82*, 231n42, 242n52, 242n62, 243n2; *83*, 242n52, 242n61; *84*, 242n68; *85*,

259

Strabo of Amaseia *(cont.)*
236n33; *2.13*, 236n33; *3.3*, 232n58; *5.2*,
229n69, 234n10, 234n19; *5.23*, 229n50
Book 15: 1.6, 237n44
Book 16: 1.2, 220n43; *1.24*, 221n58
Book 17: 3.15, 228n28
Histories F6, 236n31
Suetonius
Divine Augustus 5, 247n49
Divine Julius 2, 240n31; *4*, 242n32
Nero 24.2, 247n48
Synkellos, Georgios, *Ekloga Chronographia 332*,
222n42

Tacitus
Agricola 30–32, 242n56
Annals 3.62, 236n30; *6.33*, 247n23
Tertullian, *de anima 46*, 222n30
Theophanes of Mytilene *F1*, 237n56
Theophrastos, *Research on Plants*
4.5.5, 221n50
Thucydides *1.32–6*, 229n38; *1.129*, 221n7

Valerius Maximus *1.8.ext.13*, 243n11; *4.6.ext.2*,
243n5; *9.2.ext.3*, 237n54, 237n57; *9.13.1*,
236n38
Varro, M. Terentius, *On Agriculture 1.1.8*, 228n35
Velleius *2.4.1*, 229n41; *2.12.1*, 233n54; *2.18*,
237n52; *2.18.3*, 236n37; *2.23.2*, 239n3; *2.31*,
241n5; *2.57*, 240n54
Vitruvius *7.7.5*, 221n54; *10.5.2*, 245n66

Xenophon
Anabasis:
Book 1: 7.10, 236n19
Book 3: 5.17, 226n50
Book 4: 8.22–8, 219n8
Book 5: 5.10, 220n13; *6.15*, 219n5; *6.19*,
219n5; *6.25*, 219n5
Book 6: 1.15, 220n13, 221n49; *2.4*, 219n5
Hellenika:
Book 1: 4.7, 223n1
Kyropaideia:
Book 1: 4.5–10, 231n33
Book 6: 1.27–30, 236n19

Biblical Sources

Genesis 2:14, 226n50; 8:4, 226n50
Ezekiel 38:6, 226n63
Luke 4:1–13, 231n36

I Maccabees 6:17, 231n28
Mark 1:12–13, 231n36
Matthew 2:2, 231n22; 4:1–11, 231n36

Epigraphical Texts

IGBulg 1, part 2, no. 40, 226n61
IDélos 1497bis, 227n74; *1555*, 227n2; *1555–6*,
228n18; *1557*, 245n73; *1557–9*, 229n71;
1560, 231n44, 232n52, 245n73; *1561*,
231n45; *1562*, 231n15, 235n22; *1564–8*,
235n27; *1565*, 245n73; *1568*, 245n73;
2039–40, 235n26
IG 2.2.1334, 238n73; *2/3.2.1713*, 238n72

OGIS 251–2, 224n26; *298*, 225n21; *329*, 228n7,
228n32; *338*, 228n37; *345*, 234n66; *352*,
228n8; *356*, 243n9; *365*, 227n87; *366*,
229n54, 229n72, 245n73; *372*, 220n31; *375*,
224n2, 227n1, 228n4, 230n83; *377*, 244n21;
435, 228n37; *445*, 242n30; *771*, 226n42
SEG 37.668, 245n74
SIG 40, 221n60; *741*, 237n65; *742*, 237n65, 237n68

INDEX

For the benefit of digital users, indexed terms that span two pages (e.g., 52–53) may, on occasion, appear on only one of those pages.

Laodike, sister-wife of Mithridates IV, 74, 89–90, 103, 130, 203–4

Laodike, sister-wife of Mithridates VI, 108, 192–93

Laodike, supposed name of wife of Mithridates V, 92

Laodike, wife of Ariarathes VI, 107–8, 122–23, 124, 125, 128–29

Laodikeia, Phrygian city, 142, 143, 213

Larisa, Thessalian city, 163–64

Lemnos, Aegean island, 171, 182–83

Leokritos of Athens, 59

Leokritos, Pontic commander, 59–60, 90

Leonippos, Pontic commander, 194–95

Lepidus, M. Aemilius, Roman consul, 174

Lesbos, Aegean island, 144–45, 158, 159–60

Levant, 28, 42, 46, 47, 52, 69, 86, 185

Lex Manilia, 197–212

Libyssa, Hannibal's estate, 54, 62–63

Liguria, European region, 195–96

linen, 112, 118–19

Lion's Head, Phrygian locale, 142

Livia, wife of Augustus, 198–99

Louis XIV of France, 216

Lucania, Italian region, 175

Lucullus, L. Licinius, Roman proconsul, 164, 198–99, 202–3, 215–16
   biography and writings about, 98–99, 107, 215
   in First Mithridatic War, 154–55, 156, 157, 159–60
   in Third Mithridatic War, 169, 182 174–191, 31, 192–93, 206, 207, 208

Lusitania, European region, 169–70

Lutatius Catulus, Q., Roman consul, 174

Lutatius Paccius, Lucius, royal perfumer, 195

Lykaonia, region of Asia Minor, 109

Lykia, region of Asia Minor, 77, 108–9, 143–44, 149

Lykos, river of Pontos, 11–12, 22, 184, 200–2

Lypedron, Bithynian mountain, 56–57

Lysanias, Asian dynast, 42

Lysimacheia, Thracian city, 55

Lysimachos, successor of Alexander the Great, 29, 33–31, 36–37, 38–39, 55, 65–66

Ma, Asian goddess, 18

Macedonia, Macedonians, 26, 29, 37, 52, 63, 154–55, 158–59, 171, 174–75

Macedonian Wars, 52–53

Machares, son of Mithridates VI, 168–69, 184, 187–88, 190–91, 194, 208, 209–10

Magius, L., Roman adventurer, 170, 171, 173

Magnesia by Sipylos, Lydian city, 53

Magnesia on the Meander, city in Asia Minor, 143

Magnopolis, Pontic locale, 201

Maiotis, 22–23, 66, 114–15, 119, 209

Mallius Maltinus, Roman commissioner, 128

Mamercus, Roman legate, 180

Mancinus (Titus Manlius Malcinus?), Roman commissioner, 128

Manilius, C., Roman tribune, 206

maple, 22

Marcius Philippus, L., Roman senator, 19–20

Marcus, Roman commissioner, 52–53

Mariandynia, region of Asia Minor, 26, 27–28, 31, 33–34

Marine, false toponym, 26, 27

Marius, C., Roman leader, 122, 137, 158–59, 167–68, 169–70, 215
   in Asia Minor, 119–20, 123–24, 137
   in Jugurthine War, 121, 155, 167

Marius, M., Roman commander, 170–71, 173, 176, 182–83, 195

Maroneia, Thracian town, 154–55

Marsic (Social) War, 120–21, 129, 134, 145, 146, 153–54, 155, 162, 167, 169–70, 173, 175–76

massacre in Asia, 148

Mauretania, African region, 46–47, 170

Mausolos of Halikarnassos, 13–14

Meander, river in Asia Minor, 143

Medea, Greek mythological figure, 66

Medeios, Athenian archon, 152

Medusa, mythical Gorgon, 204

Meleagros, Greek hero, 46

Memnon, Greek historian, 98–99

Men, Asian divinity, 18

Menophanes, Pontic commander, 154–55

mercury sulphide, 23

Mesembria, city on Black Sea, 59, 62, 65

Metrodoros, Pontic commander, 71–72

Metrodoros of Skepsis, 71–72, 188, 195–96

Metrophanes, Pontic commander, 154–55, 180, 207

Miletos, Ionian city, 9–10, 12–14, 22, 27–28, 61–62, 65, 66, 113, 170, 181, 187–88

miltos, 23

mineral resources, 23, 24, 111–12, 118–19

mines, mining, 23

Misenum, Campanian locale, 91–92

Mithras of Armenia, 129

Mithridates II of Parthia, 125–26

Mithridates of Pergamon, 193

Mithridates I the Founder, of Pontos, 15–17, 25, 27–29, 33, 36

Mithridates II of Pontos, 14, 40, 42, 50–51, 53, 57–58, 67, 69–71, 86

Mithridates III of Pontos, 50, 52, 54, 71–72, 74

Mithridates IV of Pontos, 50–51, 54–55, 69–72, 74

Mithridates V of Pontos, 64, 69–71, 72–73, 84–87, 90

Pompey (Gaius Pompeius) the Great, Roman
    magistrate, 97–98, 105, 164, 170,
    198–200, 202
  in Caucasus, 208–9
  early career of, 167, 176, 186–87, 193, 195,
    197–98, 200–1
  in Third Mithridatic War, 121, 148–49, 162,
    174, 206
  triumph of, 71, 100, 193–94, 203, 210, 212
Pontius Leontinus, Aquitanian landowner, 215–16
Pontos, meaning of name, 9–10
Poredorix, Galatian tetrarch, 158
Poseidon, Greek god, 129, 176–77, 215–16
Poseidonius of Apameia, Greek polymath,
    97–98, 151–52
Priam of Troy, 20, 43
Prima Porta, imperial villa, 29
Procession of the Goddess, 18
Prometheus, Greek mythological figure, 205
prophecy, 31–32, 138
Propontis, 27, 55–56, 61–62, 87, 162–63, 173, 178,
    179, 181, 182
Prousa, Bithynian city, 179
Prousias I of Bithynia, 13–14, 42, 52, 54, 55–56,
    60–61, 62–63
Prousias II of Bithynia, 55–56, 58, 76–77, 85, 91
Prousias, Bithynian city, 27–28, 179, 193–94
Ptolemies, 17–18, 28, 38, 43–44, 46, 52, 64, 75–76,
    156, 211
Ptolemy I, 35, 37
Ptolemy II, 38, 74, 75–76, 78
Ptolemy III, 41–42, 43–44, 47–48, 87
Ptolemy IV, 46, 52, 75–76
Ptolemy V, 46, 52–53
Ptolemy VI, 46, 231
Ptolemy VIII, 46, 83–84, 86, 91–92
Ptolemy IX, 83
Ptolemy X, 195
Ptolemy XI, 195
Ptolemy XII, 164, 172, 187, 196, 211, 214
Ptolemy of Cyprus, 172, 211
Ptolemy Eupator, 231
Ptolemy Keraunos, 37
Publius, alleged Roman proconsul, 138–39
Punic Wars, 52–53, 54, 62–63, 79
Pydna, Macedonian town, 77
Pylaimenes of Paphlagonia, 87, 88
Pylaimenes, son of Nikomedes III of
    Bithynia, 120–21
Pyrrhos of Epeiros, 146, 170–71
Pythodoris of Pontos, 11, 18, 150–51, 213

queens, Skythian, 210, 212

Racine, Jean, 202–16
Raphia, Egyptian town, 46
realgar, 23
Red Sea, 208–9
Remus, founder of Rome, 146–47
Rhodes, Mediterranean island, 57, 77, 131, 180
  Black Sea interest of, 48, 57–58
  earthquake on, 41, 42, 48
  in First Mithridatic War, 142, 143, 144, 148,
    150–51, 202–3
Rhoxane, daughter of Mithridates V, 92,
    105–6, 187–88
Rhoxane, wife of Alexander the Great, 105–6
Rhyndakos River, 162–63, 181–82
Rome (city), 37–38, 54
  Campus Martius in, 191
  Capitol in, 203
  civil disorder in, 145, 170–71, 174–75
  eastern envoys to, 57, 58–59, 76, 81–82, 122, 127,
    128–29, 135, 139, 166, 168–69
  Gardens of Lucullus in, 190–91
  Greek art in, 71, 80–81
  inscriptions in, 74, 75–76, 77
  Palatine in, 170–71, 215
  Pincian in, 190–91, 198–99
  royalty sent to, 45–46, 69–71, 92, 121
  Theater of Pompey in, 199–200
  triumphs in, 165, 166, 168, 171, 190–91, 212
Romulus, founder of Rome, 146–47
Roxolanians, northern peoples, 115
Rutilius Nudus, P., Roman legate, 178–79
Rutilius Rufus, P., Roman consul, 148–50

Sallust (C. Sallustius Crispus), Roman historian,
    97–98, 187, 215
Salluvius Naso, C., Roman commander, 180
Salon, Mariandynian plain, 33–34
salt, 22–23, 67
sambouke/sambuca, siege engine, 144
Samnites. *See* Saunitians
Samos, Aegean island, 87
Samothrace, Aegean island, 183
Sangarios, river in Asia Minor, 20
Sarapis, Egyptian divinity, 131
Sardinia, Mediterranean island, 174–75, 184
Sardis, Lydian city, 44, 55
Sarmatians, northern peoples, 62, 119, 132
Satyros of Herakleia Pontika, 174–75
Saumakos, Skythian chieftain, 115–16
Saunitians, Italian peoples, 153–54
Scarlatti, Alessandro, composer, 213
Scipio, P. Cornelius, Roman proconsul, 80
scordotis or scordion, Pontic plant, 179–80